SOUTHWEST VIRGINIA CROSSROADS

AN ALMANAC OF PLACE NAMES AND PLACES TO SEE

JOE TENNIS

The Overmountain Press

JOHNSON CITY, TENNESSEE

This work is based on the best references available at the time of research. The author and publisher assume no liabilities arising from use of this book or its contents. This work does not give anyone the right to trespass on properties that may be noted as "drive-by" attractions/curiosities or those that can be seen from a public road, trail, or streambed. All personal property rights should be respected. Locations of communities listed are approximate. This book is not meant to be a strict navigational guide on rivers and should be considered only as a general-information source on public waterways.

Photo Captions
Page 1: (Top) Cumberland Gap
      (Bottom) Buffalo graze near an oil well at Ben Hur, in Lee County
Page 30: Nash's Ford at the Clinch River, in Russell County
Page 59: Hidden Valley Lake in Washington County
Page 88: (Top) Atop Whitetop Mountain
      (Bottom) Mount Rogers National Recreation Area, just off the Appalachian Trail
Page 116: The New River, near Rich Creek

All photographs reproduced in this book are copyright © 2004 by Joe Tennis

ISBN 1-57072-256-0
Copyright © 2004 by Joe Tennis
All Rights Reserved
Printed in the United States of America

1 2 3 4 5 6 7 8 9 0

For Abigail, a Southwest Virginia native

ACKNOWLEDGMENTS

For help in completing this book, foremost thanks goes to V. N. "Bud" Phillips, a Bristol author who made connections to help me get started, and to Beth Wright, my publisher, and Jason Weems, my editor, at The Overmountain Press.

For helping fill in blanks in historical research, thanks go to Dennis Reedy of Haysi; Rex McCarty in Gate City; Betty Scott at Independence; Alex Slagle of Dryden; Gerry Phillips of Pearisburg; Brenda King of Crandon; Lloyd Mathews of Pulaski; Omer C. Addington of Gate City; Ed Talbott of Grundy; Rubinette Neimann at Abingdon; Elizabeth Carpenter of Pennington Gap; Mabel E. Wimmer at Terry's Fork; Donna Hale of Council; Vonda Davis in Rye Cove; Janette Carter and Rita Forrester at Maces Spring; Eleanor Walker Jones in Chilhowie; Mary Lane of Wytheville; Ken Miller of Roanoke; Love Cox at Hillsville; C. P. Williams of Honaker; Linda Palmer of Rogers; Nola Albert in Floyd; Roger Burke in Nickelsville; Merle Crowe of Rochester, Minn.; Keith Denby of Devon, England; Jim Hoge at Burke's Garden; Jack Nida in Jonesboro, Ga.; Howard Walters of Winston-Salem, N.C.; Carlyle Clark of Jasper; Mary Vivian Daniel of Bristol, Tenn.; Roy F. Duncan of Abingdon; Melvin Dudley in Fagg; Don Francis in Marion; Dorothy Gibson Gardner in Lebanon; Louise Fortune Hall of Damascus; Dave Hart in Pulaski; John Johnson in Wytheville; Kate King in Floyd; J. C. Link at Newport; Pauline Nash of Nash's Ford; Jean Neal in Abingdon; Bill Nunley at Hidden Valley; Grace and Wyatt Ratliff at Mount Heron; Bettie Byrd St. Clair of Tazewell; Kathleen Robinson Taylor in Honaker; Bill Webb of Derby; Munsey Webb of Galax; Donald F. White in Bristol; Charles Arthur Wood of Grundy; June Ward Robertson Compton of Birmingham, Ala.; Larry Wooldridge at Blacksburg; and the staff of Stroupes Store in Wythe County.

Special thanks also goes to officials at various parks, museums, and libraries, especially Carl Mullins, superintendent at Breaks Interstate Park; Sara Zimmerman, curator of the Wilderness Road Regional Museum; Jack Collier and Carol Borneman, rangers at Cumberland Gap National Historical Park; Bob McKinney, interpretive specialist for the Mount Rogers National Recreation Area; and Jan Carlton, a librarian at Virginia Tech.

Nods of gratitude, in turn, are extended to fellow hikers, including Roscoe Osborne, a surveyor with the Clinch Ranger District of the Jefferson National Forest; Danny White, spokesperson for the Nature Conservancy of Virginia; Ralph Robertson, a volunteer promoter of Narrows; and John Wolfe, my brother-in-law in Abingdon.

Other general advice or tips came from Jan Patrick, Mike Pierry, Jr., Jack Kestner, and Bill McKee at the *Bristol Herald Courier;* Ken Heath of Marion; Daniel Rodgers in Barboursville; Frank Kilgore at St. Paul; Steve and Kim Rhodes in Christiansburg; my late mother-in-law, Louisa Chew Wolfe of Abingdon; and my parents, Richard and Jeanette Tennis, of Virginia Beach.

Most of all, I thank my wife, Mary, who constantly offered suggestions and always seemed to understand how much time this project would consume.

CONTENTS

PREFACE

Southwest Virginia Crossroads is a guide to attractions and landmarks in the sparsely populated and often overlooked southwestern corner of Virginia—from the headwaters of the Roanoke River west to the Cumberland Gap. The book is also a collection of place-names like White Gate, Frog Level, and Goose Pimple Junction, and it tells how these names came to be on maps of the Old Dominion.

Regional nicknames like "The Heart of Appalachia" and "Virginia's Southwest Blue Ridge Highlands" allude to the location of Southwest Virginia—south of West Virginia and west of the Blue Ridge. This area's rocky, rural landscape is a setting of serenity at the heart of the Southern Appalachians. Wineries, waterfalls, and mills line mountain-climbing back roads, while rivers drain primarily westward—away from the Atlantic Ocean, unlike watersheds in the rest of the Commonwealth.

In this guide, Southwest Virginia's 17 counties—Buchanan, Dickenson, Lee, Wise, Russell, Scott, Tazewell, Smyth, Washington, Bland, Carroll, Grayson, Wythe, Floyd, Giles, Montgomery, and Pulaski—and four independent cities—Norton, Bristol, Galax, and Radford—are grouped into five regions—the Western Front, Clinch Mountain Country, Holston Valley, Central Highlands, and the New River Valley.

Each region is geographically distinct—noted for the drainage of a particular river, the presence of an imposing mountain, or the region's proximity to Virginia's westernmost border. Within each region are three to five localities, including cities and counties. Each county's chapter contains alphabetical listings of its communities and towns, with stories of place-names plus what is there to see. In some instances, a particular attraction in one county may be listed under the heading "What's to See" in an adjoining county simply because it is easier to access that way.

A caveat: it may be impossible to physically find some of the communities listed in this guide. Names may appear on modern maps, but so many of these places have practically disappeared following the loss of passenger rail service, the closing of a post office, or the shutdown of a nearby mine.

In this guide, many accounts of place-names are derived from county history books published by local historical societies. More originate from information on Web sites, in magazines, books, newspapers, brochures, and historical society files, and through interviews and correspondence with historians and local residents.

In all, this guide contains several hundred entries of place-name origins. Several thousand more entries would be required to explain how every railroad crossing, hollow, corner, or stream derived its name across the roughly 7,500 square miles of Southwest Virginia.

TOURING SOUTHWEST VIRGINIA

Two major Interstate routes and numerous four-lane highways crisscross Southwest Virginia, offering outstanding views of the region's mountains.

But be forewarned—only two-lane roads lead to places of paradise like Burke's Garden, Breaks Gorge, Rocky Knob, and Whitetop Mountain. And roads that wind even more—gravel, dirt, maybe just one lane—are the primary pathways to many of Southwest Virginia's best-kept secrets.

Major roads traversing the region include:

I-81 and US-11: Most Interstate highways lack attractive scenery, proving true the old adage: "The best way to not see the state is to take the Interstate."

Yet I-81 is an exception. Largely constructed in the 1960s, this highway begins near White Pine, Tennessee, and runs north to Canada. Passing through the Commonwealth of Virginia for more than 300 miles, I-81 is mostly devoid of urban congestion, unlike I-64 running through the heart of Richmond.

Southwest of Roanoke County, it is easy to find where I-81 enters the region defined as Southwest Virginia—the highway crams its way through mountains separating the Atlantic Ocean basin from land where waters begin to flow west. Here, near Christiansburg, the asphalt channel seems to pass through a canyon. The southbound highway expands to three lanes to accommodate drivers having a hard time accelerating up the steep grades.

I-81 runs through the farms and valleys of Montgomery, Pulaski, Wythe, Smyth, and Washington counties before reaching the City of Bristol, near the Tennessee line.

Generally, I-81 parallels US-11 through the Commonwealth; at times, these north-south thoroughfares are combined. US-11 is known as the "Robert E. Lee Highway" (or "Lee Highway") in Virginia and is named for the Confederate general. In Christiansburg, at the corner of North Franklin Street and West Main Street, a stone monument commemorates the November 17, 1926, completion of the last section of Lee Highway.

In Southwest Virginia, an entire day—or longer—could be well spent exploring various downtown shops reached by US-11. Small motels and restaurants, many built in the 1950s or earlier, predate I-81 on the US-11 corridor, especially between Bristol and Abingdon. Among the road's most unique shopping outlets is the 100,000-square-foot Dixie Pottery, near Exit 13 on I-81. Open since 1957, this single-floor store sells all kinds of wicker, candles, and figurines. Next door, the Moonlite Theatre is an old-fashioned drive-in that opened in 1949 and still enjoys a brisk summertime business near Abingdon.

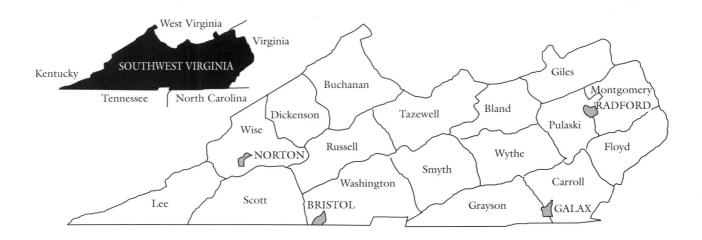

I-77 and US-52: Running from the Great Lakes to the heart of South Carolina, I-77 passes through Southwest Virginia for a little more than 60 miles.

In Bland County, a ride on I-77 offers expansive views of the Jefferson National Forest. The highway enters Virginia from the East River Mountain Tunnel on the West Virginia border and passes through the Big Walker Mountain Tunnel to reach Wythe County. I-77 also overlaps I-81 for nine curious miles near Wytheville. Here I-77 runs south while I-81 continues to run north along the same road!

At Fort Chiswell, I-77 turns south and veers across the New River, en route to North Carolina.

A "closer to the ground" view of the same corridor can be found traveling US-52, which parallels I-77 and also goes through the Jefferson National Forest. The Big Walker Mountain Scenic Byway—a 16.2-mile portion of US-52—runs across Walker Mountain and includes access at I-81 Exit 70 (Wytheville) or I-77 Exit 52 (Bland).

US-221: The mostly two-lane route of US-221 enters Southwest Virginia along the Floyd-Roanoke county line and wanders a few miles west of the Blue Ridge. The road offers great views through the agricultural valleys of Floyd, Carroll, and Grayson counties. Combined with the Blue Ridge Parkway, the route forms a round trip connecting the courthouse towns of Floyd, Hillsville, and Independence plus the City of Galax. The highway exits Virginia south of Independence and enters Alleghany County, North Carolina.

US-421: The mountain-climbing route of US-421 joins US-58 at Bristol. It overlaps US-58 for several miles, heading northwest, until the highways split in Lee County. The two-lane US-421 exits Virginia at an isolated area of Harlan County, Kentucky.

US-460: The mostly four-lane route of US-460 is a lifeline for many isolated regions of Southwest Virginia. The highway enters Buchanan County from Pike County, Kentucky, before overlapping US-19 through Tazewell County. It slips through Bluefield and detours for a short stretch through West Virginia before finding Virginia again at Glen Lyn, in Giles County. The road meanders along the scenic New River and winds through Montgomery County, providing access to Blacksburg and Christiansburg, before reaching Roanoke County.

US-19: Leaving the heart of Bristol and overlapping US-11 en route to Abingdon, US-19 heads west over Clinch Mountain while sharing its route with US-58A. US-19 finally finds a path all to itself from Hansonville to Claypool Hill, passing through the heart of Russell County, though it does share about 2.5 miles with VA-80 near Rosedale. The route later joins US-460 in Tazewell County.

Through Southwest Virginia, US-19 is a four-lane highway. The roadside scenery includes rocky plains at the base of Brumley Mountain, near Hansonville, and perfectly rounded knobs near the Town of Tazewell.

US-21: Virginia's portion of US-21, mainly two lanes, heads south from downtown Wytheville to meet the farms of Grayson County. It joins US-221 at Independence and enters Alleghany County, North Carolina, near the New River.

US-23: US-23 offers four lanes of travel from Kentucky to Tennessee and runs through Wise, Lee, and Scott counties in Southwest Virginia. This highway provides easy access to attractions in Pound, Wise, Norton, Big Stone Gap, Duffield, Clinchport, Gate City, and Weber City.

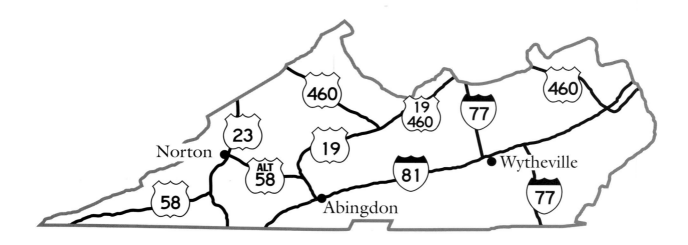

Sunrise at Rocky Knob

US-58: Originating at the Virginia-Tennessee line near Cumberland Gap, US-58 snakes along the southern border of Virginia, running about 500 miles to its terminus at the towering hotels of Virginia Beach, near the Atlantic Ocean.

Going up and down mountains and sliding around countless curves, US-58 is indeed a wild ride, especially through Southwest Virginia. The highway runs about 200 miles—a five-hour trip—from its Blue Ridge Parkway access at Meadows of Dan to the entrance of the Cumberland Gap National Historical Park.

Parts of the highway have four lanes, but most of it simply has two.

Caution: Do not get on this road if you're looking to make time, especially if you're trying to get from Hillsville to Bristol. A trip like that on US-58 might end up consuming three hours,

as opposed to the hour and a half it would take by using Interstate highways. Still, if you forego US-58, you will miss the gorgeous tumbling creeks of eastern Washington County and a close view of Whitetop Mountain, in Grayson County, on the Mount Rogers Scenic Byway.

West of Jonesville, the route is mostly four lanes. Here, US-58 splits. Its traditional path goes east to Duffield; a road called US-58 Alternate (US-58A) runs through the coal country of Wise County, crosses the Clinch River at Russell County, and again meets the main route of US-58 in Abingdon. The four-lane US-58A is generally not as scenic as the original route—US-58 passes unforgettable valley pockets at the base of Clinch Mountain as the road overlaps US-23 and US-421 in central Scott County, between Clinchport and Gate City.

GENERAL ATTRACTIONS IN SOUTHWEST VIRGINIA

Most attractions in this guide are located primarily inside one county. Yet others are regional destinations and cannot be easily categorized under one location.

Appalachian Trail: One fourth of the Appalachian Trail passes through Virginia. This 2,167-mile public footpath connects Georgia to Maine and cuts through several Southwest Virginia counties, meandering mainly in the wilderness of the Jefferson National Forest.

From the Tennessee line, the trail enters Virginia's Washington County and, within a few miles, runs down the main street of Damascus. Then it heads along Whitetop Laurel Creek in the Mount Rogers National Recreation Area before going north, slipping through Grayson, Smyth, and Wythe counties. The trail runs along the rim of Burke's Garden on the Tazewell-Bland county line and tops the spine of Brushy Mountain en route to Giles County. It then heads over Pearis Mountain and skims the West Virginia-Virginia line, before entering Craig County, Virginia, near VA-601.

The trail is marked by two-by-six-inch, vertical, white paint blazes. A double blaze—one above the other—is placed before turns, junctions, or other areas that require hikers to be alert. Side trails are marked in blue blaze.

Blue Ridge Parkway: Running about 80 miles in Southwest Virginia's Central Highlands and New River Valley, from the North Carolina line to the Roanoke Valley, the Blue Ridge Parkway bypasses fields, farms, fences, and trees thick with leaves.

This two-lane scenic road is built atop the Blue Ridge, a great wall between water-drainage basins, named for a haze that causes it to appear blue at a distance. The parkway's construction began in 1935 at a swampy area along the West Fork of Chestnut Creek at the North Carolina-Virginia line (Mile 216.9).

Maintained by the National Park Service, the parkway is designed for casual cruising. Look for mileposts, about 18 inches high, to locate destinations. But don't look for signs—there aren't any.

Blue Ridge Parkway at Low Gap

From Fancy Gap (Mile 199.5), the Blue Ridge Parkway twists its way southwest into the lower corners of Carroll and Grayson counties. Few attractions grace this quiet stretch, but an occasional overlook, like one near Mile 204, provides an aerial view into North Carolina.

Several natural and man-made attractions are located between Fancy Gap and Floyd. In this guide, individual parkway destinations, especially in that area, are listed with the closest towns.

Major Parkway Access in Southwest Virginia

Mile 165.2/Tuggle Gap: From US-221 at Floyd, follow VA-8 southeast for 6.1 miles to the parkway

Mile 177.7/Meadows of Dan: From I-77 Exit 14 at Hillsville, follow US-58 east for 23 miles to the parkway

Mile 199.5/Fancy Gap: From I-77 Exit 8, follow VA-148 east for a half mile to US-52 and follow US-52 south for one mile to the parkway

Mile 215/Low Gap: From US-58/221 in Galax, follow VA-89 south for seven miles to the parkway

Heart of Appalachia Scenic Drive: An automobile route for about 102 miles, the Heart of Appalachia Scenic Drive originates at Burke's Garden (VA-623) in Tazewell County and ends at St. Paul (US-58A) on the Russell-Wise county line. As a bike route, the span continues another 18 miles, from St. Paul's Oxbow Lake to the Guest River Gorge Trail near Coeburn. The rural route uses gravel roads, paved state highways, and a forest road. It meanders past fields of stone and natural Christmas trees along VA-640 in Russell County. VA-16, another scenic delight, roams Tazewell County's Thompson Valley. Signs for the Heart of Appalachia Scenic Drive are posted at intersections along the route.

Jefferson National Forest: Parts of the Jefferson National Forest are located in nearly all counties in Southwest Virginia. The forest—named for Thomas Jefferson, third president of the United States—contains several hiking trails and campgrounds. In this guide, individual forest destinations are listed with the closest towns.

Mount Rogers National Recreation Area: Mount Rogers National Recreation Area's 120,000 acres span five counties in Southwest Virginia, including two of this guide's geographic regions—the Holston Valley and the Central Highlands. It is headquartered at the Jennings Visitor Center in Smyth County, off VA-16, 5.8 miles south of I-81 Exit 45 at Marion. The center—named for the late W. Pat Jennings (1919-1994), a local U.S. Congressman who wrote and sponsored the legislation creating the recreation area in 1966—includes wildlife displays and trail maps. The center was built with stones, including ones that Jennings helped bring to the site.

Part of the Jefferson National Forest, the national recreation area is home to the state's highest peak, Mount Rogers, as well as mile-high Whitetop Mountain, several campgrounds, and more than 300 miles of trails suitable for hiking, biking, and horseback riding.

In this guide, the Mount Rogers National Recreation Area's individual destinations are listed with the closest towns.

New River Trail State Park: The New River Trail State Park is a multiuse recreational trail bordering the New River. The trail spans 57 miles on a mostly flat path. It follows an old railroad

The New River Trail State Park's 135-foot New River Tunnel

line that once hauled lead from Wythe County's mines, products from the Fries textile mill, and furniture made in Galax. Norfolk Southern Corp. donated the abandoned line's right-of-way to Virginia's park system in 1986, and the route became a state park in 1987. The trail's entire length opened in 1999.

The trail includes a couple of short tunnels and 30 trestles and bridges in Carroll, Grayson, Wythe, and Pulaski counties, and the City of Galax. The stretch spans about 51.5 miles from Pulaski to Galax. It splits at Fries Junction, and a spur runs 5.5 more miles to Fries.

Horseback riders, hikers, and bikers share the dirt-and-gravel path. On average, the linear park's right-of-way extends to an 80-foot width.

Parking areas are located at the Galax trailhead (US-58 at Chestnut Creek); Cliffview in Carroll County, near Galax (VA-721); Chestnut Yard in Carroll County (VA-607); Fries in Grayson County (town park, off VA-94); Byllesby Dam in Carroll County (VA-602); Ivanhoe in Wythe County (VA-639); Jackson Ferry in Wythe County (off US-52); Foster Falls in Wythe County (off VA-608); Gambetta in Carroll County (VA-793); Draper in Pulaski County (off VA-658); and the Town of Pulaski (Xaloy Way). Horse trailers can be parked at Cliffview, Fries, Foster Falls, Pulaski, and Draper.

In this guide, more information on the trail is listed with towns where attractions or accesses are most closely located.

Rivers—Fishing and Floating: Both the Clinch River and the New River extend through several Southwest Virginia counties, offering fishing and floating opportunities, from flat-water paddling to running Class III-IV rapids. In this guide, public access points are listed with the closest towns.

Home to more fish species than any other river in Virginia, the Clinch River holds small and largemouth bass, sunfish, white bass, freshwater drum, crappie, catfish, walleye, and musky. The river is considered navigable south of its confluence with Indian

Creek in Tazewell County, though Blackford, in Russell County, marks the river's northernmost formal public access. Going downstream from Blackford, established launches/takeouts are at Puckett's Hole, Nash's Ford, Cleveland, and Carterton in Russell County; at St. Paul in Wise County; and at Dungannon, Hill, Clinchport, and a remote area near Tennessee in Scott County.

Below the Virginia line, the New River meanders out of northwestern North Carolina's Alleghany County to enter Virginia's Grayson County at the mouth of Big Wilson Creek. From here, the river runs north, hovering along Grayson's south side and drifting back into North Carolina a couple of times. All along the back roads beside the river are campgrounds or places to rent canoes.

To continuously float the New River in Grayson County, look for launch/takeout points at Bridle Creek, Independence, Baywood, Riverside, Oldtown, and Fries. A launch below the Fries Dam leads to a ramp on the Byllesby Reservoir in Carroll County. Another continuous stretch runs from a ramp at Austinville in Wythe County to Allisonia in Pulaski County, where the river enters Claytor Lake. Downstream, boats can be launched below the Claytor Dam at Radford and in Montgomery County at Whitethorne. Access points in Giles County are at Pembroke, Pearisburg, Narrows, Rich Creek, and Glen Lyn.

Unfamiliar waters should always be scouted before launching a boat.

Welcome Centers: The Commonwealth of Virginia maintains welcome centers at three of its Interstate-highway entrances to Southwest Virginia. Each has restroom facilities, state highway maps, and brochures available on lodging, restaurants, and attractions. One center is on I-81 at Bristol, on the Tennessee line. Another is on I-77 at Lambsburg, on the North Carolina line. The third is on I-77 at Rocky Gap, near the West Virginia border.

In Wytheville at I-81 Exit 70, a regional visitor center for Southwest Virginia stands at 975 Tazewell St. The center is operated by the Blue Ridge Travel Association of Virginia with other partners and includes a billboard-size map of Southwest Virginia, interpretive displays, and hundreds of free brochures highlighting destinations from Christiansburg to the Cumberland Gap.

WESTERN FRONT

On Southwest Virginia's "Western Front," Cumberland Mountain and Pine Mountain provide a wall stretching from Cumberland Gap in Lee County to the Breaks Canyon on the Dickenson-Buchanan county line. These parallel ranges—overwhelming barriers to early pedestrian explorers—form the line between Virginia's westernmost territories and the Commonwealth of Kentucky.

Touring the four counties and one city comprising Southwest Virginia's Western Front can be challenging along the rattlesnake-shaped roads. A couple of four-lane highways crisscross Wise County and intersect near the City of Norton, but, on many secondary routes, expect mountains to be nothing short of steep and the valleys quite narrow.

BUCHANAN COUNTY

Buchanan County is a montage of mountains where coal mining and timber hauling are major industries in the watershed of the Levisa Fork of the Big Sandy River. The county spans 504 square miles on the borders of Kentucky and West Virginia. It was formed from parts of Tazewell and Russell counties in 1858 and named for James Buchanan, then president of the United States.

COUNCIL

Council is on VA-80, at an intersection with VA-623, in southern Buchanan County. The exact origin of its name is not known, but locals guess it stems from meetings once held here by a "war council" of Native Americans.

What's to See

William P. Harris Park: Carved out of steep mountainsides, the mile-long William P. Harris Park features ball fields, a swimming pool, tennis courts, a playground, and picnic facilities. The recreation area is named for a former Buchanan County supervisor who helped open it in 1976. For travelers along VA-80, this place provides a good spot to rest, especially for kids who need to unwind after a trip on curvy roads. On display are a red railroad caboose and an antique fire truck.

🚗 Council is about 4.5 miles southeast of Davenport on VA-80, or about 3 miles northwest of the Russell County line. The park is at the intersection of VA-620 and VA-80, near Council High School. The park entrance is on Rt. 1030.

GRUNDY

In its earliest days, Grundy was called "Mouth of Slate" for its proximity to Slate Creek, which empties into the Levisa Fork of the Big Sandy River. The present name comes from U.S. Senator Felix Grundy of Tennessee. The centrally located courthouse town is wedged between steep mountains along US-460.

A tower clock distinguishes Grundy's Buchanan County Courthouse, built with gray sandstone in 1905 at the corner of Main and Walnut streets. A 1915 fire gutted the courthouse interior, along with much of Grundy's downtown, but the courthouse was reconstructed by 1917.

Incorporated in 1876, Grundy was home to about 1,100 residents in 2000. Welcome signs boast the town as the home of Lee Smith, a novelist born here in 1944 and known for works like *Saving Grace, Oral History,* and *The Last Girls.*

For most of the 20th century, Grundy was a commerce center for surrounding coal-mining communities. Unfortunately, citizens have witnessed about one major flood each decade on the river running through town. One overflow in 1977 killed three people and damaged $100 million in property. By 2001, however, the U.S. Army Corps of Engineers had developed a plan to tear down buildings in the floodplain and reconstruct US-460. This plan also required building a floodwall and developing a new commercial district for Grundy on the opposite side of the Levisa Fork of the Big Sandy River.

The Big Sandy was named for the many sandbars in the river, but the origin of the "Levisa Fork" name is not so clear. One theory dates to the 18th-century days of famed frontiersman Daniel Boone and follows the legend of a young woman named Levisa (Luvice, Leevice) Vause (Vaux, Vass, Voss), who was taken captive at Fort Vause during a 1756 Indian raid in what is now Shawsville (see the Montgomery County chapter in the New River Valley section). Vause, by some accounts, was taken through the woods of West Virginia, Kentucky, and Ohio. According to legend, Boone found her name carved in the bark of sycamore trees and named some places and watercourses for her.

Another story concerns a Frenchman who found a painting or design here on a peeled poplar tree. That discovery may have yielded the name "La Visee" (Levisa), translated to mean "The Design." A third tale concerns a young Frenchman named Vansant and his love for a Virginia girl named "Louisa" (or Levisa), who died young. That story, once promoted in brochures by Buchanan County tourism officials, says the Frenchman visited his dead lover's homeland—Buchanan County—and named a watercourse for her. Another account says the river

Railroad caboose at William P. Harris Park in Council   Buchanan County Courthouse at Grundy

fork's original name, "Louisa," comes from Dr. Thomas Walker, an explorer who named it in 1750 for the daughter of England's King George II and sister of the Duke of Cumberland.

MAVISDALE   Local lore says Mavisdale was originally called "Maize Dale," a name derived by residents who thought of calling the area "Corn Valley" but, to be different, opted to substitute the Native American translation *maize* for the word *corn*, and to use *dale* for *valley*. Somehow, though, the name of this place along Garden Creek evolved into "Mavisdale." The community lies at the junction of VA-624 and VA-682 in central Buchanan County.

PILGRIMS KNOB   Milton Ward (1797-1878) pioneered the Pilgrims Knob area in 1833, settling at the foot of a rock-faced mountain towering 800 feet above the valley of Dismal Creek. A Ward descendant, Thomas D. Ward (1893-1956), opened a "Pilgrim Knob" post office here in eastern Buchanan County in about 1938, near

the crossroads of VA-638 and VA-680. An *S* was later added to the name, making it "Pilgrims Knob." Thomas's wife, Stella, coined the community's name to honor the area's first settlers, or pilgrims. One legend, still, says the name might have been inspired by a popular brand of coffee (locals remember "Pilot Knob") that was sold here at Thomas and Stella Ward's general store.

VANSANT   At least two theories exist on how Vansant—at US-460's southernmost junction with VA-83 in central Buchanan County—took its name. One story says a man named Vansant was a partner in a local business called Vansant Kitchen Co. A more romantic tale follows a young American girl to Europe, where she falls in love with a young Frenchman named Vansant but soon becomes ill and dies. This story says that Vansant later visited his dead lover's homeland and named a river for her (actually, a fork of the Big Sandy River) at a site where a large creek emptied into it. Perhaps Vansant's own name was used for this village, if any of this love story is true.

Bear Wallow: This scenic area takes its name from bears descending mountains and "wallowing" in a natural basin of water near a border with both Tazewell County and McDowell County, W.Va. Eastern: VA-616 at VA-637

Big Rock: In about 1932, a large rock here was blasted away during the construction of the Norfolk & Western Railway. That rock, some say, is what gave Big Rock its name. Western: VA-645, near US-460 and Rocklick Creek

Davenport: William Davenport was the first postmaster at Davenport in 1885. Southern: VA-80 at VA-600

Deel: In Buchanan County, Deel is a common family name and probably the source of the Deel community name. Basil Deel was an early postmaster here. Central: US-460, east of Vansant

Grimsleyville: James Grimsley (1878-1952) provided maps with a new town name when he opened a grocery store and the Grimsleyville post office in 1933. Southeastern: US-460, west of VA-727

Harman: The H.E. Harman family and its local coal company provided the name "Harman" in the 1930s. Northwestern: VA-609 at VA-614

Hurley: The flood-prone hamlet of Hurley was likely named for the family of Samuel Robert Hurley, a native of Scotland who settled in the Knox Creek area circa 1800. Northern: VA-643 at VA-650

Indian Gap: Skeletal remains of Indians found during a road-construction project inspired the name at Indian Gap. Southern: VA-620 at VA-662

Janey: Janey Owens was the daughter of an early postmaster at Janey. Central: US-460, near VA-684

Jewell Valley: "Jewell" is a local family name in this valley. Eastern: VA-613, near VA-636

Keen Mountain: In the 1800s, William Keen and his wife reared 11 children at Keen Mountain and lent their name to the area. Central: US-460 at Rt. 1101

Leemaster: The name "Leemaster" comes from a log cutter who worked for a local firm in 1908, the same year the Leemaster post office was established. South-central: VA-612 at VA-619

Maxie: One account says "Maxie" was a title selected by U.S. postal officials after receiving a list of suggestions for a post office name. Northwestern: VA-601 at VA-609

Mount Heron: In the 1920s, Erie Breeding Ratliff searched a geography book for a name to give a new post office, settling on "Mount Heron." Ratliff's inspiration may have come from Heron, Mont. Central: VA-624 at VA-627

Murphy: Richard Murphy was the first postmaster at Murphy. Southwestern: VA-605 at VA-663

Oakwood: Once the site of major lumber operations, Oakwood may take its name from oak harvested in the area. Central: US-460 at VA-624

Page: The name "Page" remembers the Page-Pocahontas Coal Co.—an outfit partially titled for Page, W.Va., a town named for coal operator Capt. William N. Page. Southern: VA-632, along Garden Creek

Patterson: A pair of Patterson brothers founded a coal company, and the Patterson post office was named in their honor. Central: VA-641, near VA-678

Paw Paw: Located along the Kentucky state line, the Paw Paw community takes its name from the pawpaw fruit, once known to grow plentifully along Pawpaw Creek. Northwestern: VA-643 at VA-645

Peapatch: The Peapatch region takes its name from its location—a cool, sunny ridge where peas could be grown. Eastern: VA-616 at VA-719, near McDowell County, W.Va.

Pearly: Pearly was named in the early 1900s for a daughter of local resident John Clevinger. West-central: VA-614, near VA-604

Poetown: Grundy's Poetown community was named for Poe Ratliff, a local store operator. Central: US-460 at Rt. 1005 (Poetown Rd.)

Prater: Legend says the Prater name comes from three pioneering Prater brothers—the biggest Prater settled on Big Prater Creek, while the middle-sized one (named Russell) settled on Russell Prater Creek, and the smallest lived along Little Prater Creek. Western: VA-83 at VA-604

Raitt: J. W. Raitt, a Norfolk & Western Railway engineer, is honored in the name of Raitt. Central: VA-650, near the southernmost junction with VA-651

Roseann: W. H. Leckie founded the Panther Coal Co., and Roseann was named for his daughter. Central: VA-651, near the southernmost intersection with VA-650

Roth: Norfolk & Western Railway engineer E. H. Roth once worked in Southwest Virginia, and his name is remembered at Roth. Central: VA-638, near VA-715

Rowe: John S. Rowe was an early settler here. Southern: VA-624 at VA-662

Royal City: A contest was held when it was time to name the post office at Royal City, and Walter Jackson, a store owner who sold Royal Brand shirts, won by suggesting the name "Royal City" for a new mailing address. The Royal City business district is in the southernmost corner of Grundy. Central: US-460 at Watkins St.

Shack Mills: A mill operated by Meshack Ratliff is the reason behind the name "Shack Mills." South-central: US-460 at VA-680

Slate: A bluish gray rock, slate, is on the bed of Slate Creek and gave this community its name. Central: VA-83 at VA-640

Stacy: Early landowner Benjamin Stacy is the likely source of Stacy's name. Central: VA-83 at VA-643

Thomas: John Thomas, the first roadmaster at nearby Weller railroad yard in the 1930s, lent his name to Thomas. Western: VA-650 at VA-700

Vandyke: The Vandyke area was named for first postmaster Henry Vandyke. Southern: VA-618, near VA-634

Venia: Venia Buchanan was Venia's first postmaster in 1923. Southern: VA-620, near VA-622

Vicey: The Vicey name is owed to Vicey Clevinger, the daughter of local resident J. W. Clevinger. Western: VA-83, near Dickenson County

Weller: The name Weller remembers H. C. Weller, a superintendent of the Western Division of the Norfolk & Western Railway, which arrived at Weller circa 1931. Western: US-460 at VA-700

Whitewood: This name may originate from the region's timber, possibly referring to the wood of the white oak. Eastern: VA-638, near VA-635

Wolford: John Wolford was an early settler here. Northeastern: VA-643 at VA-653

DICKENSON COUNTY

Some hard driving on winding roads leads to Dickenson County's rugged land of coal mines, roaring rivers, and scenic mountains. But remote sites like the John W. Flannagan Reservoir and Breaks Interstate Park are well worth the hunt.

Spanning about 334 square miles, Dickenson County is named for William J. Dickenson, a prominent Russell County lawyer who served in the Virginia General Assembly at the time of the county's formation in 1880.

BREAKS

What has happened at Breaks over the last 250 million years is awe-inspiring. The Russell Fork of the Big Sandy River has cut a five-mile-long gorge—as deep as 1,600 feet—through the northern end of Pine Mountain.

Still, not every part of Pine Mountain crumbled in the face of the rushing river. Just take a look at The Towers. This pyramid-shaped rock formation stubbornly stands 600 feet above the gorge floor. The Towers—surrounded on three sides by water—resisted the river and ultimately created a huge horseshoe loop along the rock-clogged waterway.

The Towers and the Breaks Gorge of the Russell Fork are preserved as the centerpieces of Breaks Interstate Park, the greatest geologic gem of Virginia's Western Front. Breaks Park sits like an island among Virginia's coal-mining communities—a cool, clean, uncluttered retreat locked away from any kind of metropolis, hidden far down narrow two-lane roads that curl and climb like the rattlesnakes of the nearby wilderness. In its isolation, and with the Jefferson National Forest at its southwest border, the park overlooks wide, expansive mountains. The view—free from the scars of strip-mining and clear-cutting—is simply stunning.

Breaks is known by a couple of nicknames—"Grand Canyon of the South" and "The Grand Canyon With Clothes On." For years, Kentuckians called it the "Breaks of Sandy," referring to the gap—or the "break"—in the mountain through which the Russell Fork flows. Yet Virginians called it the "Breaks of the Cumberlands," referring to Pine Mountain's place in the Cumberland Mountain range.

Near Kentucky, the park entrance is on VA-80, seven miles north of Haysi—or 44 miles north of four-lane US-19 at Rosedale in Russell County. The name "Breaks" also refers to a northeastern Dickenson County community along VA-80.

Park brochures boast that the Breaks Gorge is the deepest east of the Mississippi River.

Nearly 200 years after frontiersman Daniel Boone found the canyon in 1767, it remained a hard struggle to get here. In fact, the area's first hard-surface road was not built until 1951. Three years later, Breaks opened as a park shared by the commonwealths of Kentucky and Virginia. It is one of only two interstate parks in the United States and annually attracts about 400,000 visitors.

For park officials, straddling the state line is a case of good and bad. Sometimes, money resources can be pulled from both states. But Breaks can also miss out when politicians are pressured to fund only in-state parks, not one that is shared.

Most of the 4,600-acre park's development is in Dickenson County—including a swimming pool, a conference center, horse stables, hiking trails, an amphitheater, and a visitor center with displays on wildlife, coal mining, and mountain pioneers. Overnight visitors overlook conical evergreens at one block of motel rooms perched on the rim of the canyon. Other park accommodations include private cottages, a campground, and newer motel rooms.

The Southern-style food at the park's Rhododendron Restaurant is neither fancy nor expensive, but the view from the dining room is absolutely priceless. Outside, six major overlooks offer different scenes of Pine Mountain's treetops and outcrops, high above the rocky Russell Fork.

Away from the gorge is the park's 12-acre Laurel Lake, stocked with bass and bluegill and flanked by forest and marsh. Paddleboats can be rented, and a ramp is here for small boats with trolling motors.

About a mile south of the park entrance on VA-80, Garden Hole Road leads to the Garden Hole, a

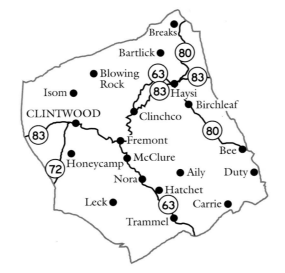

pristine spot on the Russell Fork known as a place to nab trout. Garden Hole is named for a rich spot of gently sloping land along the Russell Fork's east bank. Here, the river divides to flow around a low spot of land called Garden Island.

On weekends in October, huge flumes of water are released upstream at the John W. Flannagan Dam, allowing the park to coordinate whitewater-rafting access. Going through the Breaks Gorge, the Russell Fork's whitewater route spans about 11 miles, squeezing past rocks and house-size boulders from Bartlick (Pound River confluence along VA-611) to Elkhorn Creek in Kentucky. Takeouts are at Potter's Ford and Spruce Pine Island (both off KY-80). The river drops more than 400 feet along the length of the gorge. The names of some of this river's Class V rapids—"Maze," "Fist," "El Horrendo"—should alone be solemn hints of the Russell Fork's dangerous challenges.

CLINTWOOD

Originally called "Holly Creek," Clintwood became the seat of Dickenson County in 1882 and was incorporated in 1894. In 2000, Clintwood's population was about 1,500. The town is at

View from the Garden Hole: The Towers on the Russell Fork of the Big Sandy River

the junction of VA-83 and VA-607, near the county's center. It takes its present name from Henry Clinton Wood (nicknamed "Clint" Wood), a Scott County native and an influential member of the Virginia Senate in the 19th century. On Main Street, two-story-high columns front the brick Dickenson County Courthouse, built in 1915 near McClure Avenue.

What's to See

Birch Knob Overlook and *Mullins Pond:* Despite the fact that their names are sometimes interchanged, Pine Mountain is actually a distinct ridge from Cumberland Mountain on the Virginia-Kentucky border. In Virginia, Pine Mountain is mostly in the Jefferson National Forest; its tallest point is the 3,149-foot Birch Knob, a perch with sandy cliffs and vertical rock walls.

Birch Knob takes its name from a stand of birch trees that once stood on the knob's Kentucky side. From 1964 to 1978, the knob was the site of a 54-foot fire tower. In 2003, forest officials constructed an observation deck on the knob's Virginia side, showcasing a soaring view of Pine Mountain's gradual slide into the Old Dominion and its steep drop into the Bluegrass State.

Breaks Canyon at Breaks Interstate Park

Rock outcrop at Birch Knob

Getting to Birch Knob requires driving uphill for five miles on semi-rough forest roads. The half-acre Mullins Pond, lined with reeds, marks the halfway point. The pond's name comes from early homesteader John P. Mullins.

🚗 From VA-83 (W. Main St.) in Clintwood, follow VA-631 (Brush Creek Rd.) north for three miles. Turn right on VA-611 and follow for 2.3 miles. Turn left at a wooden shed on USFS-616 and follow uphill to reach the Mullins Pond parking lot at 2.5 miles. Bear left at the pond entrance and continue following the forest road to reach the parking area for Birch Knob Overlook in 2.4 miles. An informal overlook at "Buzzard's Roost" is 1.1 miles beyond Mullins Pond, near a monument marking the site of a 1965 airplane crash.

Blowing Rock and *Pine Mountain Trail:* Dickenson County's Blowing Rock is a natural tunnel in a rock outcrop atop Pine Mountain, with one opening about 14 feet wide and three feet high. The tunnel's other opening, much larger, is on a cliff on the mountain's Kentucky side.

The three-foot-high tunnel opening, or "blow hole," is known to create unbelievable wind effects. You can toss a hat down into the hole, then watch it blow back up, thanks to the force of the wind coming through the tunnel.

A trail leading to the Blowing Rock branches off the 28-mile-long Pine Mountain Trail, a pass linking Pound Gap to Breaks, used primarily by horseback riders. Rimming the Virginia-Kentucky line, the Pine Mountain Trail (marked in yellow blaze) lies mainly in the Jefferson National Forest, though part is on private land and may not be accessible.

The trail's Blowing Rock spur, the Counts Cabin Trail, is a moderate-to-strenuous hike that stays within the national forest. The trail continuously winds uphill, but the hike is worth the pain; the aerial view atop the Blowing Rock is a heavenly display of what lies beyond Virginia's Western Front—a sea of rolling green in Pike County, Kentucky.

🚗 From VA-83 (W. Main St.) at Clintwood, follow VA-631 (Brush Creek Rd.) north for three miles. Turn right on VA-611 and follow for 6.7 miles, passing the Blowing Rock community, to a gravel parking lot on the left. A small sign designates the hiking trail at a gated forest road.

At the trailhead, immediately pass the stone foundation of the Counts Cabin on the left. In a few yards, cross the Left Fork of the Upper Twin Branch and, also on the left, see the Hunter's Cliff, a natural rock shelter once used by hunters to escape a storm. Continue for a half mile until reaching the Counts Cabin Trail leading left, away from the gravel forest road. Follow this sometimes-strenuous trail (marked by blue blaze) for about two miles to the mountaintop. The Blowing Rock is not marked but is easily recognized as a hole in a rock, about 10 yards to the left after the spur tops the mountain and joins the Pine Mountain Trail.

Cranes Nest Campground and River Access: Originating in Wise County, the Cranes Nest River extends several miles through western Dickenson County before becoming a navigable stream near Clintwood. A paved boat ramp, open spring to fall, is on the river between the Bartley Branch (named for early settler Levi Bartley) and the Neel Branch (named for early settler Billy Neel). Next to the ramp is a handicapped-accessible fishing pier. Nearby, the 35-space Cranes Nest River Campground and a day-use playground/picnic area stay open during summer. Fees are charged through the Flannagan Reservoir office near Haysi.

🚗 From VA-607 (Main St.) in Clintwood, follow VA-83 east for 2.7 miles. Cross the bridge immediately beyond VA-649. Turn left on a gravel road and follow for 2.7 miles to the campground and picnic area. Continue for 2.5 miles beyond the campground to reach the boat ramp and pier access, on the left.

Atop the Blowing Rock, looking into Ashcamp, Kentucky, at the western edge of Dickenson County

Cumberland Mountain View Drive: Full of sharp turns twisting around trees, the Cumberland Mountain View Drive follows an often narrow paved road (VA-611), linking the general area of Breaks Interstate Park to Clintwood. This 19-mile tour borders the base of Cumberland Mountain, offering outstanding views from Maynard Ridge (named for an early settler) inside the Jefferson National Forest. Several stretches, as well, pass misty streams laced with mountain laurel, ferns, and rhododendron.

🚙 From VA-83 (W. Main St.) at Clintwood, follow VA-631 (Brush Creek Rd.) north for three miles. Turn right on VA-611. The drive ends at VA-80 about four miles south of Breaks.

Pound River Recreation Area and *Ramey Falls:* The Ramey Fork is so small that it misses a place on most maps. Yet during wet weather, this stream stages a splashy show on public land owned by the U.S. Army Corps of Engineers. Look for the fork's 18-foot-long cascade at the left side of the winding entrance road to the Pound River Recreation Area on Flannagan Reservoir. Just above the cascade, cross the stream on a flat rock and hike a trail uphill for about 100 yards to see Ramey Falls leaping in a skinny yet steady 25-foot midair plunge inside a natural amphitheater.

The 27-space Pound River Campground and a paved boat ramp, both open spring and summer, are on the Pound River portion of Flannagan Reservoir. Fees are charged through the Flannagan Reservoir office near Haysi.

🚙 From VA-83 (W. Main St.) in Clintwood, follow VA-631 (Brush Creek Rd.) north for 2.9 miles. Turn right on VA-754 and follow for 1.1 miles. Turn right on the campground entrance road. The cascades are on the left at 0.2 miles; parking is limited. Continue for another mile to the campground entrance and boat ramp.

FREMONT Fremont's name comes from John C. Fremont, a renowned western adventurer and explorer. A local theory says John Fremont was a surveyor on a small predecessor line that eventually became part of the Clinchfield Railroad in central Dickenson County.

In 1982, the old Fremont Railroad Station, once designated for destruction, was bought and renovated to pristine condition by Kenneth and Julia Herndon. The 1915 station was moved to Fremont's main crossroads, the westernmost junction of VA-63 and VA-83.

HAYSI A couple of store owners—Charles M. Hayter and Otis L. Sifers—combined the first syllables of their surnames to create the name "Haysi" when a post office was

The John W. Flannagan Reservoir, near Haysi

established here in 1900. Earlier, this northeastern Dickenson County area was called "Mouth of McClure" in reference to the point where the tiny McClure River meets the Russell Fork of the Big Sandy River. The Russell Fork was named for Russell County.

Incorporated in 1936, tree-packed mountains outline Haysi's crossroads of VA-63, VA-80, and VA-83. The town, with 200 residents, annually hosts the Russell Fork Autumn Fest during the first weekend of October.

What's to See

John W. Flannagan Dam and Reservoir: Surrounded by woods and rock bluffs, the John W. Flannagan Reservoir extends 1,145 acres across central Dickenson County. Swimmers and boats with gasoline motors are both welcome at this watery playground. And so is fishing for stocked populations of walleye and hybrid striped bass. Other bass (smallmouth and largemouth), catfish (channel and flathead), crappie, and bluegill populate the lake's clear waters.

The U.S. Army Corps of Engineers built the 250-foot-high Flannagan Dam in 1964 for flood control on the Pound and Cranes Nest rivers. The lake is named for John Williams Flannagan, Jr. (1885-1955), a U.S. Congressman representing Southwest Virginia from 1931 to 1949. Picnic shelters, numerous playgrounds, and a marina shoulder the shoreline of this beautiful retreat.

Open May to September, the Lower Twin Recreation Area features about 30 shaded campsites near a rippling stream, plus a boat ramp, a playground, and a half-mile hike on the Trail of Trees. The Spillway Launch boat ramp is open April to October. The Junction Area Ramp, near the marina, stays open year-round.

Fees are charged through the Flannagan Reservoir office near the dam.

🚗 From the Haysi Post Office, follow VA-63-South (Main St.) for 3.5 miles. Turn right on VA-614 and go a half mile to a crossroads. Veer right on VA-739 and go 0.6 miles to a left turn on a short road leading to the Spillway Launch Ramp. To find the Flannagan Reservoir office, continue straight on VA-739 past the spillway access road, go another 0.8 miles, then turn right at a traffic island. Following this route for 0.4 miles, past the office, leads to a recreation area with picnic shelters and a playground.

To reach the marina and Junction Area Ramp from the Haysi Post Office, follow VA-63-South for 3.5 miles. Turn right on VA-614 and follow for 2.6 miles. Turn right on VA-755 and follow for 0.3 miles to the lake.

To reach the Lower Twin Recreation Area from the Haysi Post Office, follow VA-63-South for 3.5 miles. Turn right on VA-614 and go a half mile. Veer right on VA-739 and go 3.2 miles, crossing Flannagan Dam. Turn left on VA-611 and go 2.6 miles. Turn left on VA-683 and follow for 0.4 miles to the entrance.

Aily: In 1890, the first postmaster at Aily was Aily Counts. Central: VA-604, between Counts Ridge and Ball Ridge

Bartlick: Early settler Bartley Belcher and numerous salt licks provided the name "Bartlick." Northeastern: VA-611 at VA-612

Bee: Honeybees did not have anything to do with naming Bee. The community was named for a young girl, Beatrice Owens. Southeastern: VA-80, near Buchanan County

Birchleaf: The Birchleaf name likely comes from the region's abundance of birch trees. In the 1880s, the area was called "Sand Lick" in reference to both a well-known salt spring and the sandy soil on Lick Creek. A post office circa 1890 was called "Birch." Eastern: VA-80 at VA-607

Blowing Rock: The name Blowing Rock comes from a nearby rock formation on Pine Mountain. The rock has a hole in it, and objects are known to blow through the outcrop from the force of the wind. Blowing Rock, a farming community, supported its own post office in the early 1900s. North-central: VA-611 at VA-619

Bucu: Zack and Zeke Sutherland tried to establish a post office at Bucu in 1883 but could not find a name that would be accepted by postal officials. Capt. Jasper S. Colley eventually supplied the winning moniker when he suggested naming the place for a patent medicine called "Buchu" but using a different spelling. Southern: VA-600, near Lick Branch

Buffalo: According to legend, John Yates killed a young buffalo near the mouth of Buffalo Creek in about 1842. It was possibly the last buffalo killed in what is now Dickenson County. Central: VA-681, near VA-63

Carrie: Carrie Kiser was assistant postmistress at Carrie when a post office was established circa 1892. Previously, Carrie was called "Roll Pone," a name originating when some hunters dropped a pone of bread that rolled down a hill near the spot where the post office was later built. Southern: VA-600 at VA-657

Clinchco: Though founded with its first post office in 1917, Clinchco was not incorporated until 1990, when its population was about 500 residents. The town owes its name to an abbreviation of the Clinchfield Coal Co. Central: VA-63 at VA-83, between Haysi and Fremont

Colley: When a post office was established in 1883, Capt. Jasper S. Colley named Colley for all of the Colleys living in the area. Colley is also the place where Dickenson County's first permanent settler, Fightin' Dick Colley, built a three-walled cabin in 1816. Eastern: VA-80 at VA-671

Counts: In 1951, Susie V. Counts was the first postmaster at Counts. Central: VA-661 at VA-670

Darwin: Boasting a couple of old-fashioned general stores, Darwin takes its name from the son of Levi Vanover, a Clintwood postmaster who applied for a post office to be located here in about 1885. Western: VA-72, near VA-637

Duty: Lemuel Duty became Duty's first postmaster in 1888. Southeastern: VA-601 at VA-602

Ervinton: When Dickenson County was established in 1880, the first county court was held at or near the mouth of Caney Creek as it enters the McClure River. Located slightly north of McClure, this area was named for early settler Micajah Ervin, an activist for the establishment of Dickenson County. The community called "Ervinton" is lost on modern maps, but its name survives as a voting district and on a local school. Central: VA-63, near VA-773

Flat Top: The area called "Flat Top" was named for a level spot of land where Castlewood residents Georgie and Johnny Banner once ranged their cattle. Southern: VA-644 at VA-652

Flemingtown: Several Flemings were among the earliest settlers at Flemingtown. W. J. Fleming, a school-board clerk, proposed building a school here in 1905. North-central: VA-689, near VA-607

Fryingpan Creek: Bordered by a stocked trout stream of the same name, the community called "Fryingpan Creek" was named by hunters who found an old iron skillet beneath a nearby cliff—a frying pan probably lost by early settlers. Eastern: VA-80 at VA-625

Georges Fork: From 1907 to 1950, Georges Fork had its own post office. Its name comes from either George Stanley (who lived near the head of the Georges Fork of the Pound River) or George French (who lived near the mouth of the same creek). Another theory says the name comes from both men. Northwestern: VA-72 at VA-83

Hatchet: At least two theories guess how the tiny Hatchet community took its name. One story says early settlers found an old tomahawk at a creek here. Another says a man named John Yates named a stream "Hatchet" after losing a new hatchet in it. Southern: VA-63 at VA-604

Hazel: Depending on which story you believe, the Hazel community takes it name either from Hazel Kiser, a daughter of Ephriam Kiser, or Hazel Rasnake, a son of Joe Rasnake. South-central: VA-63, near Russell County

Honeycamp: According to one account, Honeycamp's name comes from a 19th-century settler named Robin W. Beverly, who cut three trees filled with bees along a stream. Another story says the name comes from early hunters who kept honey in hollowed-out logs. Western: VA-633 at VA-636

Isom: A post office named for early settler Isom Mullins operated here from 1905 to 1959. Northwestern: VA-611 at VA-631

Leck: The Leck community was named for early resident Elexius "Leck" Smith. Southern: VA-644, near VA-719

Longfork: When Dickenson County was first settled, members of the Long family lived or camped on the Long Fork, a tributary of the Cranes Nest River. A community called "Longfork" later developed in the area. Western: VA-72 at VA-633

Martin Town: Local residents named "Martin" are remembered in the name "Martin Town." Southern: VA-63, near VA-715

McClure: According to one legend, in April 1774 Native Americans killed a local settler named Capt. McClure while he was pursuing an Indian named Chief Logan. McClure's body was found next to a stream presumably days after he was ambushed. Some say the village of McClure was later named to honor the slain man. Central: VA-63 at VA-714

Millard: The Millard community takes its name from Millard Rose, a neighbor of John G. Kerr, the first postmaster in 1903. The Millard post office closed in 1958. Central: VA-637 at VA-639

Nancy: A Nancy post office, established in 1908, was named for Nancy Counts Anderson. Central: VA-679, south of VA-671

Nealy Ridge: Nealy Ridge was likely named for Cornealius "Nealy" Vanover, a Clintwood man who once hunted in the area. A Nealy Ridge post office operated from 1909 to 1961. Central: VA-652 at VA-663

Nora: The Nora area was earlier called "Mouth of Open Fork" for the point where the Open Fork empties into the McClure River. Nora was also nicknamed "Tiger Town" for its rough reputation of beer joints, fighting, and wild women. Tiger Town became "Nora" in 1904 for Nora Dorton, the wife of Nora's first postmaster, W. A. Dorton. Central: southernmost crossroads of VA-63 and VA-652

Norland: One story says that Monroe Beverly and G. B. Davis named Norland in 1902 for an island in Alaska. "Norland" is short for "North Land." Northwestern: VA-624 at VA-631

continued on next page

Omaha: First postmaster Isaac A. Yates wanted the post office at Omaha to be called "Yates," but postal officials refused, saying there was already a Yates in Pennsylvania, which could confuse postal clerks. Postal officials suggested the name "Omaha," an Indian word meaning "upstream" or "above on a stream." The Omaha post office was open from 1902 to 1962. Western: VA-637 at VA-692

Open Fork: A hunter named Hamon once described the Open Fork as a stream that "opened up very pretty." Southern: VA-651, immediately south of VA-652

Osborns Gap: Osborns Gap was named for Jerry Osborn, a settler who lived at the foot of Pine Mountain. Northwestern: VA-630, near VA-624

Priest Fork: A hunter named Priest is remembered in the stream and community called Priest Fork. Southeastern: VA-682, near VA-80

Rakes Ridge: Originally from Patrick County, Va., Aaron DeHart Rakes moved here in about 1878. Rakes Ridge is at the head of the Tilda Anderson Branch of the Russell Fork of the Big Sandy River. The branch is named for Matilda ("Tilda") Anderson, who lived with her husband, Charles, at its mouth, sometime after 1843. Eastern: VA-607, near Buchanan County

Ramey Flats: Prior to 1856, Billy Ramey had 352 acres of local land surveyed at Ramey Flats. North-central: VA-742, near VA-754

Ramsey Ridge: Confederate Army veteran Rainwater Ramsey settled near what became "Ramsey Ridge" in the late 1800s. West-central: VA-643 at VA-698

Skeetrock: Sloping, slick rocks in a nearby creek helped name Skeetrock, a place where people would once skate, or "skeet." Northern: VA-744 at VA-619

Smith Ridge: The area called "Smith Ridge" is known as the site of music festivals staged by old-time mountain singer Ralph Stanley, a Grammy-winning Dickenson County native and longtime resident who once served on the county's school board. Smith Ridge takes its name from George Smith, an early settler from Russell County. West-central: VA-654 at VA-643

Splashdam: The Yellow Poplar Lumber Co. built a splash dam in 1909 to create a flood to float, or "splash," logs on the Russell Fork of the Big Sandy River. Northern: VA-613, between Haysi and the Flannagan Reservoir

Steinman: This old coal camp took its name from New York's Steinman Brothers, who purchased large coal deposits here as early as 1874. Central: VA-83, near VA-607 between Clinchco and Haysi

Stratton: Frank A. Stratton was one of the first to buy coal and timber rights in Dickenson County. Stratton also gave his name to a community when a post office opened in 1887, south of McClure. Central: VA-63 at VA-684

Tarpon: Located on a ridge, Tarpon (or "Tar Pond") takes its name from a pond once covered with a layer of pine tar. Central: VA-63 at VA-607

Tiny: Tiny is a good word to describe the Tiny community—a place perhaps named for its small size when a post office was established in the early 1900s. Southeastern: VA-600 at VA-687

Tivis: The name "Tivis" comes from Tivis Colley, father of the area's first postmaster, Fitzhugh Lee Colley. North-central: VA-611 at VA-615

Trammel: Legend says early hunters found the name "Trammel" carved on a beech tree and decided to name a stream for the missing pioneer taken captive by Native Americans. The community of Trammel was a booming 1920s-era coal camp. Southern: VA-63 at VA-626

Viers Ridge: Sometime after 1854, Lewis Viers moved to this area from Patrick County, Va., and Viers Ridge took his name. Eastern: VA-605 at VA-606

Wakenva: Between Nora and Trammel, the name "Wakenva"—a combination of West Virginia (Wa), Kentucky (ken) and Virginia (va)—was coined in 1926 when coal companies of Southwest Virginia, Kentucky, and West Virginia formed the Wakenva Coal Co. Southern: VA-63 at VA-655

West Dante: Named for its location west of Russell County's Dante community, West Dante is part of a larger region known as Sandy Ridge, named for the area's sandy clay soil. Southern: VA-627, near VA-628

LEE COUNTY

Lee County's 437 square miles are wedged into Virginia's westernmost corner, with Tennessee to the south and Kentucky to the northwest. Harshly steep mountains frame the county's northeastern corner. West of the county courthouse at Jonesville, wavy farmland fills a wide valley with meandering streams and grazing horses.

Cut from a portion of Russell County in 1792 and shaped similar to the Commonwealth of Virginia, Lee County is named for Henry "Light-Horse Harry" Lee, a Revolutionary War hero and Virginia governor from 1791-1794.

BEN HUR

Col. Auburn Lorenzo Pridemore (1837-1900), a Confederate Army soldier, originated the name "Ben Hur" to designate his own private railroad stop halfway between Pennington Gap and Jonesville. Ben Hur was named in honor of Lew Wallace's novel *Ben Hur*, which Pridemore had recently read.

Besides the funny name, this central Lee County community, along US-58A, is also known for its oil wells. One sucks green Pennsylvania crude from 2,000 feet below a grassy field off VA-647. Oil drilling in Lee County—the top oil-producing county in the state—is a diminutive dynasty shared by the Rose Hill field in the west and the Ben Hur field in the east. Deposits here are part of a geologic formation that runs from Pennsylvania to Alabama. But what is here is a far cry from the output of oil operations in Texas: Virginia's oil production reached a peak in 1983 with 65,400 barrels.

What's to See

Long Hollow Log School Museum: When the old Long Hollow School was reassembled, log by log, on the campus of Lee High School in the early 1990s, it was believed to be the last one-room schoolhouse in Lee County. The structure dates to 1858 and last served as a school in the 1950s. It was used during 1863 and 1864 for Methodist camp meetings, because Confederate troops of the 64th Virginia Regiment had taken over the Jonesville Methodist Campground. Occasionally, the school is open as a museum showcasing early life on Virginia's frontier.

🚗 Lee High School is off US-58A at the VA-645 crossroads. Use the main high school entrance and turn left behind the football stadium. Follow an uphill road for 0.1 miles. The museum is on the right.

BLACKWATER

Blackwater is in southern Lee County, below Jonesville, at the crossroads of VA-70 and VA-604. The community's original name—"Black Water Place"—was shortened when a post office was established here in the 1870s.

It is not the only Blackwater in Virginia. This village shares its name with a community in southern Virginia Beach—a Blackwater located on the opposite end of the Old Dominion, following a straight line east.

Lee County's Blackwater was named by a group of early settlers who followed streams as they first cut through the wilderness. Pioneers discovered what is now called Blackwater Creek, a watercourse filled with decayed logs, leaves, and trees that gave the water a black color.

COWAN MILL

Built sometime between 1878 and 1890, the Cowan Mill drew power from water rushing over a dam on Indian Creek. The still-standing millhouse remains a picturesque landmark of western Lee County, two miles west of Ewing. It is 0.1 miles south of US-58 on VA-698 and takes its name from Joe Cowan, who bought and rebuilt the mill in 1935. It was originally called the "Ball Mill," for Moses S. Ball, who built the first mill here.

CUMBERLAND GAP

Cumberland Mountain drifts up from a base of rounded ground in Lee County to form the imposing western wall of Virginia. In the 1700s, finding a break in this blockade—the famous Cumberland Gap—was of paramount importance for further expansion of the territories of the United States. North of this gap, near Vir-

Long Hollow Log School in Ben Hur

Cowan Mill

ginia's border with both Tennessee and Kentucky, mountains block westward passage for about 400 miles.

In 1775, the Treaty of Sycamore Shoals, signed in what is now Elizabethton, Tennessee, helped the United States obtain a large portion of the Kentucky area from the Cherokee Indians. That treaty gave the trailblazing Daniel Boone and a group of 30 men the green light to mark the Wilderness Road through the Cumberland Gap. Pioneers soon flooded into the bluegrass fields of Kentucky—as many as 300,000 between 1780 and 1810.

Animals, Native Americans, and hunters had used this natural doorway long before its discovery was credited to Dr. Thomas Walker, who mapped the gap after finding it in 1750 while on a surveying expedition. Walker named the passage for the Duke of Cumberland, son of King George II of England.

For nearly a century, this gap was paved as a route for automobiles. But, in 1996, traffic was shifted to a mile-long, $232-million tunnel through Cumberland Mountain. Subsequently, the old US-25E spanning the gap was abandoned.

In 2002, officials at the Cumberland Gap National Historical Park restored the gap to approximate how it looked in the 1790s era of Boone's Wilderness Road. Lined with transplanted seedlings of native trees, the new "Wilderness Road Trail" is a 1.5-mile path that crosses a recontoured landscape packed with enough dirt to repli-

Iron furnace at the Cumberland Gap, just a few yards inside Virginia

cate the area's original elevation—about 32 feet higher than the road blasted and paved through the gap in the 1920s.

The actual Cumberland Gap, still, is only one small part of the 20,000-acre national park, established in 1940.

Virginia's western tip is within the national park boundary at the end of a moderate, mile-long trail spiraling up the 1,990-foot-high Tri-State Peak, just a few yards west of the Cumberland Gap. A wooden pavilion marks the point where Kentucky, Tennessee, and Virginia meet.

Nearby, the park's Tennessee Road Trail leads from the Wilderness Road to an 1819 iron furnace, once used to make about six tons of iron a day. A wooden platform allows visitors to actually walk inside this stone structure, standing just a few feet above the Virginia-Tennessee line. Without hiking, the furnace can be reached from US-25E—follow posted signs through Tennessee's Town of Cumberland Gap to a National Park Service road at the corner of Pennlyn Avenue and Llewellyn Street.

Look beside the furnace for a series of small falls tumbling 100 feet on Gap Creek's stony streambed. High above this stream, look for the Pinnacle, a huge outcrop hanging off the Virginia side of Cumberland Mountain at a 2,440-foot elevation.

The well-developed Pinnacle Overlook provides a grand view of the Powell Valley in Tennessee and Virginia, the Tri-State Peak, the Cumberland Gap, and Mid-

Inside Cudjo's Cave at the Cumberland Gap National Historical Park

dlesboro, Kentucky, where the park's visitor center is located on US-25E.

The Pinnacle is in Virginia. But the only way to get there by car is to follow a paved park road through Kentucky. En route, this winding road passes attractions to interest Civil War buffs—the earthworks remains of two small forts. Both are on the park's Kentucky side and marked by cannons, though neither probably saw much action. Union and Confederate armies both manned the Cumberland Gap, but each side waited for an invasion that never came.

Still, soldiers would leave their marks—with graffiti—in an underground chamber now called the "Soldiers Cave." In the 1860s, this cavity, which is on the Virginia side of Cumberland Mountain, was used for storage and as a military hospital.

In the 1890s, a subterranean passage just below the Soldiers Cave became known as "King Solomon's Cave"—so named, according to one theory, by an English syndicate that developed businesses in the Cumberland Gap area at the time. Commercial cave tours also began in the 1890s, showing off King Solomon sights like Cleopatra's Bathtub, a shallow water pool. Sometime after 1934, a tunnel was dug to connect King Solomon's Cave with the Soldiers Cave. The newly connected caves became known singularly as "Cudjo's Cave," a name originating from the title of a popular 1863 novel by J. T. Trowbridge, in which characters explore a fictional cave in the Cumberland Mountains.

In 1992, the National Park Service acquired Cudjo's Cave after its many years as a commercial tourist attraction. Park officials removed the cave's old lighting system but added new stairways and concrete walkways. Park visitors now tour the cavern's

dripstone in the dark, using only hand-held, battery-powered lanterns to shine light on countless columns or the Soldiers Cave's most famous formation, the 45-foot-tall Pillar of Hercules, claimed to be the world's largest stalagmite. The small lights give visitors a "wild cave" tour effect and show how the damp cavern might have looked to Thomas Walker, who noted the presence of a "large Cave" in a journal entry dated April 13, 1750.

In all, more than 50 miles of hiking and biking paths—from short walks to challenging treks—cross this tri-state park. In Virginia, the moderate Lewis Hollow Trail leaves the Wilderness Road Picnic Area on US-58 near the 160-site Wilderness Road Campground. The trail heads uphill for 0.6 miles to the Skylight Cave, a grotto with a 30-foot-high entrance inside a stony embankment. Higher up, on the spine of Cumberland Mountain, a handful of primitive campsites are scattered along the park's Ridge Trail.

🚗 From the Lee County Courthouse in Jonesville, it's a 32-mile trip west on US-58 to reach the park-entrance sign at the Wilderness Road Picnic Area and Campground. Beyond that, go west for two more miles to a right turn on US-25E, then follow through the Cumberland Gap Tunnel to find the park visitor center, on the left, just before entering Middlesboro.

DRYDEN

In eastern Lee County, Dryden is a residential area near the crossroads of VA-726 and US-58A. It was earlier known as "Turkey Cove," either for an Indian chief called "Turkey Foot" or for flocks of turkeys in nearby forests. The present name comes from a Louisville & Nashville Railroad official remembered as "Captain Dryden." On the second Saturday of each September, Dryden hosts a festival called "Old Fashion Day."

ELYDALE

In western Lee County, the name "Elydale" remembers Robert Ely, who built the prominent Elydale Mansion here in 1878 along what is now US-58's westernmost intersection with VA-690, about five miles west of Ewing.

Facing Elydale School, the 12-room mansion centers the 200-acre Wilderness Road State Park and is called "Karlan," a name combination from past owners Karl and Ann Harris. Large white columns grace the front porch of this Plantation-style structure, and a grove of maples shades the front lawn. Nearby, picnic tables scattered beneath shade trees offer respite along a branch of Indian Creek.

The mansion is not far from the former path of the Louisville & Nashville Railroad, now called the "Wilderness Road Trail." A multiuse recreational path covered with crushed gravel has replaced the tracks of the chugging trains. The flat surface spans 14 miles along the approximate Wilderness Road used by frontiersman Daniel Boone to traverse Southwest Virginia in the 1770s. Trail access is available at the park or along several secondary highways.

One stop on the trail is the park's rustic replica of Martin's Station, a frontier outpost that stood a few miles east at Rose Hill in 1775. Taking its name from pioneer Joseph Martin, the original station served as a layover for early travelers on the Wilderness Road. In 2002, an army of mostly volunteers built this fort using only the kinds of tools that would have been available on Virginia's frontier in the 1770s.

Annually, the park holds the daylong Wilderness Road Festival on the second Saturday of October. A living-history event, *Raid at Martin's Station,* is held on the second weekend in May.

EWING

If you hear stories of cattle farms and oil drilling in western Lee County, you might think the Ewing clan of the CBS-TV show "Dallas" had something to do with the Ewing community's name. Still, while descriptions of the scenery may sound like Texas (and, yes, there once was a Ewing Oil Co. here), the village of Ewing takes its name from pioneer Samuel Ewing, Lee County's first sheriff. In the 1890s, a station on the Louisville & Nashville Railroad was named to honor Ewing. The community resides near the crossroads of US-58-Business and VA-724.

What's to See

White Rocks: A mile-long strand of white rock outcrops crown the spine of Cumberland Mountain. These sandstone cliffs rise above Ewing's northwestern horizon to an elevation of 3,500 feet. White Rocks can be seen for miles—from Caylor to Rose Hill—in Lee County's western corner. Kentucky is immediately beyond these rocks, marking the approximate eastern border of the Cumberland Gap National Historical Park. To the trailblazing Daniel Boone, seeing these skyline markers meant he would have to travel one more day west to reach the Cumberland Gap.

A trail inside the national park leads to the White Rocks. To find the path from US-58 at Ewing, turn north on VA-724 and go one mile. Veer left when the road forks at the entrance to the Thomas Walker Civic Park. The trail begins behind a stone picnic shelter.

JONESVILLE

Jonesville is midway between the dense mountains of eastern Lee County and the rolling Powell Valley on the county's western tip. Roads on the north side of US-58, the town's Main Street, climb steep hills and make great views easy to find.

Incorporated in 1834, Jonesville was home to about 1,000 residents in 2000. The courthouse town is the namesake of Frederick Jones, who donated land for its site in 1794. Jones is buried at the entrance to the town's Cumberland Bowl Park, a 23-acre day-use facility with a playground, a swimming pool, an amphitheater, and a picnic area at the end of Park Street, off US-58. Nearby, the Lee County Courthouse on Main Street was built in 1933 and renovated in 1978.

Two miles west of town, near US-58 at VA-652, the Jonesville Methodist Campground is a landmark listed on state and national historic registers. It's been in annual use for August revivals since 1810—except for two years during the Civil War.

What's to See

Dr. Andrew Taylor Still Memorial Park: A wooden monument at a small park near Jonesville tells the story of Dr. Andrew Taylor Still (1828-1917) and his development of osteopathic medicine. Dr. Still was born in a log cabin at the site of this park, about two miles west of the Lee County Courthouse. He lived here until 1837, when his family left for Missouri.

In 1874, after years of intense medical study, Dr. Still announced his own unique medical philosophy. He combined Greek words—*osteo,* meaning "bone," and *pathy,* meaning "feel-

White Rocks

ing"—to create a new kind of medicine called "osteopathy." Dr. Still theorized that all parts of the body were interrelated and that the body must be treated as a whole to combat disease. In 1892, Dr. Still furthered his medical mission when he founded the American School of Osteopathy in Kirksville, Missouri.

Dr. Still's birthplace cabin was moved from Lee County in 1928 to the Kirksville campus. In 1993, the cabin's original site became the Dr. Andrew Taylor Still Memorial Park, featuring eight large picnic tables under four separate shelters.

🚙 From US-58 at Jonesville, follow VA-662 southwest for 1.5 miles. The park is on the left.

KEOKEE

Settlers first called the Keokee region "Upper Crab Orchard" for the many crabapple trees growing wild in the valley. A post office using that name opened in 1872.

"Keokee" comes from Keokee Monroe Henderson Perin, the wife of Charles Perin, president of the Perin Engineering Co. of New York. Charles Perin developed Keokee's coal-mining operations in the early 1920s, a time when Keokee supported its own jewelry store, opera house, and concert band. The place later became a quiet village in the extreme northeastern corner of Lee County. It lines about a mile of VA-606 where the highway meets VA-624 three times.

What's to See

Lake Keokee Recreation Area: When the headwaters of the Powell River were impounded in 1975 to create Lake Keokee, standing timber was left protruding from the surface of the reservoir to provide habitat for fish and other wildlife, but many of those trees were removed when the lake was renovated in 2003. The Lake Keokee Recreation Area includes picnic tables, a fishing pier, a five-mile loop trail, and a paved ramp for boats with trolling motors. Overseen by the Clinch Ranger District of the Jefferson National Forest, the 92-acre lake is open year-round.

🚙 From US-58A at Pennington Gap, follow US-421 north for 2.7 miles. Turn right on VA-606 and follow northeast for 15.1 miles, going through Keokee, then turn right on VA-623. Go a half mile to a left turn on VA-876, then follow for one mile to the lake.

Alternate Route: From US-23-Business (N. Main St.) in Appalachia, follow VA-68 west for about six miles until it becomes VA-606 in Lee County, then follow for two more miles. Turn left on VA-623 and follow for a half mile. Turn left on VA-876 and follow for one mile to the lake.

NATURAL BRIDGE

The one-story-high Natural Bridge of Lee County is a 35-foot-wide limestone arch over Batie Creek. Frontiersman Daniel Boone used the structure when he built a road to Cumberland Gap in the 1770s. Boone's road later became the two lanes of VA-662 near Jonesville, two miles southwest of US-58. The bridge and the creek are in the public domain, but surrounding land is privately owned.

PENNINGTON GAP

Lee County's largest town and primary commercial center is named for one or several Penningtons, including early business leaders E. W. Pennington, William Pennington, and John W. Pennington. Formerly known as "Graham" and "Han," the Town of Pennington Gap was incorporated in 1891, about the time the Louisville & Nashville Railroad reached the area, near the crossroads of US-421 and US-58A in central Lee County. In 2000, Pennington Gap was home to about 1,800 residents.

What's to See

Cave Springs Recreation Area: Mountain air is thick and earthy at the Cave Springs Recreation Area. In the lush Jefferson National Forest, this retreat features 41 wooded campsites. A quarter-acre pond with a sandy beach and swimming area is fed by a spring below the five-foot-high opening of Cave Springs Cave, a grotto gated to protect its native bat species. The cave is visible from a 500-yard-long trail originating near Campsite 22.

The cave trail is a spur of the strenuous Stone Mountain Trail, which spans 14 miles from Cave Springs to the Roaring Branch at Big Stone Gap (see the Wise County chapter in the Western Front section).

Cave Springs is open May to September. Fees are charged through the Clinch Ranger District of the Jefferson National Forest.

🚙 From US-421-South at Pennington Gap, follow US-58A east for 2.5 miles. Turn left on VA-767 and head north for 0.7 miles. Bear right on VA-621 and follow east for 3.3 miles. Turn left at the area's entrance on VA-845.

Stone Face Rock: Called "The Guardian of the Pass" by early Native Americans, the formation jutting from a rock wall about 150 feet above US-421 creates a prominent landmark. This outcrop looks just like a face—it features a large, sloping forehead, a pointed nose, a big chin, and sunken eyes. A train tunnel passes through what looks like a neck.

Locals call it the "Stone Face Rock." It protrudes from a cliff on the southwest side of Stone Mountain in a gap formed by the North Fork of the Powell River.

Is this a natural phenomenon? Who knows? One theory says the Stone Face Rock is an ancient Cherokee Indian head carved to mark a gathering place.

🚙 From US-58A at Pennington Gap, follow US-421 north for 1.5 miles. The rock hangs over the left side of the road.

In eastern Lee County, Stickleyville grew up as a stop along the old Fincastle Turnpike, a wagon trail that once connected the Cumberland Gap to the Town of Fincastle in Botetourt County, Virginia. Stickleyville lies at the crossroads of US-58/421 and VA-612, between Powell Mountain and Wallen Ridge. It takes its name from early settler Vastine Stickley (Stoekli). The Stickley house became the "Stout Hotel," a stopover for travelers, sometime after Stickley's death in the 1850s.

What's to See

Powell Mountain Overlook: Looking south from the Lee-Scott county border at the Powell Mountain Overlook, mountains seem to roll forever across Scott County—clear down to Tennessee—from the overlook's 2,319-foot elevation.

Powell Mountain is a namesake of Ambrose Powell, an explorer who accompanied Dr. Thomas Walker through Southwest Virginia in 1750. Powell carved his name on so many trees in the region that subsequent travelers naturally lent Powell's name to the Powell River, Powell Mountain, and Powell Valley.

🚗 The overlook is on US-58/421, about two miles east of Stickleyville School, on the Lee-Scott county line.

Stone Face Rock at Pennington Gap

ROSE HILL Rose Hill was once called "Martin's Fort" or "Martin's Station" for Joseph Martin, who established a fort here in western Lee County in about 1769. Attacks by Indians, however, soon forced settlers to abandon the site. In 1775, a new "Martin's Station" was built with a half dozen cabins.

A "Rose Hill" railroad depot opened in 1890 at this area between Jonesville and Ewing. Local lore says the name originated from a nearby hill blooming with wild roses.

In the late 1990s, a four-lane version of US-58 bypassed the unincorporated town's commercial buildings along the old two-lane version of US-58, near VA-672.

Martin's Station replica at Elydale

Bonny Blue: An old coal camp of the early 1900s, Bonny Blue lies on the eastern slope of Black Mountain. Its name might be a reference to the one-star design of the Bonnie Blue Flag, which originated in the Republic of West Florida in the early 1800s. Before the adoption of the Stars and Bars, supporters of the Confederate States of America rallied under this flag, which came to symbolize rebellion. North-central: northern terminus of VA-634, near St. Charles

Calvin: Calvin Pardee, president of the Blackwood Coal and Coke Co., based his operations at Calvin after the company was organized in 1903. Northeastern: VA-756, near Keokee

Caylor: Caylor should actually be called "Taylor," but a mistake was made in about 1890 in the paperwork required to register the name of the train depot. Soon, without a correction, the wrong name showed up on maps. The Taylor name would have honored T. A. Taylor and his wife, Susan Ely Taylor. The couple either sold or donated land for Caylor's railroad station. Mrs. Taylor, incidentally, had married Mr. Taylor after the death of her first husband, Robert Ely, who built the Elydale Mansion, now the centerpiece of the nearby Wilderness Road State Park. Western: VA-690's easternmost intersection with US-58

Collier Mill: Near the Powell River, Collier Mill was named for early settler Maston Collier. Eastern: VA-640, near VA-643

Darnell Town: Raleigh Darnell operated an early store at Darnell Town. Northeastern: VA-606, between Rawhide and Keokee

Dot: Truly a small place, Dot's name spurs a lot of jokes, considering the community is hardly bigger than a dot on a map. One story says the name comes from Amanda Shelburne—known to residents here by her nickname, "Dot," when she ran the farming community's post office in the early 1900s. Central: US-58 at US-421

Fleenortown: Dr. Drury Fleenor (1813-1876) and his family founded the Fleenortown community in 1858 and established a one-room schoolhouse that doubled as a meeting place for church services. Central: VA-647, northwest of Jonesville

Gibson Station: Maj. George Gibson (1732-1819), a pioneer settler and Revolutionary War hero, built a fort—or two-story log house—known as "Gibson Station" in this vicinity in about 1785. Western: US-58 at VA-692

Hagan: In 1890, Patrick Hagan sold land to the Louisville & Nashville Railroad so a depot could be built, and the area was subsequently called "Hagan." The community borders Hardy Creek, a stream named for the families of Thomas and William Hardy, who moved to Lee County circa 1800. Western: VA-621 at VA-789

Hickory Flats: Native hickory trees and level farmland likely inspired the name "Hickory Flats." Central: VA-638 at VA-642

Hubbard Springs: Twenty-two springs of mineral water became known as "Hubbard Springs" for Eli Hubbard, who owned property in the area in 1850. In 1903, John Snodgrass established a springwater resort here; it burned in 1976 after being closed for several years. Central: VA-621, near VA-657

Jasper: One account says that Jasper was named for Jasper Edens, a local railroad employee in about 1900. At that time, the Jasper area was extensively logged, and the Jasper Depot served as a shipping point. Eastern: US-23 at VA-611

McLins Store: In the 1840s, the McLin family built an Old West-style general store at what became the McLins Store community. Many McLin family members are buried in a cemetery near the store site, a half mile west of Rose Hill. Western: US-58-Business at VA-671

Ocoonita: Located along railroad tracks, Ocoonita takes its name from an Indian princess, according to local tradition. Central: VA-621, three miles west of Ben Hur

Olinger: Founding members of the Olinger Missionary Baptist Church in 1905 included James Aaron Doc Olinger, Julia Olinger Thompson, and Phoebe Parsons Olinger. In 1907, James Aaron Doc Olinger donated land for a new church to be built in the Olinger community. Eastern: VA-621 at VA-622

Penn Lee: Penn Lee is a settlement named for the Penn Lee Coal Co., a name combining either "Penn" for Pennsylvania (the home of many coal operators) or Pennington (for nearby Pennington Gap) with "Lee" for Lee County. North-central: VA-352, between Stone Creek and St. Charles

Pocket: The North Fork of the Powell River makes a sharp turn between Pennington Gap and St. Charles, leaving what locals call a small "pocket" of land, naturally inspiring the name of the Pocket community. North-central: VA-606 at US-421

Rawhide: Called "Morris Town" in its earliest days, Rawhide was originally a company town owned by Alexander Morris. Several members of the Morris family lived in the area when young Limmie Morris nicknamed the community "Rawhide." In 1952, the Rawhide Missionary Baptist Church opened here. Northeastern: VA-624's westernmost crossroads with VA-606

Robbins Chapel: Charles Robbins moved to the Robbins Chapel area in the early 1800s. In about 1870, his son, the Rev. Zion Robbins, donated a parcel of land that became the site of Robbins Chapel United Methodist Church. Northeastern: VA-606 at VA-766

Seminary: Scenic Seminary takes its name from the Seminary United Methodist Church, a prominent brick landmark built here in 1851. Eastern: US-58A at VA-708

Shepherd Hill: A local Shepherd family was among the first settlers at Shepherd Hill. Northeastern: VA-606 at VA-625

Silver Leaf: In the 1700s, frontiersman Daniel Boone named a place "Silver Maple" for a type of tree growing in the area. In the early 1800s, resident Eli Davis renamed the community "Silver Leaf." Southwestern: VA-667 at VA-671

St. Charles: Near the border of Harlan County, Ky., St. Charles is a gateway to old coal camps. The town's title originated in 1907 from a combination of the names of coal-mine owner Charles Bondurant and his secretary, Mrs. St. John. Incorporated in 1914, St. Charles was home to about 200 residents in 2000. North-central: VA-352 at VA-628

Stone Creek: Between Pennington Gap and St. Charles, Stone Creek is named for a stone-bedded creek that empties into the North Fork of the Powell River. North-central: US-421 at VA-352

Turners Siding: "Turners Siding" refers to a fork on a railroad line named for Henry Turner, who lived in the area in the 1800s. North-central: VA-635 at VA-636, near St. Charles

Van: The Rev. John B. Van, a Baptist preacher, operated the short-lived Van post office in the late 1800s. South-central: VA-612 at VA-615

Wallen Ridge: Named for Elisha Wallen, a long hunter who roamed the region in the late 1700s, Wallen Ridge runs across southern Lee County. A village called "Wallen Ridge" is near Hancock County, Tenn. South-central: VA-613 at VA-758

Wheeler: Early pioneers of Lee County included a Wheeler family in the vicinity of the Wheeler community. Western: US-58 at VA-691

Woodway: Once called "Witt's Store" and "Tradeville Voting Precinct," Woodway took its name from an early postmaster named Wood (or Woods). Central: VA-642 at VA-785, near US-421

CITY OF NORTON

You can't get to Norton without passing through Wise County. Hemmed in by steep mountains at an elevation of 2,150 feet, this small city at the geographic heart of Wise County was first called "Prince's Flats" for William Prince, who settled here in the 1780s. The town was renamed "Eolia" in 1883 when a post office was established. By 1890, Eolia had become a railroad center during Southwest Virginia's coal boom, and the community was renamed to honor Eckstein Norton, then president of the Louisville & Nashville Railroad.

Norton was incorporated in 1894 as a Wise County town. Sixty years later, on April 6, 1954, Norton emerged as an independent city, though it was still surrounded by the county. The 2000 census counted about 3,900 residents here at the northernmost crossroads of US-23 and US-58A.

Park Avenue is Norton's main street. During Christmas, lights along the sidewalks, and icicles posted on street lamps bring the thoroughfare to life. The second week of June marks the time for the Best Friend Festival, a week-long party featuring live music and art displays.

At the heart of Norton, the Virginia-Kentucky Opry stages Saturday-night shows of country, bluegrass, rock, and gospel music. The two-hour concerts are broadcast live on Norton's WAXM-FM (93.5), a 50,000-watt radio station. The Opry opened in 1995 inside an old department store at 724 Park Ave. The cozy theater seats 241, with about 40 seats in the balcony.

What's to See

Benge's Rock and *Legion Park:* Chief Bob Benge (1760-1794) led warring raids on white settlers along the Southwest Virginia frontier. The notorious character, half white and half Cherokee, resisted the advance of white settlers into Native American homelands. He waged infamous battles, sometimes seizing white women and children, who were then adopted by various Indian groups.

According to local folklore, Benge used a large rock near Norton either as a place of meditation or as a lookout. The

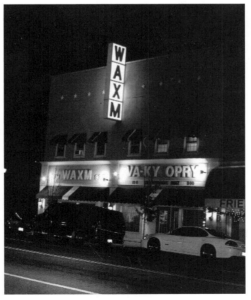

The WAXM VA-KY Opry

sharp outcrop, called "Benge's Rock," provides a sweeping view of the Stone Mountain area. A nearby tributary of the Powell River, a stream called "Benge's Branch," is dammed as part of the Norton Reservoir.

Lt. Vincent Hobbs and a group of men killed Benge in April of 1794, reportedly at a place near Norton called "Benge's Gap." Among historians, however, the exact location of Benge's death remains a cause for debate. But his demise did virtually mark the end of the early settlers' wars with Indians in Southwest Virginia's Western Front and Clinch Mountain Country. After Benge's death, these deep woods were considered much safer to settle.

The small Legion Park is located just below Benge's Rock. Operated by the Norton Parks and Recreation Department, Legion Park was named for its location, the site of an old American Legion Hall. The park includes picnic tables and a scenic trail along a mountain stream.

🚗 From US-23/58A at Norton, follow VA-619 south, toward High Knob, for a half mile to Legion Park, on the right. Benge's Rock, also on the right, is at a switchback about a quarter mile beyond the park.

Country Cabin: Bluegrass and old-time Appalachian music are mainstays onstage at the Country Cabin. But what really connects with the folks at this Norton-area night spot is the traditional "broomdance" contest. Here, one clogger in the crowd must mope around the dance floor with a broom in hand, instead of a partner. A band onstage plays an instrumental, while an announcer periodically hollers "Break!" The call is a cue to switch partners and is also a chance for the original lonely dancer to pass off the broom to somebody else. All the while, the band plays on and the whole charade collects lots of laughs.

Saturday-night dances are a long-standing routine at the Country Cabin. The Works Progress Administration built the original log Country Cabin in 1937. Kate Peters Sturgill, a local ballad singer and songwriter, later made the cramped-but-cozy cabin a community center for square dances, box suppers, and cakewalks. Sturgill's purpose was lost for many years when the cabin became a rental property and then a mattress factory. In 1978, dances resumed at this Depression-era relic listed on both state and national historic registers.

The nonprofit Appalachian Traditions oversees operations. In 2001, the group constructed a larger dance hall, also made of logs. The Country Cabin II, with 3,200 square feet, stands near the original structure.

🚗 From Norton, follow US-23-Business west for 1.5 miles, just beyond the Wise County community of Josephine. The modern dance hall is on the right. The original Country Cabin is on the left.

Flag Rock Recreation Area and *Norton Reservoir:* Old Glory sails atop a rock perch at 1,000 feet above the City of Norton. This American flag on the city's southern skyline is the focal point of the Flag Rock Recreation Area, one of the most popular destinations for day-trip and overnight recreation in Virginia's Western Front.

From a parking lot, a two-minute hike leads to a boulder-bluff overlook, guarded by chain-link fencing and some scruffy, lonesome-looking pines. This spot gives a treetop view of Flag Rock and the city. But when fog rolls in, the flag—even just 100 yards away—disappears in the mist, and the city becomes a total blur.

About the flag: Karl Matuszgyk, a German immigrant, and two friends, Herbert Bailey and Pete Keller, went camping in 1923 and decided to erect a flag here on a bluff above the town. But that wasn't easy—cutting a hole in the rock required a hammer and chisel. Since then, many flags and poles have been replaced. In 1974, with the park's dedication, the City of Norton adopted care of the site.

The Flag Rock Recreation Area features two small campgrounds and bathhouses with hot showers. Picnic sites, hiking trails, and a playground are scattered among woods and odd rock formations.

The 10-acre Norton Reservoir, accessible by trail or by road, lies adjacent to the area. The reservoir features a fishing pier and a concrete ramp for small boats (trolling motors only). The reservoir is stocked seasonally with trout. A state fishing license and a special permit issued by the City of Norton are required to fish here.

🚗 From US-23/58A at Norton, follow VA-619 south, toward High Knob, for two miles to the Flag Rock Recreation Area. The Norton Reservoir is about a half mile past the Flag Rock entrance, on the left.

The original Country Cabin, built in 1937

Fog envelops Flag Rock, overlooking the City of Norton

WISE COUNTY

Wise County boasts a rich coal-mining history, and holds vast stretches of the Jefferson National Forest at places like High Knob, Pound, and Big Stone Gap. Spanning about 405 square miles, the county's terrain is quite mountainous, pocketed with only a few small valleys. Wise is named for Henry Alexander Wise, the Virginia governor (1856-1860) at the time of its creation in 1856 from parts of Lee, Scott, and Russell counties.

APPALACHIA

For decades, the Town of Appalachia thrived as a coal-mining center and a gateway to outlying coal camps along VA-78. Incorporated in 1906 and once known as "The Magic City of Wise County," by 1923 Appalachia's population had soared to 3,700. In a 1930s brochure, the Appalachia Chamber of Commerce claimed the town was home to 4,400 people.

But the rush didn't last. Beginning in the 1950s, mechanization in the mines meant hard times for miners. Increased use of coal-mining machinery and a steady succession of mine shutdowns eventually equated to a loss of jobs and a subsequent loss of population. The town dropped to about 1,800 residents in 2000.

Still, townspeople rally around Appalachia's history. During the first weekend of each August, Appalachia celebrates its heritage with a railroad festival. And, yes, the railroad remains here in southwestern Wise County; on Pine Street, at the center of town, a car will cross no less than five sets of train tracks.

Like the name implies, Appalachia is at the heart of the Appalachian Mountains. The name "Appalachia" is derived from an Indian tribe named "Appalachee" by the Spanish in the 1500s.

Among the town's most unique structures is the Peake Building, an apartment house with street-level access on four floors. The front door faces Main Street, and the rounded brick building—named for former owner Emma Peake—also has entrances on its second, third, and fourth stories at a slope along Virginia Avenue.

The circa-1900 Bee Rock Tunnel, southwest of downtown Appalachia, once attracted attention from "Ripley's Believe It or Not." Deemed the "Shortest Railroad Tunnel in the United States" in the mid-20th century, the 47-foot, 7-inch-long bore stands on the abandoned line of the Powell River Railroad. The tunnel can be seen from US-23-Business, between Big Stone Gap and Appalachia, directly above a sign announcing Appalachia's corporate limits. Look for it in winter, when leaves are gone.

BIG STONE GAP

In the late 19th century, investors from northern states flocked to a rugged gap in Stone Mountain—the Big Stone Gap—and dreamed of creating the "Pittsburgh of the South."

Such a dream did not quite come true at Wise County's southernmost incorporated town. But Mineral City, as Big Stone Gap was once called, did thrive through coal mining, lumbering, and extracting iron ore—until natural resources proved not as rich as early investors had hoped.

This place was not another Pittsburgh.

Still, in the late 1880s, the elite of Southwest Virginia's Western Front scraped modern civilization out of a remote wilderness at Big Stone Gap. Coal-mine owners and operators built large Victorian homes along scenic Wyandotte Avenue and in neighborhoods like Poplar Hill.

One of the largest of those homes is now the Southwest Virginia Museum, a state historical park at the corner of West First Street and Wood Avenue. Through permanent and rotating exhibits, Big Stone Gap becomes the museum's model, showing the metamorphosis of the mountains with the coal industry forever changing the landscape.

Initially, this mansion-turned-museum was simply a summer retreat for Rufus Ayers (1849-1926), a Confederate Army veteran and Virginia attorney general. Ayers was instrumental in developing Big Stone Gap's coal, iron-ore, and railroad industries. The house, built from 1888 to 1895,

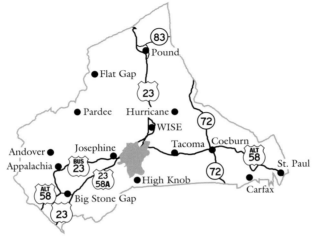

cost Ayers $25,000, a lofty sum at the time. His demands included hand-carved woodwork and hand-chiseled stonework. Later owned by various family members, one of Ayers's sons, Harry, gave up the house to pay a gambling debt. In 1929, long-time Southwest Virginia congressman C. Bascom Slemp (1870-1943) purchased the home. State officials acquired the mansion in 1946, opening the museum two years later.

Nearby, at the corner of East Third Street and Shawnee Avenue, the Harry W. Meador, Jr. Coal Museum spotlights local coal mining. This informal exhibit hall is named for Westmoreland Coal Co. vice president Harry W. Meador, Jr. (1922-1981), who personally collected and cataloged displays. Inside is a mine telephone, coal-camp photographs, and remnants of the long-gone Stonega Hospital. Outside hulks a 1960s-era continuous-mining machine. The wooden cabin housing the museum was once the library of local writer John Fox, Jr. (1862-1919).

Fox, by the way, is Big Stone Gap's foremost pride and joy. Born near Paris, Kentucky, Fox moved to town after his parents bought a small mountain retreat—now known as the John Fox, Jr. Home at 117 Shawnee Ave. Witnessing many additions, the Fox family's four-room house gradually grew until it included 22 rooms. Years later, after the nonprofit Lonesome Pine Arts and Crafts acquired it, the home opened to public tours. Fox wrote novels like *The Little Shepherd of Kingdom Come* (1903) in this house. He died of pneumonia in 1919, not long after catching a cold while visiting friends in nearby Norton.

In 1908, Fox made Big Stone Gap famous with his million-selling novel *The Trail of the Lonesome Pine,* set at a place called "The Gap" along the Kentucky-Virginia border.

In 2000, with the town's population at more than 5,000 residents, similar attention turned to the release of a Random House novel, *Big Stone Gap,* by former town resident Adriana Trigiani, whose book refers to various local landmarks.

Trigiani's book mentions *The Trail of the Lonesome Pine,* an outdoor drama based on Fox's novel. Each summer, Big Stone Gap stages productions of the often funny, sometimes crazy *Trail,* offering Fox's semi-fictitious version of how the mountains along the Virginia-Kentucky border were settled. Onstage since 1964, this easy-to-follow show stars aspiring local actors. The play follows Jack Hale, a tall, handsome mining engineer who comes to the Big Stone Gap area (or "The Gap," as this play calls it) and finds more than just coal. Hale also finds a young, barefoot mountain girl named June Tolliver and falls madly in love.

Trail is as wild as a Western, complete with heart-stopping gunshots, a family feud, threats of revenge killing, objections to an organized police force, and the hanging of a guy named Red Fox, who preaches he'll rise again from the dead, just like Jesus Christ. The Red Fox is among a few characters based on real people John Fox had met or heard about while living in Big Stone Gap. His inspiration for June Tolliver, for example, came from Elizabeth Morris, a young schoolgirl who moved to Big Stone Gap from nearby Keokee (see the Lee County chapter in the Western Front section). Morris lived in what was later dubbed the "June Tolliver House," at the corner of Clinton Avenue and Jerome Street. The brick landmark guards the gate at the outdoor playhouse and includes displays of Big Stone Gap memorabilia and antique furniture.

In its earliest days, Big Stone Gap was tagged "Three Forks" for its proximity to three forks, or streams, feeding into the Powell River. The town first incorporated as Mineral City in 1882, then Big Stone Gap in 1888.

The statue of a coal miner stands at Miner's Park, East Fifth Street at Wood Avenue. On East First Street, the much larger Bullitt Park, named in 1935 for early entrepreneur Joshua Taggart Bullitt, features picnic facilities, ball fields, and a playground.

At 619 Gilley Ave., one mile into town from US-23 Big Stone Gap Exit 1, the Interstate Railroad Private Car No. 101 serves as an information center for tourists. Built in 1870 for the South Carolina and Georgia Railroad, the car includes an observation room, two staterooms, a dining area, and a kitchen with most original fixtures intact. The car remained on rails until 1959, when the well-traveled vehicle was retired.

Immediately south of Big Stone Gap Exit 1, the 100-acre campus of Mountain Empire Community College hosts a popular festival, Home Crafts Days, on the third weekend of each October.

What's to See

Big Cherry Reservoir: Isolated on the headwaters of the South Fork of the Powell River, amid the Jefferson National Forest, Big Cherry Reservoir is a 250-acre lake owned by the Town of Big Stone Gap. It's open for boats with trolling motors. You can fish, too, but no live bait is allowed, and one of the town's paid permits is required for visitation.

🚗 From Big Stone Gap Exit 2, follow US-23/58A for seven miles north to Norton. Turn right on VA-619 and go south for four miles. Immediately past High Knob, turn right on USFS-237 and go five miles, passing several cabins, then turn right on a rough road with signs marked TOWN OF BIG STONE GAP PROPERTY. The lake is a quarter mile downhill.

Powell Valley Overlook: A handicapped-accessible walkway leads to a panoramic view of the Powell River Valley on the northwestern side of Powell Mountain. This overlook is just off the four-lane route of US-23/58A, four miles north of Big Stone Gap Exit 2.

Roaring Branch: The Stone Mountain Trail ascends a set of stone steps—away from the hot, dry pavement of US-23-Business—to enter the cool, moist climate of the Jefferson National Forest. The difficult trail bypasses many rock formations on its 14-mile way to the Cave Springs Recreation Area near Pennington Gap (see the Lee County chapter of the Western Front section). At the trailhead near Big Stone Gap are the refreshing sights and sounds of the Roaring Branch, a place where miniature waterfalls spray wispy waters on moss-covered boulders, especially during rainy springs. The small Roaring Branch parking area is on the left edge of US-23-Business, following north toward Appalachia for 0.7 miles from Big Stone Gap's northern limits.

COEBURN

A post office called "Guest's Station" was established in the Coeburn area in the late 1860s and took its name from the nearby Guest River (or Gist's River). The "Guest" comes from explorer Christopher Gist, who surveyed a 500,000-acre boundary of land south of the Ohio River in 1749. One story says Gist once camped near here at the mouth of Tom's Creek, and that campsite was later named Guest's Station.

In 1892, the name of this eastern Wise County area was changed to "Coeburn" for W. W. Coe and William E. Burns, partners in the Coeburn Land and Improvement Co. Coeburn, at the crossroads of VA-72 and US-58A, was incorporated in 1894 and home to about 2,000 people in 2000.

Small stores line Coeburn's downtown corridor on Front Street. Among them, at 409 Front St. East, is the Purely Appalachia Crafts Center, a nonprofit outlet selling locally handcrafted wares. It opened in 2000 in the former location of Lay's Furniture and Hardware. Also on Front Street, scenic arch bridges span Little Tom's Creek, a grassy stream sometimes known to run nearly dry. On Labor Day weekends, the creek's corridor becomes the site of the town's annual Guest River Rally festival.

What's to See

Guest River Gorge: Water draining out of southeastern Wise County ends up in the Guest River, roaring and tumbling over bleach-white boulders the size of cars. The 5.8-mile Guest River Gorge Trail overlooks the splashy river's flumes from behind a young-growth forest woven with informal paths leading to fishing holes. The mostly flat trail follows an abandoned rail line once used to haul coal. Compared to similar rail-to-trail projects like the Virginia Creeper Trail or New River Trail State Park, the Guest River Gorge is largely unknown and seldom crowded.

Near its start, the trail slips through the dark, damp Swede Tunnel, built in 1922 and named for its Swedish builders. Before entering the tunnel, look on the right for a 15-foot waterfall pouring down a raceway on a tiny stream. Near Mile 1.5, water spills over a 22-foot drop on Crab Orchard Branch; the 20-foot-wide cascade can be seen from a tiny trestle. At a wooden bench at Mile 3.5, Lick Log Branch drops 40 feet about 10 yards off the trail.

Only narrowly missing overhanging cliffs, the trail dead-ends near the confluence of the Guest and Clinch rivers. Established in 1994 as part of the Jefferson National Forest, the trail property boundary is 100 feet wide, or 50 feet from either side of the trail's center. To avoid trespassing, assume that not everything visible is inside the national forest.

The trail is for hiking and biking only. Horses are not allowed.

🚗 From US-58A in Coeburn, follow VA-72 south for about two miles. The entrance road is on the left and runs 1.2 miles to a large parking area at the trailhead.

Lonesome Pine International Raceway: Stock-car races are held on Saturday nights, spring to fall, as part of NASCAR's Dodge Weekly Series at the Lonesome Pine International Raceway. First opened in 1972, this 0.375-mile track is on VA-813 (Norton-Coeburn Rd.), just off US-58A. In the 1980s, the raceway closed during a local economic slump, but it reopened in 1990. Seating capacity is 6,500.

HIGH KNOB

In the Jefferson National Forest in south-central Wise County, High Knob stands at a 4,162-foot elevation between Powell Mountain and Stone Mountain. On the peak's east, water flows into the Clinch River; water on the west washes into the Powell River. On a clear day, High Knob affords views of at least four states from its observation tower. To the east, binoculars are not really needed to see the pointy spine of Virginia's Clinch Mountain—from Little Moccasin Gap in Washington County to Big Moccasin Gap in Scott County. Look for Tennessee's Bays and Chimneytop mountains on the southwest, and Black Mountain—the highest point in Kentucky—on the immediate west. It is also possible to see the mile-high peaks of North Carolina in the distant southeast, and sometimes West Virginia to the north.

High Knob's wooden tower, built in 1978, is most popular during September and October when leaves change color. During spring and summer, the view—and even the 40-foot tower itself—may be lost in a foggy haze.

Access is free, but getting there can seem tough, even on the paved road. The drive requires an elevation climb of about 2,000 feet from US-23/58A at Norton. Head south for 3.9 miles on VA-619, then turn left on USFS-238 and drive 0.4 miles to the tower's access road on the right.

Falls of Lick Log Branch, off the Guest River Gorge Trail

After 1.2 more miles heading east, USFS-238 reaches the entrance of the High Knob Recreation Area, a seldom-crowded hideaway sporting stonework built from 1938-1942 by the Civilian Conservation Corps. The recreation area has a scattering of picnic tables and grills, a campground, a bathhouse, and an amphitheater, all enclosed by dense woods and High Knob Lake, which spans only five acres and has a 300-foot swimming beach. A 1.3-mile trail encircles the reservoir and follows a forest floor full of ferns and rhododendron. Fishing for bluegill is allowed, but boating is not, because boats could spill over the lake's two-story-high concrete dam on the Mountain Fork of Big Stony Creek.

High Knob Recreation Area is open May to September. Fees are charged by the forest's Clinch Ranger District.

PARDEE   High in the western Wise County backwoods, Pardee lies at the northern terminus of VA-603, a road dead-ending near the Kentucky line. Pardee is an old coal camp named for Calvin Pardee, the president of the Blackwood Coal and Coke Co., who based his operations at Calvin in Lee County after the company was organized in 1903.

Though hard to reach, Hollywood moviemakers came here in 1979 to film footage for the movie *Coal Miner's Daughter,* a big-screen account of country singer Loretta Lynn's life. Pardee's original company store, destroyed by fire in 1940, was rebuilt and used prominently in an early part of the movie, including a scene in which actor Tommy Lee Jones, as Mooney Lynn (Loretta's husband), drives a jeep over a hill.

But visitors should not get hopes up for a tour at Pardee—every movie prop has since been torn down. Even the hill shown in the film has been altered.

POUND   People in Pound party each Memorial Day weekend during Pound Heritage Days, a festival remembering the history of this northern Wise County town. According to one theory, Pound takes its name—or nickname, "The Pound"—from a 19th-century mill used to pound grain into flour. Incorporated in 1946, Pound is located off US-23, about four miles south of the Kentucky line, at the VA-83 crossroads with US-23-Business. Its population approached nearly 1,100 residents in 2000.

What's to See

North Fork Pound Reservoir: Pound Reservoir, a winding, skinny lake with 13.5 miles of wooded shoreline, spans 154 acres on the North Fork of the Pound River. Located at the base of Pine Mountain near the Virginia-Kentucky border, the lake is surrounded by 5,000 acres of the Jefferson National Forest, though a national forest stamp is not required to fish here.

The U.S. Army Corps of Engineers built the lake in 1966. It supports a variety of fish, including largemouth, smallmouth, and spotted bass, bluegill, crappie, musky, gizzard shad, and channel catfish. From late fall to spring, the lake is usually drawn down about 10 feet from its normal summer pool.

Pound Reservoir is a no-wake zone for all boats, but gasoline motors are allowed. The boat ramp is located just beyond an overlook of the 122-foot-high dam. Near the ramp, the Laurel Fork Trail leads 1.5 miles to a primitive campground accessible only by foot or by boat.

Bordering a cove at the west end of the lake, a small beach of beige-colored sand forms the centerpiece of the Phillips Creek Recreation Area. Other destinations nearby include the Bee Bottom Picnic Area, with picnic units and playground equipment; the Cane Patch Campground, with 34 campsites, a bathhouse, an amphitheater, volleyball and basketball courts, and a playground; and the Wise Launch, a fee-free boat ramp. Most of these areas are closed during winter; fees are charged through the forest's Clinch Ranger District.

At Phillips Creek, an easy-to-moderate loop trail starts beyond the swimming beach and a pair of picnic shelters. The trail crosses the log-clogged Phillips Creek on a footbridge and scales a small portion of Pine Mountain. One short spur dead-ends at a narrow 15-foot waterfall that streams down a moss-covered rock wall. The waterfall is one mile from the far end of the recreation-area parking lot.

🚗 From US-23 at Pound, turn west on VA-630 (Old North Fork Rd.) and follow for one mile to the dam and boat-launch area. To reach the other areas from US-23, turn west on VA-671 (North Fork Rd.) and follow for 4.5 miles to the Wise Launch (on the right), 5.4 miles to Phillips Creek Recreation Area (on the right), 5.7 miles to Cane Patch (on the right), and 6.4 miles to the Bee Bottom access lane at VA-773 (on the left).

Red Fox Trail: A 1.5-mile (one way) hike on the Red Fox Trail leads to the infamous Killing Rock, the site of a grisly murder committed by three men. One of the men was Marshall B. Taylor, a doctor, preacher, and U.S. Marshal known as the "Red Fox of the Mountain."

The easy Red Fox Trail spirals through the Jefferson National Forest by following a portion of a 19th-century road used to ascend Pine Mountain through Pound Gap. Not far past the trailhead, the path crosses a small stream next to a watering trough made from an indention in a carved log and fed water from the stream through a wooden pipeline.

A mile beyond the watering trough is the Killing Rock, a small rock structure that forms a natural hiding spot. Here, on May 14, 1892, several shots exploded from behind the Killing Rock when a wagon and its seven-person entourage tried to descend Pine Mountain. Five people lay dead after the shooting. Jane Mullins, a young girl, was spared. A 14-year-old boy, John Harrison Mullins, escaped, but just barely; while fleeing the mountain, his suspenders were cut by a bullet.

Pound Reservoir

Taylor—the Red Fox—allegedly fired the shots and looted the travelers, and then he fled by sneaking across high cliffs. Reaching Norton, Taylor had his body secretly crated and shipped by freight train to Bluefield. But local law officials discovered his plan and alerted a Bluefield detective, who apprehended the Red Fox at the train.

Ultimately, Taylor was put on trial and hung to death at the Wise County courthouse in 1893, but not without some fanfare. Wise County law officials granted the Red Fox a final wish—to conduct his own funeral. The Red Fox played that final role by dressing in white and conducting a two-hour sermon, preaching that he would rise from the dead in three days, just like Jesus Christ. But Taylor never rose again—even after his body was placed in a coffin and kept at his home for three days. He was buried in an unmarked grave.

The Fleming brothers—the two men accompanying the Red Fox at the Killing Rock—fled to West Virginia after the murders occurred. One brother was killed in a battle with law officers. The other was brought to trial many years later but was acquitted because there were no living witnesses to testify against him. The legend of the Red Fox, incidentally, served as inspiration to Big Stone Gap resident John Fox, Jr., who included a character by the same name in his novel *The Trail of the Lonesome Pine*.

🚗 From Pound's northernmost junction of US-23 and US-23-Business, follow US-23 (Orby Cantrell Hwy.) north for 1.1 miles. Turn left on VA-667 (Potter Town Rd.) and go 0.7 miles to a gated road, on the left. Walk past the gate and bear left on a gravel road. Go a quarter mile to a marker for the Red Fox Trail in the woods on the right. The trail forks after about a quarter mile. Turn right and follow yellow blazes leading into a densely wooded section. Pass the watering trough and continue uphill until the trail dead-ends a mile later at an interpretive sign overlooking the Killing Rock.

ST. PAUL   St. Paul straddles the Wise-Russell county line and serves as an eastern gateway to Virginia's westernmost counties—the Western Front, along the Kentucky border. But such a title, for St. Paul, is more than a geographical reference.

In the early 1900s, a string of saloons here gained a nickname—"The Western Front"—for the region's rough reputation. Legend says St. Paul's Western Front was so infamous for gambling, drinking, fighting, and prostitution that the locals likened it to the dangerous and deadly Western Front of World War I.

The Killing Rock, where the Red Fox and his accomplices hid before attacking a wagonload of people descending Pine Mountain.

the Oxbow access, should be portaged. About two miles downriver from Oxbow, a Class II-III rapid called "St. Paul Falls" is a six-foot drop that should be portaged on the left.

The river runs about 18 miles from Matthews Park to a ramp at Dungannon (see the Scott County chapter in the Clinch Mountain Country section) on the right bank and includes more ledges and rapids; some may be formidable. A hidden highlight of floating this section, besides fishing for smallmouth bass or walleye, is Russell Creek Falls, about three miles below St. Paul Falls on the river's north-west bank, on the right. The craggy canyon surrounding the waterfall is privately owned, but the fall's 50-foot midair drop can be seen from the river or the rocky bed of Russell Creek.

🚗 Entering St. Paul on US-58A-West, turn right at the first traffic light on VA-270, then immediately turn right on Rt. 1225 (Riverside Dr.).

Oxbow Lake Park and *Sugar Hill Loop Trail:* The mile-long Oxbow Lake, shaped just like its name, was once a part of the Clinch River wrapping around St. Paul's town limits. The river was rechanneled in 1982 to prevent flooding, and the dammed portion became the 10-acre Oxbow Lake. The reservoir is the center of a small municipal park that includes a walking trail lining the lakeshore.

A concrete road leads across the Oxbow Lake Dam and stops at the head of the Sugar Hill Loop Trail, a moderate, five-mile nature walk and biking path named for a 1930s-era maple syrup operation. The Town of St. Paul maintains the grassy trail. Its midway point passes the ruins of a log home owned in the late 1700s by Francois Pierre de Tuboeuf, a French aristocrat who named this land "St. Marie on the Clinch." Two brick chimneys (not original) rise from the house's stone foundation, next to a picnic shelter built for trail users by a local Boy Scout troop.

🚗 From US-58A-West, turn left on Bush Drive, at the second traffic light in St. Paul (opposite the entrance to VA-63-North). Follow for about a quarter mile to the Oxbow Lake Park. Turn at the next right for the boat launch on Oxbow Lake. Continuing past the launch, park near a narrow road spanning the Oxbow Lake Dam. Straight ahead is a canoe launch on the Clinch River. Cross the dam on foot to reach the head of the Sugar Hill Loop Trail. At the kiosk, follow to the left at the trail-

By the year 2000, such saloons were gone, and the town, at the crossroads of US-58A and VA-63, was a clean, quiet home to about 1,000 residents.

St. Paul is Wise County's only incorporated town on the Clinch River. Here, on the first weekend of June, the Clinch River Days festival is held with canoeing, concerts, and contests.

Chartered in 1911, the Town of St. Paul began as a series of real estate ventures in the late 1800s. One proposal for this place mirrored Minnesota's twin cities of St. Paul and Minneapolis and used the Clinch River as a dividing line between what would have been two towns. But such a design drowned when the 3-C Railway went kaput and did not build a planned rail line through St. Paul.

Local residents, still, loved the name "St. Paul" and wanted it used for a post office. But that couldn't be done—a town in Carroll County (in the vicinity of Cana) was already using the name. So, for a while, the St. Paul area became known as "Estonoa," an Indian word meaning "land of the blue waters." According to legend, however, residents ultimately journeyed to Carroll County and bought the name "St. Paul" for $100.

What's to See

A. R. Matthews Memorial Park and *Clinch River Access:* Named for a local citizen, the A. R. Matthews Memorial Park features a playground, picnic facilities, tennis courts, a railroad caboose, and a public access to the Clinch River. Nearly one mile downstream from the park, a canoe launch sits on the Clinch River's right bank, near the Oxbow Lake Dam. Beware of rapids. One just below a railroad trestle, between Matthews Park and

head. After a quarter mile, look for the head of the Riverside Trail, a Sugar Hill spur overlooking the Clinch River for two miles and providing public access for fishing and boating. Two and a half miles from the kiosk on the main Sugar Hill Loop Trail, a spur on the left goes to the Guest River Gorge. Immediately beyond that spur, on the right, are the ruins of the French settlement.

WISE Years ago, Wise County's namesake courthouse town went through one name change after another. First, it was called "Big Glades," then "Gladeville" (or "Gladesville"), the name the town used when it was incorporated in 1874. All the while, mail was delivered to "Wise Court House." The post office dropped the "Court House" and became simply "Wise" in 1893—the same name the town finally began using by 1924. In 2000, 3,200 residents called this place home.

At 206 E. Main St., twin stone towers make the 1896 Wise County Courthouse an imposing example of Renaissance-revival architecture at the center of this village. Near the courthouse, several small businesses cater to students at the University of Virginia-Wise, on the east side of town where Darden Drive meets College Avenue. Founded in 1954 as a two-year school, this small branch of UVA-Charlottesville began granting four-year degrees in 1970. Until 1999, it was known as Clinch Valley College.

UVA-Wise sponsors a celebration of old-time mountain music, the Dock Boggs Festival, on the second Saturday of each September at the Country Cabin II, near Norton. The festival originated on campus in 1969 to honor Moran Lee "Dock" Boggs (1898-1971), a local singer and banjo player.

What's to See

Bear Creek Reservoir: Surrounded by evergreens, the 38-acre Bear Creek Reservoir was created in 1964 on a stream so named because pioneers had killed bears along its course. Besides being

Wise County Courthouse at Wise

a water source for the Town of Wise, Bear Creek Reservoir is a recreation spot with picnic tables and a ramp for boats with trolling motors. Both a state fishing license and a special permit, available at the reservoir office, are required to fish here. Camping, hunting, swimming, and horseback riding are prohibited.

🚗 From US-23-North, turn right at Wise's south entrance to US-23-Business (Norton Rd.) and follow into Wise for 1.3 miles. Turn right on VA-640 (Main St.) and follow for 0.6 miles. Turn right on VA-646 (Darden Dr.) and follow for 2.4 miles. Turn left on VA-829 (Sportsmans Dr.) and go 0.1 miles, then turn left on VA-682 (Browning Lane) and follow for a quarter mile to the lake.

Wise County Fairgrounds: Forget about the location credits at the end of *Coal Miner's Daughter,* the 1980 big-screen movie detailing the life of country singer Loretta Lynn. The credits read: "Filmed entirely in Kentucky and Tennessee." The problem is, that's not true.

A big chunk of filming took place at the carved-out mountainsides of Virginia's Wise County Fairgrounds during a scene in which Sissy Spacek, portraying Lynn, and Beverly D'Angelo, portraying Patsy Cline, sang onstage while it rained. Loretta Lynn giggled during a 1997 interview when she remembered visiting the movie set in Wise County: "It was just kind of funny. . . . There was Patsy Cline's bus sitting out there. And the fair said Patsy Cline and Loretta Lynn were there that night."

Beyond the movie nostalgia, the fairgrounds are busy during the Virginia-Kentucky District Fair, the scene of carnival rides and live music in early August. The long-running fair traces its beginning to a family picnic held in 1913 in downtown Wise.

🚗 From Darden Drive at Wise, follow VA-640 (Hurricane Rd.) northeast for 2.3 miles. Turn right on VA-680 (Fairgrounds Rd.). The fairgrounds are immediately on the left.

Andover: In 1919, D. B. Wentz, president of the Virginia Coal and Iron Co., named an unincorporated railroad town "Andover" for a college in New England. The area was called "Preacher" when a post office was established in 1898. Western: VA-78, near VA-686, north of Appalachia

Arno: The coal camp Arno dates to the post-World War I era, a time when Virginia's coal-mining industry attracted workers from a variety of ethnic backgrounds, including Italians. The origin of "Arno" might be attributed to an early Italian influence; "Arno" is also the name of a river and valley in Italy. Western: VA-686, between Derby and Andover

Banner: Near Coeburn, Banner is named for John Banner, a land surveyor who in 1836 received a 250-acre land patent with surveyor George Gose in this area along Little Tom's Creek. Eastern: VA-653 (Little Tom Rd.) at VA-158 (Bull Run Rd.)

Big Laurel: The Big Laurel area was probably named for the area's mountain laurel. Central: VA-626 at VA-694

Birchfield Creek: North Carolinian Jeremiah Birchfield settled on Birchfield Creek, circa 1820, and left his name on maps. Northeastern: VA-634, near VA-636

Blackwood: One story says that Blackwood's name comes from a coal town by the same name near Pottsville, Penn. Another account credits "Blackwood" to the dark waters of nearby Black Creek. A Blackwood post office was established in 1903. Central: US-23-Business at VA-674, west of Norton

Bondtown: George and Lucy Bond settled at Bondtown before the Civil War and gave their name to the area. A Bondtown post office opened in 1902. Eastern: VA-72, north end of Coeburn

Bull Run: When a bull in a grazing cattle herd turned wild, local legend says its actions inspired the name "Bull Run Creek." Eastern: US-58A, near VA-657

Carfax: According to local lore, the Carfax name comes from Floyd Hamm, a railroad worker who was known to shout, "Need more cars! That's facts!" when more coal cars were needed on the local rail line. Despite signs to the contrary in nearby Coeburn, Carfax is the hometown of bluegrass musicians Jim and Jesse McReynolds, Grand Ole Opry stars known for 1950s-era hits like "Diesel on My Tail." Southeastern: VA-657, near the Clinch River and the railroad

Cranes Nest: The Cranes Nest community takes its name from nests built by cranes on the side of a high cliff. Eastern: VA-72, half mile north of VA-652

Derby: Derby's name originated in 1922 when directors of the Stonega Coal & Coke Co. interrupted a trip to see the Kentucky Derby. The officials stopped at this coal camp and, after inspecting plans for its mining complex and unique brick homes, decided to call it "Derby." Western: northwestern terminus of VA-686

Dorchester Junction: On the western edge of Norton, Dorchester Junction shares its name with Dorchester, England. It's an example of the many coal-mining towns that borrowed names from England, a reflection of the cultural preferences of mine operators. Central: VA-621 at US-23-Business

Dry Fork: The Dry Fork community is named for the Dry Fork, a five-mile-long tributary of the Clinch River. A Dry Fork post office operated from 1871 to 1880. Southeastern: VA-659 at VA-658

Dunbar: One theory says that the Dunbar name comes from an English or Scottish village, likely Scotland's Dunbar, home of the Dunbar Castle. The coal camp was formed in 1919. Western: VA-603, south of Pardee

Duncan Gap: An early settler at Duncan Gap was Duncan Alan Stallard. East-central: VA-640 at VA-639, near Dickenson County

East Stone Gap: The East Stone Gap area takes its name from its location—east of the gap in Stone Mountain called "Big Stone Gap." Southwestern: VA-609 at VA-613

Esserville: Pennsylvania's John A. Esser formed Esser Coke Co. in the late 1800s at what became "Esserville." Central: US-23-Business, between Norton and Wise

Exeter: One story says D. B. Wentz, president of the Virginia Coal and Iron Co., named Exeter for a New England academy. Another account credits the circa-1917 coal camp as a namesake of Exeter, England. Western: VA-68 at VA-745

Flat Gap: Likely named for its flat terrain, Flat Gap sits inside a small valley on the headwaters of the Pound River. Northern: VA-671 at VA-707

Flatwoods: South of Coeburn, Flatwoods is probably named for the lay of the land—a flat, wooded area among mountains. Southeastern: VA-72, near Scott County

Franco: The Franco community was the site of its own post office, 1922-1927. Its name might be derived from its postmistress, Lizzie Franks. Eastern: VA-652, a half mile southwest of VA-650

Glamorgan: David E. Llewellyn, the first super-intendent of the Stone Gap Colliery, named Glamorgan for his homeplace of Glamorganshire, Wales. Central: US-23, near VA-625, north end of Wise

Haddonfield: This community was named for Dr. Lawrence Haddon, a native of Leicestershire, England, who came to America as a young man and moved to Wise County in 1866. Eventually settling near the Pound River, Haddon was Haddonfield's postmaster from 1895 to 1934 and also published his own newspaper here. Northeastern: VA-630, northeast of Pound

Horse Gap: During a Civil War skirmish, one warring party had all of its horses killed at a place eventually known as "Horse Gap." Northern: US-23 at US-23-Business, north end of Pound

Hurricane: A hurricane caused major destruction in this neighborhood in the early 1800s, but sources conflict on what year that storm occurred. East-central: VA-640 at VA-644

Imboden: An old coal camp on the west side of Stone Mountain, Imboden's name probably remembers Confederate Brig. Gen. John D. Imboden, who purchased vast amounts of local land for iron ore and coal speculation in about 1880. Southwestern: VA-68 and VA-804

Inman: A man named Inman from Knoxville, Tenn., opened the first coal mines at Inman. The area is bordered by Looney Creek, a stream named for early explorer Absalom Looney. Southwestern: VA-160, west end of Appalachia

Irondale: South of Big Stone Gap, Irondale likely gets its name from iron ore, first mined in this valley (or "dale") in about 1892. Southwestern: VA-609 at VA-668, near railroad

Josephine: Slightly west of Norton, Josephine is named for the wife of an official of the Intermont Coal & Coke Co. Central: VA-610 at US-23-Business

Kelly View: Between Norton and Appalachia, Kelly View overlooks the Powell River and Little Stone Mountain. The area is sometimes called "Kent Junction." The community's name likely comes from Katie Kelly or her family. Katie was the postmaster here in 1890. Central: VA-603 at US-23-Business

Lyons: Jim Lyons was one of the first settlers at Lyons. East-central: VA-649, near Dickenson County

Oreton: Like nearby Irondale, Oreton likely owes its name to wishful thinking. A post office served this area from 1899 to about 1908—a time when

continued on next page

investors flocked here with hopes that iron-ore deposits would make this an "Ore Town" (or "Oreton"). Southwestern: US-23 along railroad, about a mile north of Scott County

Ramsey: James Ramsey was a 19th-century settler here. Central: VA-74, east end of Norton

Roda: The U.S. Postal Service changed Roda's original name, "Rhoda," when the coal camp's post office opened in 1907. "Roda" is short for rhododendron, a native shrub. Western: VA-685, near VA-812

Stonega: When a post office was established in the 1890s, the P from "Stone Gap" was dropped to form the word "Stonega" (pronounced "sto-NAY-gah"). The coal camp is on the headwaters of Callahan (or "Callaham") Creek, a stream named for hunter Edward Callaham, who came here circa 1800. Western: VA-600, near VA-78

Tacoma: Once a booming coal town and busy railroad stop between Coeburn and Norton, Tacoma was first settled in the 1850s and became an incorporated town sometime during the early 1900s. Tacoma gave up its town charter in the 1920s. Local accounts say *tacoma* is a Native American word meaning either "nearest heaven" or "high ground." Central: US-58A at VA-706

Toms Creek: A thriving 1920s-era coal camp, Toms Creek was first named "Georgel" in honor of industrialist George L. Carter (1857-1936) of Carroll County. The present name comes from Thomas Gist, son of 18th-century explorer Christopher Gist. Eastern: VA-652, half mile east of VA-72

Vicco: The name "Vicco" is an acronym for the Virginia Iron, Coal & Coke Co. Eastern: VA-653, east of Coeburn

Virginia City: In the 1890s, people rushed to find black gold—coal—in Virginia City, then supporting its own post office between St. Paul and Coeburn. The coal camp's name is probably derived from a mining town in Nevada called Virginia City, where people rushed to find another kind of gold in the mid-1800s. Eastern: US-58A at VA-655

CLINCH MOUNTAIN COUNTRY

Maybe it has to do with the limestone cropping out of the rocky plains. Or maybe it's in the water emerging from the springs and creeks feeding the Clinch River. Whatever the reason, something special is in the grass of Southwest Virginia's Clinch

Mountain Country. All across Tazewell, Russell, and Scott counties, the grass just seems to be as green as grass can be, especially in majestic valleys with similar names—places like Rye Cove, The Cove, Elk Garden, or Burke's Garden.

The slow-moving Clinch River cuts through this pastoral region. Lofty, fabled Clinch Mountain—the subject of many a story and bluegrass song—dominates the eastern skyline. To the west, this area's landscape becomes denser and harsher to climb as the Cumberland Mountains mark the edge of Southwest Virginia's coalfields.

In the valley between the Cumberlands and the Clinch, modern mansions sit atop rounded knobs, and rusty-roofed barns stand among grassy fields.

Deep green, grassy fields, that is.

RUSSELL COUNTY

Steep mountains frame Russell County's northwestern edges in Virginia's coal-mining country. From the county seat at Lebanon, pastures run southeast to Clinch Mountain, over hills dotted with large rocks and roaming cattle. Russell County was formed from Washington County in 1786 and is named for Gen. William Russell, a Clinch Valley pioneer and Revolutionary War veteran. The county spans about 477 square miles.

BLACKFORD

Located between Rosedale and Honaker, the eastern Russell County community of Blackford was originally called "Black's Ford" for David Black, who developed a ford where VA-80 now crosses the Clinch River. A Blackford post office was located here in the early 1900s.

What's to See

Clinch River Access: Following the Clinch River's canoe trail downstream from Blackford, it is about seven miles to a public landing (on the right bank) at Puckett's Hole, an informal swimming area named for a local Puckett family. The Class I-III rapids on this winding stretch should possibly be portaged, depending on water levels. Another takeout is on the left bank at Nash's Ford, about nine more miles below Puckett's Hole.

🚗 From the Honaker Post Office (300 Redbud Hwy.), follow VA-80 south for 2.8 miles. Just before the Blackford bridge, turn left on VA-641, then immediately turn right at the river access.

To reach the Puckett's Hole takeout from the Honaker Post Office, follow VA-80 north for 0.1 miles, turn left on VA-645 at the town square, and go west for 2.5 miles. Turn left on VA-651 and drive one mile. Turn right on VA-652 and go 2.3 miles, then turn right on an unmarked gravel lane and follow to the river.

To reach the Nash's Ford access from Honaker, follow VA-645 west for about eight miles. Cross the river. Turn left on VA-798 and go 0.2 miles.

CARTERTON

Carterton is a central Russell County community, located where VA-614 meets the Clinch River. It takes its name from Jack Carter, a member of the Virginia House of Delegates. Carter provided several acres of right-of-way for a railroad depot here in the 1890s.

What's to See

Clinch River Access: From Cleveland, it's about a 7.5-mile float downstream on the Clinch River to a public access at Carterton. About nine more miles downstream, the St. Paul landing at A. R. Matthews Memorial Park waits on the right bank, in an area of flat water known as a place to catch walleye and sunfish.

🚗 From VA-65 at Castlewood, follow US-58A west for about 2.5 miles to St. Paul. Turn right on VA-640, which mostly parallels the river, and follow east for about eight miles. Turn left on VA-614 and follow north for 1.5 miles, then turn left on VA-855 and follow for 0.2 miles. When VA-855 becomes VA-665, turn right on an unmarked lane and follow straight to the river.

To find the St. Paul access, follow US-58A-West across the Clinch River bridge from the VA-640 intersection. Turn right on VA-270 at a stoplight in St. Paul, then turn immediately right on Riverside Drive and follow to the access at the entrance to the A. R. Matthews Memorial Park.

CASTLEWOOD

A sign on US-58A announces Castlewood's incorporation in 1991 but does not mention what happened six years later—town residents, no longer interested in supporting a government, made headlines when they voted to de-incorporate what had been, in terms of land size, Virginia's second-largest town.

The short-lived Town of Castlewood was, indeed, a vast place. It covered more than 15 square miles and included about 3,000 residents. Some critics complained Castlewood took in too much. Even the town's mayor once said there were "more cows than people" in the corporate limits.

Castlewood's name comes from Jacob Castle (or Cassell), who hunted in this area of western

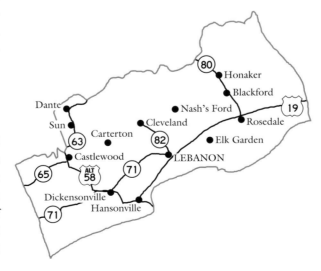

Puckett's Hole on the Clinch River, downstream from Blackford

Russell County in about 1750, roughly 20 years before the first permanent settlers arrived. According to legend, Castle traded a butcher knife and a musket to Indians for the vast area later known as "Castle's Woods" or "Cassell's Woods."

In 1786, Castlewood was the site of the first court meeting in Russell County, which took place a year before a permanent courthouse was established at nearby Dickensonville. About that same time, settlers began building mills here on a muddy stream that flows out of farmland and then pours over a 40-foot-high ledge. That waterfall can be heard—but just barely seen—from a tiny bridge on VA-640, about 0.1 miles west of the highway's westernmost intersection with VA-615. The waterfall, blocked from sight during summer by thick brush, was used to power a mill built in the 1770s and sold to Charles Bickley in about 1800. Bickley gave the community a new moniker, "Bickley's Mills," which survived as a post office name until the early 1900s.

Castlewood initially developed in a neighborhood along the Clinch River known as "Old Castlewood," in the vicinity of where VA-615 meets VA-640. Old Castlewood prospered from the time the railroad arrived here in about 1890 until the Great Depression hit in 1929. After that, businesses closed, banks failed, and the post office ultimately moved to what was called "New Castlewood," a commercially developed area at the crossroads of VA-65 and US-58A.

New Castlewood is home to a collection of small shops and restaurants. It is listed on some maps as "Banners Corner," a reference to the many families named Banner who settled the area.

CLEVELAND When it opened in 1890 in central Russell County, Cleveland's post office was named to honor President Grover Cleveland. Incorporated in 1946, Cleveland remained an active coal-mining and agricultural community through the 1950s. But, with the demise of passenger rail service, Cleveland's isolation—at the northwestern terminus of VA-82—caused economic suffering. In 2000, as the population dropped below 200 residents, many downtown buildings were left empty.

What's to See

Clinch River Access: Heading south from a public access in Cleveland, the Clinch River passes through several deep pools known for musky, catfish, and walleye fishing. About 7.5 miles from Cleveland, a river access lies on the left bank at Carterton. About 8.5 miles upstream from Cleveland, Nash's Ford provides another access to the winding river.

A picnic shelter overlooks Cleveland's public river access. Look on the opposite river bank, beyond the railroad, to see the 501-acre Cleveland Barrens, a state-owned nature preserve harboring about a dozen rare plant species. The Barrens is a buffer zone to what lies about a half mile downriver—the small Cleveland Island, owned by the Nature Conservancy as a sanctuary for rare mussel species.

🚗 From US-19-Business (Main St.) in Lebanon, follow VA-82 north for seven miles to its terminus at Cleveland. Veer left (west) on VA-600 and go 0.1 miles to a left turn on Rt. 1210, next to a public baseball field, then follow 150 yards to the river.

――――――――

Tank Hollow Falls: A small stream exits the Cleveland Barrens Natural Area Preserve on its way to the Clinch River. It pours over a 10-foot-high ledge, pauses in a small pool, and then streams down a 30-foot-high rock wall at Tank Hollow Falls. This little-known waterfall is likely named for the nearby location of Cleveland's water tank. Half of the falls is on property owned by the Town of Cleveland. The other half is in the state-owned preserve.

🚗 From US-19-Business (Main St.) in Lebanon, follow VA-82 north for 6.7 miles to Cleveland, then take the last left (Rt. 1206, which may not be marked) just before crossing the railroad tracks. Follow Rt. 1206 for 0.1 miles uphill and turn right on Rt. 1207. Go straight until Cleveland Baptist Church is on the right. Park on the shoulder of Rt. 1208, which circles the church. Here, continue straight ahead on foot, going downhill on a narrow paved lane that leads about a quarter mile to the falls.

DANTE

How the name "Dante" is pronounced has always been a subject of debate. Some say a flat-sounding "dant." Others say "daint" with a long *A*. Still more put on a French flair and pronounce it either "DON-tay" or "DAN-tay."

The name originated from William Joseph Dante (1866-1937), a Washington, D.C., native and vice president of the Dawson Coal and Coke Co., which developed the unincorporated mining town in about 1903. In the 1930s, Dante was one of

Tank Hollow Falls

Southwest Virginia's largest coal-mining centers and home to about 3,800 residents. The Clinchfield Coal Corp. housed its headquarters here for about 60 years, even though large-scale mining operations had ceased in Dante by the late 1950s.

By the 21st century, coal mining was simply a page in Dante's past. And this area, at the crossroads of VA-608 and VA-627 in the extreme northwestern corner of Russell County, evolved into a quiet residential community, hemmed in by steep ridges below the high road on VA-63.

Long before the coal mines, early settlers called the Dante area "Turkey Foot" for the shape of the valley. When Dante is viewed from the surrounding high ridges, the topographical outlay of the area resembles the foot of a turkey, with the streams of Bear Wallow, Straight Hollow, and Sawmill Hollow forming three "toes," and Lick Creek, where the streams meet, resembling a leg.

DICKENSONVILLE

Sleepy Dickensonville is a town that never grew up. The unincorporated community in western Russell County lies along one mile of US-58A, between the four-lane highway's two junctions with VA-71. Sparsely populated yet sprawling among the rolling hills of the Copper Creek valley, Dickensonville did once have a heyday; for about 30 years, it was the location of the courthouse for the original Russell County, a wide area spanning most or all of the counties in Southwest Virginia's Clinch Mountain Country and Western Front.

Dickensonville was named for Henry Dickenson, Russell County's court clerk in 1787. About that time, Dickenson (1750-1825) donated the building used for the first courthouse, a 20-by-24-foot log structure that was abandoned after it burned in 1798. A year later, county leaders apparently looked for more permanence; they used stone to construct a new place to dispatch local law.

Old Russell County Courthouse in Dickensonville

Fronted by stately columns, the large, privately owned Elk Garden Mansion dominates the community from its hillside perch on VA-656. Built in 1806 near the fort site, in the early 1900s the mansion was promoted as a drive-by tourist attraction. At that time, it housed the family of Henry Carter Stuart (1855-1933), a Wythe County native who served as Virginia's governor from 1914 to 1918.

HONAKER

Redbud trees grow to heights of about 40 feet along VA-80, the curvy, two-lane highway leading in and out of Honaker (pronounced "HO-nay-ker"). In spring, the blooming redbuds produce a bright symphony of red, lavender, magenta, and pink. But these trees, for Honaker, are more than just roadside decoration—the town calls itself the "First and Foremost Redbud Capital of the United States," or even "The Redbud Capital of the World." Each April, Honaker celebrates this claim with the Redbud Festival, featuring music, games, and tributes to the town's heritage.

As a community, Honaker's history is usually traced to about 1797, when Martin Honaker and his family settled in this vicinity, building log homes and mills. In the late 1840s, a "New Garden" post office was established here. Soon after, the place was renamed for Harvey Honaker, a town leader, postmaster,

Built in 1799, Dickensonville's courthouse was used until 1818. For years after, the stone structure was a private residence. In the mid-1850s, a brick addition doubled its size. About a century later, the county reacquired the courthouse and opened it as a historical museum. The courthouse is near Copper Creek School on US-58A.

For kids coming here on school field trips, the jail in the cellar is a favorite place to find. It's dark and gloomy, creepy and cold. The floor is bare dirt. And it looks like a true dungeon; the entrance is barred by a heavy door, and the cell is illuminated by just one window, giving an ant's view of the outside lawn.

Next door is another landmark, the Dickenson-Bundy Log House, which is actually two cabins put together in 1976 and used for selling locally made crafts. One half, the Bundy House, was built in 1790 by Thomas Bundy and his wife, Elizabeth Crank, at its original location on Moll Creek, about five miles south of Dickensonville. The second part is a 1769 cabin built on the Clinch River by one of Henry Dickenson's relatives.

ELK GARDEN

Elk once roamed the scenic pastures of Elk Garden, a central Russell County community at the crossroads of VA-656 and VA-657. In the 1770s, this rock-strewn valley was the site of a fort used as a refuge from Indian attacks.

Elk Garden Mansion, a private residence

and grandson of Martin Honaker. Bolstered by local coal-mining and timber industries, the town prospered after the Norfolk & Western Railway arrived in 1889. Honaker became an important stop halfway between Richlands and Cleveland, two nearby towns on the line connecting Bluefield to Norton.

From 1894 to 1905, Honaker was home to Old Dominion College, an institution probably related to a college using the same name at Richlands (see the Tazewell County chapter in the Clinch Mountain Country section). Honaker's college was housed in a three-story building that stood at the intersection of Main Street and Lockhart Circle.

Honaker was incorporated in 1919. Unlike its financially troubled college, though, the town survived the 20th century. But, eventually, Honaker's growth waned—just like the bloom of the redbuds in the heat of summer. Honaker began suffering economic woes in the 1950s with a reduction in rail traffic and, later, with a significant decline in the local coal-mining industry. By 2000, less than 1,000 people lived here.

Still, the town remains abuzz. It's a commerce center for northeastern Russell County, especially during weekday afternoons, as commuters shuttle to Honaker's handful of eateries and about two dozen small retailers.

What's to See

Dye's Vineyards: A sign says tiny Dye's Vineyards is "Russell County's Oldest Winery." But don't get the wrong idea. This place is not old at all compared to wineries in Virginia's Shenandoah Valley. Proprietor Ken Dye began growing French hybrid grapes here, at the foot of Big A Mountain, in 1989, and Dye's Vineyards opened in 1996. Names of wines made here, like Richlands Red or Russell Rose, reflect the local landscape.

🚗 From US-19 at Rosedale, follow VA-80 north to Honaker. Continue five miles past Honaker and turn left on VA-620. The winery is on the right.

LEBANON

Smooth knobs roll like waves on the headwaters of Big Cedar Creek, a rocky, bubbling watercourse flowing down Clinch Mountain on its way through Lebanon. Cedar trees gave the creek its name and also inspired the name of Lebanon, the seat of Russell County since 1818. Town founders compared the cedars here to the Biblical cedars of a more famous Lebanon—the one bordering Israel. Cedars in that faraway Lebanon were used in the construction of Solomon's temple in ancient Jerusalem.

Russell County's Lebanon (pronounced "LEB-a-nun") was named in 1819, soon after the county seat was moved here from Dickensonville. The Russell County Courthouse, 121 E. Main St., is a stately brick structure topped with a cupola, a clock, and a weather vane. The courthouse was constructed in 1874,

two years after a fire destroyed a previous courthouse built here circa 1850. Residents salvaged parts of the 1850s-era courthouse for the construction of the new one.

Incorporated in 1873, Lebanon is situated at the heart of the county, where US-19 meets VA-82. In 1892, the town became home to Russell College, an institution located on the present-day site of Lebanon Middle School, off US-19-Business. The college closed in 1909. During its short life, Russell College officials bragged of its "quiet, retired location" in the 1895-1896 course catalog: "Away from the confusion, the stifling air, the impure water, and the deadly contagion of the city, in the midst of green fields, fresh air, pure water, purpling hills, and towering mountains, our location is an ideal one for the highest culture and most perfect development of mind and body."

Amid the "green fields" and "purpling hills," Lebanon remained primarily a farming community until the 1950s—about the time it attracted a series of modern stores and housing subdivisions. In later decades, the town survived the economic decline of Virginia's coal industry and falling cattle prices by attracting new retail outlets and a handful of restaurants, while developing industrial sites on the outskirts of town. Lebanon was home to about 3,300 residents in 2000.

What's to See

Pinnacle Natural Area Preserve: Photographers love visiting the Pinnacle Natural Area Preserve to capture the mood of the Big Falls. This 15-foot drop on Big Cedar Creek creates a wide and majestic blend of water crashing atop several layers of erosion-resistant sandstone. The frothy falls are at the center of a state-owned preserve, a 435-acre tract named for an imposing spire of dolomite. The Pinnacle is an outcrop rising about 400 feet over Big Cedar Creek.

The Pinnacle Natural Area Preserve is open for public visitation. But to reach its lower parking lot, you must drive through Big Cedar Creek on a concrete ford. This can be dangerous when the creek runs high in spring, and it can be impossible during winter weather.

Still, building a bridge for vehicles above the creek's water level is not on the agenda for state officials, who manage this area as part of the Virginia Department of Conservation and Recreation. The mission here, instead, is to protect rare plant species, like glade spurge, and to provide a sanctuary for rare animals, like the two-foot-long hellbender, a salamander that usually comes out only at night.

Visitors who may be leery of water do not necessarily have to drive through the trout-stocked creek to reach the lower parking lot. A footbridge provides an alternative crossing from an upper parking lot to a short trail leading to the mile-long access road that runs from the concrete ford to the lower parking area.

The Pinnacle. This dolomitic outcrop rises above Big Cedar Creek

From that lower area, it's a quarter-mile hike to the Big Falls. Beyond that, the trail goes another quarter mile before eventually splitting three ways. Each spur is less than a mile; one path leads to an overlook of the Pinnacle, another heads to the confluence of Big Cedar Creek and the Clinch River, and a third trail climbs to an overlook on Copper Ridge.

Facilities are minimal but include handicapped-accessible restrooms and a picnic shelter at the lower parking area.

🚗 From US-19-Business at Lebanon, head northwest on VA-82 for 1.1 miles. Turn right on VA-640 (Glade Hollow Rd.) and go 4.2 miles. Turn left on VA-721 (gravel), immediately past Oak Grove Baptist Church, and proceed 0.8 miles to the area's upper parking lot, on the left. The road continues for another mile (after fording the creek) to reach the lower parking area. The trail to the Big Falls begins at the lower parking lot on an old roadbed blocked by rocks.

NASH'S FORD

A local Nash family lived near a crossing of the Clinch River, a scenic spot marked by a river bridge on VA-645, at the center of Russell County. In the late 1800s, Fullen Nash shuttled passengers here on a rowboat ferry.

What's to See

Clinch River Access: Rocky shoals percolate water immediately above a canoe landing and fishing area on the Clinch River at Nash's Ford. Floating downstream from here, it is about 8.5 miles to another public access at Cleveland, on the right bank.

🚗 From the railroad crossing on VA-82 at Cleveland, follow VA-82 southeast for 1.7 miles. Turn left on VA-645 and go five miles. Turn right on VA-798 at Nash's Ford Baptist Church and go 0.2 miles to the river.

Alternate Route: From US-19-Business (Main St.) in Lebanon, follow VA-82 northwest for 1.1 miles. Turn right on VA-640 and follow for 2.8 miles. Turn left on VA-740 and follow for 2.2 miles. Bear right on VA-645 and follow for 0.8 miles to the river access road (VA-798) on the right.

ROSEDALE

For many years in the 20th century, Rosedale was known best as "Oaks Garage," a reference to a long-gone service station at the Rosedale crossroads—where VA-80 heads northwest from US-19 in eastern Russell County. The current name is believed to originate from the area's Rosedale Plantation. One story says the plantation was named for the couple who owned it—she was "Rose," and he was "Dale." If not, the name may simply be a word meaning "Rose Valley."

Artrip: James Artrip came to the Artrip area in the 1780s. His descendants later operated the Artrip General Store along the banks of the Clinch River. Central: VA-661, near VA-663

Barnett: A man known as "Uncle Barnett" Reylonds (maybe Reynolds) is remembered in the name of Barnett, a community between Lebanon and Rosedale. Barnett was probably named in 1891, when a post office was established here. Central: VA-776, near US-19

Belfast Mills: In the 1780s, settlers from Belfast, Ireland, established several mills in an area that became known as "Belfast Mills," or simply "Belfast." Southeastern: VA-603 at VA-642, near US-19

Bolton: Between Hansonville and Dickensonville, Bolton takes its name from postal worker Chad Bolton. Its post office operated from 1890 to 1903. Central: US-58A at VA-613

Carbo: Once called "Kiser" for the family of early settler Dick Kiser, the Carbo community was renamed when the U.S. Government operated the area's Carbo Coal and Coke Co. plant in 1917, making chemicals for use during World War I. Central: VA-664 at VA-616, near railroad

Clifton: The tiny Clifton community shares its name with a house called "Clifton," built in the late 1700s by local surveyor Henry Smith. Eastern: VA-640, near Little River

Corn Valley: At the foothills of Clinch Mountain, Corn Valley is an agricultural region named for areas of high-volume corn production. The Corn Valley post office operated from 1924 to 1958. Southeastern: VA-619, east of VA-80

Coulwood: In the early 1900s, Coulwood was the name of a post office. But the local railroad depot was called "Finney," paying homage to store owner Lilburn Finney. The name "Coulwood" might be a play on "Coalwood," the name of a coal-mining town in nearby McDowell County, W.Va. Central: VA-620 at VA-646, near railroad

Counts: The Counts community might be named for the family of early settler John Counts (1765-1843), who purchased land in 1787 and built what may have been the first house in the greater Cleveland area. The name, also, could be a reference to B. F. Counts, the postmaster here in the 1880s. Central: VA-628, near VA-700

Drill: Hundreds of coal miners lived at Drill in rows of company homes in the 1920s. The camp was named for water gushing from a deeply drilled artesian well during an early coal prospect near Lewis Creek. Northern: VA-622 at VA-624

Dye: A residential area, Dye was named for a local Dye family. Northeastern: VA-617 at VA-632

Fugates Hill: This community's name pays reference to the family of John Fugate, one of the area's first settlers. In 1786, Fugate built a two-story log house here. Southwestern: VA-613, along Big Moccasin Creek

Fullers: Moving here in 1798, Stephen Fuller was among the earliest arrivals of the Fuller family in northern Russell County. The community called "Fullers" is likely named for this man or his family. North-central: VA-615 at VA-712

Gardner: East of Honaker, Gardner owes its name to Zaddock Nutter Gardner, who built a three-story mill here in about 1850 and served as the community's first postmaster. Gardner's Mill once stood near a railroad flag stop called "Gardner." Northeastern: VA-67 at VA-637

Gibsonville: Families named Gibson settled between Dickensonville and Lebanon. By 1855, a Gibsonville post office opened in the vicinity. Andrew Perry Gibson (1817-1890) helped distribute mail. Central: VA-71, near VA-614

Grassy Creek: Among Russell County's earliest settlers was a group from North Carolina that had once lived in a place where several streams were called "Grassy Creek." Coming here, it was natural for these settlers to use the same name. A Grassy Creek post office was open in the agricultural community in the 1850s. Western: VA-71 at VA-678, near Scott County

Gravel Lick: A salt lick for animals and the gravel bed of Gravel Lick Creek are what likely inspired the name "Gravel Lick." Northwestern: VA-615 at VA-691

Hamlin: Across the Clinch River from Old Castlewood, between St. Paul and Dante, Hamlin's name could be owed to early settler Henry Hamlin or his family. Hamlin lived in this vicinity in about 1780. Northwestern: VA-615 at VA-870

Hansonville: Towering Brumley Mountain rises on the eastern skyline of Hansonville, a community named for settler David Hanson, who came here in about 1823. South-central: US-19 at US-58A

Hickory Junction: Slightly north of Honaker, Hickory Junction was once a railroad stop, or junction, where passengers waited for trains beside two hickory trees. Northeastern: VA-624 at VA-637

House and Barn Mountain: Rock outcrops resemble a house and a barn atop House and Barn Mountain, a distinctive sight for miles in Russell

County. Eastern: east of VA-80 and north of US-19, near Tazewell County

Jessees Mill: Southwest of Cleveland, Jessees Mill is named for Andrew Jackson Jessee, who built a mill in about 1890 using yellow poplar grown on his farm. The mill remained in operation until 1932. Central: VA-640 at VA-645

Laurel: At a community called "Laurel," the Laurel Branch feeds into Lewis Creek, a stream named for early settler William Lewis. Laurel is a shrub that grows wild on the branch's banks. Northeastern: VA-624 at VA-639

Mew: The word *mew* means "hideaway" or "secret place." In Russell County, Mew is a residential area surrounded by farms. Western: VA-65 at VA-611

Putnam: On the eastern edge of Honaker, this place takes its name from Allen Putnam Perley, superintendent at a local band mill during Honaker's lumber boom in the early 1900s. Northeastern: VA-637 at VA-709

Rockdell: Countless outcrops in fields along the rocky bed of Loop Creek likely inspired the name "Rockdell." This farming community supported its own post office in the early 1900s. The name "Loop Creek" comes from the stream's origin in nearby Corn Valley, where mountains seem to enclose flatter areas in the form of a loop. Southeastern: VA-80 at VA-619

South Clinchfield: A post office operated at South Clinchfield from 1919 to 1959. The coal-mining town was named for the Clinchfield Coal Co. Central: VA-600, near VA-615

Spring City: Far from having enough residents to be a city, Spring City was probably named for the many springs in the farming community's surrounding hills. Central: VA-82 at VA-662, north of Lebanon

Swords Creek: Two long hunters, Henry and Michael Sword, settled along Swords Creek and gave a name to the community. Later, circa 1900, the railroad town's wild reputation gave Swords Creek an infamous nickname, "Butcher Knife," based on stories of unsolved murders and other violent incidents. Northeastern: VA-67 at VA-633

Sun: Fred Phillips arranged to have this mile-long community's name designated as "Sun" on maps and a road sign in about 1956. The change was necessary so Phillips's large auto-parts retail business, located here, could revise its marketing slogan to be: "Phillips Auto Warehouse: Everything under the sun . . . in Sun." Northwestern: VA-63, between St. Paul and Dante

SCOTT COUNTY

Trees shroud Scott County's portion of Clinch Mountain like rumpled fur on a bear's back. Stretching east to west, this shaggy wall stands between places called Hiltons and Snowflake and poses a barrier between the bulk of Scott County's 539 square miles and the county's southeastern corner, on the Tennessee line below Weber City. Cut from parts of Russell, Washington, and Lee counties in 1814, Scott County was named for Gen. Winfield Scott in recognition of his victories during the War of 1812.

CLINCHPORT

Clinchport faced one disaster after another in the 20th century. First came a fire in 1945 that gutted much of the downtown district. Then came the death knell—a 1977 flood on the Clinch River that destroyed nearly everything in town.

Originally incorporated in 1894, Clinchport grew as a port for loggers who dodged river rocks while rolling timber downstream. It also became a thriving railroad and agricultural center at the Clinch River's confluence with Stock Creek in central Scott County.

The town is named for the river. But several theories exist on how the Clinch River and Clinch Mountain took their names. One story says "Clinch" comes from a large, athletic hunter named Clinch (Clinche), who was thrown from his horse into the river while retreating from Indians circa 1749; Clinch managed to drown one of his Indian attackers, even after his fall. Yet another story says the name is for an Irishman who fell off a raft and cried, "Clinch me! Clinch me!"

Clinchport's first incorporation was repealed in 1915, but the town was rechartered in 1940. For years here, a wooden boardwalk connected general stores, a bank, and a barbershop, all along VA-65, the main drag through town. But all of that was wiped out when the river surged out of its banks on April 4, 1977. About 80 homes in the greater Clinchport area were flooded. Some washed downriver through the submerged suburbs. Later, when floodwaters receded, business dried up in the town limits.

The 1990 census counted 67 residents in town. That same year, Clinchport won fame by electing the country's youngest mayor, 18-year-old Michael Mullins, whose two-year stint won him an appearance on NBC-TV's "Late Night With David Letterman."

What's to See

Clinch River Access: Thick and hairy vegetation sways upward from the bed of the slow-moving Clinch River off the banks of Clinchport. The river here is easily navigable for canoeists. Shoving off from the paved ramp at Clinchport, boaters can expect to find ledges on the river bottom just before passing the US-23/58/421 bridge at Speers Ferry. About nine miles downstream from that bridge, near the Tennessee line, a public river access sits on the left bank. This route passes an occasional shoal but no big rapids.

🚗 From US-23/58/421, follow VA-65 northeast for one mile to the Clinchport ramp, on the right. A small boat landing downstream from Clinchport, near the Tennessee line, is off VA-627, about 8.5 miles southwest of the Clinch River bridge on US-23/58/421.

DUFFIELD

In northwestern Scott County, Duffield is home to a couple of shopping centers, a couple of motels, and an industrial park. Still, as an incorporated town, Duffield is among the smallest in Virginia, with a population of less than 100, according to the 2000 census.

Duffield's main intersection lies where US-58/421 splits from US-23 and heads west. At this junction is what looks like the old Duffield train depot. But it's not, despite the DUFFIELD DEPOT sign hanging out front. Another thing—it was never even a train station. Hollywood moviemakers had the Christmas-tree-green building constructed in nearby Wise County for a scene in 1980's big-screen hit *Coal Miner's Daughter*. In the movie, the depot is labeled "Van Lear" for a town in Eastern Kentucky where country music singer Loretta Lynn (portrayed by actress Sissy Spacek) says

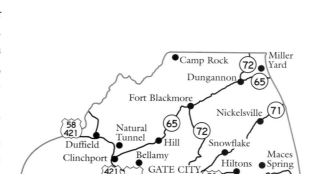

goodbye to her father as she boards a train to join her husband in Washington State. Years later, long after the film was released, Duffield resident Kenny Fannon dug this abandoned prop out of some woods, and then he rebuilt it on his property, off US-23/58/421, near Duffield's primary crossroads.

Incorporated in 1894, Duffield's name originated either from Sam Henry Duff, an early settler who came here in about 1818 from Mount Airy, North Carolina, or Robert Duff, a pioneer who lived in a log cabin known as "Duffield."

A stream little bigger than a drainage ditch—what maps note as the North Fork of the Clinch River—slices through town. Another North Fork, however, is on maps at the river's head in Tazewell County.

Each Labor Day weekend, Duffield holds its Duffield Daze festival.

Hollywood leftovers in Scott County—the Duffield Train Station, a prop from the movie *Coal Miner's Daughter*

DUNGANNON

Settled as early as the 1770s along the Clinch River, Dungannon was first called "Hunter's Ford" and, later, "Osborne's Ford," for Stephen Osborne (Osborn), who obtained a land grant here in 1786. Another early settler, Patrick Porter, built a mill on the waterfall of Fall Creek in 1774. Fall Creek's 35-foot-high falls can be seen, but just barely, from a public highway in Dungannon, off the right shoulder of VA-774, 0.1 miles southeast of VA-65.

The name "Dungannon" comes from Patrick Hagan, who came to Scott County in about 1844 to join his uncle, Joseph Hagan. Patrick Hagan (1828-1917) became a prominent lawyer and eventually amassed large holdings of timberlands, including Osborne's Ford. By the early 1900s, Hagan had changed the name of this place to pay homage to his family's hometown in Ireland. He also designed the town plan.

Incorporated since 1918, Dungannon's older business buildings lack the polish and paint of early years. But the town's residents—more than 300, according to the 2000 census—still support a handful of scattered stores at this crossroads of VA-65 and VA-72 in northeastern Scott County.

What's to See

Bark Camp Recreation Area: Nestled in the Jefferson National Forest, Bark Camp Recreation Area includes a 48-acre lake with a paved ramp for boats with trolling motors. Mowed grassy areas line part of the lakeshore. The Virginia Department of Game and Inland Fisheries dammed this reservoir on Little Stony Creek in the mid-1950s. It was earliest known as either "Corder Bottom Lake" or "Scott-Wise Lake." Stumps and trees were left on the lake bottom to provide a habitat for fish.

The area includes an amphitheater, picnic tables, hiking trails, as well as a handicapped-accessible fishing pier where anglers try hooking largemouth bass, bluegill, and rainbow trout. Camping facilities—some 20 spaces—are open May to September. Fees are charged through the Clinch Ranger District of the Jefferson National Forest.

🚗 The route to Bark Camp from Dungannon uses steep gravel roads through the Jefferson National Forest. From VA-65, follow VA-72 north through Dungannon for a half mile. Turn left on VA-653 and follow for 1.7 miles. Turn right on VA-706 and follow for 3.5 miles. Turn right on VA-822 and follow for 2.7 miles to the mile-long entrance road on the left.

Alternate Route: From US-58A at Tacoma, between Norton and Coeburn in Wise County, follow VA-706 south for 4.1 miles, turn left on VA-699 and follow for 0.3 miles, then turn right on VA-822 and go 1.7 miles to the entrance.

Clinch River Access: Going downstream from Dungannon, the Clinch River passes deep pools harboring a wide variety of fish, including musky, sunfish, walleye, catfish, and smallmouth bass. It is a 12-mile float from Dungannon to the VA-72 bridge at Fort Blackmore, then eight more miles to a public access at Hill.

🚗 From VA-72 at Dungannon, follow VA-65 northeast for 0.1 miles. Turn right on Rt. 1006 (Wilder St.) just before the Clinch River bridge, then immediately turn left on Rt. 1007 (Fourth Ave.) and follow to the boat ramp and fishing area.

Falls of Little Stony and *Hanging Rock Picnic Area:* Little Stony Creek is a little more acrobatic than the average stream in the Jefferson National Forest. In a mountain-laurel thicket, the creek cruises below a man-made footbridge, then immediately jumps a small cliff. It makes a dramatic 24-foot midair plunge into a shallow pool, less than a quarter mile from the head of the Little Stony National Recreation Trail.

But, wait—there's more. Several hundred yards below this drop, the creek hops a 12-foot-high ledge to form a twin fall; one side shoots through a rock flume, while the other fans into a midair spray and cascades over a wide stairway of rock. After another quarter mile, the slow-flowing creek drops yet again, this time cascading for 30 feet over a wall of black rock.

Blazed in yellow, the trail to the Falls of Little Stony goes along a narrow-gauge railbed constructed in the early 1900s to haul logs to a sawmill at Dungannon. It runs through a gorge 400 feet deep and 1,700 feet wide. Off its beaten path, just yards beyond the 30-foot cascade, the adventurous can turn left after crossing a bridge, follow an informal spur for 75 yards, and see the 18-foot-high but sometimes near-dry Laurel Branch Cascades. Without any detours, the main trail runs 2.8 miles, constantly keeping the creek in sight. The southern terminus is the national forest's Hanging Rock Picnic Area, a fee area open spring to fall with picnic tables, grills, a large shelter, and a large outcrop that seemingly hangs on a rock wall, high above the trout-stocked Little Stony Creek.

A stunning aerial view of the Little Stony Creek Gorge can be seen from Bear Rock, once a locally famous make-out point for couples, according to a forest official. Hikers at the Bear Rock Overlook, off USFS-701, should watch for loose rocks and cracks between rocks; it's easy to lose your footing on the short trail leading to the cliff. Originally, Bear Rock was known as "Dan Ramey Bear Cliff" and was named for a trapper who caught two bear cubs here.

🚗 From VA-65 at Dungannon, follow VA-72 north for 2.5 miles to the Hanging Rock Picnic Area entrance, on the left.

To find the Falls of Little Stony, follow VA-72 north for about six miles beyond Hanging Rock, passing into Wise County. Turn left on VA-664 and follow for about one mile. Turn left on USFS-700 and follow for about two miles. Where the road forks, bear left on USFS-701 (the route may not be marked). After a quarter mile, see the parking area for Bear Rock on the left. Continue for a half mile past Bear Rock on USFS-701 to a parking area, on the left, near a trailhead providing the easiest access to the falls.

Alternate Route: To reach the falls from US-58A at Coeburn in Wise County, follow VA-72 south for about three miles. Turn right on VA-664 and go one mile. Turn left on USFS-700 and go two miles. Bear left at USFS-701 and go less than a mile to the trail parking area.

FORT BLACKMORE

Fort Blackmore takes its name from Blackmore's Fort, an early pioneer settlement. Established in 1771-1772, this fort was built on land owned by Capt. John Blackmore.

Details of its physical size are not recorded, but it is known that the fort bordered the north side of the Clinch River on an ancient elevated floodplain. The structure was torn down, or destroyed, sometime in the early 1800s.

In the mid-1990s, an imaginative replica of Blackmore's Fort was constructed with tree-bark fencing resembling an old-time palisade. Used for history lessons, the replica is on the yard of the Fort Blackmore Elementary School, off VA-619. The school is near the southwesternmost junction of VA-65 and VA-72, Fort Blackmore's main crossroads.

Big Stony Creek meets the Clinch River here in central Scott County. The first Fort Blackmore post office opened in 1859. Prior to that, a post office called "Stony Creek" operated in this vicinity as early as 1847.

What's to See

Chimney Rock: Rising about 360 feet from the Chimney Rock Fork of Big Stony Creek—a rushing, rocky, roaring watercourse—Chimney Rock is among the most remote sites in Scott County's portion of the Jefferson National Forest. And finding it isn't easy. This quarter-mile-long pinnacle stands at the center of a small gorge. Partially lined with scraggly trees, the formation looks similar to The Towers of Breaks Interstate Park in Dickenson County. But, unlike The Towers, the Chimney Rock juts out of a surrounding thick forest in four prongs, not one.

Sometime in the 1970s, a trail was initiated to the formation, but lack of funding halted the project. Without a well-established trail, getting to this hidden treasure requires a hike through thickets of sticker vines and atop fallen logs. Alongside part of the Chimney Rock Fork, hikers should look for the former path of a narrow-gauge railroad once used for logging. Above this path is a small cliff that can be climbed to provide a straight-ahead view of the Chimney Rock, unobstructed by tree cover.

Chimney Rock is located on topographic maps available through the Clinch Ranger District of the Jefferson National Forest.

🚗 From VA-65/72 at Fort Blackmore, follow VA-619 north for about 10 miles, then turn right on USFS-704, near the Wise County line. Follow USFS-704 for about 1.8 miles, then turn right on USFS-2610 (marked as a "narrow, rough road") and, bearing right when the road forks, follow for about two more miles until the road ends. From here, follow forest maps through the woods to locate the Chimney Rock.

Devil's Bathtub and Waterfall: The noisy waters of the Devils Fork of Big Stony Creek have carved a hole about 20 feet long and eight feet wide in solid rock, known as "The Devil's Bathtub." And the name fits; the 12-foot-deep depression in the creek

Upper Falls of Little Stony Creek

Lower Falls of Little Stony Creek

Middle Falls of Little Stony Creek

41

Chimney Rock. Four prongs like this rise from a remote gorge in northern Scott County

Devil's Bathtub, near Fort Blackmore

bed is shaped just like a bathtub. An eight-foot-high cascade drips into the basin like a faucet. Local tradition says the tub is named for the devil because its clear-as-ice water is "cold as hell." Downstream from the tub, water files through a narrow raceway and spits into a crystal clear swimming hole. Because this pool is approached first on the 2.2-mile-long Devils Fork Trail, hikers often mistake it for the Devil's Bathtub.

The Devils Fork Trail is mostly flat in the Jefferson National Forest, but it crosses the stream about 10 times along an old road once used to transport coal and logs. Jumping over rocks works only part of the time, so hikers should expect to get their feet wet. About a half mile beyond the bathtub, the trail reaches another sight—the 25-foot-high Devils Fork Falls, which snakes down a cliff in a sheer vertical drop. The falls are about 200 feet off the trail and hidden, a little, in the woods.

🚗 From VA-65/72 at Fort Blackmore, follow VA-619 north for about five miles, bearing to the right at the Glen Carter Memorial Bridge. At the crossroads of VA-619 and VA-657, turn left onto a one-lane bridge to follow VA-619 for about a quarter mile. Turn left on a gravel lane next to a white house and a chain-link fence. Follow this gravel road for about a half mile, bearing to the right when the road forks, then, after another 0.1 miles, bear left when the road forks again and leads to the small parking area.

The gated road above the parking lot is the trail. After a quarter mile, the trail crosses a stream. At a sharp curve about 50 yards farther, a sign designates USFS-619. Bear left here to follow the trail for 20 yards, then bear right and follow the trail marked with yellow blaze as it goes up the creek. After about two miles, pass the swimming hole. Continue on the trail for several more yards to a small sign pointing to the Devil's Bathtub, at the center of the creek bed. To find the waterfall, follow the trail for a half mile beyond the bathtub. Pass two large rock walls on the left, and look for the falls on the right.

GATE CITY At the junction of US-23/58/421 and VA-71, Gate City is Scott County's courthouse town and was named for its proximity to Big Moccasin

Devils Fork Falls, just beyond the Devil's Bathtub

Dating to 1829, the brick Scott County Courthouse at 104 E. Jackson St. stands near the Moccasin Avenue intersection. On the front lawn, a unique, black iron statue made by World War II veteran Jim Spears depicts a soldier wearing a military uniform.

Also near the center of town is Shoemaker Elementary School, situated on a hillside where college students once walked on the campus of Shoemaker College. This college was founded in 1897 after the death of Col. James L. Shoemaker, a Gate City businessman whose lengthy will stipulated that he wanted part of his $30,000 estate used to establish an educational institution here. Unfortunately, there was not enough money to keep the college open very long. Financial difficulties forced it to close in 1906; the brick college building burned in 1957.

HILL A man named Hill once operated a local tavern, or hotel, during the stagecoach era and left his name on a central Scott County community near the crossroads of VA-609 and VA-645. Hill's post office was called either "Hill's Station" or "Hill Station" beginning in the 1890s, then just plain "Hill."

What's to See

Clinch River Access: The float down the Clinch River from Hill to Clinchport is a five-mile scenic route slipping past shady banks. The water is full of rocks—even boulders—but rapids are small and few. During summer, Natural Tunnel State Park in Scott County sponsors canoe trips on this stretch.

🚗 From US-23/58/421 at Clinchport, follow VA-65 northeast for 6.5 miles. Turn right on VA-645, cross the bridge, then turn left on VA-729 and follow for a quarter mile to the river.

HILTONS Near the crossroads of VA-709 and US-58/421, Hiltons was once known as "Fulkerson," so named for Abraham Fulkerson, a Revolutionary War veteran who settled on 100 acres in the Hiltons area of southeastern Scott County. Fulkerson, incidentally, is the name of the magisterial district in the county's southeastern corner. The current name dates to about 1889 and probably honors early postmasters John H. Hilton and Enos B. Hilton or their families.

MACES SPRING A man remembered only by his last name, Mace, lived in southeastern Scott County during the 1800s and owned property containing three springs, each producing a different kind of water. A post office in the area, near the crossroads of VA-614 and VA-691, became known as "Mace's Spring" (1888-1893), then "Maces Spring" (1893-1954). At the base of Clinch

Gap, which lies at its south side. This gap in Clinch Mountain once inspired the town's nickname, "Gateway to the West." About 2,200 people called Gate City home in 2000.

Laid out in 1815, the town's main east-west thoroughfare was named "Jackson Street" for Andrew Jackson, a U.S. president then known as a military hero for his service in the War of 1812. Gate City was initially known as "Winfield" for Gen. Winfield Scott, another War of 1812 hero. Winfield later became "Estillville" to honor Benjamin Estill, a judge who helped establish Scott County. Estillville became "Gate City" in about 1886 and was incorporated in 1892.

Parts of downtown Gate City can be seen in the 1984 movie *The River,* a drama starring Mel Gibson and Sissy Spacek. One scene filmed here shows a Jackson Street sign pointing the way to Kingsport, Nickelsville, and Bristol. But visitors may hardly recognize the town they see on-screen. In the mid-1990s, the real-life setting changed when Gate City put a fresh face on the downtown corridor, with new sidewalks, trees, and antique-looking lampposts.

Mountain, Maces Spring is part of Poor Valley, an area named not for economics but its poor quality of soil.

What's to See

Carter Fold: The story of the Carter Fold is the story of Janette Carter. Born on July 2, 1923, this woman never got rich from the music of The Carter Family—her clan's famous group of early country music performers. But, throughout a hard life of working in kitchens and factories, this spirited-yet-easygoing and seemingly tireless woman would maintain a love for traditional Appalachian mountain music.

Janette Carter inherited that love from her parents, especially her father, Alvin Pleasant Delaney Carter. Known as "A. P.," he was born in a log cabin in 1891 in an area called Little Valley, near Maces Spring. Growing up, A. P. Carter often roamed the mountains of Southwest Virginia, finding inspiration for songs from hymns or traditional folk tunes.

A. P. Carter and his brother Ezra (or "Eck") married a pair of first cousins, Sara and Maybelle, respectively. Later, A. P., Sara, and Maybelle would go on to make music history; the trio became "The Carter Family" sometime in 1926.

Not long after a talent scout discovered the Carters in nearby Bristol in August 1927, the group's vocal harmony, Sara's Autoharp playing, A. P.'s songwriting, and Maybelle's widely imitated "chicken scratch" guitar style became signatures of country music. The Carters recorded about 300 songs, from blues and ballads to hymns. A 1928 tune, "Wildwood Flower," sold one million copies. Initially, this "First Family of Country Music" never ventured far from their Clinch Mountain homes to make appearances, aside from relocating to Del Rio, Texas, in 1938 to perform on a radio show for a few years.

The original trio broke up in 1943. A. P. Carter spent the last years of his life playing music with his children, including Janette, a child dancer with The Carter Family. After A. P. died in 1960, music fans flocked to Maces Spring and begged Janette to sing the family's songs or tell stories. The fans also wanted to see where A. P. Carter was buried, at Mount Vernon United Methodist Church off VA-614. And, yet, Janette herself wanted to uphold a promise to her dying father: she wanted to keep her family's music alive.

So, in 1974, Janette opened the door to her inheritance—the A. P. Carter Store, a small place her father had operated in the late 1940s. Janette transformed the wooden floors of that empty building into a music hall to perform what she called "old-time Carter Family music." Soon, the store's Saturday shows overflowed with fans and musicians. In 1976, to accommodate larger gatherings, Janette and her brother, Joe, built a barn next door and called it "The Carter Fold." Its nothing-fancy interior seats about 1,000, and its rustic, plain appearance suits the simplicity of the acoustic music performed by various acts.

Well, almost everything is acoustic. Johnny Cash, a country music legend and husband of June Carter Cash, one of Maybelle's daughters, made surprise appearances here to perform his regular show with an electric amplifier. Often, in interviews, Janette Carter explained the exception, saying Cash "was electrified before I knew him." Still, Cash's concerts—and benefit shows by Marty Stuart, a country singer once married to one of Cash's daughters—have been the only electric exceptions at the Carter Fold.

The rule onstage is "old-time Carter Family music." That means old-time Appalachian songs, like the original Carter Family played. Hearing music at the Carter Fold, still, is only part of the fun. Watch—or join—the all-ages audience as it crowds the tiny dance floor to do a little flat-footin' during Saturday-night shows.

The old store building, next to the Carter Fold, houses a museum of Carter family memorabilia, including pictures, records, newspaper clippings, and show costumes. In 2003, A. P. Carter's circa-1890 birthplace cabin was dismantled at its location on a Scott County farm about three miles away and rebuilt near the Carter Fold.

Annually, on the first Saturday of August, the Carter Fold stages the Memorial Festival to commemorate the anniversary of The Carter Family's first recordings in Bristol.

🚗 From the Gate City exit on I-81 (Exit 1) in Bristol, follow US-58/421 west for 17 miles to Hiltons. Turn right on VA-709, then turn almost immediately right on VA-614 (A. P. Carter Hwy.) and follow for three miles to Maces Spring. The Carter Fold is on the left.

A. P. Carter's general store is now a country music museum

NATURAL TUNNEL

Railroad buffs and geologists love Natural Tunnel, as do typical tourists roaming Virginia's mountains.

In central Scott County, the Natural Tunnel spans 850 feet beneath Purchase Ridge. The feature formed about one million years ago as groundwater bearing carbonic acid percolated through cracks in a wall made of limestone and dolomitic bedrock. The water created a cave as the regional water table gradually dropped. Ultimately, Stock Creek was rerouted underground, and the creek widened the tunnel through erosion.

Politician Williams Jennings Bryan (1860-1925) made the tunnel famous when he visited the region in the 1880s and declared it the "Eighth Wonder of the World." Later, Natural Tunnel Caves and Chasms operated a lodge and restaurant for guests here in the 1930s. The property was acquired by the state and developed as the Natural Tunnel State Park in the late 1960s.

This natural phenomenon is used as a railroad passage. It also lends its name to the Natural Tunnel community, where a post office existed in the 1860s. Natural Tunnel—the park or the place—can be found by going 3.5 miles south of Duffield on US-23/58/421, then following VA-871 east for one mile.

One park trail (0.3 miles one way) leads downhill to the tunnel's face in Stock Creek Gorge, where vertical walls of limestone rise more than 400 feet. For a fee, you can take a six-minute-long, 536-foot chairlift ride that passes overtop this trail. Both the chairlift and the trail end at a deep, semicircular basin known as the gorge's "amphitheater." A platform at the edge of the railroad tracks provides a close-up view of the Natural Tunnel's swirling, round entrance and, occasionally, a passing train.

The 850-acre park extends much farther than the tunnel. It also includes a large swimming pool, picnic sites, an amphitheater, a campground, and a visitor center with railroad photographs and geological exhibits. Behind the center, a universally accessible trail leads to an aerial overlook of the tunnel. This path is easygoing on asphalt, but its straight-up ascension of Tunnel Hill equals a bit more workout than it looks, especially if you follow it for almost a half mile to Lover's Leap.

Lover's Leap is a cliff named for the legend of two Indian lovers. Park brochures promote a simple story of a Cherokee maiden and a Shawnee warrior who fell in love but could not marry, because their respective tribes each claimed this area as a hunting ground. The pair leapt to their deaths from Lover's Leap in hopes of being together in the afterlife.

Another account, remembered in Edward A. Pollard's 1870 book *The Virginia Tourist*, places the Lover's Leap legend in the 1790s, when a Wyandot chief promised his daughter to the chief of a neighboring tribe. But the daughter, Masoa, wanted to remain with her lover, a young warrior of her own tribe.

On the day of the planned wedding, Masoa escaped and came to this high perch with her lover. The two were soon found, and a crowd numbering several hundred gathered in the canyon below. Masoa began preaching her heart's desire. But not everyone was swayed by her speech—the jilted and jealous chief of the neighboring tribe reacted by firing an arrow into the breast of Masoa's lover. Uttering a wild shriek, Masoa grabbed her dying lover's body and leapt to her death on the rocks below the cliff. Then the young brother of Masoa instantly struck the murderous chief with the deadly blow of a tomahawk.

Natural Tunnel

NICKELSVILLE

Surrounded by farms in northeastern Scott County, Nickelsville is a town of about 450 residents. It was named for the family of James Nickels, Sr. (1781-1869), an early landowner whose sons William and Walter operated a store and post office here in the 1830s. Originally incorporated as "Nicholsville" in 1902, the town adopted the current spelling in 1938. On the last weekend of June, look for the annual Nickelsville Days, a festival held near the town's main crossroads of VA-71 and VA-682.

What's to See

Bush Mill: Built in about 1896, the water-powered Bush Mill sits on the banks of the Amos Branch of Copper Creek and is sometimes called "Bond Mill" for S. H. Bond, who owned it for a few years in the early 1900s. The "Bush" is for Valentine Bush, who built the mill on a limestone foundation with help from his sons, Stephen and William, and W. T. Frazier. Its waterwheel is 30 feet in diameter. The Nickelsville Ruritan Club maintains the county-owned mill. Demonstrations, along with sales of cornmeal, are held on the first Saturday of each October during the club's annual fall festival.

🚗 From VA-71 at Nickelsville, follow VA-680 west for one mile. The mill is at the crossroads of VA-680 and VA-681.

Kilgore Fort House: Built sometime between 1782 and 1790, the Kilgore Fort House is considered the oldest surviving structure in Scott County. It was once a link in a chain of early Southwest Virginia fort houses built for protection from attacks by Native Americans. The two-story cabin consists of hand-hewn logs solidified with limestone and mortar. In the early 1800s, it was the home of Robert Kilgore, a Primitive Baptist preacher who often held religious services here. Privately owned, the house is listed on both state and national historic registers.

🚗 The drive-by attraction is 1.2 miles south of Nickelsville on VA-71, near a Copper Creek bridge.

RYE COVE

Wild rye growing in central Scott County lent its name to Rye Cove, an agricultural community at the crossroads of VA-649 and VA-650. Yet the name "Rye Cove" designates more than just a road crossing. The name also identifies the largest valley in Scott County, stretching six miles long and four miles wide. Similar to Burke's Garden in Tazewell County, Rye Cove is ringed by mountain walls at all sides.

Perhaps this setting seemed like natural protection to pioneer settlers, who built the long-gone Rye Cove Fort here in the 1770s. Even so, these mountain walls did not block Indians from finding the Rye Cove Fort and attacking it with deadly force in 1776.

The mountains encircling Rye Cove also could not hold back a cyclone on May 2, 1929. That afternoon, a tornado killed 12 schoolchildren and one teacher. The phenomenon left 54 people with injuries and destroyed Rye Cove Consolidated School. Classes in the community were not held again for a year, when Rye Cove Memorial High School opened in 1930.

WEBER CITY

No Webers are involved in the name of Weber City, a southern Scott County town near the Tennessee border.

Bush Mill at Nickelsville

The town's name, actually, comes from a joke by the late Frank M. Parker, Sr. This businessman is credited with naming Weber City after hearing a skit on the old radio show "Amos and Andy" in the 1930s. In one episode, a character promoted a real estate development in a place called "Weber City." Finding inspiration there, Parker erected a WELCOME TO WEBER CITY sign at his service station on US-23, near Chapel Street. At first, Parker's sign seemed like a joke to residents. But, in 1954, that joke became reality when the town here was incorporated as "Weber City."

Weber City supports a few dozen small businesses and spans about two miles along US-23—from the US-58/421 crossroads to a bridge crossing the North Fork of the Holston River. This town, which had about 1,300 residents in 2000, is primarily a bedroom community for the much larger industrial city of Kingsport, Tennessee, about two miles south.

What's to See

Big Moccasin Gap and *Anderson Block House Monument:* In terms of crossing Clinch Mountain, Big Moccasin Gap must have looked like a godsend to Daniel Boone when the trailblazer passed through in 1769.

Here, between Weber City and Gate City, towering Clinch Mountain drops more than 1,800 feet from its high point above

Kilgore Fort House at Nickelsville

it with dread and in numbers. Routinely, early travelers would gather about four miles southeast of the gap at the Anderson Block House, a frontier outpost. Capt. John Anderson built the Block House sometime before 1782. Here, travelers waited until collecting in large enough numbers to defend themselves as they passed through the gap. In 1876, the Block House was consumed in a fire. A monument later marked its location, and construction began in 2003 on a Block House replica at Scott County's Natural Tunnel State Park near Duffield.

🚗 Big Moccasin Gap is at the crossroads of US-23 and US-58/421, between Weber City and Gate City. To reach the Anderson Block House Monument from the gap, follow US-58/421 east for a quarter mile. Turn right on VA-224 and continue for about 2.5 miles south, then turn left on VA-704. Follow for a half mile and turn left on VA-606. The monument is on the right, about 0.1 miles north of VA-704.

nearby Hiltons. The gap allows room for Big Moccasin Creek, as well as railroad tracks and the four lanes of US-23/58/421. This natural mountain pass is the only way to get to the Scott County courthouse from the county's lower southeastern corner.

At the gap, in 1815, the first court of Scott County was held at the home of Benjamin T. Hollins. A small monument marks this spot at the crossroads of US-23 and US-58/421. Nearby, on the gap's northwestern side, is a wayside area with picnic tables.

A Scott County post office here in the 1810s was known as "Moqueson Gap" or "Mockinson Gap." The spelling had evolved to "Moccasin Gap" by the early 1900s. Traditionally, the name is owed to early travelers who found the footprints of moccasins along the creek near the gap.

Boone used the gap to build the Wilderness Road through the region in the 1770s. Unfortunately, the gap also provided an ideal place for attack by hidden enemies, so pioneer settlers approached

---

Homeplace Mountain Farm and Museum: Opened in 1996, the Homeplace Mountain Farm and Museum is comprised of 19th-century buildings—mostly log structures—that founder Rex McCarty collected from places across Scott County. Many were once smokehouses, and none are particularly historic. But these buildings do give a glimpse of the architecture and lifestyle of mountain settlers, circa 1840.

🚗 From US-23 at Weber City, follow US-58/421 east for about a quarter mile. Turn right on VA-224 and follow for a half mile. The Homeplace is on the left.

SCOTT COUNTY CROSSROADS

Bellamy: Between Moccasin Ridge and the Copper Creek Knobs, this community likely takes its name from William H. Bellamy, the first postmaster in 1901. Central: VA-627 at VA-643

Bruno: From 1902 to 1907, Bruno supported its own post office where Roberts Creek crosses US-58/421 at a hairpin curve, near a rustic country store. About four miles east of Bruno, also on US-58/421, a post office called "Fido" was open from 1879 to 1907. Both Bruno and Fido, according to local tradition, took their names from somebody's dogs. Southeastern: US-58/421 at VA-859

Camp Rock: Inside the Jefferson National Forest, Camp Rock is a cliff shelter used by hunting parties during early settlement in the late 1700s. The rock's elevation is about 4,000 feet, the highest point in Scott County. Northern: VA-619 at Wise County line

Daniel Boone: Local tradition says explorer Daniel Boone once drank from a spring at a small settlement named for him. In the 1770s, Boone blazed a trail through Southwest Virginia from Big Mocassin Gap to Cumberland Gap. South-central: VA-870, near VA-643

Duncan Mill: At the eastern edge of Rye Cove, Duncan Mill was named for a long-gone gristmill destroyed during a tornado on May 2, 1929. John Duncan built the original log mill on Cove Creek in about 1835. George W. Johnson, Duncan's son-in-law, later replaced it with a more modern structure. Central: VA-649 at VA-656

Fairview: A view of rolling hills likely inspired the name "Fairview." Southwestern: VA-600 at VA-622

Holston Springs: A mile west of Weber City, a springwater resort opened at Holston Springs in about 1809. For recreation, hotel guests rowed boats on the nearby North Fork of the Holston River. In the mid-1880s, the 24-room Holston Springs resort hotel was sold to Rufus Ayers (1849-1926), the industrialist whose large home at Big Stone Gap later became the Southwest Virginia Museum. The Holston Springs hotel, once Ayers's personal showplace, burned down in 1914. Southern: VA-614 at VA-714

Jennings Mission: Abram and Victoria Jennings donated land for the Jennings Mission Church of Jesus Christ in the 1920s and gave their name to the area. South-central: VA-788, near VA-870

McConnell: The name of the McConnell community in the Copper Creek valley is probably derived from its first postmaster, Henry McConnell, in 1885. Some say Copper Creek was named for copperhead snakes. Central: VA-670 at VA-671

Miller Yard: A Miller Yard post office operated from 1924 to 1948. The name comes from H. L. Miller, president of the Interstate Railroad in the 1920s, when this railroad yard was established. Northeastern: VA-608 at Clinch River

Nottingham: The Nottingham community probably owes its name to the family of G. H. and Martha Nottingham. The couple deeded land to establish a church here in 1899. Southern: US-58/421 at VA-614

Pattonsville: The Rev. Samuel Patton was a prominent early minister in Scott County and is remembered in the name "Pattonsville." Western: VA-604 at VA-638

Pendleton Island: The shallow Clinch River slips around Pendleton Island, a sanctuary owned by the Nature Conservancy of Virginia and once deemed the richest 300 yards of mussel diversity on the planet. The water here supports 40 different mussel species, including the green-blossom pearly mussel, believed to live only at this vicinity. Named for a local Pendleton family, the island is actually a collection of three wooded isles rising over 33 acres of riverbed. Farmers once grew corn here, carrying crops to the mainland by horse and cart when the river was low. A post office called "Pendleton" operated in the 1830s. Central: Clinch River, one mile downstream of VA-72 bridge at Fort Blackmore

Shelleys: Miniature waterfalls on the Ketron Branch of Cove Creek tumble down rock stairs at heights of about seven feet alongside US-58/421, one mile east of the Shelleys crossroads. This community of cattle farms was named for early landowner Joel Shelley. Southeastern: easternmost crossroads of US-58/421 and VA-617

Silica: An early-1900s business that dug silica sand out of nearby Clinch Mountain left behind the name "Silica." Southeastern: VA-614, near Washington County

Slant: Land naturally slopes toward the Clinch River at Slant. Still, the area is alternately known as "Starnes," "Starnes Bluff," or even "Starnes Slant." The "Starnes" name comes from Frederick Starnes, who settled at Slant in the late 1700s. Central: VA-65 at VA-662

Snowflake: It doesn't snow in Snowflake any more than in other parts of Scott County. But one account says a snowstorm in the 1880s, when the Snowflake post office was established, inspired the community's name. A different tale, still, says Snowflake took its name because it looked like snow had fallen here after nearly everyone painted their houses white. Central: VA-71 at VA-671

Speers Ferry: Prominent landowner Joshua Speer, Sr., established a ferry across the Clinch River in 1833 and gave his name to the Speers Ferry community. The ferry was discontinued in 1925 after a highway bridge opened. Central: US-23/58/421 bridge over Clinch River

Stanleytown: An early settler, most likely Richard Stanley (1750-1838) or his son George, inspired the name "Stanleytown." Northwestern: VA-653 at VA-722

Sunbright: Tradition says the name "Sunbright" originated from the railroad stop's location, a tiny valley where the sun shines bright among dense mountains. Northwestern: VA-653 at VA-871

Twin Springs: A pair of springs naturally inspired the name "Twin Springs." Northeastern: VA-671 at VA-680

Yuma: In 1886, residents of Yuma produced a list of possible names for a post office. The one they liked the most—the name of an Indian tribe in southwestern Arizona—came from a suggestion by the county's superintendent of schools, W. D. Smith. Southern: VA-614 at VA-640

TAZEWELL COUNTY

Tazewell County contains the headwaters of the Clinch River, in an unbelievably scenic area that has remained largely agricultural—and unspoiled—since settlers began arriving here in the mid-1700s. Spanning 520 square miles, Tazewell County was formed in 1799 from parts of Russell and Wythe counties and is named for Virginia's Henry Tazewell, a U.S. Senator from 1794 to 1799.

BLUEFIELD

Bluefield is a town with a Siamese twin in another state. There is a Bluefield in Virginia and a larger one in West Virginia.

In the early 1860s, Virginia's Bluefield was called "Pin Hook." The small settlement was later renamed "Harman," in honor of Confederate war hero Col. E. H. Harman. The town experienced its first real growth as "Graham," named in 1884 for Thomas Graham, a Philadelphia engineer who surveyed the area for the Norfolk & Western Railway. The name "Graham" is still on churches, parks, and stores in this railroad town.

In 1924, voters decided to change the name to "Bluefield" to match the adjacent town in West Virginia. Along the way, the Baptist-affiliated Bluefield College also took the name. Originally a two-year institution, the school, at 3000 College Dr., has been granting bachelor's degrees since 1977.

Several stories are told on how the name "Bluefield" originated. One theory says the moniker comes from a species of chicory that has a dark blue flower. Another says it is for the area's proximity to the Bluestone River, named for the blue limestone in the river, which gives a clear blue color to the stream.

According to yet another account, the original name of Bluefield, West Virginia, was "Higginbotham's Summit," for John D. Higginbotham, whose farm adjoined one belonging to Joseph Davidson. With the arrival of the railroad in 1883, a post office was moved to the Higginbotham farm and named "Bluefield" by Hattie Hannah in reference to the bluegrass fields on the Davidson and Higginbotham farms.

On US-460, a sign says WELCOME TO THE BLUEFIELDS. Like the two Bristols of Virginia and Tennessee, the two Bluefields of the Virginias share resources, such as the Greater Bluefield Chamber of Commerce, which promotes the low-average-temperature area as "Nature's Air-Conditioned City." In 1939, chamber manager Eddie Steele came up with the idea to give out free lemonade on the streets whenever the temperature reached 90 degrees here. Serving lemonade has been good publicity ever since, though the lemonade rarely flows. The fact is, two years passed before the first cup was poured, in 1941. And, due to mild temperatures, lemonade was served only once from 1960 to 1982. But then came 1988, a hot year that required serving lemonade a record 17 times!

Unlike Bristol, the Bluefield marriage does not appear as physically evident as Bristol's State Street, which runs along the Tennessee-Virginia border. The Bluefields, instead, are connected at the state line on US-19. Virginia's Bluefield is at VA-102's crossroads with US-19, while Bluefield, West Virginia, surrounds the vicinity where US-52 meets US-19.

In 2000, Virginia's Bluefield counted a population of about 5,000. Nicknamed "Virginia's Tallest Town" for its elevation at 3,800 feet above sea level, it partially serves as a suburb for its West Virginia counterpart, which boasts more than twice as many people.

What's to See

Graham Recreation Park: Open since 1988, Graham Recreation Park is a 57-acre day-use facility featuring picnic shelters, a playground, a gazebo, an amphitheater, a baseball field, tennis courts, and a short hiking trail. The Town of Bluefield operates the park.

🚗 From Bluefield Exit 1 on US-460, follow US-19 north for a half mile. The park entrance is on the right at Rt. 1530.

BURKE'S GARDEN

From the air, Burke's Garden looks like a volcano, or maybe an extinct lake. Geologically, Burke's Garden is a single valley, rimmed on all sides by Garden Mountain, at Tazewell County's southeastern corner. The valley is shaped like a bowl ten miles long and five miles wide. Native Americans called Burke's Garden "The Great Swamp," likely because it was a bog too wet for crops. Some theories say this valley was once a water basin, and that tiny Burke's Garden Creek drained the valley through tiny Garden Mountain Gap. Another theory says Garden Mountain once was a 6,500-foot-high dome. But water cracked the summit's sandstone cap and continually eroded the dome until a valley of flat land formed at the center of the mountain. Some Burke's Garden residents tell stories of cave-ins, saying Garden Mountain's erosion has yet to yield.

By car, Burke's Garden is most easily accessible through Garden Mountain Gap, where two lanes of asphalt (VA-623) pass beside Burke's Garden Creek and enter from the main body of Tazewell County (from VA-61), after six miles of hairpin curves and steep upgrades. On the south side, a gravel portion of VA-623 climbs up and over Garden Mountain to reach Bland County on an even more perilous journey.

The average elevation at Burke's Garden is about 3,100 feet. The area's highest point, Beartown, stands about 1,000 feet higher and took its name because bears were once known to descend the peak and eat local farmers' sheep. Beartown is now a roadless wilderness area of about 6,000 acres in the Jefferson National Forest.

The Burke's Garden name comes from hunter James Burk, a native of Limerick, Ireland, who spelled his last name without an *E*. According to legend, Burk chased a wounded elk into the wilderness here in about 1748 and found an old Indian campground. Burk ate a few potatoes on his first visit to the valley, then covered the peelings with dirt so Indians could not track him. Explorers reached the campground the following year and found a large, sprouting bed of potatoes. The explorers jokingly referenced this place as "Burk's Garden."

A Virginia historical marker stands alongside VA-623 at what is believed to be the actual site of Burk's potato garden. Near that marker are white directional signs, looking like pieces of a white picket fence. Each sign lists a name and distance to a family's farm. Such informal markers were first posted here in the 1950s.

German Lutherans, migrating from Pennsylvania, settled here in the late 1700s. A little more than a century later, Burke's Garden supported a population of 1,500, when large sheep and cattle farms needed lots of hands. Yet another century later, increased use of machinery contributed to a smaller head count as people left to find other work. The population steadied around 300 in the 1990s.

Signs point the way to farms and homes in Burke's Garden

Crooked roads put a barrier on this 20,000-acre community and keep out signs of modern civilization, like newspaper deliveries, cable television, and door-to-door solicitors. This island-style isolation is part of the Garden's charm. It is partly why several Amish families bought land and called the Garden home in the 1990s. Coming from Maryland and Pennsylvania, they raised crops and conducted farm business without telephones and automobiles. They traveled by buggy. They operated their own school and sold goods to tourists. But they didn't stay long; by 1999, the last family had departed Burke's Garden, saying they were unable to find more land so their children could stay here, too.

Rarely does land change hands in Burke's Garden. It is usually passed generation to generation through the same bloodline, though occasional exceptions occur. Commonly in the 1980s, heirs settled estates by subdividing old farms and creating small tracts called "farmettes."

One hundred years earlier, however, subdivision was far from the case when wealthy businessman George Washington Vanderbilt tried to buy his way into Burke's Garden and found no one would sell him land. Vanderbilt ultimately went to Asheville, North Carolina, and built what he had planned for Burke's Garden—Biltmore Estate, America's largest private home.

As far as the weather goes, Burke's Garden is cold. It is sometimes 10 degrees colder than nearby Tazewell. But residents here seem used to stuff like snow, where it's measured in feet, not inches. On record, it's snowed here every month of the year except July and August.

Still, snow usually doesn't fall on the last Saturday in September, when the community unites for its annual fall festival. That's when crowds gather at the community center, and tourists jam roads by the thousands to see this non-commercialized place nicknamed "God's Thumbprint" or "Garden Spot of the World."

CEDAR BLUFF

Cedar Bluff is an incorporated town nestled below cedar-covered bluffs on US-460 in western Tazewell County. For many years, Cedar Bluff—or at least a part of the town—was known as "Indian" or "Mouth of Indian" for its proximity to Indian Creek, which empties here into the shoals of the Clinch River. The name "Indian Creek" remembers an incident in which Indians killed early settler Joseph Ray and his family along the creek in about 1789.

Originally incorporated in 1895, Cedar Bluff was reincorporated under a new charter in 1912. The 2000 census counted about 1,100 residents here. On the third Saturday of each September, Cedar Bluff celebrates its heritage with a festival of arts and crafts, plus soapmaking and blacksmithing demonstrations, near the town square, on US-460-Business.

What's to See

Cedar Bluff Overlook Park: Picnic shelters and a small play area center the Cedar Bluff Overlook Park on the side of The Cuts—looming rock walls that were carved to build the four-lane version of US-19/460 near winding railroad tracks and the Clinch River. This park sits at an elevation of 2,142 feet and is overseen by the Town of Cedar Bluff.

🚗 From US-19/460-East at Cedar Bluff, turn right on VA-816 (Hurt Buggy Rd.), then turn almost immediately right at the park entrance.

Historic Grist Mill and Restaurant: Waters of the Clinch River rush over a nearly four-foot-high milldam alongside the Historic Grist Mill and Restaurant in Cedar Bluff. Ray Childress bought this mill in 1976 and, after extensive renovation, opened it in 1998 as an upscale eatery, located off US-460-Business.

The mill dates to 1858; fire destroyed a portion of the original wooden structure. W. J. Higginbotham rebuilt the mill in 1883. A century later, Childress rebuilt it even more, while also rechanneling the river to prevent floods and constructing a floodwall packed with local stones, fossils, and rock.

The intricate interior of the millhouse is a shiny showcase of fine oak and cherry. Handcrafted trim outlines a balcony above the main dining room. Floor-to-ceiling windows overlook fish jumping from the glistening river. Milling demonstrations are offered in the restaurant's mill room, where corn can be ground with power generated by the 24-foot waterwheel.

CLAYPOOL HILL

Known for its modern shopping mall in southwestern Tazewell County, Claypool Hill was named for James and Jeremiah Claypool, a pair of 18th-century settlers from Pennsylvania. A couple of miles south of Cedar Bluff and Richlands, the community sits at a major crossroads, where US-19 joins US-460.

Historic Grist Mill and Restaurant in Cedar Bluff

What's to See

Southwest Virginia Community College: Fondly nicknamed "Wardell Tech" for its proximity to the Wardell community, Southwest Virginia Community College was founded in 1967 as one of the first two community colleges in Virginia. Each spring, the hillside campus is home base for the Festival of the Arts, a series of concerts, plays, lectures, and art exhibits.

The main college entrance, off US-19, is five miles southwest of Claypool Hill on the Tazewell-Russell county line. A recreation area includes a railroad caboose, picnic facilities, playground equipment, and ball fields. The college's community center features a permanent piece of imposing artwork—a 30-foot-high brick mural fashioned in the mid-1990s by artist Johnny Hagerman, one of the school's graduates. Hagerman used more than 8,000 bricks to compose this three-dimensional sculpture. It depicts the story of "Jack and the Beanstalk," as interpreted in a 1993 drawing by comic book artist Charles Vess.

THE COVE

Locals living in The Cove boast of the place's magical beauty, saying it rivals the breathtaking scenery of nearby Burke's Garden.

And, well, it does. Part of the larger geographic region known as Thompson Valley, The Cove is a community of large farms where sheep nibble bluegrass on rocky slopes with gentle elevation climbs. Clinch Mountain provides the backdrop of what may be the most scenic farmland in Southwest Virginia.

Located in central Tazewell County along VA-91, near two intersections with VA-608, The Cove is listed on some maps as "Ward Cove," a name referring to David Ward, who settled here in about 1769.

What's to See

Cove Center: The Cove is where most of the filming for the 1994 big-screen movie *Lassie* took place. Actors Richard Farnsworth and Helen Slater trouped in here during the winter of 1993-1994 with movie crews and Howard, the collie that portrays Lassie. But despite the gorgeous scenery captured, Tazewell County did not win any credits at the end of the movie to let viewers know where it was made.

Local resident Mag Peery taught the film's school-age actors and won an on-screen role as a schoolteacher. Peery performed her supporting role at the Cove Center, an old brick school building that had been made into a community center. The center was featured in a panoramic shot at the end of the film and served as the story setting of "Franklin Falls," a fictitious Virginia town.

🚗 From US-19/460 at Claypool Hill, follow US-19 southwest for about three miles. Turn left (south) on VA-609 (near Wardell) and follow southeast for about seven miles. Turn right on VA-91 and go south for one mile. The Cove Center is on the left.

FALLS MILLS

Between railroad tracks and VA-102, the Bluestone River jumps a 15-foot-high cliff; water constantly cascades through three chutes, giving a whitewater facade to slippery steps. These are the falls of Falls

Clinch Mountain fades behind a field of hay bales at The Cove.

Cove Center, used in the 1994 film *Lassie*

Mills, formed by a natural dam on the river and once used to power a mill in the 1800s. In northeastern Tazewell County, the falls are a drive-by attraction on VA-102, about 500 feet north of a crossroads with VA-782, or 3.3 miles north of US-19 at Bluefield. You can see the falls clearly in winter when trees are missing leaves. Accessing the falls beyond the public roadway may be trespassing.

FROG LEVEL

For Frog Level, the jokes began one night in the 1930s when Jack Witten went fishing with a buddy on Plum Creek, a ditch-size watercourse named for wild plum trees growing along its banks. That night was both foggy and froggy. And, according to local lore, Witten heard so many frogs croaking that he figured the fog was low enough to be "at frog level." Hence a funny name was born for this little town in central Tazewell County.

Throughout the 1930s, Witten told the whole county about this tiny place in "Frog Level News," a column he penned for the local *Clinch Valley News*. Witten wrote about such stuff as the Frog Level Bridge Club, a group of good ole boys who played poker beneath a bridge that crosses Plum Creek.

Decades later, the name and the jokes remain. Frog Level is on most maps, and an official highway sign marks the community at the junction of US-19/460-Business and VA-91. At the Frog Level crossroads sits a grass median known as Frog Level's "Center Square."

The square is just a jump from the Frog Level Service Station, home of the Frog Level Yacht Club. But don't be fooled by this name. There is no marina on nearby, near-dry Plum Creek, and certainly no yachts. The fact is, the Frog Level Yacht Club is an all-joke organization. The club is really no more than a name on some souvenir T-shirts for sale at the service station, a business once known as the last combination beer bar/convenience store/gas station in Virginia, until the store's owner removed the gas tanks in the mid-1990s to increase parking space.

The store was built in 1932. Sixty-five years later, in 1997, the Frog Level Service Station won almost 15 seconds of fame during a short scene in the CBS-TV movie *Country Justice*, starring actor George C. Scott. The movie was filmed at various sites in Buchanan and Tazewell counties.

LIBERTY

Known as "Knob" when it was settled in the late 1700s, the village of Liberty owes its present name to Liberty Hill Church, a nondenominational house of worship founded in the mid-1800s. In the late 1800s, Liberty's Thornleigh Tavern helped the village become a gathering place for travelers. The tavern also spawned nearby businesses.

But then came the flood—the "June Tide" of 1901. Water suddenly spouted from the ground, out of a series of caves, and formed a lake as deep as eight feet here. The waters reached the second stories of buildings, destroying homes and businesses.

Fortunately, no one was killed. But people were apparently ready for the end. According to one account, a very stout minister's wife found herself caught on the second-floor balcony of her home, where she told rescuers that if she had to go, then she would go with the Bible in her hand. Yet, when the woman was rescued, it was found that in all the excitement she had picked up a copy of the Sears and Roebuck catalog instead.

Liberty, as a town, was never rebuilt. A century later, it was a quiet community with a very small population along VA-91, at an intersection with VA-608 in central Tazewell County.

PAINT LICK

Early settlers dubbed the name "Paint Lick" on what became a farming community in southwestern Tazewell County, near the crossroads of VA-609 and VA-603. The name is for both the presence of a salt lick and a line of about 30 ancient glyphs on a large rock outcrop atop Paint Lick Mountain.

Painted in a red medium using iron oxide, the glyphs, which are listed on both state and national historic registers, are of unknown origin, but archeologists believe Native Americans painted them sometime before European settlement, circa 1400-1700. Explorers discovered the paintings as early as the 1790s. By 2000, the mysterious images were fading and hardly legible, possibly due to acid-rain pollution.

On a privately owned site, the paintings range in height from a couple of inches to a couple of feet. The most famous figure, commonly called the "Running Target," looks like a bull's-eye with feet and is similar to a design found in rock art all over the Western Hemisphere, including Mexico.

POCAHONTAS

The discovery of coal on land owned by Jordan Nelson forever changed northeastern Tazewell County and created the Town of Pocahontas.

This town's story began in the 1870s with Capt. Isaiah A. Welch. He surveyed an area near the Bluestone River at the edge of West Virginia and discovered Jordan Nelson digging coal from a 13-foot outcrop. Nelson sold coal for a penny a bushel, though he was cautioned, either by his wife or a neighbor, not to give away too much, fearing the coal supply would eventually be exhausted.

In about 1881, a Philadelphia man, probably an investor, suggested that this developing coal camp should be called "Pocahontas," to honor the Indian girl who in 1608 saved the life of Capt. John Smith, an early Jamestown settler. The name "Pocahontas," once translated as "a bright stream between two hills," is now believed to mean "Little Wanton" or "The Playful One."

Large-scale mining began in Pocahontas in 1882. The Norfolk & Western Railway shipped the first carload of coal in 1883. And the first mayor of Pocahontas was elected in 1884, after openly buying votes with cash and commodities.

Such an incredulous act was indicative of the wildness of Pocahontas in its earliest days. For one, many miners were heavy drinkers and would rely on "blind tigers" for drinks; before alcohol was made legal here, miners would drop a quarter in a slot to get a drink of uncertain quality, delivered by the hand of a person they could not see. Later, liquor licenses arrived, and untold amounts of booze flowed from more than 20 saloons.

Yet Pocahontas also possessed an air of sophistication, evidenced by the likes of its 1895 opera house.

Early mine practices were risky; in 1884, an explosion killed 114 men at the Pocahontas East Mine. Undaunted, Pocahontas kept growing. In 1904, with a population of 4,000, the town was the largest in Tazewell County. But by 1955 the Pocahontas coal mines were closed, after yielding more than 44 million tons of coal. The town's population had dwindled to less than 500 by 2000, leaving many antique and architecturally intriguing buildings empty here at the north end of VA-102, making much of Pocahontas look like a ghost town.

What's to See

Pocahontas Exhibition Mine and Museum: From April to October, visitors can inspect 14-foot-high coal seams at the Pocahontas Exhibition Mine. A regular 45-minute tour walks through coal-mining history, starting with the hand-digging era of picks and shovels, transportation by mule, and mining by candlelight. Such practices were common when this 875-foot passage-way—the Pocahontas "Baby Mine"—began operations in 1882.

In 1938, the man-made grotto became the world's first coal mine open to tourists. Inside, it is damp, dark, and dusty. It is also cold—the mine's temperature stays at 52 degrees, year-round. Near the mine's entrance, a museum remembers Pocahontas with vintage photographs and coal-mining displays.

🚙 From US-19 in Bluefield, follow VA-102 north for about nine miles (passing through West Virginia for about three miles) to reach Pocahontas. In town, turn right on VA-644 and follow for about a quarter mile. Turn right on VA-659 and follow to the mine.

RICHLANDS   When the stock market crashed in 1893, so did the infant Town of Richlands— just three years after the Clinch Valley Coal & Iron Co. began developing the burg with squarely outlined streets. Company officials had dreamed that the untapped timber, coal, and iron deposits might make this region the "Pittsburgh of the South." Dreams aside, the Richlands area retained its familiar title, given years earlier for the fertile "rich lands" along the Clinch River when this was primarily a farming community.

In an early 1890s brochure, the Richlands Land Co. advertised the area, boasting CHEAP COAL! CHEAP IRON! LOW COST OF MANUFACTURE! PURE WATER! HEALTHY CLIMATE. The same brochure described the Clinch River as "a stream of some hundred feet in width and having at all seasons of the year sufficient water for a large city." Richlands was incorporated in 1892, but it never became the large city this brochure promised it could be.

Entrance to the Pocahontas Exhibition Mine in northeastern Tazewell County

At once, it seemed, the stock market crash sent panic through Clinch Valley Coal & Iron Co. officials, who immediately followed investors' orders to cease business operations and dismantle the large rolling mill, built to finish iron. The company's fabulously furnished Hotel Richlands, meanwhile, not only went belly-up but was later looted, with townspeople carrying away everything from chandeliers and carpeting to sterling silver and china.

For Richlands, the road to recovery would be long. Among other developments, the Hotel Richlands became the site of the short-lived Old Dominion College. This school was likely an extension of the Old Dominion College in nearby Honaker, which local historians note operated at about the same time. Both colleges had closed by the early 1900s.

Ultimately, as the 20th century progressed, so did Richlands. Near the crossroads of US-460 and VA-67, the town, calling itself "The Center of a Friendly Circle," became a shopping-center and bedroom community for the coal-mining region of Russell, Tazewell, and Buchanan counties. And its population, by 2000, had grown to more than 4,100.

Among the town's registered historic landmarks is the site of the old headquarters of the Clinch Valley Coal & Iron Co., at 102 Suffolk Ave. Built in 1890, this house serves as the town's library. The site of the old Hotel Richlands, meanwhile, burned a few years after the college closed. Once rebuilt and used as a hospital, it was later demolished to make room for a new town hall. In 2003, the Coal Miners Memorial, 200 Washington Sq., opened at this site.

TAZEWELL

Across the landscape of early Southwest Virginia, differences were often settled with fisticuffs, or even guns. Christiansburg, the county seat of Montgomery County, is the site of the last legal duel fought in Virginia. Tazewell, the courthouse town of Tazewell County, is infamous for a similar claim: a fistfight ended a quarrel over the location of the county courthouse. But that fight, lasting hours, is not something county historians try to hide. In fact, the brawl is bragged about in Tazewell tourism brochures.

In 1800, a town was laid out at the center of Tazewell County. Incorporated in 1866, the town became known as "Jeffersonville," for President Thomas Jefferson. At the time, though, mail was delivered to a post office called "Tazewell Court House." Eventually, mail addressed to Jeffersonville would not be delivered, so the town became "Tazewell" in 1892 to match the county.

Not everyone seems to remember that this town's name honors a Virginia politician named Henry Tazewell. In modern times, a few businesses have adopted a different "Taz"—the Tazmanian Devil, a Warner Brothers cartoon personality whose car-

icature is painted on various signs in this town of about 4,200 residents.

The Tazewell County Courthouse was built in 1874 with a Colonial Revival style. The courthouse is on Main Street, between Moore and Court streets, and includes a front lawn with a large statue, erected in 1903 to recognize local Confederate soldiers.

The Clinch River flows through Tazewell near the intersection of VA-61 and US-19/460-Business.

What's to See

Cavitt's Creek Park and *Lake Jack Witten:* Picnic shelters at the 164-acre Cavitt's Creek Park afford an aerial view of the 52-acre Lake Jack Witten. Named for a local doctor and state politician, this reservoir features a dock for fishing (bass, trout, catfish, walleye, and bluegill) and a paved ramp for boats with trolling motors. Gravel roads and walking trails encircle the lake's wooded shoreline.

🚗 From Tazewell Exit 4 on US-19/460, follow VA-645 north (opposite the town) for 2.5 miles. Turn right on Rt. 1030 and follow for a half mile to the park entrance.

Historic Crab Orchard Museum & Pioneer Park: Inside Tazewell County's most popular attraction waits a collection of pottery, pipes, furniture, jewelry, rifles, and mining tools, as well as a wedding dress made into a Confederate battle flag.

But, hey—that's only the interior. Outside, the Crab Orchard Museum & Pioneer Park is a reconstructed pioneer village, set among perfectly rounded hills speckled with weeping willows and outlined by split-rail fences. On the outskirts of the village stands Fort Witten, a pioneer-fort reconstruction commissioned in 1926 by the Daughters of the American Revolution. The original Fort Witten (also "Witten's Fort" and "Big Crab Orchard Fort") was built by Thomas Witten in the 1770s and served as a neighborhood place of refuge. Crab Orchard is named for the presence of a crabapple orchard.

Reconstructed Fort Witten

The museum opened in 1982. The non-profit facility features exhibits on Native Americans, Southwest Virginia pioneers, and local industries like coal mining and railroads. In summer, demonstrations of blacksmithing, candle making, and musketry are held.

Nearby, the small Higginbotham House Museum contains local artifacts and Native American relics once belonging to the late A. Jefferson "Jeff" Higginbotham, Jr., a longtime contributor to the Crab Orchard Museum collection. Higginbotham, a farmer, kept many treasures for himself and housed a collection of guns, arrows, china, silver, and woodwork in an 1811 log-and-stone cabin—his own private museum. In 1998, the cabin opened to the general public, usually by appointment. The museum's well-manicured grounds are alone an attraction; ornamental gardens include a water fountain, Japanese umbrella trees, and an arched footbridge spanning rock-walled banks of the Clinch River.

🚗 The Crab Orchard Museum is three miles southwest of Tazewell, at the corner of US-19/460 and US-19/460-Business. To reach the Higginbotham House from the Crab Orchard Museum at US-19/460, turn north on VA-632 and go 0.1 miles to Pisgah United Methodist Church. Turn left on VA-693 and then immediately turn right at the Higginbotham entrance.

Split-rail fences outline the Pioneer Park, outside the Historic Crab Orchard Museum

---

Lincolnshire Park: A dam on the Lincolnshire Branch of the Clinch River forms a 25-acre lake, with a ramp for boats with trolling motors. A trail lines the grassy shore. The lake is part of Tazewell's Lincolnshire Park, a 104-acre multiuse recreation area featuring ball fields, a swimming pool, a playground, picnic shelters, a railroad caboose, and a jogging path. The origin of the park's name is unclear; early deeds refer to the Lincolnshire area as "Linking Shears."

🚗 From Tazewell Exit 3 on US-19/460, follow VA-61 east for 0.8 miles. Lincolnshire Park is on the left.

WARDELL Members of the Ward family—including John T. Ward, a postmaster in 1901—are the inspiration behind the "Wardell" name in western Tazewell County. For years, the Wardell post office operated at the Wardell Store, a weathered, old building off VA-609 (Wardell Road), about a quarter mile south of US-19. It was established as a general store in 1874.

And then came Hollywood. Moviemakers showed up in Tazewell County in 1993 to film the big-screen production *Lassie*, released the following year. Along the way, Wardell became the setting for the fictitious town called Franklin Falls, Virginia. One scene was shot outside the Wardell Store. Film props included a Franklin Falls sign, showered with hair spray simply to make it look old and rusty.

The *Lassie* role kept Wardell on the map. Later, the store became the site of the Highland Bull Pub, a watering hole where, curiously, patrons sign $1 bills, then tape them anywhere they can find a spot—on the walls, on the ceiling, or on the unfinished cedar logs used as ceiling support poles.

The Wardell Store, seen in the 1994 movie *Lassie*

Abbs Valley: Absalom Looney, a hunter from Augusta County, Va., roamed the 10-mile-long Abbs Valley in about 1766 and left his name on the landscape. Northeastern: VA-644 at VA-758

Amonate: The Pocahontas Fuel Co. brought the name "Amonate" to an area near McDowell County, W.Va., when it opened new coal mines in 1924. "Amonate" is one of the names used by the Indian princess Pocahontas. Northern: VA-624 at VA-643

Asberrys: The Asberrys name honors a local family, including Mary Asberry, the first Asberrys postmaster in 1879. It's part of tiny Freestone Valley, named because its soil is free from stones. Southern: VA-16 at VA-601

Bailey: Jesse Bailey served as Bailey's first postmaster in 1895. Bailey is part of Wrights Valley, named for early explorer Peter Wright. Eastern: VA-650 (Wrights Valley Rd.) at VA-656 (Bailey Switch Rd.)

Bandy: William W. "Billy" Bandy arrived at the Bandy area in the late 1800s and basically populated the place as the father of 19 children. Northwestern: VA-624 at VA-627

Baptist Valley: Home to residences, churches, and tiny businesses, Baptist Valley spreads out for about two miles either east or west from its crossroads at Rourke's Gap, named for James Roark (or "Rourke"), an early Tazewell County settler. Baptist Valley's name comes from early Baptist settlers who moved here, some before 1776, to escape religious persecution. Central: VA-637 at VA-631

Ben Bolt: Thomas Dunn English is responsible for giving the name "Ben Bolt" to a neighborhood on the eastern edge of Tazewell. In 1842, the politician wrote a poem for the premiere issue of *The Atlantic Monthly*, with inspiration from a young woman named Alice Wynne. His work, "Sweet Alice, Ben Bolt," was converted into a popular song in the 1850s. English wrote it while sitting outside the Peery-Wynne Homeplace (or "Ben Bolt House"). The area around the brick house was later called "Ben Bolt" in reference to the poem. Central: VA-61 at Ben Bolt Ave.

Bishop: Walter A. Bishop served as chief engineer of the Pocahontas Fuel Co. from 1923-1949, and his name is remembered at Bishop, a 1930s-era coal camp. An early post office in this vicinity was called "Shraders," named for the family of Henry Shrader, a local farmer in the 1800s. Northern: VA-16, near McDowell County, W.Va.

Boissevain: Three miles west of Pocahontas, Boissevain takes its name from G. L. Boissevain, chairman of the board of the Pocahontas Colleries Co. Northeastern: VA-644 at VA-657

Busthead: The name "Busthead" has to do with some homemade hooch. In the days before Prohibition, some moonshiners won infamy for making a potion so strong, it would "bust your head" or "make your head bust," according to local accounts. Central: VA-627 at VA-631

Cliffield: Cliffield's name comes from the topography of the land; this community stretches across several fields and ends at a cliff overlooking the Clinch River. Central: US-19/460 at VA-639

Coaldan: From 1906 to 1932, Coaldan supported its own post office. The place-name may come from the combination of the coal mined here and "dan," the first syllable of the surname of first postmaster George R. Daniels. The "dan" may refer to a small truck or sledge used for mining. Northwestern: VA-67, between Jewell Ridge and Richlands

Cove Creek: This community gets its name from nearby Cove Creek, a wild trout stream that empties into the Clear Fork of Wolf Creek. Southeastern: VA-61 at VA-662

Doran: A manufacturing center named for Joseph I. Doran, general counsel of the Norfolk & Western Railway, Doran was established in 1890 on the Clinch River. Western: US-460's westernmost crossroads at VA-67

Drytown: A lack of springs and wells prompted early settlers to name this community "Drytown." Central: VA-678, near US-19/460

Five Oaks: In the 1800s, Five Oaks derived its name from five large oak trees that stood near railroad tracks, slightly north of Tazewell. Central: VA-645, near US-19/460

Gratton: In about 1853, the farming community of Gratton was known as "Croftsville" for David Croft, a local landowner. The name was changed to "Gratton" when a post office was established in 1882, but the exact origin of that name seems unknown. One possibility: the word *gratton*, in Devon, England, is used to describe a sheltered field that receives an early growth of spring grass. Southeastern: VA-61 at VA-623

Harman: Charles G. Harman served as Harman's first postmaster in 1883. Northwestern: VA-612 at VA-627, near Bandy

Horsepen: Cherokee Indians against the early settlement of white men in the Tazewell County area once made regular raids with the intent of capturing horses. The Indians corralled their stolen horses at what became known as the "horsepen." In later years, settlers remembered that pen for a community name. Northern: VA-644 at VA-692, near McDowell County, W.Va.

Jewell Ridge: Atop a 3,500-foot summit, Jewell Ridge originated in 1910 as a uniquely developed coal-mining camp, with houses situated on the ridge so mine dust would not hit the camp, unlike coal towns at lower elevations. It is named for a local Jewell family, with one account specifically citing Josh Jewell, saying his daughter Effie was the first baby born at Jewell Ridge. Northwestern: VA-620, near the northern terminus of VA-67

Maiden Spring: According to legend, the Maiden Spring portion of Thompson Valley was named when early settler Rees Bowen saw a young doe (or "maiden") feeding on moss between rocks where a spring gushes. Central: VA-91 at VA-609

Maxwell: James Maxwell, of Northern Ireland, settled in the Maxwell area sometime after 1772. Soon after, John Deskins came to Tazewell County, and his name was remembered at Deskin Mountain, southwest of Maxwell. Central: VA-637 at VA-698

Mouth of Laurel: The Laurel Fork meets Indian Creek at a place naturally called "Mouth of Laurel," slightly northeast of Cedar Bluff. Northwestern: VA-627 at VA-630

Mud Fork: Settled largely by freed slaves immediately after the Civil War, the community of Mud Fork likely takes its name from the nearby muddy bottom of the Mud Fork of the Bluestone River. North-central: VA-643 at VA-655

North Tazewell: Known as "Kelly" or "Kelly's Mills" in the 1890s, North Tazewell was incorporated as its own town in 1894 and flourished for years as the site of a Norfolk & Western Railway station. In 1963, the town dissolved during a merger with the nearby Town of Tazewell, though North Tazewell retains a distinction from the older part of town. Central: VA-16 at VA-61

Pisgah: A post office operated in the 1890s at Pisgah, a place taking its name from the Pisgah United Methodist Church. This congregation first met in 1793; the present church building dates to 1889. The name is a Biblical reference to Pisgah Peak, from which Moses saw the Promised Land. Central: VA-693 at VA-632

Pounding Mill: A massive limestone quarry is Pounding Mill's most prominent landmark, but the "Pounding Mill" name comes from a long-gone mill that stood here in the 1800s and was infamously known for the pounding noises made by its machinery. Western: US-19/460 at VA-637

Raven: Fred and Hubert Raven were two community leaders in nearby Richlands during the 1890s, when Raven was named for them. Northwestern: VA-67, near Russell County

continued on next page

Red Ash: When coal from local mines was burned at Red Ash, the ashes would be a reddish color. Northwestern: VA-804 (Red Ash Camp Rd.), near US-460

St. Clair: Between Tazewell and Bluefield, the St. Clair community is named for Alexander St. Clair, a prominent banker whose brick home, built here in 1880, is listed on both state and national historic registers. Eastern: US-19, near VA-650

Sayersville: In 1879, David G. Sayers served as the first postmaster of Sayersville. North-central: VA-637 at VA-643

Shawver Mill: Christopher Shawver and his wife, Susannah, owned a mill on the Clear Fork of Wolf Creek prior to 1860, likely giving this community its name. Southeastern: VA-614 at VA-61

Shortt Gap: Clarence B. Shortt was the first postmaster at Shortt Gap in 1928. Northwestern: US-460 at Buchanan County line

Springville: A large number of springs flow on the headwaters of the Bluestone River at Springville. Eastern: VA-680 at US-19/460

Steelesburg: Sometimes spelled "Steelsburg" or "Steeleburg," this neighborhood was named for George W. Steele, a landowner in the early 1800s. Southwestern: VA-719, near US-19

Stony Ridge: Between Bishop and Tazewell, this community is named for Stony Ridge, a stone-topped mountain separating Abbs Valley from Baptist Valley. Northern: VA-16 at VA-830

Tannersville: A farming community named for a local tannery, Tannersville was settled in the mid-1800s. It is inside the small portion of Tazewell County that drains into the Holston River. Southwestern: VA-607 (Little Tumbling Creek Rd.) at VA-601 (Freestone Valley Rd.)

Thompson Valley: A 17-mile-long agricultural area lying between Rich and Clinch mountains, Thompson Valley is named for William Thompson, who settled here in about 1772. The community's main crossroads lie southwest of Tazewell. Southern: VA-16 at VA-604

Tip Top: Named for its lofty 2,780-foot elevation on the Norfolk & Western Railway, Tip Top was the location of the short-lived and long-gone Iron Lithia Springs Resort, circa 1892. Eastern: VA-650 at VA-655

Wittens Mills: Northeast of Tazewell, Wittens Mills takes its name from Thomas W. Witten, who built a mill here with his son-in-law, Richard Smoot, after the Civil War. Central: VA-651 at the North Fork of the Clinch River

Yards: A Yards post office was established in 1888. The name came from the area's railroad yards. Northeastern: VA-102, near Mercer County, W.Va.

HOLSTON VALLEY

Three river forks drain Southwest Virginia's Holston Valley. The muddy Middle Fork of the Holston runs through the heart of Smyth County, along I-81, and eventually finds the cleaner-flowing South Fork in the backwoods of Washington County, at the northern gateway to South Holston Lake. The North Fork of the Holston, meanwhile, hugs Clinch Mountain from its headwaters in Bland County through Smyth, Washington, and Scott counties in Virginia. And, strangely, either side of Clinch Mountain is part of the North Fork watershed—from Little Moccasin Gap in Washington County to Big Moccasin Gap in Scott County.

Nearly all of the water in Smyth and Washington counties flows into the Holston River. The same goes for the City of Bristol, a unique two-state town built on the banks of Beaver Creek, one of the upper Holston River's longest tributaries.

CITY OF BRISTOL

Two cities named "Bristol"—one in Virginia, the other in Tennessee—are joined in a single downtown district. State Street, the cities' main thoroughfare, runs along the Tennessee-Virginia state line. Brass plates noting Virginia on one side and Tennessee on the other divide the two lanes of traffic. From here, Virginia's Bristol fans to the north, while Tennessee's Bristol spreads to the south. East of the downtown corridor, the state line cuts through East Hill Cemetery. A long-standing rumor says some people here have their heads buried in Virginia and their feet in Tennessee.

But, in Bristol, nobody makes a big deal about boundaries. Time to time, city officials show cooperation across state lines; they like to shake hands with one person in Virginia, another in Tennessee. But no real distinction is made among residents—it's all one city, as far as they're concerned.

The two Bristols share the same post office, library, hospital, newspaper, and chamber of commerce. Yet each city maintains its own police force, school system, and city council. This situation is clearly a marriage; welcome signs show the bond on roadsides in either city—the shapes of Tennessee and Virginia are joined at Bristol.

Yet years before anybody hung a sign saying "Bristol" here, a post office called "Sapling Grove" opened in 1839 on the Virginia side of town. Sapling Grove was a stop along the Great Stage Road (the Wilderness Road). But small Sapling Grove did not just naturally grow into modern-day Bristol, at least not without the help of developer Joseph R. Anderson.

Anderson wanted to span a city across the state line near Sapling Grove, where Washington County, Virginia, meets Sullivan County, Tennessee. In about 1852, he mapped out a town on 100 acres of his own land. Then he sold lots, with half in Virginia, and the other half in Tennessee. He named this single town for Bris-

tol, England. Two years later, early settler Samuel Goodson formed another town, Goodsonville, in a section that is now part of modern-day Bristol, Virginia.

The railroad reached the area in 1856. That year, in Virginia, the two tiny towns—Goodsonville and Bristol—were incorporated as the single Town of Goodson, inside Washington County. Still, practically everyone called the town "Bristol," the name that remained on the railroad depot. In 1890, Goodson became the independent City of Bristol. The new city's name matched the adjacent community of Bristol, Tennessee.

The two towns met at Main Street, more commonly known as "Mud Street," due to its reputation for washouts. But the street's actual location was in Tennessee, not Virginia. The state line, then, ran along the north sidewalk, smack against buildings on the Virginia side. After many disputes, in 1881 the governments of both towns passed a resolution to place the dividing line at the center of the road. That agreement, however, was not made official until 1901, when Tennessee ceded the northern half of the road to Virginia. That's when a new state line was drawn along what became State Street.

Constructed with steel in 1910, the 60-foot-wide Bristol Sign arches above State Street, spanning the state line. The sign was moved in 1915 to its present site, near the railroad crossing. Initially, its slogan said: PUSH—THAT'S BRISTOL. Comically, however, the sign's letters would often burn out, resulting in embarrassments such as PU—THAT'S BRISTOL or SH—THAT'S BRISTOL. The wording changed in 1921, when a contest was held to create a new slogan. James T. Cecil provided what's been the catchphrase for the twin cities ever since: BRISTOL VA-TENN—A GOOD PLACE TO LIVE.

For decades, Bristol prospered as a major rail center and shopping destination in the four-state area of Virginia, Tennessee, North Carolina, and Kentucky. Hotels, department stores, and restaurants lined Old Bristol, the vicinity of State Street. The downtown brimmed shoulder to shoulder with sidewalk pedestrians.

But Bristol's story changed after passenger rail service stopped in the late 1960s. Within a dozen years, the traditional downtown slumped as large retail establishments moved out, cropping up closer to I-81, which skirts the city's western edge. Retailers and restaurants gradually relocated to

Beaver Creek at Sugar Hollow

The Bristol Sign spans the Tennessee-Virginia state line. Brass plates (inset) mark the division on the road below.

fill this reservoir. Until 1997, when the City of Bristol opened the golf course, this lake was the centerpiece of Clear Creek Park, a quiet place known for rolling hills dotted with weeping willows. Golfers aside, the lake is still a destination for diehard fishermen and canoeists. A small fishing pier overlooks a tiny island, where putting greens are at a safe distance. Open to the public, the pier is a great site for hooking bluegill or enjoying a fight with a carp.

🚗 From US-11/19 (Lee Hwy.) near I-81 Exit 7, follow VA-659 (Clear Creek Rd.) north for one mile. Veer right on VA-645 and follow for 1.5 miles to the golf-course entrance. Turn left on VA-625 and follow

the Bristol Mall, off I-81 Exit 1, and to a previously undeveloped area of north Bristol, off I-81 Exit 7.

Still, State Street survived, and was revamped in the 1980s as part of the national Main Street program. Rows of century-old State Street structures were renovated and refreshed as specialty shops and antique stores on a half-mile-long corridor lined with fluffy trees and park benches. Bristol's stately stone-and-brick passenger-train station, constructed in 1902 near State Street's intersection with Randall Street Expressway, was made into a shopping mall in the 1980s. It was later acquired by the nonprofit Train Station Foundation for a long-term restoration project.

About 18,000 people lived in Virginia's Bristol in 2000, compared to nearly 25,000 on the Tennessee side.

Various festivals celebrate Bristol's dual-state identity, often with block parties on State Street. Each spring and summer, the biggest hoopla happens when major NASCAR races are held at the 160,000-seat Bristol Motor Speedway. Opened in 1961 as Bristol International Raceway, the half-mile track is on the Tennessee side of town, about six miles south of Virginia on US-11E (Volunteer Parkway).

What's to See

Clear Creek Lake: Surrounded by an 18-hole public golf course, Clear Creek Lake is open only to boats with trolling motors. No boat ramp is available, but maybe that is fitting. Any boater, after all, would have to watch for flying golf balls when venturing onto this 46-acre water hole created by the Tennessee Valley Authority (TVA) in 1965.

The lake's 51-foot-high dam holds back the narrow, mud-bottomed Clear Creek, spilling down from Walker Mountain to

north for a half mile to the golf clubhouse, or continue another quarter mile to the parking lot at the fishing pier.

Country Music Monument, Mural, and *Museum:* Bristol claims many firsts and footnotes in the story of country music.

For one, Bristol is the hometown of Tennessee Ernie Ford (1919-1991), an entertainer best known for starring in NBC-TV's "The Ford Show" (1956-1961) and for singing the 1955 hit "Sixteen Tons." Ford's birthplace, two blocks below the Virginia line at 1223 Anderson St., is shown by appointment through contacts with the Bristol Convention and Visitors Bureau.

Bristol was also once the home of Dave Loggins, a singer known for the 1974 acoustic pop classic "Please Come to Boston." Loggins, a 1965 graduate of Bristol Virginia High School, earned a place in the Nashville Songwriters Association International Hall of Fame on the strength of country music hits he wrote for Alabama ("40 Hour Week"), Wynonna Judd ("She Is His Only Need"), and others.

Still, Loggins and Ford are almost afterthoughts considering what happened in this town during July and August of 1927.

That summer, Ralph Peer, a talent scout for the Victor Talking Machine Co., arrived from New York City on a search for "hillbilly music," on the advice of Ernest V. "Pop" Stoneman, a musician from the Galax area. Stoneman had launched his own career with Peer two years earlier. Now, in Bristol, Peer wanted to find more singers like Stoneman.

So, on the Tennessee side of State Street, just a few feet below the state line, Peer set up a makeshift studio at the since-demolished vacant warehouse of the Taylor-Christian Hat Co.

Birthplace of Country Music Mural on Bristol's State Street

Peer placed an advertisement in the *Bristol Herald Courier*. In response, a parade of string bands, singers, and fiddlers showed up, each wanting to make their music immortal.

But two acts were heard louder than the rest—The Carter Family and Jimmie Rodgers. Peer discovered both of these early country music stars in Bristol. And, by doing so, he produced what music historians call the "Big Bang of Country Music."

Prior to Peer's recording sessions in Bristol, country music had existed only in an embryonic form, composed largely of string-band recordings and fiddle tunes. And nobody was calling it "country music," at least not just yet. In fact, it was not until the arrival of The Carter Family and Rodgers—in their separate careers—that the fledgling musical form began to achieve a style that still resonates.

The Carter Family transformed the guitar into a lead instrument and used tight vocal harmonies to accent their carefully crafted compositions about love, mountains, and natural disasters. This home-oriented bunch from Virginia's Scott County arrived in Bristol on August 1, 1927, and recorded a handful of songs in two days, including "Single Girl, Married Girl" and "Bury Me Under the Weeping Willow."

On the other hand, Jimmie Rodgers, a native of Meridian, Mississippi, was a wild-living former railroad worker. He had a

personality discord with his backing band and split the group in Asheville, North Carolina, just hours before he arrived in Bristol as a solo act on August 4. That afternoon in Bristol, Rodgers recorded two songs, "The Soldier's Sweetheart" and "Sleep, Baby, Sleep," just enough to introduce the world to his unique style. Rodgers (1897-1933) blended blues and yodeling with stories of women and the railroad. His music made him a superstar during his short life and ultimately influenced generations of honky-tonk players, from Merle Haggard to Lynyrd Skynyrd.

In 1971, a man-size monument was placed at the corner of State Street and Edgemont Avenue, the former site of the Taylor-Christian building. The monument notes that the 1927 sessions produced "the first country and western music to be distributed nationwide." Fifteen years later, local artist Tim White painted the Mount Rushmore of Bristol—a giant mural depicting the key players of the 1927 sessions. The mural is just barely in Tennessee, on the side of the Lark Amusements building on State Street's 800 block. The mural shows Peer, the Carters, Rodgers, and Stoneman with his wife, Hattie, and boldly claims that these are the "First Country Music Recordings."

In 1998, the U.S. Congress was convinced of just such a claim. A congressional resolution passed noting Bristol as the "Birthplace of Country Music," in recognition of Peer's discoveries of both The Carter Family, widely noted as the "First Family of Country Music," and Rodgers, known as the "Father of Country Music."

The following year, the nonprofit Birthplace of Country Music Alliance Museum opened at the Bristol Mall, off the Gate City Highway (US-421), with exhibits of photos, records, and instruments. Besides the 1927 sessions, museum displays feature Ford, Loggins, and Bristol's 1950s-era "Farm and Fun Time" show, a live radio program that fostered the early careers of bluegrass performers like the Stanley Brothers, who grew up near Stratton in Dickenson County.

Bristol's country music museum mentions another claim to fame—singer Kenny Chesney, whose recording career began in 1990 on the Virginia side of town. Chesney, then an East Tennessee State University student at nearby Johnson City, made a self-financed debut album at Classic Recording Studio (13 Moore St.), about two blocks from where Rodgers and the Carters were discovered. The Luttrell, Tennessee, native later rose to national prominence, scoring a string of No. 1 country music hits ("How Forever Feels," "She's Got It All") beginning in the late 1990s.

The museum regularly holds concerts at a small stage fronting the mural. An annual music festival, the Rhythm and Roots Reunion, is held at various sites across Bristol on the third weekend of September.

Cumberland Square Park: An amphitheater is often used for summer concerts at the Cumberland Square Park, at the corner of Lee and Cumberland streets in downtown Bristol. The park's immaculately clean lawn includes a military memorial with life-size statues fashioned by artist Mariah Kirby-Smith in 1994. The statues depict images of World War II, including a nurse, an Army infantry soldier, a Navy seaman, a Marine, and an Army Air Force captain.

Beaver Creek hugs the north side of the park on one of its widest stretches. Past this park, the creek runs for three blocks through a tunnel, constructed in 1925-1927 beneath Piedmont Avenue, before it sees light again on the Tennessee side of town, between Seventh and Eighth streets.

As early as the 1770s, Bristol's pioneers settled on the banks of Beaver Creek, first calling it "Shallow Creek." Waters were so clean in those days that the creek—in the vicinity of this park—was used as a fishing hole and a place to bathe. Yet, a century later, as Bristol grew with the rise of the local railroad industry, Beaver Creek became a drain for the town's trash.

But times change. By the dawn of the 21st century, "Beaver Creek Cleanup" days were common, and a grassroots effort unfolded to redevelop the creek's corridor.

Sugar Hollow Recreation Area: How the 400-acre Sugar Hollow Recreation Area won its attractive name is a lesson in public relations. This city-owned park is the site of the 85-foot-high Beaver Creek Dam, a 1,588-foot-long grassy spine that makes a great jogging path affording aerial views of north Bristol's commercial district. Constructed in 1965, the dam holds back Beaver Creek, a 21-mile-long watercourse draining both Bristols. This creek originates about six miles upstream, at a spring in a marshy field off VA-611 (Providence Road) in Washington County.

Sugar Hollow probably should have been called "Beaver Creek Recreation Area" when it opened in 1981. But it wasn't, because the name "Sugar Hollow" did not mean anything to anyone—unlike Beaver Creek, which once held a nasty reputation for flooding Bristol, not to mention smelling bad and looking worse. The creek can be muddy as it flows through Sugar Hollow, but it is free from trash. It makes a great complement to the park's concrete walking paths and wooden footbridges.

Above the dam, an extensive trail system leads through wooded ridges, where it is easy to explore a cool young forest of white pines. The park also features ball fields, a playground, a fee-entry picnic area, and an amphitheater. Bristol's parks and recreation department operates Sugar Hollow's 75-space campground. Its woodsy feel seems much more remote than it actually is, just a couple of miles from the mad rush of traffic on I-81.

🚗 From I-81 Exit 7, follow Old Airport Road for 0.1 miles north to the Lee Highway intersection. Turn right and follow US-11/19 (Lee Hwy.) for a half mile to the park on the left.

Virginia Intermont College: Before moving to Bristol in 1891-1893, Virginia Intermont College got its start in Glade Spring in 1884 as the "Southwest Virginia Female Institute." J. R. Harrison, a Baptist minister, founded this college for women. Yet within a few years, the school outgrew its original campus, and the name changed to simply "Virginia Institute" soon after the move to Bristol. In 1922, the school adopted the "Intermont" name to reflect its location "in the mountains." The private liberal arts college admitted men as degree-seeking students in 1972 and also began awarding four-year degrees. The student population is less than 1,000 on its campus of brick buildings at 1013 Moore St., near the center of the city.

SMYTH COUNTY

Smyth County lies on the headwaters of both the Holston and New rivers, in a land shouldered by Clinch Mountain on the northwest and Mount Rogers, the state's highest peak, on the southeast. Smyth County is home to Hungry Mother State Park in Marion and the inviting Town of Saltville, a place famous for its Civil War role as the "Salt Capital of the Confederacy." Formed in 1832 from parts of Washington and Wythe counties, Smyth County was named in honor of Gen. Alexander Smyth, a Virginia Congressman from 1817 to 1830. The county spans about 452 square miles.

ATKINS

About two miles north of Marion on US-11, the name "Atkins" abbreviates the earlier titles "Atkins Tank" and "Atkins Switch," both 19th-century references to the railroad passing through this community. This central Smyth County area likely remembers the name of Thompson Atkins, an early landowner.

What's to See

Cullop's Tavern: Cullop's Tavern is believed to be haunted by weird noises and flying bedcovers, what may be the reactions of more than one ghost. Frederick Cullop, a German who came to Atkins from Pennsylvania, operated a stagecoach tavern here prior to 1815; some accounts date the construction of this two-story limestone structure as early as 1805.

According to legend, at age 53 Cullop committed suicide at this house and, for years, his spirit haunted the place. Later, Thomas Jefferson Snavely bought the house and built a frame ell onto the structure. According to another legend, Snavely also died here after he accidentally consumed horse medicine.

Cullop's Tavern is listed on both state and national historic registers. The drive-by attraction is on US-11, near VA-622, just off I-81 Exit 50.

CHILHOWIE

Apples remain a big deal in Chilhowie, even though much of the region's apple production fell in the 1970s and many of its dozen or so orchards have since become housing subdivisions. At the dawn of the 21st century, only one, Duncan's Orchard, remained in business near Chilhowie. Still, the absence of orchards does not stop this town from celebrating its apple-growing heritage. Each September, the Chilhowie Com-

munity Apple Festival brings a feast of food and crafts highlighted by a marching-band contest and an old-fashioned beauty pageant.

Incorporated in 1913, Chilhowie takes its name from a Native American word meaning "valley of many deer." In 2000, about 1,800 people lived here in west-central Smyth County, near I-81 Exit 35.

Col. James Patton surveyed the area in 1748. Soon after, as early as 1754, a two-story structure was built here. Called the "Town House," it was used as a fort and later a tavern on the Great Stage Road. Now in ruins, only a chimney can be seen at the Town House site, and only during winter. The Town House is immediately west of a Food City grocery store at the main Chilhowie crossroads of US-11 and VA-107.

The community, for a while, was known as "Greever's Switch," either for a railroad siding built on Hiram Greever's property, or for Bob Greever, the first train-station agent after the railroad arrived in 1856.

The railroad built Chilhowie. In fact, most buildings on Main Street faced the railroad, until 1909, when the Bank of Chilhowie and many other downtown buildings caught fire. When reconstructed, new buildings on the 100 block of Main Street were made to face the road used by cars.

Chilhowie's Society Row also once faced the railroad. But a 1977 flood on the Middle Fork of the Holston River changed that, when high water destroyed the line of stately homes. Years later, this site became the Chilhowie Recreation Park, with picnic shelters, ball fields, and a playground. The park lines Railroad Avenue, immediately northeast of VA-107 (Whitetop Road). An informal

Cullop's Tavern, a historic landmark at Atkins

canoe launch is on the Middle Fork, near a railroad bridge at the park's far northeastern end. The takeout is near the baseball field, less than one mile downstream. This river route, basically flat and narrow, is noted for smallmouth bass fishing.

GROSECLOSE

In the early 1800s, John Groseclose operated a gristmill in east-central Smyth County. He also lent his name to the Groseclose community, near the crossroads of US-11 and VA-679.

What's to See

Settlers Museum of Southwest Virginia: The story told at the Settlers Museum of Southwest Virginia explains how Pennsylvanians primarily settled the mountains of Southwest Virginia. The story is spelled out in 3-D on a topographic map in the museum's visitor center. The Blue Ridge Mountains blocked residents of early Virginia settlements like Jamestown and Williamsburg from easily accessing the far end of the Old Dominion. But the Great Valley of Virginia opened the door to folks from Pennsylvania. From there, Germans and Scotch-Irish shuttled south, along the Great Stage Road.

Newcomers sought fresh land in Southwest Virginia beginning in the late 1700s, bringing cultural preferences for religion and food with them. Many Germans settled along the Smyth-Wythe county line and founded Lutheran churches. They also grew lots of cabbage, a mainstay of traditional German menus. In the late 1800s, the area surrounding Groseclose and nearby Rural Retreat in Wythe County became widely known for its cabbage farms.

One such cabbage farm, owned by the late George Phillippi, is the centerpiece of the nonprofit Settlers Museum, open March to November. Outbuildings— including a granary, a woodhouse, a corncrib, and a barn—skirt a two-story farmhouse built in 1890. The museum's costumed interpreters regularly demonstrate farm skills, like repairing a wagon or saddle, on a lawn beneath a canopy of oaks. Also here is a restored one-room schoolhouse built in 1894 and furnished with antique desks.

🚗 From I-81 Exit 54, follow US-11 south for 0.1 miles. Turn left on VA-683 (Phillippi Hollow Rd.) and follow for 1.5 miles. Turn left on VA-615 (Rocky Hollow Rd.) and go a quarter mile to the museum on the right.

MARION

Just before the close of the 20th century, Marion sought a return to its glory days. Town leaders instituted an ambitious "Streetscape" plan as part of the Smyth County courthouse town's Virginia Main Street program. The Streetscape design included the restoration of Marion's Main Street to its 1940s visage, with new streetlamps, fresh sidewalks, and shade trees.

The face-lift was definitely needed. Like many places along US-11 in Virginia, Marion's downtown slowly began deteriorating in the 1960s after north-south traffic moved off US-11 and shifted onto the parallel span of I-81. Over time, too, newer shopping centers peeled customers away from traditional outlets near the county courthouse.

Streetscape helped the downtown prove its resilience. In turn, the county courthouse, 109 W. Main St., became known for festivals and concerts held on its lawn. The 1905 courthouse was built with bricks and limestone. Nearby, the Lincoln Theatre, 117 E. Main St., was built in 1929 and named for local businessman C. C. Lincoln, Sr. Within walking distance of Main Street, exhibits at the Smyth County Museum, 105 E. Strother St., include vintage clothing, Civil War flags, maps, and relics from a silent-movie house. The historical museum occupies a circa-1908 brick school building.

Earlier called "Royal Oak," Marion was incorporated in 1849 and named for Gen. Francis Marion, a Revolutionary War hero from South Carolina known as "The Swamp Fox." The 2000 census counted about 6,300 residents here.

What's to See

Hungry Mother State Park: Hungry Mother possesses what is undeniably the weirdest name of any state park in the Old Dominion, but how this 2,215-acre paradise came to be called "Hungry Mother"—and what that name really means—seems to be anybody's guess.

State officials mentioned names like "Southwest Virginia State Park" or "Forest Lake State Park" when planning the facility in September 1933. Then, suddenly and without any explanation, the proposed park was referred to as "Hungry Mother" in an October 17 article in the *Marion Democrat,* a local newspaper. Smyth County historian Mack Sturgill once suggested the park's new name and its accompanying legend were "coined and packaged" by a group of Marion men, including Robert Lane

Rowboat tests the waters of Hungry Mother Lake, north of Marion

How the original "Hungers Mother" became "Hungry Mother" is one mystery. Another is how the park's tallest summit took its name. The knob is called "Marleys Top" on the 1929 Unaka National Forest map; earlier maps show it as "Mollie's Knob" or "Molly's Knob."

Park visitors, regardless of the name, love the view atop the 3,270-foot Molly's Knob, despite the strenuous hike getting there. Below the knob, the park includes a campground bordering Hungry Mother Creek, as well as cabins planted inside an evergreen forest.

Hungry Mother Lake stretches over 108 acres, from one side of the park to the other. The lake includes a ramp for boats with trolling motors, plus a pier to fish for walleye, musky, crappie, channel catfish, and sunfish. A 580-foot swimming beach, built with 1,500 tons of Virginia Beach sand, lies along the lakeshore. In mid-July, when the beach is packed practically shoulder to shoulder, the park's annual arts and crafts festival is held near Hungry Mother's lakefront restaurant, where walls of photos and newspaper articles explain the role of the Civilian Conservation Corps in creating Hungry Mother State Park in the 1930s.

An entry fee is charged per vehicle at the main gate off VA-16 (Park Boulevard), four miles north of US-11 at Marion.

Anderson, editor of the *Marion Democrat* and a son of famous fiction writer Sherwood Anderson.

Outside the park headquarters, a sign tries to explain the legend of the Hungry Mother name: "Molly Marley's husband was killed at a New River settlement by raiding Indians. She and her child were captured and taken to the Tazewell area. Soon thereafter, she escaped with her child. Eventually, after eating only berries for many days, Molly collapsed at the foot of the mountain now known as Molly's Knob. The child wandered down a creek and came to a group of houses. He could only say, 'Hungry Mother!' Searchers found Molly's body by the creek, which became known as Hungry Mother Creek. From this, the park gets its name."

Nobody really knows if the park's version of the story is true. But the late Goodridge Wilson, a Marion author, did uncover local accounts related to the legend. One concerns Confederate veteran William Copenhaver, who remembered his grandmother's story about a woman escaping from Indians and collapsing along a creek with her small child, who cried, "Hungry, Mammy!" Additionally, Wilson found a connection in the account of a 1755 raid at the Samuel Stalnaker cabin, which stood at or near the mouth of Hungry Mother Creek, and he discovered that generations of Stalnaker descendants had kept alive a story of a woman and her starving child.

In 1774, Robert and John Crow made a survey documenting the creek, calling it "Hungers Mother." In 1929, about seven years prior to the park's opening, a Unaka National Forest map had changed the name to "Hungry Mother Creek."

Mountain Dew Birthplace: In October, Marion celebrates Mountain Dew Days, a festival honoring one of the town's biggest claims to fame. The late William H. "Bill" Jones formulated the flavor of the soft drink Mountain Dew in Marion, following a series of experiments in the early 1960s at Marion's Tip Corp.

Though Marion claims to be the birthplace of Mountain Dew, the story doesn't begin there. Mountain Dew had existed for years prior to Jones's involvement. Two brothers, Barney and Allie (aka "Ollie" or "Ally") Hartman of Knoxville, Tennessee, originated the lime green beverage as a mixer in the late 1940s. That mixer was redeveloped in 1954 as a soft drink called "Mountain Dew," bottled at Tri-City Beverage in Johnson City, Tennessee, by businessman Charles Gordon, in association with the Hartman brothers. Gordon and the Hartman brothers later sold the original formula and the "Mountain Dew" name to Bill Jones.

By 1961, Jones had acquired all rights to the product and introduced a new Mountain Dew on local store shelves. Sales of the drink soon attracted the interests of the Pepsi-Cola Co., which acquired the Tip Corp. and Mountain Dew in 1964. The Tip Corp. building, now the site of Hungate Business Services, is at 517 N. Main St. (US-11).

Sherwood Anderson Sites: When he came to town in the late 1920s, the internationally known author Sherwood Anderson (1876-1941) was quite a character on the streets of Marion. Originally from Camden, Ohio, Anderson moved in 1925 to Troutdale (see the Grayson County chapter in the Central Highlands section). Two years later, he purchased two weekly newspapers in Marion, the *Smyth County News* and the *Marion Democrat*. At the time, Anderson was known best for *Winesberg, Ohio*, a 1919 short-story collection lauded for its innovative style.

In Marion, Anderson operated his newspapers in a 1924 brick structure at 111 N. Park St. Called the "Sherwood Anderson building" by most people, the edifice features unique rounded windows on its second floor. Anderson used his writing skills as an editor and as the ghostwriter behind fictional reporter Buck Fever, who made observations about everyday life in Smyth County.

In 1933, Anderson married Eleanor Copenhaver, a Marion woman who became his fourth wife. In his final years, Anderson lived in Troutdale and also in Marion, where he stayed at Rosemont, his wife's home, which formerly stood at the site of the Marion Volunteer Fire Department Hall at the corner of Main Street and North Jones Street. Anderson died from peritonitis while on a good-will mission trip to South America. He is buried at Marion's Round Hill Cemetery, and the author's unique sail-shaped tombstone bears the words: LIFE NOT DEATH IS THE GREAT ADVENTURE.

🚗 To reach the Round Hill Cemetery from the Smyth County Courthouse on Main Street, follow Park Street south for about 0.3 miles. At the top of the hill, bear right onto Cemetery Street. Enter the cemetery and follow a one-way, one-lane road for 0.2 miles to Anderson's headstone, on the right, about 10 yards below the Lincoln mausoleum.

RICH VALLEY

Between Walker Mountain and Brushy Mountain, Rich Valley is named for its rich soil and grazing land. The valley stretches across Washington and Smyth counties, but the community most commonly called "Rich Valley" is centered at VA-630 and VA-42 in north-central Smyth County. Each August, the community's Rich Valley Fair and Horse Show features equestrian contests, carnival rides, and concerts.

SALTVILLE

Saltville's name comes from—of all things—its salt. As early as 10,000 B.C., prehistoric animals, like the woolly mammoth and the mastodon, were attracted to a now extinct salt lake in Saltville's portion of northwestern Smyth County. Pioneers settled the Saltville Valley in the late 1700s, a time when the area's saline deposits were treasured for more than just a tabletop condiment. At that time, salt was important as a preservative for food, especially meat, long before the advent of refrigeration.

In 1892, Saltville became the company town of the Mathieson Alkali Works, which used the area's underground salt resources to make chemicals. The company eventually became known as the Olin Corp. and made such chemicals as hydrazine, used to transport a moon-bound rocket in 1969. Olin also operated a nine-mile-long aerial tramway to haul buckets of salt above the town.

Now the tramway is gone, and so is the Olin Corp. In 1972, after company officials determined they could not meet the Virginia Water Control Board's environmental requirements for discharged waste, Olin closed its Saltville plant, putting 1,000 people out of work.

Saltville survived the loss. In some ways, it also thrived. This intriguing hamlet spanning into both Smyth and Washington counties became a popular day-trip destination for tourists, especially during Saltville's annual Labor Day Celebration. About 2,200 residents lived here in 2000.

Incorporated in 1896, Saltville's primary crossroads is where VA-91 meets VA-107, about eight miles north of I-81. In places, the town looks like a toy train village; buildings at the town square, like the community library, resemble make-believe models. Adding to the ambiance, just west of the library is a remnant of Olin's aerial tramway: two pairs of salt buckets hang from a post near the intersection of Palmer Avenue and Main Street. Nearby is an exhibit of two 1890s-era steam locomotives used here by the Mathieson Alkali Works.

What's to See

Battlefield Overlook: Salt produced at Saltville during the Civil War was paramount to keeping the Confederacy alive, because it was used to preserve food. Saltville, in turn, became known as the "Salt Capital of the Confederacy," a title still posted on the town's welcome signs.

One of the many fortifications built in Saltville during the Civil War remains visible at an overlook of a VA-91 bridge spanning the North Fork of the Holston River. Confederate soldiers dug these defense trenches to protect the town's salt-making operations. The overlook and trenches are now part of a town park commemorating the two times Saltville came under fire during the Civil War.

Overlooking Saltville from VA-107

The First Battle of Saltville occurred when Union Gen. Stephen Burbridge launched an attack on October 2, 1864. After six hours of fighting, Burbridge retreated from Saltville when his troops could not break the Confederate wall of defense. Burbridge skipped town without claiming all of his wounded, notably a regiment of wounded and dead black soldiers that had fought on the battle's front line. Later, some Confederate soldiers, acting independently, killed either a dozen or as many 155, according to various accounts, of those wounded black soldiers on the battlefield or at a field hospital.

About three months later, Union forces commanded by Gen. George Stoneman attacked the town and, this time, destroyed the saltworks during the Second Battle of Saltville, on December 20-21, 1864. Still, Stoneman's damage was not permanent. The kettles at the saltworks operated again at full capacity within three weeks.

From VA-107 in Saltville, turn right (northeast) on VA-91 (E. Main St.) and follow for 0.4 miles. Turn right on Buckeye Street and follow for 0.3 miles to the overlook on the left.

Clinch Mountain Wildlife Management Area: Talk about a good recipe for a mountain paradise. Start with a wild-running stream bulging with boulders. Stock it with trout. Then let it run over a series of small waterfalls, including one that makes a midair drop of about 15 feet. Add a 300-acre lake with a sandy bottom at an elevation of 3,600 feet and include a ramp for boats with trolling motors. Now mix in a diverse forest floor with elevations ranging about 3,000 feet, from high to low. And spread out that forest at the four-county meeting point of Smyth, Tazewell, Russell, and Washington counties. Final product: the Clinch Mountain Wildlife Management Area.

This outdoorsman's paradise, overseen by the Virginia Department of Game and Inland Fisheries, is popular for fishing (brook trout, smallmouth bass, and rock bass at Laurel Bed Lake) and hunting (deer, turkey, bear, grouse, squirrel, rabbit, and duck). But it also pays the casual traveler to brave this area's dirt-and-gravel roads simply to see the waterfalls on Big Tumbling Creek.

To a trout looking for a hideout, this creek couldn't get any better—water continuously trips over small ledges. It rides on riffles and ruffles, and makes a midair leap of 15 feet at the Big Falls. Immediately tumbling again, this time over a series of stairsteps, the creek is soon fed the passions of another stream at Twin Hollows Falls, a Y-shaped twin cataract dropping 35 feet from a mountainside at Russell County's extreme southeastern corner. Behind a veil of trees, Twin Hollows Falls and Big Tumbling Creek meet at the base of an eight-foot-high cascade.

High above the falls, Laurel Bed Creek drains Tazewell County and flows into Laurel Bed Lake, a placid reservoir constructed in 1967-1968 atop Clinch Mountain, in a bog area of Russell County. Within five miles of the lake is the area's 19-site primitive campground.

The wildlife-management area, in total, spans 25,477 acres. More than 22,000 acres are contiguous. The remainder comprises several small tracts, primarily along the North Fork of the Holston River.

One caveat: a four-wheel-drive vehicle may be necessary to navigate the area's switchbacks during certain times of year. Fees are charged to fish on the

Big Falls of Big Tumbling Creek, at the Clinch Mountain Wildlife Management Area

stocked trout sections of Big Tumbling Creek. An office for the wildlife-management area is at the entrance on VA-747.

🚗 From VA-107 in Saltville, turn left (southwest) on VA-91 (E. Main St.) and follow for 0.2 miles. Turn right on VA-634 (Allison Gap Rd.) and follow for 1.4 miles. Bear left (east) on VA-613 and go 3.9 miles. Turn right on VA-747 to enter the area, and continue straight. The wildlife-management area's headquarters are at Mile 2.1. Bear right on switchbacks leading up the mountain at Mile 3.1. Twin Hollows Falls are on the left at Mile 4.5. Big Falls are at Mile 4.6. A spur road leading to an overlook of a small waterfall is at Mile 4.7. The road forks at Mile 4.9—the left fork leads two miles to Laurel Bed Lake; continuing on the right fork for 2.8 miles leads to the campground.

Saltville's King-Stuart House

King-Stuart House: In the early 1860s, William Alexander Stuart, the eldest brother of famed Confederate Gen. James Ewell Brown "Jeb" Stuart, acquired a share of King Salt Works, a salt-manufacturing company. The purchase included a log cabin built circa 1795 as a residence for William King, an Irish immigrant who helped develop Saltville's salt-mining industry. The two-story cabin, known as the "King-Stuart House," is owned by the Town of Saltville.

Following Jeb Stuart's death on May 12, 1864, after the Battle of Yellow Tavern, the general's widow, Flora, moved to this cabin to live with William and other Stuart family members. Flora taught school in a ground-floor room before leaving Saltville and eventually moving to Staunton, Virginia.

The cabin is a drive-by attraction, but tours are available by appointment through the Town of Saltville.

🚗 From VA-107 in Saltville, turn left (southwest) on VA-91 and go 1.7 miles. Turn left on Stuart Drive, just past the Salt Park, and follow for 0.1 miles.

Madam Russell Methodist Church and Cabin: Elizabeth Henry Campbell Russell (1749-1825) was a sister of Patrick Henry, the early American statesman famously remembered for his plea, "Give me liberty or give me death!"

During her lifetime, Elizabeth was best known as "Madam Russell." She was a tireless champion of Methodism in Southwest Virginia and often hosted pioneer itinerant Methodist ministers at her Saltville home. Some accounts say that the nearby Methodist-affiliated Emory & Henry College at

Emory (see the Washington County chapter of the Holston Valley section) might be partly named for her.

Elizabeth's first husband was Gen. William Campbell, whose father, Charles, was among Saltville's first landowners. Following Gen. Campbell's death, Elizabeth married Gen. William Russell, the man for whom Russell County is named. In 1788, the Russells moved to Saltville and constructed a two-story log home that stood until 1908. A reconstruction of the Russell cabin was built in 1974, using old photographs as a guide. The cabin stands next to the Madam Russell Methodist Church.

🚗 From VA-107 in Saltville, turn left (southwest) on VA-91 (E. Main St.) and go 0.3 miles. Bear right at the town square and continue 0.1 miles to 207 W. Main St., on the right.

———————————————

Museum of the Middle Appalachians: Woolly mammoths and mastodons called Saltville home at the end of the last Ice Age. These animals harbored in the shallow, 300-acre Lake Totten, an extinct body of water that once covered the floor of the Saltville Valley. Scientists exploring for prehistoric fossils in the bed of the long-gone lake named the feature for the family of Charlie Bill Totten, a town employee who began assisting archeologists here in the 1960s.

Annually, archeologists hold fossil digs in Saltville, usually in early August, near the town's Well Fields Park. Discoveries from these digs are on display at Saltville's nonprofit Museum of the Middle Appalachians.

The museum, housed in the circa-1949 Salt Theatre building, is an ideal place to start any Saltville tour. A 16-foot-long model of the Saltville Valley centers the main gallery. A 10-foot-high cast model of a mastodon skeleton stands above this display, a representation of the kind of big beasts that once roamed Saltville.

Beyond these and other exhibits, the museum is known for its mascots, Woolly and Little Salty. Each year, on the Saturday before Groundhog Day, Saltville celebrates Woolly Mammoth Day. This holiday is a museum fund-raiser starring Woolly, an 11-foot-tall replica of a prehistoric woolly mammoth. Hundreds gather in Saltville to hear Woolly decide when winter will end, just like the famous groundhog Punxsutawney Phil in Punxsutawney, Pennsylvania.

Woolly's 28-foot-long carcass is covered with brown, flame-resistant baling twine and sits atop a 1969 International pickup truck. Woolly moves by a hidden web of cables, ropes, and pulleys. A miniature version—the mammoth's baby, named "Little Salty"—was hatched on July 4, 1996, as part of a museum promotion. Little Salty stands about five feet tall.

🚗 From VA-107 in Saltville, turn left (southwest) on VA-91 (E. Main St.) and go 0.3 miles, bearing left at 123 Palmer Ave.

———————————————

Palmer Mill Playhouse: Little is known about George Palmer's original gristmill. It stood in Saltville for a few years in the late 19th century, sometime after Palmer, a businessman from Syracuse, New York, moved to Saltville in 1858 and became well-known for his huge herd of registered shorthorn cattle.

A few surviving pictures of Palmer's mill and the remains of the millpond inspired a group of Saltville residents to voluntarily build a stone-and-wood replica in 1999. The new Palmer Mill stands about 60 feet from the original mill's foundation. The three-story operation relies on the original millpond to turn its 20-foot-high waterwheel. The modern mill, an arts center, is used by the nonprofit Salt Theatre Corp. to stage various public theatrical performances. The playhouse seats 130.

🚗 From VA-107 in Saltville, turn left (southwest) on VA-91 (E. Main St.) and go 0.3 miles. Bear left on Palmer Avenue and follow for 0.7 miles. The mill is on the right, near the Madison Street intersection.

Little Salty, a make-believe woolly mammoth, guards the entrance to Saltville's Museum of the Middle Appalachians

Palmer Mill Playhouse at Saltville

Salt Park: A survey expedition by Charles Campbell in 1748 passed through Saltville and took note of the area's saline springs. The Saltville area subsequently became known as "Buffalo Lick," "Little Lick," and "Salt Lick."

Still, the area's first commercial salt-excavation business, launched by Arthur Campbell, did not start operations until 1782. Campbell used pumps to extract brine, and furnaces were then used to boil the solution in kettles, removing the salt from the water. The resulting product was later dried and stored in structures called "salt houses."

William King, an Irish immigrant who settled in Saltville in the early 1790s, had a different idea about getting salt. King had worked a while for the Preston Salt Works, Campbell's former company, before going into business for himself. In 1799, King dug what is claimed to have been the first salt mine in the United States. King's kind of mine, however, was no success; the 200-foot shaft kept filling with water and mud. King soon reverted to the salt-making ways of others—boiling brine.

King did eventually become a successful salt baron. He loaded salt on flatboats and sent them down the winding North Fork of the Holston River to markets in Tennessee and Alabama. About 60 miles downstream from Saltville, King landed near what is now the Netherland Inn in Kingsport, Tennessee. Here, in 1802, he constructed "King's Boatyard" (or "King's Port") where the river's north fork meets its south fork. In 1822, this area was briefly incorporated as "Kingsport," but that initial incorporation was short-lived.

In Saltville, the town's Salt Park occupies the former site of King's first salt mine. The Salt Park's outdoor exhibits include cast-iron salt kettles, a salt-well pump used to extract brine, and a working reconstruction of a 19th-century salt furnace.

🚗 From VA-107 in Saltville, turn left (southwest) on VA-91 and go 1.4 miles to King Avenue. The park is on the right at the Washington-Smyth county line.

Saltville Overlook: In any season, the Saltville Overlook on VA-107 provides a pretty picture of the Saltville Valley. The wall of Clinch Mountain and practically all of Saltville can be seen from this roadside perch, including rows of homes that still give the impression of Saltville as a company town. One such line of houses along VA-91 in Washington County was named "Smoky Row," because smoke would hover above the homes as steam trains chugged uphill.

🚗 The overlook is on VA-107, 1.4 miles south of the VA-91 intersection.

Well Fields Park: Despite the connotations of its name, Saltville is not like Salt Lake City, Utah, where the salty brine of the Great Salt Lake can be smelled for miles and miles. But at least one part of Saltville does strangely resemble the salt-heavy backwaters of the Virginia coast, almost as if a little piece of the Chesapeake Bay landed at the east side of Clinch Mountain. Salt-loving marsh and plants, including black grass and spearscale, rim the pools of Saltville's Well Fields Park, the site of salt excavations for several decades. Here, brine was extracted with pumps, then boiled to extract salt.

The well-fields area, alternately known as the "Salt Ponds," is now a town park with picnic tables. The ponds are popular fishing holes as well as stopping points for migrating geese and ducks. The well fields are part of the watershed of old Lake Totten, a natural lake drained in the late 1840s by Col. Thomas Preston to build a road across the swampy ground.

Comers Creek Falls, near the Grayson-Smyth county line

71

🚗 From VA-107 in Saltville, turn left (southwest) on VA-91 (E. Main St.) and follow for 0.3 miles. Bear left on Palmer Avenue and follow for a half mile. Turn right on Lake Drive to enter the park.

Rowland Creek Falls in the Mount Rogers National Recreation Area

SUGAR GROVE

Sugar Grove is a village on the northern rim of the Mount Rogers National Recreation Area. The main crossroads is where VA-16 meets VA-601 in south-central Smyth County. The name is derived from this scenic area's abundant sugar maples.

What's to See

Comers Creek Falls: Comers Creek Falls tumbles about 15 feet on a rock wall inside the Mount Rogers National Recreation Area. Below the falls, noisy Comers Creek drains Hurricane Mountain to meet the South Fork of the Holston River.

🚗 From Sugar Grove, follow VA-16 south for 5.5 miles to the Grayson County line. Turn right on VA-741 (Homestead Rd.) and follow for a half mile. The trailhead is on the right and is marked by a small brown sign next to a fence in a grassy field. Follow the trail downhill for about 0.3 miles, then turn right on a short spur marked with white blaze. The spur leads to a footbridge overlooking the waterfall.

Rowland Creek Falls: Finding Rowland Creek Falls might be hard, even with an established trail in the Mount Rogers National Recreation Area. The trailhead, for one, is not marked. And, from the nearest main highway, you must follow a winding maze of back roads to the trail, part of an 11.8-mile loop known as the Rowland Creek Falls Circuit.

The trek to the falls is worth the work. This rushing stream majestically steps down a mountainside on a rock stairway. Its 150-foot-long descent, shouldered by boulders, centers a symphony of green composed by rhododendron, firs, and ferns.

🚗 From VA-16 at Sugar Grove, head west on VA-601 for 3.5 miles, until VA-601 becomes VA-670 at Teas. Follow VA-670 for another 4.4 miles and veer left on VA-656. Go 1.7 miles and turn left on VA-668, which turns into USFS-643. Follow the gravel forest road for 0.1 miles (passing a road immediately on the right) to park at earthen mounds marked by large rocks at the right side of the road (about 50 yards before the road veers sharply to the left). This is the unmarked trailhead. Look for the trail—a wide path in a forest of young pines—and follow orange blazes. After a half mile, cross a small stream and see a small cascade (on the left). Continue climbing a steeper ascent on a skinny, spiraling section for another mile until finding the falls on the right. Try bushwhacking down the mountain, off the trail, to find a clear vantage point.

Adwolfe: The name "Adwolfe" (sometimes "Adwolf") is a name combination for Addison Wolfe (1831-1905), a local storeowner and farmer. Western: VA-657 at VA-660

Allison Gap: Brothers Ben, Dave, and Sam Allison were among the early settlers at Allison Gap, and their family inspired a name for this residential community. Northwestern: VA-613 (Allison Gap Rd.) at VA-634 (Lick Skillet Rd.)

Attoway: Some Atkins brothers built a tool-handle factory at Attoway, probably in the 19th century. But the area's post office could not be named for these brothers, because an Atkins already existed in Smyth County. So this spot became Attoway, a name suggested by postal officials. Previously, the area was called "Falling Waters." The word "Attoway" might be a colloquialism for "that-a-way." Central: VA-16 at VA-689

Broadford: The first Broadford post office opened in 1831. It took its name from a broad ford crossing an island on the North Fork of the Holston River. The community's post office later moved one mile east, near Laurel Creek, and the original site was renamed "Old Broad Ford." Northern: VA-42 at VA-91, near Tazewell County

Broady Bottom: Gen. William Campbell lived at Seven Mile Ford, and his family had vast landholdings at Saltville. The general died in 1781, about a year after leading an American victory at the Battle of King's Mountain in South Carolina. One of Campbell's slaves, John Broady, often accompanied him on military expeditions and later was inherited by Campbell's daughter, Sarah, and her husband, Gen. Francis Preston. The Prestons granted Broady his freedom in 1793, following a request originally made by Campbell; they also gave Broady a piece of land that became known as "Broady Bottom." Northwestern: northeast area of Saltville, north of North Fork of the Holston River, near VA-91

Buckeye Hollow: Several buckeye trees stood here when this community near Saltville needed a name. Northwestern: VA-635 at VA-776

Camp: Bordering the Mount Rogers National Recreation Area, Camp is a small residential community with a name originating when the spot was a favorite campground for covered-wagon travelers. Southeastern: VA-612 at USFS-16

Carlock Creek: David Carlock and his family were among the early settlers of this area near Chilhowie. West-central: VA-637, near VA-638

Cedar Branch: An abundance of cedar trees once grew along this tributary of the North Fork of the Holston River. According to legend, Cedar Branch ran red with blood during the First Battle of Saltville in October 1864. Northwestern: VA-632, near VA-91

Cedar Springs: Named for its many springs and cedar trees, the Cedar Springs community is in the small part of Smyth County that drains to the New River. Eastern: VA-614 at VA-749

Chatham Hill: According to legend, Chatham Hill takes its name from the Earl of Chatham of England, a man who defended the American colonies in their fight for independence. North-central: VA-16 bridge at the North Fork of the Holston River

Cleghorn Valley: John Cleghorn settled here in the early 1900s. West-central: VA-617, near VA-637

Davis Valley: The "Davis" of Davis Valley can be traced to James Davis, who settled in this vicinity circa 1748. The area, which is crossed by the Appalachian Trail, was earlier called "Davis Fancy." East-central: VA-617 at VA-602

Furnace Hill: Staley Creek passes through Furnace Hill, an area named for an iron furnace built in 1860 but destroyed by Union soldiers in 1864. The name of Staley Creek likely comes from pioneer settler Abram Staley. Central: VA-16, near VA-712

Henrytown: The name "Henrytown" refers to a pair of Henry brothers who owned land along the North Fork of the Holston River sometime after the Civil War. The original site of Henrytown was located northwest of the river; it was torn down to form a chemical waste impoundment called a "muck dam." Henrytown is now southeast of the river. Northwestern: Saltville's Henrytown Rd.

Lick Skillet: One folk tale says mountaintop views of the curvy roads going in and out of Lick Skillet make the hamlet look like a big black skillet. A similar story says Lick Skillet's roads run around like the edge of a skillet. Northwestern: VA-634 (Lick Skillet Rd.) at VA-733 (Cove St.)

McCready: In the early 1800s, Thomas McCready owned land at McCready (or "McCready's Gap"), between Broadford and Saltville. Northwestern: VA-91 (Saltville Hwy.) at VA-743 (Clark St.)

Nebo: Formerly called "Olympia," Nebo is a tiny community near the North Fork of the Holston River. "Nebo" is a Biblical name referenced in Deuteronomy 34:1 as the mountain from which Moses surveyed the Promised Land. Northeastern: VA-620 at VA-622

North Holston: The nearby North Fork of the Holston River lends its name to this neighborhood. Northwestern: VA-91 at Rainbow Ave.

Perryville: Charles M. Perry helped operate Saltville's Mathieson Alkali Works circa 1900 and gave his name to Perryville. The Saltville suburb is sometimes called "New Perryville," because the original Perryville was eradicated in the 1950s to form a chemical-waste impoundment. Northwestern: VA-611 (Perryville Rd.)

Quarry: South of Saltville, the Quarry community is named for a rock quarry that operated in the vicinity from 1902 to 1924. Northwestern: VA-610 (Old Quarry Rd.) and VA-696 (Mountain Rd.)

St. Clair Bottom: Perhaps more accurately called "Sinclair Bottom," the St. Clair Bottom community derives its name from Charles Sinclair, a hunter and trapper who in 1748 received about 1,000 acres of land in this vicinity from Col. James Patton. West-central: VA-600 at VA-660

Seven Mile Ford: A highway ford crossing the Middle Fork of the Holston River was named "Seven Mile Ford" for its location, seven miles from another ford on the river at Marion. Central: US-11 at VA-643, near I-81 Exit 39

Summit: The location of Summit Missionary Baptist Church—on a grassy summit—is probably where the small Summit community found its name. Southeastern: VA-612 at VA-614

Teas: Founded in 1910, a short-lived extract plant made acid for tanning leather at Teas, a place named for plant superintendent W. H. Teas. The community is part of Rye Valley, named for wild rye, a species of grass. Immediately east of Teas is an area called "Roberts Mill," which takes its name from a mill operated by A. B. Roberts from 1922 to 1935 on the South Fork of the Holston River. South-central: VA-601 at VA-670

Thomas Bridge: The Thomas Bridge community owes its name to the family of Abijah Thomas, a mid-1800s industrialist who created the area's Holston Woolen Mills. West-central: VA-650 bridge over the South Fork of the Holston River

Wassum Valley: A clue to this name may come from early settlers named Wassum. In 1891, David Wassum helped organize the area's Wassum Valley Baptist Church. Central: VA-645, near VA-664

WASHINGTON COUNTY

Washington County spans about 566 square miles in the valleys of the Holston River's three forks. The spry old courthouse town of Abingdon centers the county culturally, politically, and geographically.

Formed in 1776, Washington County was named for Gen. George Washington (1732-1799), later to become the country's first president. Its central valley is easily accessible by both I-81 and US-11, which run parallel through rolling farmland. Roads along Washington County's mountainous shoulders are crooked and constantly climbing.

ABINGDON

Abingdon seamlessly mixes a thriving arts culture with historical attractions, recreation sites, modern shopping conveniences, and a gorgeous mountain setting. All the while, this central Washington County hamlet at US-11's northernmost junction with US-58—home to about 7,800 residents—is able to retain a small-town charm.

Sometime between 1774 and 1776, settler Joseph Black erected a fort in Abingdon, and the place was called "Black's Fort" when the first court of Washington County was held in 1777. Chartered in 1778, Abingdon claims to be the oldest incorporated town on a stream that drains to the Mississippi River.

The most common story says Abingdon's name comes from early settlers' wish to honor Martha Washington's ancestral home of Abingdon Parish, in England. But stories also say that the name originates from pioneer Daniel Boone's former residence at Abington, Pennsylvania, or that early settler William Campbell named the place for his friend Lord Abingdon, an English nobleman.

Abingdon lacks big city lights, especially along its well-kept Main Street, a romantic thoroughfare with antique shops and sharp steeples. Inside Abingdon's 20-block historic area, tree-lined brick sidewalks along Main Street connect about two dozen 19th-century buildings and six structures dating to the 1700s. The Washington County Courthouse dominates this downtown district with its towering cupola. Standing on a hill, the circa-1869 courthouse, 189 E. Main St., was built to replace an earlier structure, burned in 1864 by a lone, disgruntled Union soldier in the Civil War.

Behind the courthouse lies Plumb Alley, nearly hidden between Abingdon's parallel spans of Main Street and the mostly residential Valley Street. So named because it runs "plumb through town," Plumb Alley allows no room for passing cars. But the thoroughfare's narrow size does not matter to the thousands who flock here on the last Saturday before each Memorial Day, when the road is closed to cars during the Plumb Alley Day craft fair.

According to legend, a pack of wolves emerged from a cave on Plumb Alley in 1760 and attacked Daniel Boone's dogs; the frontiersman subsequently called the area "Wolf Hills." Now the entrance to Plumb Alley's Wolf Cave is gated and off-limits to the public, but visitors can peruse the Cave House Craft Shop, located in the 1857 Adam Hickman House, a Victorian structure above the subterranean hole. The Cave House, 279 E. Main St., sells crafts like caned chairs, quilts, and stained glass.

In August, visitors can spend about two weeks looking for crafts, art, antiques, and more during the town's annual Virginia Highlands Festival. First held in 1949, this extravaganza attracts about 100,000 visitors a year, easily filling up Abingdon's hotels, motels, and bed-and-breakfasts.

Year-round, you'll find the doors open at Abingdon's art galleries, including the Starving Artist Café, 134 Wall St., a restaurant with rotating art exhibits. Nearby, the Fields-Penn 1860 House Museum, 208 W. Main St., showcases life in antebellum Abingdon. The brick Fields-Penn House was named for first owner James Fields and latter-day owner George Penn.

Clearly, the brightest beacon of Abingdon's arts culture is the nonprofit William King Regional Arts Center, 415 Academy Dr. This three-story center—with working artist studios and museum-standard galleries—is housed at the former campus of William King High School. The brick school building, built in 1913 atop a natural overlook, was named for William King, an early Saltville-area businessman.

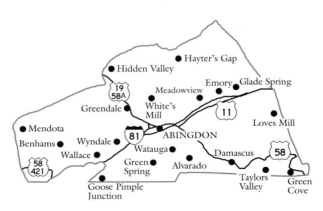

The Arts Depot, 314 Depot Sq., is another nonprofit gallery with working artist studios. Open since 1990, the Arts Depot is housed inside a train depot built in 1869-1870. Next door, the Historical Society of Washington County Library lays claim to another old depot, Abingdon's circa-1909 railway passenger station, at 306 Depot Sq. The society's library contains an extensive collection of books, papers, and personal recollections. As a museum, the 1909 depot features its own history, including an original ticket window and a collection of O. Winston Link photographs chronicling the 1950s steam-train era on the Abingdon Branch of the Norfolk & Western Railway.

Standing behind the Washington County Public Library, 205 Oak Hill St., the Alexander Breckenridge Cabin may be the oldest surviving building on the headwaters of the Holston River. Constructed in 1769, this log building was restored in 1984 after it was moved to Abingdon from its original location in Washington County, near Stone Mill Road at Spoon Gap Road.

Just a few blocks away, the Parson Cummings Cabin stands at Sinking Spring Cemetery, at the corner of Valley Street and Russell Road. The circa-1773 log house, relocated here in 1971, was the living quarters of the Rev. Charles Cummings, the first minister of Abingdon's Sinking Spring Presbyterian Church.

The Alexander Breckenridge and Parson Cummings cabins both predate the town's incorporation. But a restaurant called The Tavern, 222 E. Main St., is considered Abingdon's oldest structure, because the box-shaped building stands on its original site.

Built in 1779, The Tavern was once a bank, an overnight inn, a bakery, and a private residence. The building served as the first post office in Abingdon, and an original mail slot is still in place. During the Civil War, The Tavern served as a small hospital for Confederate and Union soldiers. Numbers designating patients' beds were drawn in charcoal on the plastered walls of the third-floor attic, a place that is sometimes shown to curious restaurant patrons. But . . . watch out! That attic could be haunted. Once, a repairman told restaurant owner Max Hermann that those charcoal numbers lit up blood red when the lights failed here.

What's to See

Abingdon Vineyard and Winery: Founded in 2001 along the South Fork of the Holston River, the Abingdon Vineyard and Winery includes a 10-acre vineyard and a two-story winery. A tasting room is open spring to fall.

🚗 From I-81 Exit 19, follow US-58 east for five miles. Turn right on VA-722 and go 1.8 miles. Bear left on VA-710 (Alvarado Rd.) and follow for a half mile to the entrance, just beyond a hairpin turn, at 20530 Alvarado Rd.

Barter Theatre: Time was, you could trade ham for *Hamlet* at the site of an old Presbyterian church in Abingdon.

This story began when Bob Porterfield, a young actor, left New York City for his native Southwest Virginia. He brought home a group of 22 unemployed actor friends. Like so many others during the Great Depression, Porterfield did not have much. But he did have a dream—he wanted to start a theater in Abingdon, despite the cash-poor times.

The personable Porterfield persisted in his plan by adopting a barter system. Crazy as it sounded, Porterfield opened his theater's doors in exchange for produce, like corn or potatoes. The policy at Porterfield's newly constituted Barter Theatre said simply: "With vegetables you cannot sell, you can buy a good laugh."

On June 10, 1933, the Barter's first show featured John Golden's *After Tomorrow*. Farmers, for years, continued to line up here with their vegetables, fruits, and meats. Just as incredible, the Barter survived on a shoestring budget for more than a decade before receiving state financial assistance. It won the State Theatre of Virginia title in 1946.

In time, too, money became the standard charge for admission, though Lady Bird Johnson showed up as late as 1965 and successfully traded a potted plant for an admission ticket.

Barter Theatre in Abingdon

The Barter Theatre building, 133 W. Main St., is a prominent Abingdon landmark. Originally constructed in 1830-1832 by the congregation of Sinking Spring Presbyterian Church, the brick structure became the home of theatrical productions staged by the Sons of Temperance during the mid-1800s. It was later used as an opera house, a town hall, a fire department, and a jail. In the 1950s, Porterfield redecorated the theater's interior, using furnishings salvaged from New York's now-demolished Empire Theatre. In 1996, a $1.7-million renovation enlarged the lobby and expanded the auditorium to 507 plush seats.

At the corner of South Church and Main streets, the Barter Stage II is a smaller and more intimate playhouse in a circa-1829 structure also once used as a church. Shows here or at Barter's main stage run year-round, with dramas, comedies, and musicals staged during afternoons and evenings.

Barter's popular productions provide a natural proving ground for up-and-coming thespians. Since Porterfield's time, hundreds of budding actors have come and moved on. Barter alumni include Ned Beatty, Ernest Borgnine, Wayne Knight, Larry Linville, Patricia Neal, and Gregory Peck.

The repertory theatre continues to attract actors from distant cities. While in town, the "Barter Players" live at the Barter Inn, once home to Abingdon's Stonewall Jackson College, an institution established in 1868 and closed in about 1930. The college's ghostly campus buildings off Court Street date to 1915 and also house the Barter Theatre's extensive costume shop.

Martha Washington Inn: Abingdon's Martha Washington Inn is overflowing with lavish amenities, architectural charm, and a whole lot of history—not to mention ghosts.

A wrought-iron fence and a fountain-centered courtyard guard the inn, often called simply the "Martha," making this antique a can't-miss landmark at 150 W. Main St. Horse-drawn-carriage rides use the circular driveway as a take-off point, and the inn's wide front porch is the scene of many celebrations.

In 1832, the Martha's central building—a three-story brick structure—was constructed as a private residence for Gen. Francis Preston, his wife, Sarah, and their family of nine children. The building was sold in 1858 to the Holston Conference of the Methodist Church, which established the Martha Washington College for Women here in 1860.

Abingdon's Martha Washington Inn

Soon after, the Civil War interrupted college life. Students turned into nurses when the Martha became a hospital for both Confederate and Union soldiers. College courses resumed after the war, but the school closed by the time the Martha's building turned 100 years old, and the student population was consolidated with nearby Emory & Henry College.

Later, in 1934, the Martha housed actors for the newly opened Barter Theatre, which faces the inn on Main Street. In 1935, the Martha opened as a hotel that has since operated through a succession of owners. The hotel's service, like its antique furnishings, has traditionally remained first-class.

At various times, guided tours of the stately hotel include interpretations of its Civil War-era ghost stories. One tale involves a young Confederate gunned down by Union soldiers; his blood stained the floor at the feet of his college-girl sweetheart. All attempts to remove the bloodstains were unsuccessful. Stories say the stains just kept reappearing. The marked floor, outside what is now the Governor's Suite, was eventually covered with carpet.

Another ghost story follows a college girl named Beth, who nursed Capt. John Stoves, a wounded Union officer. One night, Stoves called out, "Play something, Beth, I'm going." With trembling fingers, Beth played a melody on her violin. Stoves died, and, shortly after, so did Beth, a victim of typhoid fever. Patrons and staff insist Beth's haunting violin melodies can be heard on the inn's third floor during full-moon nights.

Morgan-McClure Motorsports Museum: Abingdon is home to NASCAR's Morgan-McClure racing team, established in 1983. Actual race cars showcase the team at a motorsports museum at the north side of town, off I-81 Exit 22, at 26502 Newbanks Rd. Named for founders Tim Morgan and Larry McClure, the team's past drivers include Mark Martin, Sterling Marlin, and Ernie Irvan.

South Holston Lake: Heavy stone pillars support a steel-and-wood railroad trestle on the Virginia Creeper Trail where the Holston River's middle and south forks unite. This isolated area is the northern gateway to South Holston Lake, a 7,580-acre water hole managed by the (TVA). However, more than two thirds of this lake lies in Tennessee, so South Holston seems to get little mention in Virginia travel guides.

Still, there is plenty of room to roam. Some 10 navigable miles of the lake's river channel winds through Washington County and continues another 14 miles to Tennessee's South Holston Dam. In 1942, TVA began construction on the South Holston Dam in order to control flooding along the South Fork. Paused to defer resources to the war effort, work resumed in 1947. The first valleys of what is now the lake bed began flooding in 1948, and the dam was completed in 1950.

In Virginia, South Holston Lake covers about 1,600 acres and is not nearly as expansive as the mile-wide waters in Tennessee's Sullivan County. But Washington County's lake views can be equally exciting. Much of the eastern shore is national-forest land, and the lake's west side is home to fancy houses outlined with lavish decking and lattice-laced gazebos.

South Holston Lake is ideal for all kinds of boating, though compact craft with trolling motors or small gas engines will find staying in Virginia more accommodating than venturing to the more heavily traveled Tennessee side. Virginia boaters seeking quiet cruises, also, should slate summer weekdays, when fewer personal-watercraft drivers are ripping up the lake's glistening blue-green surface.

From the river forks' confluence, fishing boats can travel upstream only a half mile on the Holston's middle fork, during spring's high-water season, before hitting rocks on the riverbed. Boats can travel farther up the South Fork. But boaters need caution when trolling through the mini-forest of skinny trees growing on the river bottom between the trestle and a set of rapids at the river's confluence with Louse Creek. This bayou scene is a popular haunt of fishermen.

Traveling downstream, the lake widens, narrows, and then fattens again on the six-mile stretch between the trestle and Avens Bridge (named for a local Avens family) on VA-670. South of Avens Bridge, pontoon boats are standard and water skiers common. You might even see a small yacht.

Keep this in mind: Virginia does not end past a Tennessee-state-line sign nailed to a tree at the tip of a small peninsula at Washington County Park. Traveling downstream past that marker, turn immediately right and follow back into Virginia at Spring Creek, an inlet seen alongside VA-75, near the Tennessee line.

Prime time for boating is spring and early summer, when water levels are highest. Spring, too, is best when fishing for largemouth and smallmouth bass, crappie, bluegill, trout, walleye, catfish, or musky. But remember that you will need a license from both Virginia and Tennessee if your plans include criss-crossing the state line with a fishing pole.

Trees grow out of the riverbed on the South Fork of the Holston River at the headwaters of South Holston Lake

Usually in August, the TVA draws down the lake level for power generation and flood control. Water is navigable year-round, but the Virginia side gets so low by mid-September that it may be impossible to access the lake's public boat ramp at Whitaker Hollow.

The water remains deep at the 55-acre Washington County Park, which overlooks a wide stretch of the lake at the Tennessee-Virginia line. Lots of picnic tables and two large shelters are scattered throughout the woods, and a "swim at your own risk" area lines the shore. There's a swimming pool, an amphitheater, a playground, and a boat ramp. More than 100 campsites for tents and trailers are also here, but vacancies are rare.

🚗 A public boat ramp provides access to the lake at Avens, near Green Spring. From I-81 Exit 17 in Abingdon, follow VA-75 south for about 3.5 miles, turn left on VA-672, and follow for about 2.5 miles to the Avens ramp on the left.

Another fee-free ramp, plus picnic tables and a swimming area, is at Whitaker Hollow, a more remote and secluded site. To get there from I-81 Exit 19 in Abingdon, follow US-58 east for about five miles. Turn right on VA-722 and follow for about 1.8 miles, then continue straight for about two miles after the road becomes VA-710 (Alvarado Rd.). Turn right on VA-674 and follow for one mile to a right turn on VA-664 (gravel). Continue for about 1.5 miles on VA-664 to the Whitaker Hollow entrance on the right.

At Green Spring, a TVA public access provides space for fishing or to hand-launch small boats where Wolf Creek meets the lake. To get there from I-81 Exit 17, follow VA-75 south for about 6.5 miles. Turn left on VA-670 and follow for one mile. Turn right on VA-664 (Lake Rd.) and follow to the access, on the left, about 30 yards after crossing a creek bridge.

To reach Washington County Park from I-81 Exit 17 in Abingdon, follow VA-75 south for 8.4 miles. Turn left on VA-663 (County Park Rd.) and follow for 0.8 miles to the entrance on the right.

Virginia Creeper Trail: You can hike it. You can bike it. You can take it by horseback or on cross-country skis. Zipping across most of eastern Washington County, the Virginia Creeper Trail is a multiuse recreation trail linking downtown Abingdon to the North Carolina border near Grayson County's Whitetop community.

The 34-mile trail is the former path of the Virginia-Carolina Railway, later known as the Abingdon Branch of the Norfolk & Western Railway. Trains ran here from 1900 to 1977. The trail opened a decade after the railroad's demise and has spurred a series of rental cottages, bed-and-breakfasts, and bicycle-rental shops along its route.

The trail begins in Abingdon at an old steam locomotive used on the rail line, which came to be called the "Virginia Creeper" either from the Virginia Creeper vines that grow along the route or from early steam locomotives slowly creeping up the railroad's steep grades. Views virtually anywhere here are awesome, especially on the trail's 100 trestles and bridges, including a 529-foot span crossing the headwaters of South Holston Lake.

East of Damascus, the trail lies mostly within the Mount Rogers National Recreation Area, boasting incredible scenery as it continually climbs uphill to Whitetop. Mountain-bike riders love starting at Whitetop and coasting 17 miles downhill to Damascus, as the trail's elevation drops about 1,500 feet. Several Damascus businesses rent bikes and offer shuttles to the trailhead near Whitetop.

Running through farms and forests, the trail is basically flat from Abingdon to Damascus and is welcome to folks strolling with a dog on a leash. On this stretch, the trail right-of-way belongs to the towns, giving the public a right to use it, though most of the land is privately held.

🚗 Parking access is available at the corner of A Street and Green Springs Road in Abingdon; along VA-677 at Watauga; near the Holston River bridge on VA-710 at Alvarado; on US-58

Long trestles aid passage along the Virginia Creeper Trail

at the Damascus Community Park; along US-58 at Straight Branch and Whitetop Laurel Creek (4.6 miles east of Damascus Community Park); at the junction of VA-725 and VA-726 in Taylors Valley; off VA-728, south of US-58, at Creek Junction; along VA-600 at the Green Cove Depot; and off VA-726 at the Whitetop Station in Grayson County. Maps are available at the Abingdon Visitor Center, 335 Cummings St.

The Virginia Creeper Trail crosses this 529-foot trestle at the headwaters of South Holston Lake, where the Holston River's middle and south forks unite.

ALVARADO

It's not clear how a place called "Barron" in central Washington County became "Alvarado." One theory suggests that some young men once visited relatives in Texas, where another Alvarado is located near Dallas, and later suggested renaming this community for the Texas town. Sparsely populated, Alvarado supported its own post office until 1962. The community is located along VA-710, near VA-674, at a popular fishing spot on the South Fork of the Holston River.

The South Fork meets the Holston's middle fork about a mile west of Alvarado. At this site, in 1801, an early settler named Hugh Neely laid out a town called "Carrickfergus," a name likely originating from the port city of Carrickfergus in Northern Ireland. Space along the Holston's riverbanks was set aside for boat landings and shipping barges, and in 1802, the Virginia General Assembly passed an act establishing the town. But land didn't sell, and Carrickfergus soon faded away.

DAMASCUS

Shade trees and sidewalks line US-58, the main street of Damascus, as the road winds past stores, restaurants, and homes. This scenic drive is full of snapshot opportunities in this town, which was home to about 1,000 residents in 2000.

Still, this road is not the main attraction in Damascus. Look, instead, for the town's trails, including the Appalachian Trail, known to hikers as the "AT." This village boasts so many biking and hiking paths that it calls itself the "Town of Many Trails." In return, AT users have dubbed Damascus the "Friendliest Town on the Trail," a title that town leaders have lovingly embraced. Each spring, during the weekend after Mother's Day, Damascus throws a big bash called "Appalachian Trail Days." This festival includes a parade and a reunion for AT hikers along an in-town section of the trail that follows the sidewalks of US-58.

The famous AT also passes through Damascus Community Park, a green space at the corner of West Laurel Avenue (US-58) and South Beaverdam Avenue, marked by a gazebo, a playground, and a large railroad trestle providing access to the Virginia Creeper Trail. From spring to fall, the U.S. Forest Service uses a railroad caboose at the park to distribute brochures on the Mount Rogers National Recreation Area.

Damascus is at the confluence of Laurel and Beaverdam creeks, where VA-91 meets US-58, at the edge of the Iron Mountains and Feathercamp Ridge. The area was once known as "Mock's Mill" for a gristmill owned by early settler Henry Mock. The town took its current name, which honors the ancient Asian capital of Syria, when Confederate Brig. Gen. John D. Imboden (1823-1895) bought a bulk of Damascus land from the Mock family in 1886. Imboden believed the town would become a famous steel-producing city. Unfortunately, the area's iron deposits turned up only on the surface.

The mountains near Damascus, however, were covered with hardwoods. In about 1901, Damascus was established as a stop on the Virginia-Carolina Railway. At the time, extensive lumbering stripped virgin timber from surrounding peaks, in what is now the Mount Rogers National Recreation Area in southeastern Washington County. Incorporated in 1904, Damascus adopted a nickname, "The Little Swiss Town," during the early 1900s, when it was a chief commerce center for local lumber operations.

About a century after the railroad arrived, young-growth forest covered the ridges enclosing Damascus, providing a scenic skyline to this "Town of Many Trails." In turn, bike-rental outlets, plus bed-and-breakfasts and a coffee shop, opened here, signaling new chapters in the town's history.

What's to See

Beartree Recreation Area: Situated at a 3,010-foot elevation, the Beartree Recreation Area includes picnic shelters, a campground for tents and trailers, handicapped-accessible trails, and a bathhouse. The shiny blue waters of the 11-acre Beartree Lake—with a sandy beach and two fishing piers—are the area's main attraction. Fishing includes bluegill, sunfish, and smallmouth bass. Surrounded by evergreens, the lake is open year-round and stocked with rainbow trout, usually in fall and spring. Boats can also be launched, but only with trolling motors and only by hand; there is no boat ramp. The beach and campground are closed during winter. Fees are charged through the Mount Rogers National Recreation Area.

Local folklore, incidentally, says that the name "Bear Tree" comes from a tree here used as a scratching post by bears.

🚘 From Damascus Community Park, follow US-58 east for 8.2 miles and turn left at the entrance on USFS-837. The anglers' parking lot is immediately on the right. Continue straight to the parking lot for the beach, bathhouse, and campground.

Chestnut Mountain Waterfall: Jagged cliffs caked green with moss stand beside the Chestnut Mountain Waterfall, a rocky ripple of water that spits and sputters for a height of nearly 20 feet. This drive-by attraction borders a narrow, unpaved road at Chestnut Mountain. Prior to the 1930s blight, the American chestnut was a prominent species in this area.

🚘 From Damascus Community Park, follow US-58 east for 1.5 miles. Turn right on VA-91 and go south for 2.3 miles. Turn left on VA-725 (Taylor Valley Rd.) and go 2.6 miles. Turn right on VA-726 (Chestnut Mountain Rd.) and go two miles to the falls on the right.

Falls of Alvarado Road: On a narrow country lane near Damascus, a thin stream tumbles for 15 feet over mossy rocks, forming the Falls of Alvarado Road. The drive-by attraction makes for a good photo. Going beyond the roadway is trespassing.

🚘 From Damascus Community Park, follow US-58 west for 3.3 miles. Turn left on VA-711 (Alvarado Rd.) and follow for 0.6 miles. The waterfall is on the left.

Straight Branch Falls: The tumbling, trout-stocked waters of the Straight Branch consistently cascade along the west leg of the Mount Rogers Scenic Byway (US-58). Beside one bend in the road, the stream pours over a 14-foot-high cliff to form Straight Branch Falls. This branch of Whitetop Laurel Creek drains Straight Mountain.

🚘 From Damascus Community Park, follow US-58 east for 6.3 miles (or 1.7 miles east of a Virginia Creeper Trail parking lot at Straight Branch). The falls are behind a guardrail on the left. A highway pull-off is 15 yards beyond the falls.

Whitetop Laurel Creek: In the Mount Rogers National Recreation Area, Whitetop Laurel Creek is a rippling stream paralleling the Virginia Creeper Trail. It is stocked with trout and is nationally noted by fly fishermen for its clean water.

It is also simply scenic. The creek makes a frothy plunge for a total drop of 10 feet at the small Whitetop Laurel Falls. A little more than a mile upstream, Whitetop Laurel runs deep in calm water at the Creeper Pool, a natural swimming hole bordered by large rock overhangs and a sandy beach. Late morning is the best time to find full sunlight. Other times, the clear pool—full of underwater boulders—is simply a shady spot to cool overheated trail users.

🚘 From Damascus Community Park, go 4.6 miles east on US-58 to the Virginia Creeper Trail parking lot at Straight Branch. To reach the Creeper Pool, turn left on the trail and go east for a quarter mile, then cross Trestle No. 22 and turn right on an informal path ending at the creek. To find Whitetop Laurel Falls, turn right on the trail and go west for nearly one mile, then look 20 yards below Trestle No. 21.

EMORY Emory, like Emory & Henry College, takes its name from Bishop John Emory, who promoted Methodism in rural areas in the region. The origin of the school's "Henry," however, remains a debate among scholars. Some say it's for early American statesmen Patrick Henry, while others contend it's for Henry's sister, Elizabeth Henry Campbell Russell, who lived at nearby Saltville (see the Smyth County chapter of the Holston Valley section) and was an early leader of Methodism in Southwest Virginia.

Most everything here at the crossroads of VA-609 and VA-737 in eastern Washington County is related to Emory & Henry College. A good example is Emory's 1912 train depot, a space renovated to house the school's art exhibits.

Straight Branch Falls east of Damascus, just off US-58

Whitetop Laurel Falls

Founded in 1836, Emory & Henry is home to less than 1,000 students. Sidewalks on the picture-perfect campus form mazes between huge oaks and brick buildings, just a half mile from I-81 Exit 26. Centering the campus, the 1958 college chapel boasts beauty and elegance. It's a favorite for couples wanting traditional wedding ceremonies, but its popularity is so great that reservations may be needed a year in advance.

GLADE SPRING

Incorporated in 1875, Glade Spring is centered by a once-thriving town square, a commercial district that has faced a problem with prosperity since railroad commerce dried up here in the 1950s. The problem is simple—town-square buildings face train tracks, not the main highway. For decades, town leaders and business owners have sought new life for the square. In the 1990s, one plan involved summer bluegrass shows staged at the town square's Joe White Memorial Park, a green space named for a local fireman.

Prior to the railroad's 1856 arrival here in northeastern Washington County, what is listed on maps as "Old Glade Spring" existed as a village along the Great Stage Road, near US-11's intersection with VA-91. About two miles north, the present Glade Spring, home to about 1,400 residents in 2000, lies on the opposite side of I-81 at Exit 29. Ironically, Old Glade Spring could be "New Glade Spring," judging from its rapid commercial development along I-81 during the early 21st century.

Glade Spring's railroad depot was initially called "Passawatami," an Indian word meaning "this is the place" or "here is the trail."

Though the exact derivation is unclear, Glade Spring—called "Glade Springs" by some—may owe its name to a single spring at the head of a long glade near the site of the Old Glade Spring Presbyterian Church on US-11. Other stories say the name is owed to either of two sets of seven springs located just outside the town limits. Yet another tale says Native Americans once camped here at a place called "Glade of the Springs."

One set of seven springs, east of town off VA-753, was once the site of the Washington Springs Hotel, built by Dr. Edmund Longley in the antebellum era. The resort served springwater for decades. But the hotel, after being closed for years, burned in the mid-1970s.

Another set of seven springs is on the west side of VA-750, about two miles north of VA-609 (Hillman Hwy.) and just past an intersection with Seven Springs Road. Sometime in the 1940s, World War I veteran L. Curtiss Vinson covered each of these springs with meticulously designed stone models of church buildings. The intriguing models stand on private property but can be seen from the public highway.

GOOSE PIMPLE JUNCTION

Legend says that the noise of an estranged couple fighting inside a hilltop home was once scary enough to give you goose pimples at the junction of VA-649 (Junction Drive) and VA-650 (Old Jonesboro Road) in south-central Washington County.

In 1955, residents L. B. Nease and Russ Taylor erected the neighborhood's first sign saying "Goose Pimple Junction." Since then, about a dozen more signs have been erected to replace stolen ones. Each lists the unincorporated community's population, tallied using a surveying method unlike any government census—you simply count the houses you see from the sign. Goose Pimple Junction's population was 29 on the first sign. It later climbed to 197 in 1975 but dropped below 160 through the 1990s.

GREEN COVE

Painted white with forest green trim, the tiny Green Cove Depot was built in 1914 for $2,600 and housed a post office until 1958. Though silent to train traffic since 1977, it remains the center of the

Green Cove community in the southeastern corner of Washington County. The family of former Green Cove station agent William M. Buchanan donated the Green Cove Depot to the U.S. Forest Service in 1991. The restored structure became a visitor center for Virginia Creeper Trail users in the Mount Rogers National Recreation Area and is usually open April to October. On sale are snacks, maps, and soda.

Green Cove was named for big pine timber standing in a cove between rounded hills. To find the Green Cove Depot, go 15 miles east of Damascus on US-58 and turn right on VA-600. The depot is on the right, less than a half mile from the turn.

GREENDALE

Greendale is situated in a green valley, or "dale," at the central Washington County junction of US-19/58A and VA-700. A Greendale post office operated from 1873 to 1963.

What's to See

Falls Hill Waterfall Loop: Two nearly identical waterfalls are situated on the sides of a narrow state highway in the vicinity of Greendale. Both falls are horsetail forms, always maintaining contact with a bedrock surface. And both are on small creeks draining to the North Fork of the Holston River. The falls rush down a wavy strand of rock on Falls Hill Creek. After an initial 35-foot drop, the creek levels, then falls another 20 feet. Nearby, falls on Cabin Creek descend about 35 feet on a slightly steeper set of rock ledges.

The falls are drive-by attractions on private property, but both can be easily seen from the gravel highway, especially during winter. Accessing the falls beyond the road may be trespassing.

🚗 From US-11 in Abingdon, follow US-19 northwest for 4.5 miles to a stoplight at Greendale. Turn right on VA-775 and follow for about 0.1 miles east to VA-700. Continue east on VA-700 for one mile and turn left on the first entrance to VA-684 (Fall Hill Rd.), which soon parallels Cabin Creek and slips into

Green Cove Depot, along the Virginia Creeper Trail

a forested area. The Cabin Creek Falls are on the left at Mile 1.7. The North Fork of the Holston River is at Mile 2.2. Beyond, the road climbs through another forested area. The Falls Hill Falls are on the left at Mile 3.3. Continue straight to rejoin VA-700 at Mile 3.8.

Garrett Creek Cascades: Garrett Creek descends a series of small rock stairs, then cascades about 25 feet over a sheet of resistant rock at a 20-foot width. The creek eventually empties into the North Fork of the Holston River. The falls are a drive-by attraction on private property but can be easily seen from a state highway. Accessing the falls beyond the road may be trespassing.

🚗 From US-11 in Abingdon, follow US-19 northwest for 4.5 miles to a stoplight at Greendale. Turn left on VA-700 and head west for about 1.5 miles. Turn right on VA-611 (Garrett Creek Rd.) and follow this road as it steadily descends in elevation and increasingly narrows. After one mile, VA-611 crosses a one-lane bridge and turns to gravel. It crosses another bridge as the roadside creek dramatically begins to tumble. The cascades are on the left at 1.4 miles.

HIDDEN VALLEY

In western Washington County, Hidden Valley is named for a small valley atop Brumley Mountain. Just below, on the mountain's west side, the Hidden Valley residential community lies along VA-690. The community is alternately known as "Little Moccasin Gap" for its proximity to a Clinch Mountain gap where US-19/58A runs to Russell County.

The John Douglas Wayside is about one mile south of VA-690's entrance to Hidden Valley on US-19/58A. This public facility includes a stone-and-wood picnic shelter overlooking the roaring waters of Little Moccasin Creek. The wayside's name honors a scout who was killed here by Indians in 1776 while on his way from Black's Fort (now Abingdon, in Washington County) to Castle's Woods (now Castlewood, in Russell County) to warn settlers of an impending Indian raid.

What's to See

Chestnut Grove Community Church: The Chestnut Grove Community Church looks like other pretty chapels scattered across Southwest Virginia. But the story of some young men who started a renowned gospel group here makes the 1890 structure especially intriguing.

Singing a cappella in the late 1940s—a time when most others used instrumental accompaniment—became the trademark of the Chestnut Grove Quartet. The group's style influenced countless folk and bluegrass musicians. During one 18-month period in the 1960s, the Chestnut Grove Quartet made four independent LPs and sold 50,000 copies of their records—a *huge* number for an unsigned gospel group—while playing shows in Virginia, Ohio, Tennessee, Kentucky, Pennsylvania, and the Carolinas. Still, on Sundays, members of the quartet always returned to sing at the community church during regular services, despite having to drive all night from distant shows.

In 1994, Rebel Records released a 15-song collection of the original group's music, with assistance from the National Council for the Traditional Arts. In 1999, original member Bill Nunley, at age 84, opened the Chestnut Grove Community Church as a museum to celebrate the quartet's work.

🚗 From US-11 in Abingdon, follow US-19 northwest for 10 miles and turn right on VA-690 (Hidden Valley Rd.). The church is on the left, about a half mile farther.

Hidden Valley Wildlife Management Area: Hidden Valley Lake forms the centerpiece of the 6,400-acre Hidden Valley Wildlife Management Area but lies "hidden" at a 3,600-foot elevation atop Brumley Mountain. Created in 1964, the 61-acre Hidden Valley Lake is surrounded by a moist rhododendron forest, grassy fields, and marshy shorelines. The lake's deepest waters—about 20 feet—are near its dam on the headwaters of Big Brumley Creek. Fishing includes smallmouth and largemouth bass, sunfish, bluegill, and northern pike. A popular angling spot for boaters (with trolling motors only) is near a marsh island located directly across the lake from a concrete ramp.

Managed by the Virginia Department of Game and Inland Fisheries, the wildlife area includes informal picnic and camping areas. Several trails wind through the forest. One path originates at a yellow gate at the upper parking lot and follows the placid waters of Big Brumley Creek below the dam. The trail runs over old railroad ties, evidence of when this area was logged in the early 1900s.

🚗 From US-11 in Abingdon, follow US-19 northwest for 10 miles and turn right on VA-690 (Hidden Valley Rd.). Follow

Chestnut Grove Community Church at Hidden Valley

for about four miles (on a nearly straight-up ascent) to a gravel road at the area's entrance. After going another mile, turn right on a short drive to reach the boat ramp, or continue to the next right to reach a camping area, or take the third right turn to find the dam.

HOLSTON Native Americans called the Holston River "Hogoheegee," and early explorers called it "Indian River." The present name comes from Stephen Holstein, who in 1749 built a canoe and drifted away, eventually sailing to the Mississippi River, according to legend. Settlers renamed the river "Holston," spelling it like they pronounced Holstein's name.

At the crossroads of US-19/58A and VA-802 in north-central Washington County, a community called "Holston" borders the river's north fork, near Little Moccasin Creek. Holston supported its own post office from 1831 to 1966.

A couple miles west, the Prices Mill settlement bordered the river during the Civil War. The mill provided power to the area with a dam, and Price's Factory turned wood into furniture. A Price's Factory post office was open from 1859 to 1866. The mill and factory owner, James Price, was postmaster.

MEADOWVIEW During the late 1800s, William Campbell Edmondson opened the first store and served as the first postmaster at Edmondson's Meadows, in east-central Washington County. What was later known as "Meadow View" prospered as a railroad town in the early 1900s, and regular Saturday-night dances enlivened the town square, near the crossroads of VA-80 and VA-609.

Meadowview was incorporated in 1914, but its government lasted only a few years. According to one account, when a citizen here was shot by one of the town's law-enforcement officers, the leaders voted to un-incorporate the town, because they feared a lawsuit.

With the loss of passenger rail service a few decades later, Meadowview's town square began to fade. Buildings continually deteriorated for years, until 1994, when a crew polished the outer facades with fresh paint. Such a splash made everything look better. But Meadowview remained a sleepy respite off I-81 Exit 24, between Abingdon and Emory.

What's to See

Falls of Chestnut Ridge: Alongside a narrow road north of Meadowview, a small stream slips down Chestnut Ridge. After tumbling for about 10 yards, the water forms a 25-foot-high cascade inside a small ravine. This waterfall can be easily seen during winter, below the road and behind a guardrail. Accessing the falls beyond the public roadway is trespassing.

From I-81 Exit 24 at Meadowview, follow VA-80 west for 3.5 miles. Turn right on VA-745 (Old Saltworks Rd.) and go 2.2 miles. Turn left on VA-686 and go 1.3 miles. The falls are on the right, near a wide spot in the road.

Falls of Logan Creek: Logan Creek probably takes its name from James Logan, who moved to the area between Hayter's Gap and the North Fork of the Holston River in 1769. The creek is one of several tributaries of the North Fork with a waterfall at the side of a state highway. Logan Creek drops about 35 feet, flowing between the vertical walls of a rocky gorge and a rock bluff at the edge of VA-80. The falls, a drive-by attraction, can be seen best during winter. Accessing the falls beyond the public roadway may be trespassing.

From I-81 Exit 24 at Meadowview, follow VA-80 west for seven miles. The falls are on the right, 0.1 miles before crossing a bridge over the North Fork of the Holston River. From the Hayter's Gap Community Center, the falls are one mile southeast on VA-80, just past an intersection with VA-611.

MENDOTA

Clinch Mountain's towering wall of treetops dwarfs Mendota, providing a beautiful backdrop to the farming community's pastureland along the North Fork of the Holston River. In the mid-1800s, landowner Adam Hickman named this area "Kinderhook"—a name that still survives as northwestern Washington County's magisterial district—for his former home in New York. Henry C. Holly, a merchant, later named the town "Mendota," an Indian word for "bend in the river."

Near Mendota's main crossroads of VA-614 and VA-802, the brick Bank of Mendota building included a doctor's office, an apartment, and a post office when it was constructed in 1918, the year the Virginia General Assembly granted Mendota status as an incorporated town. But the bank went bankrupt in 1930. Then went the town itself; the Mendota town charter was surrendered in 1942. Six decades later, a post office remained open at Mendota, but old town buildings were either gone or crumbling.

What's to See

Barn Rock: In Mendota's Pine Grove section, the late Frank Osborne showed how Southwest Virginia's outcrops could be creatively used when he built a barn in the 1940s with a 12-foot-high rock for a wall. At first, this was a shed and a corncrib. Osborne later combined the structures into what's called the "Barn Rock Barn." Privately owned, it's a drive-by curiosity.

From US-11 in Abingdon, follow US-19 northwest for 7.5 miles. Turn left on VA-802 (Mendota Rd.) and follow west for 11.8 miles. Turn left on VA-621 (Barnrock Rd.) and follow

Barn Rock Barn, near Mendota

for 0.3 miles, then veer left on VA-614. The barn is about 100 yards on the right, just past Pine Grove Baptist Church.

Alternate Route: From the Mendota Post Office, follow VA-802 east for about two miles. Turn right on VA-621 and follow for 0.3 miles. Turn left on VA-614. The barn is on the right.

TAYLORS VALLEY

Each year, the Taylors Valley community of southeastern Washington County celebrates the Fourth of July with a parade. Practically every resident participates, and many build floats. But, until it is time to line up, there is a big hush-hush on what the neighbors are building in their garages. Some residents have even been known to playfully shoo each other away, just so surprises are not spoiled, or ideas borrowed. The holiday parade draws hundreds to the mountain-locked hamlet of Taylors Valley, home to about 150 people and said to have been named for a local Taylor family. A post office was established here in 1906.

Unfortunately, a problem lies in getting to Taylors Valley. The easiest route follows VA-91 into Tennessee from Damascus. About one mile south of Virginia on TN-91, turn left at a sign pointing to Taylors Valley. Then follow this road for a little more than two miles to the junction of VA-725 and VA-726.

WHITE'S MILL

Romantic in its archaic architecture, built mostly from yellow poplar and capped with a forest green roof, White's Mill takes its name from the family of Col. James White, who acquired land surrounding a mill in this area in 1838. Milling here in central Washington County dates to 1796-1797, when Thomas Moffett hired John Lewark, a shipbuilder, to construct a gristmill. The existing White's Mill on Toole Creek may be the same as Moffett's. But some historians say that this mill was built by White's family, circa 1840. The mill's actual year of construction is not recorded.

White's Mill, a landmark near Abingdon

The water-powered mill's almost constant business selling cornmeal ended in 1998, and its metal waterwheel was left at a standstill. In 2001, the nonprofit White's Mill Foundation, Inc. acquired the structure, later opening it for tours. It's on both state and national historic registers.

To the north of White's Mill, look for the Falls of Toole Creek, a little-known natural treasure. Here, Toole Creek searches its way to the North Fork of the Holston River, taking several drops on the right side of the highway. The first is a 30-foot downhill rush behind a guardrail and barbed-wire fence. The roadside stream then levels for a mile and curves, crashing for about 45 feet and forming a 10-foot cascade at its confluence with a feeder branch boasting its own 12-foot waterfall.

🚗 From Valley Street in Abingdon, go 4.2 miles north on VA-692 (White's Mill Rd.) and you'll see White's Mill on the left.

To find the Falls of Toole Creek from White's Mill, turn right on VA-700 (Rich Valley Rd.) and go 0.4 miles, then turn left on VA-692 (Toole Creek Rd.) and simply watch the water.

The falls are a drive-by attraction. Not all can be easily seen. Accessing the falls beyond the road may be trespassing, but you can try a drive when trees are missing leaves. The falls produce a refreshing roar even during dry weather.

Alum Wells: A man remembered as "Dr. Lancaster" served water from a low-yielding alum spring in the late 1800s. Local legend says one of the doctor's sons, frustrated by the slow-moving spring, tried to increase its flow with dynamite, but the explosion dissipated the spring's output. The Alum Wells spa, at the foot of Clinch Mountain, soon closed. Northwestern: VA-872 (Alum Wells Rd.) at VA-802 (Mendota Rd.)

Benhams: Tradition says this community's name is probably owed to a local Indian fighter named Benham. Possibly, the name is a reference to John Benham, who settled in the Mendota area on the North Fork of the Holston River and constructed a fort near here in 1769. Benham, who died in 1800, owned 1,000 acres along the North Fork, about four miles below the village of Holston. A Benhams post office operated from 1880 to 1959. Southwestern: VA-627 at VA-700

Bethel: In 1881, a church built between Abingdon and Damascus was called "Bethel," a term meaning "house of God." Central: VA-708, near VA-710

Blacksburg: The origin of the name "Blacksburg" is owed to the popularity of the community's blacksmith. East-central: US-11 at VA-736 (Indian Run Rd.)

Blackwell: Joseph D. Blackwell sold land in 1902 so a church could be built. Ironically, that sale also meant shutting down Mr. Blackwell's moonshine still, because its location was in violation of a state law prohibiting stills within one mile of churches. "Blackwell," however, became a fixture on local maps. Northeastern: VA-700 at VA-746

Brumley Gap: Scenic Brumley Gap may derive its name from Richard Brumley, who lived on 80 acres along the North Fork of the Holston River in 1773. Thomas Brumley (possibly "Bramley") was another early settler and owned 200 acres of Washington County land in 1781. North-central: VA-687 at VA-689

Burson Place: A neighborhood near Benhams was named "Burson Place" for Bristol attorney John Edward Burson (1847-1920), a local landowner buried atop a wooded knoll in the vicinity. Southwestern: VA-633 (Reedy Creek Rd.) at VA-640 (Benhams Rd.)

Cedarville: A Cedarville post office operated at an inn along the Great Stage Road in the 1850s. An abundance of cedar trees inspired the name. Central: US-11 at VA-80

Cleveland: Addison King built a mill on Spring Creek in the 1850s, and a "King's Mill" post office operated in the area from 1872 to 1903. Still, the King's Mill area gradually became known as "Cleveland" after 1891, when the neighborhood's one-room Cleveland Academy was named for President Grover Cleveland. The school once stood near Cleveland Presbyterian Church, off VA-653. South-central: VA-665 at VA-663

Clinchburg: Named for nearby Clinch Mountain, Clinchburg grew up in the 1920s as the company town of the Holston River Lumber Co. The company's lumber operation sawed out in 1932, and houses built here on the mountainous landscape were either sold at public auction or torn down. Clinchburg later became a quiet suburb of Abingdon and Saltville. Northeastern: VA-745 at VA-748

Craigs Mill: In 1853, Robert C. Craig served as the first postmaster at Craigs Mill and likely gave his name to this isolated community along Smith Creek. Northwestern: VA-614, near VA-625

Creek Junction: Green Cove Creek joins Whitetop Laurel Creek at the aptly named Creek Junction. This picturesque place along the Virginia Creeper Trail was once a stop on the Abingdon Branch of the Norfolk & Western Railway. Southeastern: VA-728, south of US-58

DeBusk Mill: Built sometime after the Civil War, the DeBusk Mill was named for a local DeBusk family and was once called "Ebbing Springs Roller Mill." It's on the Middle Fork of the Holston River and was used to make livestock feed until the mid-1960s. East-central: VA-736, about one mile east of VA-91

Denton Valley: During the 1790s, brothers David and James Denton settled in what became known as "Denton Valley," an area on the southeastern side of the South Fork of the Holston River, near Sullivan County, Tenn. The river channel is now part of South Holston Lake. South-central: VA-670 at VA-673

Duncanville: In 1853, farmer Henry Duncan moved to an area between Brumley Gap and Hayter's Gap. He fathered 18 children and gave his name to tiny Duncanville (or "Duncansville"). In 2000, Duncanville's 1889 one-room schoolhouse was moved to Abingdon's Stanley Road and became a museum open for tours during August's Virginia Highlands Festival. North-central: VA-689 (Brumley Gap Rd.), immediately east of Brumley Creek bridge

Fleenors: In the late 1700s, pioneers of Washington County included Nicholas, Casper, John, and Michael Fleenor. Their descendants lent their surname to a farming community called "Fleenors." John D. Fleenor served as the first postmaster here in 1888. Fleenors Memorial Church, established in 1897, is a local landmark. West-central: VA-784 at VA-700

Friendship: Friendship supported its own post office for about three decades, beginning in 1876. Local lore says the name is owed to this farming community's friendly folks. Eastern: VA-714 at VA-762

Green Spring: Known to some as "Green Springs," the Green Spring community is an ever-increasing residential area, bolstered by its proximity to South Holston Lake. Local landmarks include the Green Spring Presbyterian Church, a prominent brick structure built in 1923. A log church built sometime before 1782 predated the church's brick building and stood near a footpath used by pioneers traveling along Wolf Creek. Green stones found in a nearby spring gave that first church, and the community, its name. South-central: VA-75 at VA-670

Hayter's Gap: Abraham Hayter surveyed a small gap on Clinch Mountain in 1782, but the actual community called "Hayter's Gap" was settled to the southeast, at a gap in Little Mountain. Northern: VA-80 (Hayters Gap Rd.) at VA-689 (Brumley Gap Rd.)

Keywood: In May 1788, Stephen Keywood's two-story log home became the site of the first Methodist Conference held west of the Blue Ridge Mountains. Centuries later, the log home is gone, but Keywood's name survives on maps. Northeastern: VA-748 at VA-750

Konnarock: A common story says *konnarock* is a Native American word for "high rock," used here in reference to a cliff on nearby Whitetop Mountain. Yet a conflicting tale says early travelers would pass by a rock cliff on Whitetop Mountain and call it "Corner Rock," a name that may have evolved into "Konna-rock."

In 1906, Konnarock became the company town of the Hassinger Lumber Co. and, for a while, boasted 2,000 residents, a large mill, a company store, and a hotel. Konnarock later became a sparsely populated community bordering the Mount Rogers National Recreation Area. Southeastern: VA-603, near Smyth County

Laureldale: Tennessee Laurel Creek flows north to meet Whitetop Laurel Creek at Laureldale, a tiny valley southeast of Damascus. Southeastern: VA-91, about a half mile south of US-58

Lime Hill: Lime Hill was likely named for the lime quarry that operated in the vicinity during the 1920s. Southwestern: VA-617 (Lime Hill Rd.) at VA-700 (Rich Valley Rd.)

Lodi: The California town made famous by Creedence Clearwater Revival's 1969 rock 'n' roll hit "Lodi" might also be responsible for a name given

continued on next page

to a Washington County crossroads. Actually, the true derivation is unclear. But one guess follows a pair of 19th-century residents who left here for Lodi, Calif., in search for gold. Upon their return, the pair renamed this farming community (formerly called "Liberty Hall") for a local academy. A Lodi post office operated until 1935. Eastern: VA-91 at VA-731

Loves Mill: In 1837, Leonidas Love became the first postmaster at Loves Mill, on the South Fork of the Holston River. Love was a mill operator and noted mechanical genius. But, according to legend, he was killed in a fight over a plug of tobacco. East-central: VA-607 at VA-762, near Smyth County

Masada: Opening in 1895 and closing in 1904, the Masada post office derived its name from the community's Masada Methodist Church, a congregation founded by William Meek "Squire Bill" Widener, who operated a gristmill here on Rush Creek. The name "Masada" refers to an ancient fort in Israel that fell to the Romans circa A.D. 73, marking the demise of Israel for nearly 1,900 years. Eastern: VA-605 at VA-733

McKee's Store: William McKee (1894-1965) and the general store he operated in the early 1900s are remembered in the name "McKee's Store." The neighborhood is also called "Kelly Chapel," for the site of a church built in 1857 and named for a local Kelly family. East-central: VA-608 at VA-736

Mongle Spring: J. B. Mongle operated a store in the late 1800s at the Mongle Spring community, an area near the North Fork of the Holston River once known for its mountain springwater. Central: VA-611 (North Fork River Rd.), two miles east of US-19/58A

Osceola: According to legend, a Seminole chief named "O'sceola" once camped in the Osceola area. South-central: US-58, near VA-722

Parks Mill: David Parks purchased property in Washington County in 1810 and later built a gristmill known as "Parks Mill." In the 1890s, the Parks Mill area became "Clip" when a short-lived

post office was named for a dog belonging to Virginia Lowry Parks. South-central: VA-672, near VA-676

Plasterco: The Buena Vista Plaster Co., founded in 1808, gave the name "Plasterco" to an area near Saltville. *Buena vista* is Spanish for "beautiful view." Northeastern: VA-91 at VA-745

Rhea Valley: Many Rhea families live in Washington County, likely giving their name to Rhea Valley, an area near Damascus. Southeastern: VA-708 at VA-719

Rocktown: An agricultural community, Rocktown takes its name from either Boston G. Rock (1836-1881), a farmer who settled in Washington County during the mid-1800s, or his son Samuel J. Rock (1871-1962), a general-store owner at Rocktown for more than 50 years. West-central: VA-625 (Jasper Creek Rd.) at VA-700 (Rich Valley Rd.)

Roetown: Near Damascus, a local Roe family is remembered in the name "Roetown." Southeastern: US-58 at VA-715

Shortsville: Between Meadowview and Abingdon, Shortsville owes its name to Americus D. Lafayette Shortt (Short), a butcher and tanner who was Shortsville's postmaster in 1886. Shortsville is on the headwaters of Maiden Creek, a scenic stream alongside VA-741 (Maiden Creek Rd.) with small waterfalls dropping heights of about eight feet. The creek is likely named for the family of Charles E. Maiden, the postmaster here in 1883. East-central: VA-703 at VA-741

Spoon Gap: John and Mary Spoon lived in Washington County in the 1830s and gave their name to the Spoon Gap community, situated among the Great Knobs, a ridgeline between Abingdon and South Holston Lake. Central: VA-670, along Spoon Gap Creek

Three Springs: The name "Three Springs" likely comes from the number of springs near Stoffel Creek, at the southwestern base of Walker Mountain. Southwestern: US-58/421 at VA-633

Vails Mill: Vails Mill took its name from a mill Henry Vail operated in the early 1900s. Southeastern: US-58 at VA-718

Wallace: Situated immediately north of Bristol, the Wallace community became a rail stop some time after 1856 and was called "Wallace's Switch," for the Rev. W. P. Wallace, a local minister. It was earlier known as "Goforth's" for a mill operated by Major Goforth. Southern: VA-645 (Wallace Pike), between two intersections with VA-659

Watauga: In 1901, Watauga was established as a stop on the Virginia-Carolina Railway. Between VA-75 and US-58, the area remained primarily a farming community until the 1980s, when its sprawling hillsides and meandering streams attracted large residential developments. One interpretation says "Watauga" comes from the Creek *wetoga*, a word meaning "broken waters." South-central: VA-677 at VA-675

Widener Valley: Several families named Widener settled what came to be known as "Widener Valley." Among the earliest pioneers was John Widener, a German who immigrated to the United States in about 1767. Eastern: VA-605, northeast of Damascus

Wyndale: The exact derivation of Wyndale's name may be unknown, but one story says the title originated from Norfolk & Western Railway authorities, who dropped the previous name, "Montgomery's Switch," to prevent confusion with Montgomery, W.Va. The "Montgomery" name came from S. W. Montgomery, who donated land for a depot. Before that, Wyndale was called "Prestons." A folk tale says "Wyndale" was derived from the fact that the valley was on the path of a wind channel coming up a straight line of tracks from Wallace. Perhaps the name is a play on "Wind Dale," meaning "windy valley." Central: VA-645 at VA-869

Yellow Springs: Some children once played in a spring where yellow gravel was found, near an old log schoolhouse. This discovery lent the surrounding community a name, "Yellow Springs." Central: VA-80 at VA-743

CENTRAL HIGHLANDS

Mile-high Mount Rogers looms above the Christmas-tree farms and red silos dotting the Central Highlands of Southwest Virginia. Pockets of the Jefferson National Forest and the Mount Rogers National Recreation Area provide plenty of tree cover and places to explore in this area of Wythe, Carroll, Bland, and Grayson counties and the City of Galax. I-77 and I-81 make travel convenient in the Central Highlands. But, off those highways, much of the region remains refreshingly remote.

BLAND COUNTY

Bland County is a sparsely populated agricultural community spanning 360 square miles. Blanketed by the Jefferson National Forest along the West Virginia state line, most of Bland County is blocked, behind Big Walker Mountain, from the rest of Southwest Virginia's Central Highlands. Formed in 1861 from parts of Wythe, Tazewell, and Giles counties, Bland County is named for Richard Bland (1710-1776), a Revolutionary War patriot.

BASTIAN   In central Bland County, Bastian takes its name from F. E. Bastian, manager of a local railroad that helped establish the Virginia Hardwood Lumber Co. as a major industry here in the 1920s. An earlier name, "Parkersburg," honored Parker Hornbarger, who owned land near Bastian's crossroads of US-52 and VA-615.

What's to See

Wolf Creek Indian Village and Museum: Hidden behind a mask of trees, just yards from I-77, is a life-size model of an ancient Native American village. Costumed interpreters demonstrate how to make blowguns or arrowheads inside 20-foot-high wigwams covered with fiberglass resembling rawhide.

Though clearly a tourist attraction, the Wolf Creek Indian Village and Museum is far from a hokey, just-off-the-highway place that sells wooden nickels. This nonprofit operation, instead, offers an educational experience.

State archeologist Howard A. MacCord, Sr., spent four weeks of 1970 digging along the banks of Wolf Creek and discovered evidence of an unidentified tribe's village. At the time, Bland County was being reshaped by the construction of I-77. Wolf Creek needed to be rerouted, and the site of this archeological find lay in the path of progress.

MacCord's excavation uncovered the remains of 14 skeletons in shallow graves. He also found pits and post molds (stains in the ground where wooden posts used to be). In all, MacCord found enough evidence to map a circular village with about a dozen wigwams surrounded by a palisade, which could have been built here as early as 1215. In the 1990s, after the Bland County Historical Society acquired property along Wolf Creek, MacCord's report was used—along with some federal grants and the labor of local Boy Scouts—to

painstakingly build an authentic replica of the village about 200 feet from the original site, now lying beneath the bed of the rerouted Wolf Creek.

Tours of the village are held every day except for major holidays and heavy snow days. Admission is charged.

🚗 From I-77 Exit 58, follow US-52 north for 0.2 miles. The museum complex is on the right.

Wolf Creek Picnic Area: You could spend an afternoon chasing waterfalls—well, at least looking for tiny tumbles—in the leafy woods of Round Mountain, where countless streams drain to a wide and free-flowing section of Wolf Creek. The streams crisscross the Wolf Creek Nature Trail at the Wolf Creek Picnic Area, a Jefferson National Forest facility with scattered picnic tables and grills.

🚗 From I-77 Exit 58, follow US-52 south for 0.1 miles. Turn right on VA-614 and go 3.4 miles to the picnic area, on the left.

BLAND   This community honors Richard Bland in its name, just like Bland County. But it was not always this way at the crossroads of US-52 and VA-42. Bland was earlier called "Crab Orchard" for Crab Orchard Creek. The town was later named "Seddon" for James Alexander Seddon (1815-1880), a member of the U.S. House of Representatives in the 1840s.

Built of brick in 1889 and topped with a huge belfry, the Bland County Courthouse at Bland replaced a courthouse that burned on the same site in 1888. The courthouse is on VA-98, between town routes 1002 and 1003. On the front lawn stands a statue erected in 1911 to honor Confederate soldiers.

Rocky Gap
Hicksville   77   Hollybrook
Bastian
Crandon
BLAND
52
Sharon
Springs
Ceres

Wigwams are replicated at the Wolf Creek Indian Village, near Bastian

Bland County Courthouse

BLAND COUNTY CROSSROADS

Camp Laurel: Near Mercer County, W.Va., Camp Laurel likely takes its name from its proximity to Laurel Creek, a stocked trout stream. Northwestern: VA-613, between River Mountain and Buckhorn Mountain

Ceres: In 1879, Capt. H. C. Groseclose named Ceres for the Roman goddess of agriculture. The farming community was earlier known as "Bear Garden." Western: VA-42 at VA-625

Clear Fork: The Clear Fork community is in a valley named for the Clear Fork of Wolf Creek, a stream known for its clear-running waters. Northwestern: VA-61, between Buckhorn Mountain and Rich Mountain

Crandon: One account says 19th-century settler George Wohlford named Crandon for a word meaning "green hills." Wohlford's grandson Charles Wohlford served as Crandon's first postmaster circa 1897. Southeastern: easternmost crossroads of VA-42 at VA-608

Dry Fork: Settled primarily by freed slaves in about 1880, this isolated community lies along a stream called "Dry Fork." Northeastern: VA-613, near East River Mountain

Grapefield: About four miles east of Tazewell County, Grapefield likely takes its name from a site where grapes were grown. Western: VA-614, between Rich Mountain and Round Mountain

Hicksville: When Hicksville Methodist Church was founded in the early 1800s, its name remembered Joseph Hicks, an early local settler. Northern: US-52 at VA-642

Hollybrook: A brook lined with holly trees inspired the names of the Holly Brook farm and the Hollybrook community. East-central: VA-606 at VA-608

Kimberling: Edwin S. Booth of New York built a hotel at Kimberling in 1854. Kimberling Springs, a resort serving springwater lauded for its medicinal value, operated here until 1880, likely taking its name from the several Kimberling (Kimberlin) families who settled early in Bland County. East-central: VA-612 at VA-627

Mechanicsburg: Established in 1830, Mechanicsburg once supported its own bank, printing shop, tailor shop, carpenter shop, and carding mill. The community's name, according to one idea, originated from the area's large number of machinists, or "mechanics." Southeastern: VA-738 at VA-42

Niday: One theory says Niday was named for the Niday (Nida) family, probably a descendant of Adam and Hannah Niday. Northeastern: VA-61 at VA-644

North Gap: North Gap was named for a gap in Buckhorn Mountain, about a mile north of Rocky Gap. North-central: VA-613 at US-52

Point Pleasant: Also known as "The Slide," Point Pleasant is in the valley of Helveys Mill Creek at a point settlers must have considered pleasant. The origin of "The Slide" is unclear, but one story says the name comes from an otter slide at the old Helvey Mill, an operation run by a local Helvey family, while another says "The Slide" originated when Confederate soldiers shot marbles on the creek bank, making it very slippery. Southeastern: westernmost crossroads of VA-42 and VA-608

Rocky Gap: The community of Rocky Gap was named for a rocky pass between Rich Mountain and Wolf Creek Mountain. North-central: VA-61 at US-52

Sharon Springs: In about 1821, a church was built at Sharon Springs, on the headwaters of the North Fork of the Holston River. Later, the community was the site of Sharon Alum and Chalybeate Springs, a late-1800s resort hotel that specialized in mountain springwater and had its own bowling alley. Locals believe the name "Sharon Springs" comes from the Biblical Rose of Sharon, found in Song of Solomon 2:1, in which the girl talking to King Solomon proclaims, "*I am* the rose of Sharon, *and* the lily of the valleys." Western: VA-42 at VA-623-North

South Gap: Situated along Wilderness Creek, the South Gap community was likely named for its location south of Rocky Gap. North-central: VA-606 at US-52

Suiter: In 1830, Alex Suitor (Suiter) acquired 1,100 acres of land in the Suiter vicinity, along Hunting Camp Creek. Western: VA-615 at VA-618

CARROLL COUNTY

Carroll County was formed from Grayson County in 1842. On record, the county's name honors Charles Carroll, the last surviving signer of the Declaration of Independence. But there is another story. John Carroll, a state legislator, rallied in 1841 to create this 477-square-mile county, to be named in his honor. Carroll won his wish, but his political nemesis, John Blair, who had once held Carroll's office, rushed to get the state bill passed to read that the "Carroll" in the county's name would honor Charles Carroll, not John.

CANA In the late 1800s, a post office here in southeastern Carroll County was named, according to one theory, for Cana of Galilee, a biblical town in Israel. Yet another story says the name originates from Cana Thomas, an early postmaster. Still, at about the same time, Cana—or part of the area—was called "St. Paul," now the name of a school at Cana. The name "St. Paul," according to legend, was sold for $100 to residents of Wise County who wanted to use that name for a town on the Clinch River.

To tourists, Cana is known for Produce Alley, a string of open-air produce markets, assorted gift shops, and restaurants along three miles of US-52, just above the North Carolina line.

What's to See

Lovill's Creek Lake: Surrounded by woods and farmland, the 55-acre Lovill's Creek Lake is locked inside a natural ravine created by Lovill's Creek. Open to the public, lake facilities include a ramp for boats with trolling motors, a small dock, hiking trails, and picnic tables. The lake harbors bluegill, channel catfish, crappie, largemouth bass, and sunfish. The origin of the lake's name, however, is unclear; early land records refer to the creek as "Lovings" or "Lovens."

🚗 From the Cana Post Office, follow US-52 (Fancy Gap Hwy.) south for 1.1 miles. Turn left on VA-686 (Epworth Rd.) and follow for one mile. Turn left on a gravel entrance and follow for 0.3 miles to the lake.

FANCY GAP The story of Fancy Gap follows Col. Ira Coltrane, who, in his boyhood, drove a team of horses across the mountains of south-central Carroll County. Coltrane took one possible route over the Blue Ridge and later deemed it more advantageous than the regularly used Good Spur Road. Coltrane named his new-

found gap "fancy" for its beauty. A road was built through the region in the 1850s, and, about a decade later, the name "Fancy Gap" was given to a post office.

Located where VA-683 crosses US-52, Fancy Gap is next to the Blue Ridge Parkway, which has attracted several tourist-oriented souvenir shops and antique stores to the area.

What's to See

Blue Ridge Music Center: Ground was broken in 2000 for the $10-million Blue Ridge Music Center, operated by the National Park Service under the direction of the National Council for the Traditional Arts. The center features a large amphitheater and live performances of traditional Appalachian music. The facility is at Blue Ridge Parkway Mile 213, about 13.5 miles south of the parkway's Fancy Gap entrance on US-52.

The site is near Fisher Peak, a 3,609-foot summit named for a member of a crew surveying on the Virginia-North Carolina line in the mid-1700s. Legend says Mr. Fisher died from heat exhaustion after drinking too much cold water here.

Devil's Den Nature Preserve: You might call it a mixture of heaven and hell. Above ground, the grassy meadow called "Devil's Den Acres" is a sublime setting—a cleared field, dotted with picnic tables and drenched in sunshine, just minutes from the Blue Ridge Parkway. Dipping into the surrounding thorny woods, you find the Devil's Den, a cave carved inside the Blue Ridge with a name inspired by mystery, legend, and a network of seemingly endless channels. A folk tale says a man once spent a week inside this fault cave and came out three miles down the mountain. Exactly where the cave goes, it seems, is unknown.

A nonprofit foundation oversees the Devil's Den as part of the 250-acre Devil's Den Nature Pre-

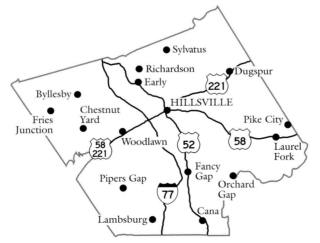

Lovill's Creek Lake, near Cana

serve. Visitors can explore the cave at their own risk. But getting in requires sliding 40 feet into a huge hole shielded by a hanging cliff.

🚗 From I-77 Exit 8, follow VA-148 (Chances Creek Rd.) east for a half mile. Turn right on US-52 (Fancy Gap Hwy.) and follow for one mile, passing below the Blue Ridge Parkway, then take an immediate right on VA-608 (Old Appalachian Trail) and follow for 1.3 miles to a left turn on VA-843 (Cemetery Rd.). Proceed a quarter mile to a gate marking the preserve at the Morris Family Cemetery. The trail to Devil's Den Cave starts in the woods, on the left, immediately beyond the cemetery. After a quarter mile, find a spur going left off the main trail. Pass a bench, then follow to the right of an outcrop for about 20 yards on a path to the cave opening.

Groundhog Mountain Overlook: Perched at a 3,030-foot elevation, the Blue Ridge Parkway's Groundhog Mountain Overlook includes an observation tower made to look like an old tobacco barn. The rustic log structure stands on an open meadow—probably good for a groundhog's home—and provides a great view of the humpback shape of Buffalo Mountain in southern Floyd County. The site also features a picnic area with grills and a display of wooden rail fences.

🚗 At Blue Ridge Parkway Mile 188.8, the overlook is 10.7 miles north of the parkway's Fancy Gap entrance on US-52.

Puckett Cabin: Orelena Hawks Puckett (1837-1939) helped deliver more than 1,000 babies as a midwife. But, ironically, none of Puckett's own 24 children (yes, she bore two dozen babies) survived beyond infancy. Puckett and her husband lived in a log cabin on a site that has since been developed by the National Park Service as an attraction at Mile 189.9 of the Blue Ridge Parkway.

🚗 To find the Puckett Cabin, follow the parkway north for 9.6 miles from the Fancy Gap entrance on US-52.

HILLSVILLE

When Labor Day weekend hits Hillsville, the unpretentious courthouse town expands to a population rivaling Virginia's biggest east-coast cities. State police, during the late 1990s, estimated that as many as 700,000 people passed through the Hillsville area during its four-day Labor Day Gun Show and Flea Market. During this time, the otherwise sleepy suburb at the center of Carroll County is catapulted into a circus of continuous traffic jams. By daybreak, it's not uncommon for traffic to be backed up more than a mile along US-58. By midday, driving US-58 through Hillsville is virtually impossible.

Visiting any other time of year, this town at the crossroads of US-58 and US-52 looks ghostly empty, which may be fitting. That is, there is a good chance Hillsville may have a few ghosts, namely at the 1872 Carroll County House, 515 N. Main St., where a courtroom nightmare left five people dead and unfairly shrouded Hillsville in infamy for most of the 20th century.

On that fateful day, March 14, 1912, trouble was expected as mountaineers rode into town during Floyd Allen's trial in Carroll County's circuit court. Allen had tried to free two relatives who were in jail for disturbing a church meeting, and afterward he was charged for interfering with an officer of the law. The judge sentenced Allen to a year in jail.

But Allen replied, "I ain't a-goin'," and, within an instant, members of his family produced guns and started shooting in the courthouse, which was packed with 300 people. Indeed, all hell broke loose. The judge was killed, along with the commonwealth's attorney, the sheriff, the jury foreman, and a witness for the prosecution. And then, like a scene from the Wild West, the Allen clan rode off into the hills. Floyd's brother J. Sidna Allen eventually got as far as Des Moines, Iowa, where he remained until detectives captured him the following September. All other participating members of the Allen clan were eventually caught and sentenced.

Puckett Cabin, just off the Blue Ridge Parkway near Fancy Gap

J. Sidna Allen also lost his dream house. Standing five miles south of Hillsville on US-52, near VA-685, the J. Sidna Allen House was built in 1911 for about $13,000. The home dominates a landscape of rolling fields, sitting on a high point with a panoramic view. Once the finest home in Carroll County, it is adorned with all kinds of Queen Anne-style grandeur. The architectural ornamentation, possibly inspired by Allen's visit to Chicago in 1898, includes stained-glass windows and a conical tower rising at the center of a wraparound front porch. Inside, intricate woodwork is featured on fireplace mantels.

J. Sidna Allen and his wife, Bettie, lived in this house for less than a year. After Allen was convicted for his role in the courtroom massacre, the state confiscated the place, and it was later sold to a succession of private owners. Sometimes, though, the registered historic landmark is open for tours through contacts with the Carroll County Chamber of Commerce.

J. Sidna Allen House

Guided tours are also sometimes offered at the Old Carroll County Courthouse, a prominent landmark topped with an octagonal cupola. The county's current courthouse, 605 Pine St., was built in 1998.

The Carroll County Historical Society Museum, 307 N. Main St., includes an elaborate carved-wood depiction of the courtroom tragedy, as well as more-sedate displays like a buggy and a spinning wheel.

If you want to buy a buggy, a spinning wheel, or just about anything else you can imagine, come to Hillsville when the flea market happens on Labor Day weekends. This sprawling event began in 1968 as a small gun show held to raise funds to repair the roof on a building owned by Hillsville's Grover W. King VFW Post No. 1115, on US-58 (West Stuart Drive). The VFW still sponsors its own flea market, but its annual fund-raiser faces competition as landowners rent nearby shaggy fields to sellers hawking everything from beer cans and gas pumps to antiques and art. Rain or shine, the flea market flourishes. It's a village of vendors. Normally, on any given day of the market, Hillsville's pop-

Old Carroll County Courthouse in Hillsville

ulation swells 100 times beyond the 2,600 residents the census said lived here in 2000.

No doubt, too, out-of-town shoppers guess the hills of this curvy-contoured town are the reason behind its name. But Hillsville actually owes its name to at least one person named Hill. One account says it's for the family of John and Susannah Hill, and another cites the James J. Hill family. The name could be for William C. Hill, a postmaster here in the 1820s, when the area was known as "Cranberry Plains."

The town became "Hillsville" in the late 1820s or early 1830s, though it was also briefly known as "Carrollton" following the formation of the county, and the town's designation as the county seat in 1842. "Carrollton" honored John Carroll, a state legislator who had pushed for the county's creation. But that name never really caught on, because residents were already used to "Hillsville."

The town seal celebrates the town's existence "since 1878." But residents did not favor Hillsville's initial incorporation, due to a lack of money and few services provided, and they soon had the original charter repealed. In 1900, Hillsville was incorporated again, but this, like the first incorporation, also proved unpopular, and the town then went for years without an active government. Stability finally arrived in 1940, when Hillsville's government was rechartered.

What's to See

Byllesby Reservoir: A couple of small creeks feed into the New River near a paved boat ramp on the 335-acre Byllesby Reservoir, a quiet lake suitable for canoes or small boats with outboard motors. The lake was formed in 1913 with the creation of Byllesby Dam. The lakeshore is lined with marsh and rock bluffs. Fishing includes smallmouth bass and walleye.

🚗 From I-77 Exit 14 at Hillsville, follow US-58/221 west for 4.4 miles. Turn right on VA-887 (Glendale Rd.) and follow west for 2.9 miles. Turn right on VA-635 (Hebron Rd.) and go

4.6 miles. Turn left on VA-736 (River Hill Rd.) and go 1.1 miles. Turn right on VA-793, then bear immediately left on VA-736 (River Hill Rd.) and follow for 2.1 miles to the river.

Carroll County Recreation Park: Ball fields, a playground, a swimming pool, and picnic shelters comprise the small Carroll County Recreation Park, operated by the county's recreation department. The pool is open Memorial Day to Labor Day. Fees are charged.

🚐 From I-77 Exit 14, follow US-58/221 west for 0.2 miles. Turn left on VA-706 (Farmer's Market Dr.), then immediately turn right on VA-689 (Ball Park Dr.).

Chestnut Creek Falls: Chestnut Creek flumes over a mound of resistant rock on a 25-foot-wide, 10-foot-high ledge and then makes a hard plunge into a quiet pool. This is Chestnut Creek Falls, just off the New River Trail State Park.

🚐 From I-77 Exit 14 at Hillsville, follow US-58/221 west for 4.4 miles. Turn right on VA-887 (Glendale Rd.) and follow west for 2.9 miles. Turn right on VA-635 (Hebron Rd.) and follow north for 3.9 miles. Turn left on VA-607 (Iron Ridge Rd.) and follow for 1.5 miles to the parking area on the left.

At Mile 45.5, follow the trail from the parking-lot side of the road and immediately pass a kiosk on the left. The falls are at Mile 46.3, also on the left.

New River Recreation Area: The Mount Rogers National Recreation Area holds sharp contrasts between its western high country's wind-swept balds and the junglelike foliage bordering the New River. It's hard to picture the two places having much in common other than the Mount Rogers name.

The New River Recreation Area, on Mount Rogers's eastern end, lies adjacent to the New River Trail State Park. The site includes a 16-space campground and picnic tables alongside the rocky river above Buck Dam. Mowed banks offer easy access for anglers and canoeists. River fishing includes smallmouth bass and walleye. Fees are charged through the Mount Rogers National Recreation Area's office at the Jennings Visitor Center in Smyth County.

🚐 From I-77 Exit 14 at Hillsville, follow US-58/221 west for 9.7 miles and enter Galax. Turn right on VA-

887 (Glendale Rd.) and go 0.6 miles. Turn left on VA-721 (Cliffside Rd.) and go 1.1 miles. Turn right on VA-607 and go 0.3 miles. Turn left on VA-721 (Fries Rd.) and go 2.3 miles to reach a New River bridge. Bear left beyond the bridge and continue for 2.2 miles, passing through the Town of Fries on West Main Street. Turn right on VA-94 and go north for 6.3 miles. Turn right on VA-602 (Byllesby Rd.) and go 3.5 miles to the New River Trail parking area at the VA-737 (Buck Dam Rd.) intersection. Turn left on VA-737 and go 2.1 miles to the campground, on the right.

Alternate Route: From I-81 Exit 80 at Fort Chiswell in Wythe County, follow US-52 south for 1.2 miles. Turn right on VA-94 and go 13.1 miles. Turn left on VA-602 and follow 3.5 miles to Byllesby Dam.

LAMBSBURG

Lambsburg may owe its name to a trio of Lambs—Wilmot Lamb was an early settler here in southern Carroll County, near the North Carolina line; Jehu Carmen Lamb was a gunsmith who settled here in about 1860; and Mariam A. Lamb, a daughter of Jehu Lamb, served as the first postmaster in 1866. The community, at the junction of VA-696 and VA-620, was first called "Lambsburgh"; the H was dropped in 1894.

What's to See

Stewarts Creek Wildlife Management Area: Look for clear mountain streams, rock outcrops, and thick woods—places hunters like to search in pursuit of deer, grouse, turkey, or squirrel—at the Stewarts Creek Wildlife Management Area. Overseen by the Virginia Department of Game and Inland Fisheries, this 1,087-acre tract lies along the north and south forks of Stewarts

Buck Dam on the New River

Chestnut Creek Falls, near the New River Trail State Park

festival called "Stompin' '76." A wild crowd of 100,000 people—maybe even 250,000 (estimates vary)—showed up here for a three-day festival of rock and bluegrass music, featuring performers John Prine, Bonnie Raitt, Nitty Gritty Dirt Band, Doc Watson, and others.

The overflowing festival, running August 6-8, backed up traffic and added mountains of trash to Pot Rock's already mountainous landscape. Tack on tales of nudity, drugs, and property damage, and it comes as no surprise that, by the end of 1976, the Carroll County Board of Supervisors had passed an ordinance banning any other kind of outdoor music festival.

Pot Rock takes its name from a large pot-like rock found here. Native Americans once used holes in rocks like these to grind corn.

Creek, a stream named for the Stuart families that settled here or received early land grants. Among the family members was Archibald Stuart, the father of Confederate Gen. Jeb Stuart.

Fishermen can hook native brook trout, but this rugged area has many restrictions. Single-hook artificial lures must be used, no live bait is allowed, and all fish must be immediately released back to the stream.

Trails follow old logging roads. Hikers can see wildflowers or rhododendron during spring bloom.

🚗 From I-77 Exit 1 at Lambsburg, follow VA-620 northwest for 1.5 miles. Turn left on VA-696 (Chestnut Grove Rd.) and follow for 0.7 miles, then bear right on VA-795 (Parkwood Rd.) and follow for 1.5 miles, bearing right again on a one-lane road and fording a creek at the area's entrance.

The upper parking area is off the Blue Ridge Parkway. Between mileposts 209 and 210, turn south on VA-716 and follow for 0.1 miles. Turn left on VA-715 and follow for a quarter mile, then turn right on VA-975 and follow for 0.3 miles, bearing left at the entrance.

POT ROCK

Hillsville's flea-market madness is not the only story about a huge crowd descending on Carroll County. In 1976, the Pot Rock community, located along VA-635 (Pot Rock Rd.), near Crooked Creek in northwestern Carroll County, was the site of a Woodstock-style

WOODLAWN

In west-central Carroll County, Woodlawn takes its name from Col. James Wood of Virginia's Frederick County. In 1756, Wood received a 2,800-acre land grant near what is now US-58/221's intersection with VA-620.

What's to See

Crooked Creek Wildlife Management Area: Managed by the Virginia Department of Game and Inland Fisheries, the Crooked Creek Wildlife Management Area is a mix of forest and open land spanning 1,800 acres. Hunting and hiking are welcome, as is fishing for both native and stocked trout, for a fee.

🚗 From I-77 Exit 14 at Hillsville, follow US-58/221 west for 3.4 miles to Woodlawn, then follow VA-620 (Forest Oak Rd.) south for four miles.

Harmon Museum: From antique military guns to ancient farm tools and vintage newspapers, the single-room Harmon Museum displays all kinds of collectibles relating to the history of Carroll County and Southwest Virginia. The museum opened in 1983 and is named for the collection of G. H. Harmon.

🚗 From I-77 Exit 14 at Hillsville, follow US-58/221 west for 3.4 miles to Woodlawn, at a junction with VA-620. The museum is on the right.

Buck: In 1912-1913, the Appalachian Power Co. built two 50-foot-high dams on the New River, one at Buck and another three miles upstream at Byllesby. The remote Buck Dam was named for a partner in New York's Vile, Blackwell and Buck engineering firm. Northwestern: northern terminus of VA-737, off New River Trail

Byllesby: The area near the New River's Byllesby Dam was once a passenger stop on the rail line that later became the New River Trail State Park. In about 1913, the Byllesby Dam took its name from H. M. Byllesby and Co., a Chicago investment firm that helped start the Appalachian Power Co., which built the dam. Northwestern: VA-602 at VA-737, off New River Trail

Chestnut Yard: When Chestnut Yard was established as a Norfolk & Western Railway stop along Chestnut Creek in about 1900, the creek was known for the chestnut trees growing along its banks. Western: VA-607 at New River Trail

Cliffview: Northeast of Galax, the Cliffview community borders cliffs along Chestnut Creek, near a ranger's station for the New River Trail State Park. Cliffside, a 1902 mansion built by Thomas Felts for his wife, Ethel, overlooks the community. West-central: VA-721 (Cliffview Rd.) at New River Trail

Corinth: Early settlers called a place "Corinth," short for the Bible's Book of Corinthians. Northwestern: VA-740 (Oak Grove Rd.) at VA-847 (Corinth Rd.)

Crooked Oak: An early school built near an unusually bent and twisted oak tree inspired this community's name. Southeastern: US-58 at VA-680 (Crooked Oak Rd.)

Dugspur: Sometime before the Civil War, an early east-west passageway was developed from a "spur" that had to be "dug" by hand with picks, mattocks, and shovels. After the spur here was completed, the area became known as the "Dug Spur." Northeastern: US-221 at VA-638

Early: The first postmaster here in 1899 was James L. Early. Northern: VA-749 at US-52

Five Forks: Five roads joined, or forked, at this crossroads. Central: VA-743 at VA-803

Fries Junction: At Fries Junction, the Norfolk & Western Railway split, with one spur going to Fries, and the main line heading to Galax. Fries Junction later became part of the New River Trail State Park built on the old railbed. It's the site of the trail's longest trestle, spanning 1,089 feet across the New River. Northwestern: Mile 39.8 of the New River Trail

Gardner Mills: A. W. Gardner built a mill at Gardner Mills, near Hillsville, in 1914. Central: VA-703 (Gardner's Mill Rd.), south of US-58/221

Gladesboro: Glades of cranberry bogs inspired the name "Gladesboro." A post office was established here in the late 1800s. Southeastern: VA-654 at VA-677

Grayson: Visitors once sought springwater to cure various ailments at Grayson Sulphur Springs, a resort founded circa 1835. At the time, Carroll County was still a part of Grayson County. By 1913, the business at Grayson had closed, and the site was flooded with the construction of the Byllesby Dam on the New River. Part of the name still survives, however, as Carroll County's Sulphur Springs voting district. Northwestern: Mile 38 of the New River Trail State Park, near Brush Creek's confluence with the New River

Hebron: The most prominent landmark of the Hebron community is the Hebron Church of Christ. "Hebron" is a Biblical name referenced in Numbers 13:22 as an ancient city. Western: VA-635 (Hebron Rd.) at VA-607 (Mallard Dr.)

Laurel Fork: An evergreen shrub, laurel, grows abundantly along the Laurel Fork, a watercourse near this community. Eastern: US-58 at VA-638

Oak Grove: People once gathered for religious services beneath a grove of oak trees, making it natural to name the local community "Oak Grove." Northwestern: VA-740 (Oak Grove Rd.), near VA-810 (Frost Rd.)

Orchard Gap: Local apple and cherry orchards inspired this name. Southeastern: VA-608 at VA-691, near Blue Ridge Parkway

Pike City: In the 1840s, Pike City originated as a stop, or "city," on the old Danville and Wytheville Turnpike. Eastern: VA-632, near Floyd County

Pipers Gap: Col. James H. Piper, an engineer on the Southwest Turnpike in the 1840s, is credited with locating a road across the Blue Ridge from Grayson Court House, now Old Town, to Mount Airy, N.C., through Pipers Gap. The actual Pipers Gap cleaves the Blue Ridge where VA-620 crosses the Blue Ridge Parkway, about four miles southeast of the Pipers Gap community. Southwestern: VA-97 at VA-713

Red Hill: An abundance of red clay gave Red Hill its name. Eastern: US-58 at VA-674

Richardson: L. Alice Richardson was the first postmaster here in 1898. North-central: VA-749 at VA-772

Riverhill: A scenic residential community, Riverhill is located on a grassy hillside near the New River. Northwestern: VA-736 at VA-793

Shorts Creek: An early settler named Short once lived in a log house along a stream that became known as "Shorts Creek." Northern: US-52, near VA-745

Snake Creek: One story says Snake Creek's name comes from trappers who found a black snake frozen to death in a cliff outcrop between two springs. Central: VA-670 at VA-674

Sylvatus: Prominent early resident Sylvatus Smith is immortalized in the name of Sylvatus, an 1890s-era lead-mining community. Northeastern: VA-693 at VA-100

Volunteer Gap: Two stories circulate about Volunteer Gap's name. One owes the "volunteer" to men who joined the Confederate Army and traveled across the Blue Ridge here, while another says residents volunteered to put a road here. Southeastern: VA-670 at VA-608, near Blue Ridge Parkway

Wolf Glade: Commonly called "Gladeville," the Wolf Glade community is bordered by two creeks named for glades of cranberries that once grew in abundance across Carroll County. West-central: VA-635 at VA-887

CITY OF GALAX

Snuggled between Grayson and Carroll counties, the City of Galax is an industrial center noted for its furniture factories, though the municipality began as a real-estate venture by a group of local businessmen. By the end of 1903, this group had persuaded Norfolk & Western Railway officials to extend its line to the new settlement, then called "Bonaparte." In 1906, Galax was incorporated as a town, named for the Galax plant, a mountain evergreen that grows locally. Galax is used in floral arrangements and was among the first rail cargo to be shipped from here in 1904.

The railroad lines that brought prosperity to Galax have since become the multiuse New River Trail State Park. A red caboose in the heart of Galax marks its southern terminus, about 10 miles west of I-77 Exit 14, on US-58/221. From a parking area near VA-89, the trail enters woods and winds north along Chestnut Creek. It eventually goes to Austinville, Foster Falls, and Pulaski.

Galax calls itself the "World's Capital of Old-Time Mountain Music," namely for its Old Fiddlers Convention, established in 1935. The festival crowds the 28-acre Felts Park on Main Street during the second week of August. The event attracts thousands to the park's 3,000-seat amphitheater and still more to the festival's camping area, where musicians and dancers sometimes perform impromptu shows while practicing. On Fridays, the Galax Downtown Association offers more music, sponsoring "Blue Ridge Backroads," a series featuring bluegrass and old-time Appalachian musicians performing for live radio broadcasts on WBRF-FM (98.1). The shows take place at the 450-seat Rex Theatre, 113 Grayson St.

An independent city since 1954, Galax was home to about 6,800 residents in 2000.

Galax, the World's Capital of Old-Time Mountain Music

What's to See

Jeff Matthews Memorial Museum: The Jeff Matthews Memorial Museum, 606 W. Stuart Dr., is named for a Galax hardware-store owner whose 10,000-piece collection of Native American relics forms the cornerstone of exhibits. The 8,000-square-foot museum includes displays of an old-time general store and an early dentist's office, plus photos and biographies of Virginia's Civil War generals.

Just inside the front door waits an almost intimidating collection of big-game trophies, donated by local resident Glenn Pless. These stuffed heads and skins of various North American animals still seem capable of roaring. Outside are pioneer cabins, built in the mid-1800s and moved to the museum grounds from a nearby site on the New River.

Rooftop of Virginia Craft Shop: Open since 1967, the Rooftop of Virginia Craft Shop, 206 N. Main St., is a consignment shop housed in a stately brick church building. A variety of locally made pottery, carvings, and quilts are sold. The shop is a project of the Rooftop of Virginia Community Action Program, formed in 1965 to help low-income residents.

Cabin at Jeff Matthews Memorial Museum

GRAYSON COUNTY

William Grayson, one of Virginia's first two U.S. senators, is remembered in the name of Grayson County, a 446-square-mile, triangular region along the North Carolina line. Established in 1792 from Wythe County, Grayson County was not organized until 1793, the date claimed on the county seal. About a half century later, the area was torn in two with the creation of Carroll County. Thousands of acres of evergreens in the Mount Rogers National Recreation Area dominate Grayson County's northern border.

BAYWOOD

In southeastern Grayson County, Baywood lies at the crossroads of VA-624 and VA-626. Once called "Hampton Cross Roads" or "Hampton Valley" for circa-1830 settlers Griggs and Phyllis Sutherland Hampton, local tradition says that in the late 1800s resident Arch Moore renamed the community "Baywood," for the bay tree. On the first Saturday of each October, the community hosts a fall festival.

What's to See

New River Access: A public boat landing at Baywood leads to a quiet stretch of the New River below the US-58/221 bridge. A float downstream from here includes a few Class I-II rapids before reaching another public access eight miles downstream at Riverside, on the left bank.

🚗 The river access road is immediately east of the US-58/221 bridge, two miles west of Baywood, or about six miles east of Independence.

BRIDLE CREEK

A folk story says an early settler found his bridle on the banks of Bridle Creek, after following the trail of a thief who had stolen his horse, which ultimately turned up on Horse Creek in Ashe County, North Carolina.

A Bridle Creek post office operated for about a century, until 1950, near the crossroads of VA-601 and US-58 in south-central Grayson County. A fall festival is held at Bridle Creek on the third Saturday of each October.

COMERS ROCK

One theory on Comers Rock's name says that a trapper named Comer once lived in a cabin near this mountaintop rock. Another story says the rock was simply named for the many Comers who settled in north-central Grayson County.

The community of Comers Rock is at the crossroads of VA-658 and VA-672, about two miles southwest of the actual rock called "Comers." A Comers Rock post office was open until 1962.

What's to See

Comers Rock Recreation Area and *Hale Lake:* Ah, the view: that's what makes Comers Rock such a jewel. But don't tell everybody; let this jewel remain hidden. Comers Rock sits on the Grayson-Wythe county line at an ear-popping 4,102-foot elevation. Here, wooden rails mark the site of a long-gone lookout tower built circa 1928 atop the Comers Rock outcrop.

The lookout is a half mile from the Comers Rock Recreation Area, a primitive campground and picnic site. It is among the least used facilities in the Mount Rogers National Recreation Area. What you can see here, however, rivals what people fight crowds to find in the Great Smoky Mountains of Tennessee or Virginia's Shenandoah Valley.

To the north, Comers Rock overlooks the tree-topped mountains of Wythe County, folded in chunky waves on the endless horizon. It's just as unforgettable but very different looking south; pockets of green curves appear in Elk Creek's bowl between Buck Mountain, Point Lookout Mountain, and the Iron Mountains of central Grayson County.

About two miles west of the Comers Rock Recreation Area is Hale Lake, a five-acre fishing hole where minnows and tadpoles feed along forested banks. A half-mile-long loop trail encircles the lake, which is sometimes stocked with trout.

🚗 From US-58 in Independence, follow US-21 north for about 14 miles. Turn left on USFS-57 (Hales Lake Rd.) at the Grayson-Wythe county line and head west for 3.6 miles to the campground. Continue west for a quarter mile to the Comers Rock Overlook road on the right. The overlook road leads a quarter mile

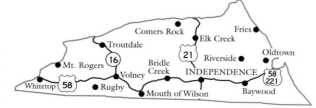

Overlooking Wythe County from Comers Rock

But first: the name of this old factory town has nothing to do with what you order with a hamburger. The name—pronounced like *freeze*—originated from Col. Francis Henry Fries, who came here from North Carolina and built a 39-foot-high rock dam across the New River in 1902-1903. Below the dam, the water is low and rocky. Above the dam, the river looks like a little lake. Col. Fries used the dam to power a textile mill, housed in a large brick building on the riverbank. The mill, in operation until the late 1980s, made Fries a busy railroad stop—a place where cotton arrived raw and was transformed into cloth.

Incorporated in 1902, Fries is situated along VA-94, about a mile southwest of the Carroll County line. In 2000, the town was home to about 600 residents.

A historical marker at the center of town notes Fries's place in the embryonic years of country music. Fries is the hometown of Henry Whitter, a fiddler who went to New York City in March 1923 to record two songs, "The Wreck on the Southern Old 97" and "Lonesome Road Blues."

Whitter's efforts inspired another local musician, Ernest V. "Pop" Stoneman, who heard Whitter's music and figured he could do just as well. Stoneman sought his own recording career in 1924 and had released records by 1925. Whitter's and Stoneman's talent lured a scout to Bristol, Tennessee, in 1927, but their efforts—and ultimately their credit in giving birth to country music—would be overshadowed by the discovery at the Bristol sessions of star acts Jimmie Rodgers and The Carter Family.

Still, in Fries, old-time mountain music like Whitter's remains alive. Here, on the third weekend of each August, the Fries Volunteer Fire Department holds the Fries Fiddlers Convention.

uphill to a circular driveway, where stone steps reach the overlook platform within a few yards. To find Hale Lake, follow USFS-57 1.5 miles west of the overlook road to a gravel parking lot on the left.

Alternate Route: From VA-658 (Comers Rock Rd.) at the Comers Rock community, follow VA-672 (Blue Spring Rd.) north for 2.3 miles. Turn right on USFS-57 and follow east, reaching Hale Lake in a half mile, the overlook road at two miles, and the campground at 2.2 miles.

ELK CREEK

Two communities, Elk Creek and Lower Elk Creek, lie along a New River tributary called Elk Creek. This stream flows beside VA-660, between the Iron Mountains and Point Lookout Mountain, in north-central Grayson County.

The name likely originates from the wild elk that once inhabited the region. Still, one account specifically targets famed hunter James Burk. According to what may be a tall tale, Burk chose to name this stream "Elk Creek" because he began chasing an elk here that later led him up and down mountains to finally reach Burke's Garden, several miles north in Tazewell County, in about 1748.

Along a straight stretch of US-21, large farms dominate the wide meadows of the Elk Creek community. Here, on the last full weekend in June, look for the Grayson County Fiddlers Convention at Elk Creek School, off VA-658.

FRIES

In Fries, an entrance sign brags that the river-hugging town is "Where The Trail Begins," in reference to the New River Trail State Park. And, yes, one part of the trail does begin at a red caboose here in northeastern Grayson County, just as much as it starts in nearby Galax or, more than 40 miles north, at Dora Junction, on the outskirts of Pulaski.

This sign welcomes visitors to Fries.

What's to See

New River Access: A major access to the New River Trail State Park originates in Fries at Trail Mile 45.3. Near the trailhead is a public access on the river's rocky, rippling waters. Passing a few rapids, the New River runs seven miles from Fries to a ramp at the Byllesby Reservoir, on the right bank, near Riverhill in Carroll County.

Beware of water rising rapidly at the Fries Dam, immediately upstream from the Fries landing.

🚗 From US-21 in Independence, follow US-58/221 east for 2.5 miles. Turn left on VA-274 and follow for 7.5 miles. Turn left on VA-94 and follow for five miles into Fries. Pass the Fries Dam and bear right on West Main Street when entering town. Turn right on Riverview Avenue and follow to the river access at a small town park near the Fire House Drive intersection.

INDEPENDENCE

Since the early 1980s, the people of Independence have been doing a funny thing—they put outhouses on wheels and roll them down public streets during the town's Grand Privy Race. The outhouse outings gather a lot of attention as the centerpiece of the town's Mountain Foliage Festival, held on the second Saturday of each October.

Most other times, though, Independence simply sits quiet at the crossroads of US-21 and US-58/221 in south-central Grayson County. Incorporated in 1934, in 2000 this county seat was home to nearly 1,000 residents, about a dozen stores, and not one but two courthouses, representing architecture from both the beginning and the end of the 20th century.

Grayson County's red-brick 1908 courthouse—a commanding presence—stands at 107 E. Main St. The building rises from a neatly trimmed lawn, and conical towers at its four corners point to the sky. It was listed on both state and national landmark registers in the late 1970s. Still, this majestic building once faced the wrecking ball, just after the 1979-1981 construction of the modern Grayson County Courthouse on nearby Davis Street.

Residents vehemently objected to tearing down the old courthouse. The county government, in response, put the building on the auction block. A local businessman, Dan Baldwin, bought it for $110,000 and then donated it to a nonprofit foundation. The old courthouse later became a community center, and a former courtroom was converted into a 200-seat auditorium bearing Baldwin's name.

Inside, courthouse halls display historic photographs, The Vault Museum exhibits early mountain life, and The Treasury sells locally made arts and crafts. Outside, the courthouse's front lawn includes a 25-foot marble monument of an infantryman at

1908 Grayson County Courthouse in Independence

parade rest, constructed in 1911 to honor local Confederate soldiers. The courthouse lawn, at the town's main junction, is usually quiet.

The Independence area's quiet nature is what inspired its name. Rewind to 1850. Back then, people were at odds on where the county seat should be after Carroll County's formation had wiped away Grayson County's eastern half. One group wanted the courthouse to remain where it was, at Oldtown. Another band lobbied to move the seat to Elk Creek. Residents in the county's southern area, meanwhile, said they wanted to remain independent and refused to take sides.

The final decision came on the advice of three commissioners from adjacent counties. This panel suggested that the courthouse should be located on a site centering Grayson County—what is now Independence, a town named for the quiet, independent group.

What's to See

Grayson County Recreation Park and *Peach Bottom Falls:* Wooded areas for picnics and hikes outline the Grayson County Recreation Park, a site with ball fields, tennis courts, and a paved walking track.

Nearby is a cataract known as either "Power House Falls" or "Peach Bottom Falls." An S-shaped slide down a rock raceway with several drops and cascades, the falls descend 100 feet on Peach Bottom Creek. In the early 1900s, Garnett Davis used this waterfall to power a mill at a structure known as the "Power House," which also provided some electricity to the Town of Independence. Prior to Davis, Matthew Dickey operated an iron furnace here. Located on private property, the falls are a drive-by attraction but can be viewed from the road (just barely) when trees are missing leaves.

🚗 From US-21 in Independence, follow US-58/221 east for nearly a mile. Turn left on Rt. 1124 (Morton Dr.) and follow for nearly a half mile. Turn right on VA-685 (Powerhouse Rd.)

and follow for 0.7 miles. The park is on the right at Rt. 1135 (County Park Ln.). Continue east on VA-685 for 0.2 miles to see the falls on the left, near a bridge.

New River Access: From the mouth of Bridle Creek to the Independence boat landing near the US-21/221 bridge, the New River extends 10 miles on a particularly rocky stretch, with Class II-III rapids, lots of ledges, and a five-mile detour through Alleghany County, North Carolina. Continuing downstream from Independence, the next 12 miles roll over a few Class I-II rapids in southern Grayson County. Then, after another detour through Alleghany County, the canoe trail reaches the Baywood landing, on the right.

From US-21 in Independence, follow US-58 west for 2.5 miles. Turn left on VA-711 (Battlefield Dr.) and follow south for four miles to the Bridle Creek landing, on the left, immediately beyond the VA-601 (Cox's Chapel Rd.) intersection.

To reach the Independence landing from US-58 in Independence, head south on US-21/221 for three miles. Turn right on VA-701 (Old River Ln.). After 0.7 miles, VA-701 approaches the river and becomes VA-700. Continue for a half mile to the landing, on the right.

MOUNT ROGERS

Mount Rogers is named for William Barton Rogers, a 19th-century scientist who initiated the first comprehensive study of Virginia's geology. The 5,729-foot peak was earlier called "Balsam Mountain" for its native balsam firs. Hikers on the Appalachian Trail can reach the mile-high mountain from either Elk Garden on the west or Grayson Highlands State Park on the east. It's about a four-mile walk, either way, to the half-mile trail that ascends the summit.

A spruce-fir forest fragrantly marks the crest of Mount Rogers, the highest point in Virginia. Consistently moist and often covered with clouds, the environment here resembles a rainforest. Green moss drapes almost every rock and limb, and the woods are so quiet that even a finger snap will produce an echo. But the trees are also so thick that the summit lacks any kind of scenic view.

MOUTH OF WILSON

In central Grayson County, near the junction of US-58 and VA-16-South, Mouth of Wilson is a community named for the point where Big Wilson Creek empties into the New River. The creek's name is derived from a surveyor named Wilson, a member of Peter Jefferson's 1749 surveying party along the North Carolina-Virginia line. Mr. Wilson died from a stomach disorder and was buried near this creek, named for him by other surveyors.

What's to See

New River Access: A public access at Mouth of Wilson leads to a lazy stretch of the New River where you can fish for smallmouth bass. But boat trips are short; within a mile, this section stops at a dangerous fall over the Fields Dam, a 13-foot-high barrier constructed in the late 1920s by Fields Electric to provide power to a local woolen mill and the Mouth of Wilson community.

From VA-16-South at Mouth of Wilson, follow US-58 east for one mile. The river access road is on the right, immediately beyond a junction with VA-93 (County Line Rd.).

OLDTOWN

Established as the seat of Grayson County in the late 1790s, the county's first official courthouse stood at Oldtown in the days when Grayson and Carroll counties were one. For years, the area was known as Greenville, though mail was addressed to "Grayson Court House." After the creation of Carroll County in 1842 and the eventual establishment of a more centrally located courthouse at Independence in 1850, this neighborhood in eastern Grayson County adopted a new name—"Old Grayson Court House," later changed to "Old Town."

County business was conducted for nearly two decades in Oldtown's Old Grayson County Courthouse. The circa-1830s brick structure stands among rolling farmland at Oldtown's main

Rock outcrops in the woods at the 5,729-foot Mount Rogers, Virginia's highest point

Old Grayson County Courthouse at Oldtown, now a private residence

junction, where VA-634 (Justice Rd.) meets VA-640 (Greenville Rd.). Four chimneys sprout from the two-story courthouse. The building was restored as a private residence in the late 1980s and is listed on both state and national historic registers.

What's to See

New River Access: From the public access at Oldtown, the New River runs past small islands and Class I rapids for about three miles before it reaches the dangerous Fries Dam, a 39-foot drop that must be portaged on the left bank, at a public wayside. Fishing here includes bluegill and largemouth bass.

🚗 From US-21 in Independence, follow US-58/221 east for about 11 miles. Turn left on VA-94, then immediately turn right on VA-882 (Nuckolls Curve Rd.) and follow for 0.2 miles. Turn left on VA-634 (Justice Rd.) and follow north for one mile to the Oldtown community. Turn right on VA-640 (Greenville Rd.) and follow for 0.1 miles through Oldtown. Turn left on VA-634 (Water Wheel Rd.) and follow north for about 1.3 miles. Turn left on VA-641 (Pattons Mill Ln.) and follow for 1.5 miles to the river access road, on the left.

RIVERSIDE

The Riverside area of eastern Grayson County is simply that—at the side of the New River, near the crossroads of VA-94 and VA-274.

What's to See

New River Access: The New River is wide and grassy and includes a few islands downstream from a public boat landing and fishing area at Riverside. Six miles of quiet waters stretch from here to another landing at Oldtown, on the right bank, about two miles beyond a bridge on VA-94.

🚗 From US-21 in Independence, follow US-58/221 east for 2.5 miles. Turn left on VA-274 and follow for 7.5 miles to the river access road on the right, just before reaching the VA-94 and VA-274 intersection.

RUGBY

Rugby was once known as "Greers," probably for the first postmaster here, Edwin Greer, whose service began in 1879. The area's rugged mountain scenery is believed to be—at least partially—the inspiration for the name "Rugby." Near the crossroads of VA-725 and VA-743, a post office at Rugby was open until 1965.

What's to See

Grayson Highlands State Park: East Coast residents could visit Grayson Highlands State Park to save money and miles on a venture to the Rocky Mountains. The reason? The rock-topped mountains of this 4,935-acre park resemble the Rockies. A Canadian-style forest and windswept balds highlight vistas free from the visual pollution of city lights, strip mines, trains, or highways. Not to mention that it's cool, too. A hot day here is 85 degrees with low humidity, and breezes never seem to end atop the countless craggy outcrops.

The park's well-maintained trails follow old railroad beds used in the early 1900s to extract virgin timber. One old logging line is now the Rhododendron Trail. The trail starts at Massie Gap, a place named for Lee Massey, an early settler who unfortunately could not get his name spelled correctly by mapmakers in the late 1800s. The Rhododendron Trail exits the park to meet the Appalachian Trail. Along its way, grassy slopes are freckled with evergreens and wildflowers, plus the bright bloom of rhododendron in mid-June.

Watch for wild ponies running among the rocks here and in the adjacent Mount Rogers National Recreation Area. A little more than 100 ponies live at this heaven on the high plains. The late Bill Pugh, a horse breeder from nearby Smyth County, released a small herd to graze on the high country's open balds in 1974, around the time the original name, "Mount Rogers State Park," was changed to "Grayson Highlands."

Over the years, the ponies did well, feeding on wild grasses. They are known to greet trail hikers with friendly nibbles on shirts or camera bags. But resist the urge to pack an extra apple—the official line from park officials is to not feed the animals.

Once a year, the Wilburn Ridge Pony Association, a volunteer group, rounds up ponies for sale at auction during the Grayson Highlands Fall Festival. The ponies fetch $100 to $500 apiece, and the money raised pays for the veterinary care of the remaining herd. The fall festival is held on the last full weekend of September; a typical Southwest Virginia celebration, making apple butter takes center stage, while mountain music sweetens the air.

Away from Massie Gap, the park's 1.9-mile Cabin Creek Trail slips into dark, moist woods. The path passes a 25-foot-high waterfall rushing down a rock wall and swirling into a clear pool. Flat boulders face the falls and provide a natural point for picnics. Several yards farther on the Cabin Creek Trail, the path makes a wide swath to the right, and a sign points the way to another waterfall. But this cataract tumbles 50 feet through a mish-mash of stones that clog most views of the water flow.

Cabin Creek, by the way, is named for a cabin that once straddled the stream.

Big Pinnacle overlooks Massie Gap at Grayson Highlands State Park

On the opposite side of the park, the 1.8-mile Wilson Creek Trail starts at the campground entrance and scurries through a shady forest for nearly a mile before reaching Wilson Creek's series of falls and cascades. The stream's steady tumble provides a great stage for debating ways to categorize waterfalls. One fast flume drops 25 feet. A wide cascade slides for about 30 feet on solid rock. Others are airborne for just a few feet.

Trail maps are available at the park's gated entrance, off VA-362, or at its interpretive center, planted high atop Haw Orchard Mountain. The center, about four miles north of the park entrance, includes a consignment crafts shop and exhibits of early mountain life.

The interpretive center's back door leads to the Twin Pinnacles Trail, an easy-to-moderate, 1.6-mile loop through a spruce-fir forest. On this trail, the Little Pinnacle faces a sweeping blend of North Carolina peaks. An airplane-style view can also be found at the jagged folds of the house-size Big Pinnacle, a second jewel crowning the 5,089-foot Haw Orchard Mountain. Kids of all ages love to follow the Big Pinnacle's tough 500-foot spur off the main trail. They climb the rock outcrop and shout far below to the people at Massie Gap, just to hear the echo.

Grayson Highlands State Park amenities include a large campground, picnic shelters, overnight horse stables, and a country store selling basic camping supplies. An entry fee is charged per vehicle at the main gate, off US-58 about halfway between Whitetop and Mouth of Wilson.

🚗 From the crossroads of VA-16 and US-58 at Volney, follow US-58 west for about eight miles to the park entrance, on the right, at VA-362.

TROUTDALE   A sign in Troutdale once touted the town's population at 248, its elevation at 3,300 feet, and its motto—"Highest Incorporated Town in Virginia." Sounds a

Grayson Highlands State Park merges into the Mount Rogers National Recreation Area with little distinction, at an elevation nearly one mile high

Cabin Creek Falls at Grayson Highlands State Park

boundaries extend one mile in all directions from Troutdale's center, forming a perfect circle.

What's to See

Fox Creek Falls: In a corner of the Mount Rogers National Recreation Area, Fox Creek bubbles through pools of clear water stocked with trout. The mountain stream sounds like thundering applause where it flumes for 10 feet through a well-chiseled chute of bedrock. After landing in a quiet pool, the creek almost immediately forms whitewater again at Fox Creek Falls, a 15-foot-high cascade. The falls can be seen, just barely, from the Mount Rogers Scenic Byway (VA-603).

🚗 From VA-16 (Troutdale Hwy.) at Troutdale, go west on VA-603 (Fairwood Rd.) for 1.7 miles. The falls are on the right. Look for an informal trail at a small parking area.

Ripshin: In 1925, Sherwood Anderson discovered the cool climate of Troutdale when heading north to escape the New Orleans heat. A year later, the nationally acclaimed writer from Camden, Ohio, built a stone-and-log home called "Ripshin" on the outskirts of Troutdale. Until his death in 1941, Anderson split his time between Ripshin and his wife's home in Marion (see the Smyth County chapter of the Holston Valley section). Ripshin was named for a nearby creek and is listed on both state and national historic registers. The privately owned house is a drive-by attraction.

🚗 From VA-16 at the main Troutdale crossroads, follow VA-603 (Ripshin Rd.) east for 2.4 miles. Turn right on VA-732 (Laurel Creek Rd.) and follow for about 0.1 miles to Ripshin. The house is immediately on the left past a small bridge. Anderson's small writing cabin is nestled in the woods off VA-732, opposite the main house, near the VA-603 crossroads.

WHITETOP

Whitetop Mountain stands tall above a tight-knit community settled at its southern edge. Long a place of isolation, in the mid-1800s this village was called "White Top," the name on its original post office. By the early 1900s, "Whitetop" was spelled as one word, though the area was known as "Whitetop City" in the 1920s, when it was a center for huge lumber operations. The Whitetop Train Station, at 3,576 feet above sea level, became famous as the highest area served by passenger trains east of the Mississippi River.

Lumber operations spelled success through the 1930s, but decades passed before Whitetop's next chapter of prosperity began. In the 1970s, Christmas-tree production became a way of

little like Bluefield's claim as "Virginia's Tallest Town." Yet a promotional brochure offers a clarification: "Troutdale claims the highest elevation [about 3,200 feet downtown and 4,016 on the northern edge] and the smallest population [about 276] of any incorporated town in Virginia."

As a town, Troutdale dates to 1906, though its first post office opened in 1882. The valley, or "dale," was named for the abundance of trout in nearby Fox Creek. Troutdale grew as a lumbering center at the crossroads of VA-16 and VA-603 in western Grayson County. In 1920, the town's 2,800 residents supported hotels, a theater, a furniture factory, the Bank of Troutdale, and even the town's own newspaper. But the lumber boom fell just like the timber, especially after the blight that decimated the American chestnut tree in the 1930s. In 1934, the railroad tracks leading here were removed.

Decades later, with all the sawdust settled, Troutdale had evolved into a residential and retirement community near the Mount Rogers National Recreation Area. Curiously, town

life in Whitetop. Such roots stem from the 1960s, when local farmer Byron Sexton experimented with seedling transplants, and local resident George West pulled evergreens off Mount Rogers to sell as Christmas trees. Growing and harvesting trees for decorative purposes later became Grayson County's largest industry. Almost everywhere, neatly spaced rows of evergreens line the roadsides at Whitetop. The Christmas-tree farms make it look and smell like Yuletide never ends.

Local farmers specialize in growing the Fraser fir, considered a "Cadillac" for its long life and high dollar value. Frasers are similar to the Balsam fir, which grow naturally atop Whitetop Mountain, the community's fabled landmark.

Whitetop Mountain—where the boundaries of Washington, Smyth, and Grayson counties merge a mile high—is named for the summit's vast field of light colored grass, which makes the mountain look snow covered at a distance. This field also inspired the peak's original name, "Meadow Mountain."

In the Whitetop community, an annual maple-syrup festival attracts crowds of about 6,000 and signals spring's arrival. The festival began as a way to celebrate the local tradition of tapping trees to make syrup from boiled sugar water. Always on the last weekend in March, the festivities serve as a "welcome back" to visitors who come here each summer to escape city heat but won't brave mountain roads when winter ice slicks switchbacks.

Festival tours include a trip along VA-754 to the community's Sugar House, built in 1975 to bottle syrup and molasses to raise funds at festivals supporting the Mount Rogers Volunteer Fire Department. Tours also stop at nearby Elk Garden for tree-tapping demonstrations at Whitetop's maple orchard.

Not all of the festival's syrup is made at Whitetop. In the late 1990s, organizers struggled to find volunteers to tap trees and work in the Sugar House. To subsidize demand, syrup was imported from Vermont. But the crowds don't seem to care—they just keep coming back to the mountain.

Visitors are clearly in love with the syrup festival and the one that follows on the third Sunday of May. The May event celebrates the ramp, a wild lily that blooms in spring at Whitetop and other places with altitudes above 3,000 feet. Old-timers used to say that eating a batch of ramps in spring would purify your blood. But the onion-like plant stains your breath with such an odor that even your grandmother won't kiss you. Even so, Whitetop folks make a big, funny deal out of the ramp. Each year, a contest is held to see who can eat the most, and prizes include cash and a bottle of mouthwash.

One more time, for one more festival, the community unites to serve molasses at the Mount Rogers Volunteer Fire Department on the second Sunday in October, just as the local leaves stage a grand show for autumn.

And what a colorful show this mountain makes.

What's to See

Whitetop Mountain: Virginia's highest navigable road ascends Whitetop Mountain, unfolding breathtaking views of North Carolina on a true skyline drive. The gravel forest road makes wide-swinging switchbacks at the meadow atop the 5,520-foot summit. One spur leads to a circular drive, and another ends at a set of radio towers. Car radios, incidentally, seem otherworldly up here, able to pick up stations that broadcast from all over the Carolinas, Virginia, and Tennessee.

A gated road about 300 yards below the radio towers leads to a secluded outcrop. To find the feature, walk past the gate for 150 yards, then turn right on the Lovers Leap Trail, which marches 75 yards downhill to a large rock overlooking Virginia's Holston Valley.

Whitetop Mountain is part of the Mount Rogers National Recreation Area. The Appalachian Trail crosses the peak.

🚗 From Volney, at the crossroads of VA-16 and US-58, follow US-58 west for about 17 miles to the Whitetop Post Office on US-58. Turn right on VA-600 and head north for 1.5 miles. Turn left on USFS-89. Follow for about three miles to reach the top of the mountain.

Whitetop Station: The original Whitetop Train Station stood at Whitetop from about 1912, when rail service arrived, until

Looking out from mile-high Whitetop Mountain

Whitetop Station, a replica of a train depot, greets users of the Virginia Creeper Trail

trains stopped running here in 1977. In 2000, U.S. Forest Service officials built a replica of the Whitetop station as an interpretive center. The $350,000 project complemented the Virginia Creeper Trail, an increasingly popular 34-mile recreation path on a former rail line, leading downhill from Whitetop to the western trailhead at Abingdon (see the Washington County chapter of the Holston Valley section). Painted blinding white with green trim, Whitetop's 1,500-square-foot station—usually staffed April to October—includes a souvenir shop and displays of Whitetop's rail history.

🚗 From Volney, at the crossroads of VA-16 and US-58, follow US-58 west for about 18 miles to the Mount Rogers Volunteer Fire Department. Turn left on VA-755 and follow south for 1.7 miles to the Virginia Creeper Trail crossing. Turn left on VA-726. The station is immediately on the left.

WILBURN RIDGE

On the southeast side of Mount Rogers, rocky Wilburn Ridge lies along the Appalachian Trail, near Grayson Highlands State Park. Here, at an elevation of about 5,000 feet, tree growth is dwarfed by strong winds, and rocks are composed of residual rhyolite, evidence of ancient volcanic activity.

The ridge is the namesake of Wilburn Waters, a famed 19th-century hunter of Indian and French Huguenot lineage. Waters came to the Mount Rogers area from Wilkes County, North Carolina, after hearing that the area overflowed with game. He became a local folk hero. One story about Waters claims that after he attacked a wounded buck, he saved himself by wrestling with it; another says Waters once followed the trail of a 400-pound bear and killed it in deep snow on Pond Mountain; and still another relates that Waters once captured an enormous wolf, tied it up, and attempted to take it home alive.

Wilburn Ridge, a rocky summit in Grayson County

Carsonville: James Carson became the first post-master at Carsonville circa 1857. Eastern: VA-694 at VA-695

Cox's Chapel: The Cox's Chapel community originated in 1832 with the founding of a chapel named for the descendants of Lt. David Cox. This Revolutionary War veteran settled in the area in the late 1700s. South-central: VA-601 at VA-708

Delhart: When Arthur Hampton built a store in Grayson County, he changed the name of what had been called "Rector's Crossroads," for brothers Isom and Fielden Rector, to "Dalhart." This new name honored a Texas town where Hampton once lived. Dalhart, Tex., was named for a combination of the counties—Dallam and Hartley—where the town is located. A post office at Grayson County's Dalhart was open from 1904 to 1911. But, somehow, the name has now evolved into "Delhart." Southeastern: VA-622 at VA-624

Elk Garden: The name "Elk Garden" originated from the wild elk once roaming the area. About four miles northeast along the Appalachian Trail, a spur ascends Mount Rogers, Virginia's highest peak. The unpopulated Elk Garden, boasting an elevation of 4,500 feet, lies within the Mount Rogers National Recreation Area. Southwestern: VA-600 at Appalachian Trail, near Smyth County

Fairwood: Two miles west of Troutdale, Fairwood began as an early 20th-century lumbering town, likely named for wood harvested along Fox Creek. The town's timber harvests were exhausted by the 1930s, and the place evolved into a cattle-farming community, nestled at the foot of Pine Mountain. Fairwood is now simply a destination for hikers and horseback riders as part of the Mount Rogers National Recreation Area. Western: VA-603 at USFS-613 (Pine Mountain Rd.)

Fallville: On the southern edge of the Iron Mountains, the small falls on Elk Creek's Knob Fork could be the source of the name "Fallville." A Fallville post office was open circa 1900. Northeastern: VA-805 (Spring Valley Rd.) at VA-891 (Fallville Rd.)

Flat Ridge: A flat area surrounded by a ridge naturally inspired the name "Flat Ridge." A post office operated here from the 1870s to 1958. Central: VA-601 at VA-675

Fox: Stocked with trout, Fox Creek begins on Hurricane Mountain at the Grayson-Smyth county border. It runs east to the New River and passes near the Fox community. Like the creek, Fox takes its name from a legend concerning an early hunter who lost track of a fox while chasing it toward the creek. Western: US-58 at VA-711

Gold Hill: Capt. Melville Cox once operated a small gold mine near the site of the Gold Hill Baptist Church. But getting the gold to a market at Marion, in Smyth County, required a seven-day journey with a wagon. Ultimately, Cox decided his gold was not worth the expense of mining. The mine was later used as a dump by the agricultural community's one-room school. Southern: VA-681, south of US-58

Grant: One story says a resident wanted to call the Grant post office "High Meadows." But postal officials in post-Civil War Washington, D.C., objected to that name. They said that a post office could be opened at this location only if it was called "Grant," presumably to honor Ulysses S. Grant, commander of the Union forces during the Civil War and president of the United States from 1869 to 1877. Western: VA-730 at VA-16

Longs Gap: William Long, Sr., moved to Longs Gap in about 1790 and established a general store and gristmill on his extensive landholdings. Central: US-21 at VA-611

Low Gap: One story credits the name "Low Gap" to a low-elevation mountain gap in the Blue Ridge. Southeastern: VA-89 at Blue Ridge Parkway

Peach Bottom: Early settlers' peach orchards inspired the name "Peach Bottom." A Peach Bottom post office existed here, though not continuously, from about 1844 to 1939. Southeastern: VA-628 at VA-629

Potato Creek: Tradition says famed hunter James Burk carried potatoes wherever he went, and his visit to an area called "Potato Creek" must have been no exception. Early settlers allegedly found potatoes floating in a creek here and assumed Burk had something to do with it. South-central: VA-708 (Potato Creek Rd.), south of New River, near Alleghany County, N.C.

Providence: Methodists constructed the first Providence Chapel in this neighborhood circa 1837. A more modern church at Providence was built in 1886. Eastern: VA-94 at VA-867

Reavistown: Two Reavis brothers, John and Sandy, came to the Reavistown area in about 1852 and developed a blacksmith shop and a gristmill. Eastern: VA-94 at US-58/221

Roberts Cove: Stories say that William Roberts fell ill on a hunting trip, probably in the 1780s, and was left behind at a place where he decided to settle. Ultimately, that area became "Roberts Cove" for Roberts and his sons, who were among the region's first residents. Central: VA-672 at VA-674, south of Brushy Ridge

Saddle Creek: Local tradition says an early settler followed the trail of a horse thief and found his horse's saddle on the banks of Saddle Creek, near what became the Saddle Creek community. Central: VA-682 at VA-683

Scales: In the early 1900s, farmers grazed their cattle in meadows and weighed them on a set of scales inside what is now the Mount Rogers National Recreation Area. This scenic spot, called "Scales," is popular among primitive campers and horseback riders. Western: USFS-613 (Pine Mountain Rd.) at the Appalachian Trail

Spring Valley: Settled as early as 1765, Spring Valley was named for its many springs. In 1793, Grayson County's first court met in this vicinity at a barn belonging to William Bourne. Northeastern: VA-777 at VA-805

Volney: In about 1894, Elijah Hash helped establish a post office between Whitetop and Mouth of Wilson, and then he named it for his son Volney. Southern: US-58 at VA-16-North

WYTHE COUNTY

Formed in 1789 from a part of Montgomery County, Wythe County was organized in 1790 and named for George Wythe, a Williamsburg lawyer and signer of the Declaration of Independence. The county is centered by Wytheville, a courthouse town nicknamed "The Hub of Southwest Virginia." Such a moniker could also fit Wythe County. It spans 464 square miles where Southwest Virginia's two interstate highways meet, overlap, and split like an odd-shaped X at the center of Southwest Virginia's Central Highlands.

AUSTINVILLE

Austinville was known simply as "Lead Mines" when its natural resources provided lead for patriots during the Revolutionary War. From 1772 to 1776, Lead Mines served as the courthouse town of Virginia's now defunct Fincastle County, which once included all of Southwest Virginia and Eastern Kentucky.

The name "Fincastle" comes from Lord Fincastle, the eldest son of Lord Dunmore, royal governor of Virginia. Fincastle County ceased to exist in 1776 with the creation of Montgomery and Washington counties as well as the County of Kentucky, now the Commonwealth of Kentucky.

A granite monument marks the site of the Austinville area's first lead mines and also the site of the old Fincastle County Courthouse. The stone monument stands off VA-619 (Austinville Rd.), about 0.1 miles southeast of an intersection with VA-631 (Walton Furnace Rd.). Here, in southeastern Wythe County, the Committee of Safety of Fincastle County drafted a forerunner of the Declaration of Independence—the Fincastle Resolutions—on January 20, 1775. The resolutions stated local grievances against the British government and boldly declared citizens' determination to never surrender their rights and privileges granted to them as Virginians.

Sometime after 1789, Austinville took its present name from the family of Moses Austin, who operated the Austinville lead mines for a few years. Stephen Austin (1793-1836), a son of Moses, was born here. As an adult, he became a political leader and a Texas pioneer. Stephen Austin commanded Texas military forces in the Texas Revolution, and his own name is honored at Austin, the Texas capital.

Three flags—representing Virginia, the United States, and Texas—fly on poles at the Stephen F. Austin Memorial Park. This small green space near Austinville's

main crossroads of VA-69 and VA-636 honors Austin—"The Father of Texas"—with a nine-foot-high granite monument.

What's to See

New River Access: For a scenic 3.5-mile trip, go downstream on the New River from a paved boat ramp at Austinville to a landing at Foster Falls, headquarters for the New River Trail State Park. The water is flat as the river runs through Austinville, but rapids crop up between the mouth of Galena Creek and the I-77 bridge.

🚗 From I-77 Exit 24, follow VA-69 west for 3.9 miles. The river access road is on the right, just beyond the New River Trail State Park and the Stephen F. Austin Memorial Park.

Alternate Route: From I-81 Exit 80, follow US-52 south for 5.2 miles. Turn right on VA-619 (Austinville Rd.) and follow for 2.5 miles. Turn left on VA-636 (Store Hill Rd.) and follow for 0.2 miles. The river access is on the left, just beyond the New River bridge.

CRIPPLE CREEK

Cripple Creek's heritage comes alive on the fourth Saturday of each May during the town's Homecoming Celebration Day. The party partly remembers when Cripple Creek was a center of iron-ore mining, circa 1900, a time when its population swelled to about 1,500. A century later, the south-central Wythe County neighborhood near the crossroads of VA-602 and VA-721 was home to about 200 people.

One story says that Cripple Creek's name comes from early hunter James Burk, who chased and crippled an elk on this creek before tracking the animal all the way to Burke's Garden in Tazewell County, circa 1748. Locals brag this is the same place immortalized in James Thompson's 1872 song "Goin' Up Cripple Creek," a folk and bluegrass standard.

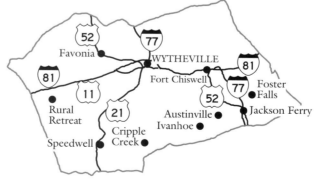

FORT CHISWELL

John Chiswell gets credit for finding the rich lead deposits of Wythe County. Legend claims that this entrepreneur from eastern Virginia fled from Indians in about 1756 and hid along the New River near present-day Austinville, where he found lead in a cave later known as "Chiswell's Hole."

Chiswell's discovery ultimately led to the development of Wythe County's long-running lead-mining industry; the mines at Austinville remained open until 1981. John Chiswell was honored in the name of Fort Chiswell, a military outpost established by Col. William Byrd III circa 1760 and used until about 1794. During the American Revolution, Fort Chiswell was a strategic point in the defense of the nearby lead mines at Austinville. The fort stood along the Wilderness Road, an ancient north-south highway that followed the general routes of modern I-81 and US-11.

In 1779, a town was laid out at Fort Chiswell, but it did not fully develop during the decade that Fort Chiswell served as the seat of the original Montgomery County. Fort Chiswell's courthouse was removed in 1790 with the organization of Wythe County. Two centuries later, the name was used by shopping centers, such as the Old Fort Antique Mall. But, by then, part of the actual fort site was gone, destroyed by the construction of I-81 in eastern Wythe County.

The pyramid-shaped Fort Chiswell Monument does make an effort to remember history. Embedded with millstones, the 12-foot-high structure marks the vicinity of the actual fort, a half mile north of I-81 Exit 80, along a service road, on the western side of the Interstate highway.

FOSTER FALLS

Foster Falls is an old riverside settlement in Wythe County's southeastern corner. Part of its name remembers early landowner William Foster (or Thomas Foster, by another account), but the second half of the name—the "Falls"—might be a misnomer. No big waterfall drops here; the name refers to a quarter-mile-long set of shoals on the New River.

In the late 1800s, the economy of Foster Falls ("Fosters Falls" on early maps) depended on both agriculture and rail traffic. Once providing about 70 jobs, an iron furnace built in 1881 and used until 1914 still stands here. Near the crossroads of VA-608 and VA-623, the community also once supported a large hotel and a gristmill.

What's to See

New River Trail State Park and *New River Access:* Foster Falls Depot may still be a name on a map, but the heart of the old railroad town is a campground and recreation site at Mile 24 of the New River Trail State Park. The Foster Falls Depot,

Traffic on I-81 rushes past the Fort Chiswell Monument

built sometime after the railroad arrived here in 1886, is a museum. Concessions include horse, canoe, and bicycle rentals.

Two public river accesses are located about one mile apart at Foster Falls. A popular run starts at the upper access and rides the Class III-IV Foster Falls rapids down to the lower river entry.

Trail use is free. A parking fee is charged.

🚗 From I-77 Exit 24, follow VA-69 east for 0.2 miles to US-52, then follow US-52 north for 1.3 miles. Turn right on VA-608 and follow 1.8 miles, turning left at VA-623.

IVANHOE

"Ivanhoe" was not always the name of the community at the crossroads of VA-94 and VA-733, near the New River and the Carroll County border, in south-central Wythe County. The area was first known as "Red Bluff" (1840s), then "Brown Hill" (1856-1882), and then "Van Liew" in honor of Charles S. and Cornelius S. Van Liew, the postmasters here in the 1880s. The name changed to "Ivanhoe Furnace" in 1884, then simply "Ivanhoe" in 1890.

According to tradition, "Ivanhoe" comes from the wife of a local company official; she finished reading Sir Walter Scott's novel *Ivanhoe* sometime after an iron furnace was established here, and she wanted to rename the community after the book. On the first weekend of each July, Ivanhoe hosts the Jubilee Festival.

JACKSON FERRY   Like a lighthouse staked on a high bank, the Shot Tower of Wythe County stands guard over the New River. For years, Thomas Jackson (1762-1824) piled stones to build this 75-foot-tall fortress on a 20-foot square base. The circa 1807 tower was used to make lead shot for firearm ammunition. The shot was later shipped on the New River to hunters or traders.

To make shot, lead was melted at the top of the tower and poured through sieves of various sizes. The hot lead then fell 150 feet through a shaft, from the tower top to a large kettle of water far below the tower's base. Jackson figured the long fall was necessary to properly mold the shot into a round form. The kettle at the bottom, filled with water from the river, served as a cushion to break the fall. Seventy-five feet below the tower's base, Jackson used a tunnel with an opening near the riverbank to access the kettle and retrieve the finished product.

In the 1800s, Jackson also kept busy operating the Jackson Ferry for passengers crossing the New River just below the Shot Tower, at the approximate point of US-52's New River bridge in southeastern Wythe County.

After the tower stood unused for decades, the Lead Mines Ruritan Club donated the tower to the Commonwealth of Virginia, and it opened to the public as the centerpiece of the tiny Shot Tower Historical State Park. The tower is one of only three still standing in the United States.

🚗 To find the Shot Tower Historical State Park from I-77 Exit 24, follow VA-69 east for 0.2 miles to US-52, then follow US-52 north for 1.2 miles. Turn left on Shot Tower Road and go a half mile to the park.

Thomas Jackson built the Shot Tower in about 1807.

RURAL RETREAT   When the railroad arrived at Rural Retreat in 1856, the depot was called "Mount Airy." But that name, given to a nearby German settlement in the early 1800s, was eventually dropped to end confusion with Mount Airy, North Carolina. The depot was renamed Rural Retreat circa 1866 to match a nearby post office that had opened in the 1830s, when this rural area was a retreat for stagecoach travelers.

Rural Retreat was incorporated in 1911. Around that time, the town claimed to be the "Cabbage Capital of the World," or simply the "Cabbage Capital of the South," in reference to the amount of the heady vegetable exported from local farms. The 2000 census counted about 1,400 residents living here in western Wythe County, near the crossroads of VA-90 and VA-616.

What's to See

Dr. Pepper Sites: Dr. Charles Taylor Pepper (1830-1903) was buried at Rural Retreat's Mountain View Cemetery. And, by nearly all accounts, Pepper is the man for whom the world-famous soft drink Dr Pepper is named. But stories do not agree on practically anything after that, including by whom, when, or where the formula for that soft drink was concocted.

Locals maintain that Dr. Pepper, a pharmacist, had a fondness for mixing herbs, roots, and soda to create his own soft drink flavors, perhaps even the soft drink potion that became Dr Pepper. He sold his mixtures at his Rural Retreat drugstore, a landmark that stood at the corner of North Main Street and West Railroad Avenue until 1999, when fire destroyed it.

Born in Montgomery County, Virginia, Dr. Pepper was a grandson of Samuel Pepper, the man for whom Southwest Virginia's Peppers Ferry Road is named (running across Montgomery, Pulaski, and Wythe counties). In the 1850s, Dr. Pepper moved to Bristol, Tennessee, where he and his brother, Dr. J. G. Pepper, operated the Pepper Brothers Drug Store on the 500 block of the Tennessee side of State Street, approximately where the offices of Theatre Bristol (506 State St.) are now located. While in Bristol, Dr. Pepper also served the Confederacy for two years as an acting surgeon at a Civil War hospital.

Dr. Pepper moved to Rural Retreat in 1879 and opened a new drugstore. At some point, either in Bristol or Rural Retreat,

Pepper hired Wade Morrison (1852-1924) as an assistant druggist. Stories say that Morrison later left Pepper's practice and moved to Waco, Texas, where he created the soft drink formula for Dr Pepper and named it for his old boss. A footnote to that tale says that Morrison fell in love with Pepper's daughter, Ruth, and that she insisted the drink be named for her father. But that footnote is likely erroneous, because the daughter (born 1874) would have been just a child at the time Morrison settled in the Lone Star State in the 1880s.

Yet, another account says Charles C. Alderton worked at Morrison's drugstore in Waco, and that Alderton actually fine-tuned the formula in about 1885, before Dr Pepper was mass-produced and bottled.

Rural Retreat remains in conflict with Waco over the "Home of Dr Pepper" claims. But, for sure, Rural Retreat is the final resting place of Dr. Charles Taylor Pepper. His six-foot-high, pointed tombstone stands on a hill at Mountain View Cemetery, a pleasant place with a spectacular view of Brushy Mountain on the northwestern horizon.

From I-81 Exit 60, follow VA-90 southeast for 1.7 miles to the railroad tracks. At the center of town, the old store site is at the corner of North Main Street and West Railroad Avenue, across from the railroad depot and immediately right of the town's railroad caboose. To reach Mountain View Cemetery from here, follow VA-749 (S. Main St.) for 0.3 miles south of the tracks. Turn right on VA-615 (Cemetery Rd.) and follow for 0.3 miles, then turn right at the cemetery sign and a flagpole. Dr. Pepper's gravestone is about 20 yards to the left of the flagpole.

Rural Retreat Lake Park: Grassy hills, marsh, and woods line the shore of Rural Retreat Lake, a 90-acre getaway surrounded by a 330-acre municipal park. A 72-space campground

Dr. Charles Pepper—the man who gave his name to the soft drink Dr Pepper—is buried at Rural Retreat's Mountain View Cemetery.

stays open spring to fall, near a swimming pool, a stocked trout pond, three miles of nature trails, and a playground.

The water is 35 feet deep at this inviting impoundment on the headwaters of the South Fork of Reed Creek. Lake fishing includes largemouth bass, crappie, musky, bluegill, northern pike, and channel catfish. Boats can be rented, and a concrete ramp is available for boats with trolling motors.

From I-81 Exit 60, follow VA-90 southeast for 1.7 miles to reach the railroad tracks at Rural Retreat, then continue straight on VA-749 (S. Main St.) for 1.6 miles. Turn right on VA-677 (Rural Retreat Lake Rd.) and follow for 1.4 miles. Turn left on VA-678 (Lake Rd.) at the park entrance.

Wythe Raceway: Summer Saturday nights are filled with stock cars stirring up clouds of dust at Wythe Raceway. Amateur drivers mash the gas to 100 mph and maneuver turns on high banks rising 30 degrees. All the while, dust spreads on the crowd, huddled on large bleachers or camped along grassy embankments overlooking the half-mile, oval dirt track built in 1970.

From I-81-South at Exit 60, turn right off the ramp, then turn immediately right on Radio Drive. Follow for 1.5 miles and turn left at the entrance on Racetrack Road.

SPEEDWELL Speedwell is any one of a variety of the plants of the genus *Veronica* and is characterized by small, usually blue clusters of flowers. Speedwell is known to grow in abundance in southwestern Wythe County and, according to an early historian's theory, is probably why the Speedwell community, near US-21 at VA-619, adopted its name.

What's to See

Raven Cliff Furnace: The two-story-high Raven Cliff Furnace stands alongside Cripple

Rural Retreat Lake

Creek at a site where iron furnaces operated as early as 1810. The furnace is named for the ravens nesting on a nearby cliff and is representative of the many iron furnaces that once roared all over southern Wythe County. Rebuilt in 1861, the stone furnace was last used in the early 1900s and is part of the Raven Cliff Campground and Picnic Area, a retreat with 20 primitive campsites inside the Mount Rogers National Recreation Area. An entry fee is charged.

🚗 From US-21 at Speedwell, follow VA-619 east for seven miles and turn right on the campground access road. An easy, half-mile trail to the furnace begins at a gate, opposite a parking area and information kiosk at the end of the gravel campground road. Veer right on a large footbridge and follow through a grassy meadow to the furnace.

WYTHEVILLE

Wytheville kicks off the third Saturday of each June with its weeklong Chautauqua Festival. The celebration's name is a throwback to the late 1920s, when Wytheville regularly hosted Chautauqua Gatherings, led by traveling caravans of performers and educators known as *chautauquas* (the chautauqua movement began in 1874 at New York's Lake Chatauqua). In 1985, members of the Wythe Arts Council resurrected the chautauqua idea with musical performances and workshops held at the Elizabeth Brown Memorial Park, off Fourth Street. The festival's hot-air balloon rally has, in turn, so commonly come to symbolize Wytheville that the town's 500,000-gallon water tower is painted to resemble one of the soaring, colorful globes.

The tower stands aside I-81, announcing Wytheville's name as a welcome to visitors. One mile north, traffic creates a continuous buzz beside the multitiered dining room of the 210-seat Wohlfahrt Haus Dinner Theatre. Resembling a Bavarian village, this lavish, 19,000-square-foot facility opened in 1999 at 170 Malin Dr., just off I-81 Exit 73. Founder Peggy Sutphin provided the name; "Wohlfahrt" (pronounced "WOOL-fert") honors Sutphin's German ancestor Johann Wilhelm Ludwig Wohlfahrt, who immigrated to America from Germany in 1750 and whose descendants eventually settled in Wythe and Bland counties.

Situated along I-81 and that highway's overlap with I-77, Wytheville's location is part of what defines the town. The bright lights of many motels and restaurants hug the highways and give an impression that this place is much larger than it is—a village of less than 8,000 residents, according to the 2000 census.

In the late 1700s, early settler Jesse Evans named the town "Abbeville" in honor of his South Carolina birthplace. In 1792, Abbeville was renamed "Evansham" to honor Jesse. Evansham became known alternately as "Wythe Court House" until 1839, when it was incorporated as Wytheville, a name matching the county it centers.

The setting of the Log House 1776 Restaurant, 510 E. Main St., focuses on what the town looked like in its infancy. This rambling log building is centered by a two-room, two-story tenant house. In the mid-1970s, owner James Green renovated the structure, first removing an exterior mask of white weatherboard, later uncovering an account saying that construction of the house began in 1776. Local historians, meanwhile, have traced the cabin's construction to at least 1784, a date noted with a brass plate on the front porch.

The Log House is part of Wytheville's well-marked downtown walking tour. Another stop is the circa-1901 Wythe County Courthouse, 225 S. Fourth St., a Classical Revival structure with large columns at its front steps. Near the courthouse, the Millwald Theatre was built in 1928 on the Main Street block between Tazewell and Fourth streets. "Millwald" is a combination of the names of former owners Morris Miller and Rolfe Ewald.

The Big Pencil, a unique town landmark, hangs outside Wytheville Office Supply, 146 W. Main St. First erected in 1959 at a nearby location by businessman John Campbell Findlay (1911-1977), this gigantic aluminum pencil—an attention-getting business emblem kept in place by steel cables—is nearly 31 feet long.

The Bolling Building stands across the street from the Big Pencil. First Lady Edith Bolling Wilson, a daughter of Wytheville Judge William Holcombe Bolling, was born here on October 15, 1872, inside a second-story apartment directly above 145 E. Main St. Edith made her mark in American history soon after marrying President Woodrow Wilson (1856-1924). In 1919, President Wilson collapsed during a cross-country speaking tour, and Edith became "America's first woman president" by making decisions on which matters should concern her husband during the last 18 months of his second term.

Raven Cliff Furnace

Outside the Bolling Building, sidewalks border Main Street, making this a good place for a stroll. The ease of foot travel is owed to Thomas Jefferson Boyd (1804-1893), a surveyor whose design left Wytheville's Main Street wide and roomy. Once a mayor, Boyd is known as "The Father of Wytheville," and his name is on a general-history museum operated by the town at 295 Tazewell St., with displays like antique carriages, farm tools, military uniforms, and a permanent exhibit on the Civil War.

The town also operates the Haller-Gibboney Rock House Museum, 205 Tazewell St. Built in 1822-1823, this was the handsome home of Dr. John Haller, Wytheville's first resident physician. The Rock House contains more than 1,400 items, including antique furniture and Native American artifacts.

The Civil War's Battle of Wytheville bruised the two-story Rock House. A bullet hole still punctures a window frame, and a bloodstain still darkens a hardwood floor—a marker of when the limestone structure was a hospital for Confederate wounded.

Buildings on Tazewell Street near the Rock House were burned during the battle on July 18, 1863. But a Union cavalry detachment ultimately failed in its attempt to destroy the railroad, thanks to 26-year-old Molly Tynes's brave flight on horseback. Tynes rode 40 miles from Tazewell County to warn Wytheville's Confederates that the Union Army was approaching. The subsequent battle, known as "Toland's Raid," was thwarted when a guard of old men, boys, and a small number of Confederate troops killed Union Col. John T. Toland as he led a federal force of about 900 soldiers through town.

What's to See

Big Bend Picnic Area: Built by the Civilian Conservation Corps in the 1940s, the primitive and secluded Big Bend Picnic Area is set among rocky, grassy fields atop Walker Mountain, at a 3,950-foot elevation. Part of the Jefferson National Forest, the area harbors a handful of scattered picnic tables, grills, and stone fireplaces. Big Bend is known for rhododendron, blooming in summer, and its bird's-eye view of Wythe County. The "Big Bend" name likely stems from the big bend, or curve, that Walker Mountain makes here along the Bland-Wythe county line.

🚗 From I-81 Exit 70 in Wytheville, follow US-52 north for 12 miles

The Big Pencil hangs above Wytheville's Main Street

to the top of Walker Mountain. Turn right on USFS-206 (gravel) and follow for four miles. The entrance is on the left.

Big Survey Wildlife Management Area: Sand Mountain joins Lick, Swecker, and Stuart mountains on a towering tract spanning 8,300 acres at Wytheville's south side. The state acquired this wooded area for $3 million, and in 2001 the Big Survey Wildlife Management Area opened. The name commends the area's high-altitude vistas, where surrounding land can be surveyed for miles in many directions. Crossed by VA-640, Big Survey is overseen by the Virginia Department of Game and Inland Fisheries and is open for exploration on foot through a network of old roadbeds.

🚗 From I-81 Exit 67 in Wytheville, follow US-11 north for 3.4 miles. Turn right on US-21 and follow south for 2.3 miles. Turn left on VA-696 (Barrett Mill Rd.) and follow for 0.7 miles to a trail starting at a gated road, on the right. Follow this road for two miles to the top of Sand Mountain to find a natural overlook among rock outcrops. Posted signs mark the property boundaries.

Big Walker Lookout and *Monster Rock Trail:* Lofty views of Wythe County's Stony Fork watershed await discovery atop either the Big Walker Lookout or the natural seat of the Monster Rock in the Jefferson National Forest. Both sites are on the spine of Walker Mountain, named for Dr. Thomas Walker (1715-1794), a man from eastern Virginia who led survey expeditions into Southwest Virginia in the mid-1700s.

The Monster Rock is just what its name implies—a monstrous rock. The 14-foot-high outcrop hangs at a 45-degree angle above the terminus of the Monster Rock Trail, a mile-long, uphill maze tracing the Tennessee Valley Divide on the Bland-Wythe county line.

The Monster Rock Trail begins near Big Walker Lookout, an observation tower built to attract tourists in 1947. At 3,405 feet, the turquoise tower provides panoramic views far above treetops, though the 100-foot climb—straight into the sky—on the sturdy steel structure can feel spooky during a stiff breeze.

The tower is open spring to fall. A fee is charged to climb the tower; trail access is free.

Wytheville's Rock House, built circa 1822-1823

🚐 From I-81 Exit 70 in Wytheville, follow US-52 north for about 12 miles to the Big Walker Lookout, on the Bland County line at VA-621. To reach the Monster Rock from US-52-North at the tower, turn left on VA-621 and follow west for about 50 yards to a parking lot at the left edge of the road. Yellow blazes mark the trail, which starts as a grassy lane going uphill.

Virginia City Pioneer Town & Gem Mine: Actually, nobody is mining the side of Walker Mountain at the Virginia City Gem Mine. Visitors, instead, sift through imported mine ore using a sluice and screens to search for stones like rubies or shiny chunks of fool's gold (pyrite). Buckets of mine ore come from places around the world. The Gem Mine is open April to October.

The Jefferson National Forest surrounds Virginia City. From 1972 to 1981, this 244-acre site was the home of Dry Gulch Junction, an amusement park with an Old West-theme. Buildings from Dry Gulch Junction's make-believe town overlook the gem mine's sluice shelters. In 2000, renovations began, converting the old structures into outlets for craftspeople.

🚐 From I-81 Exit 70 in Wytheville, follow US-52 north for nine miles. A train silhouette marks the entrance on the right.

Barren Springs: James Barron was an early merchant at Barren Springs. In the 1850s, the post office was known as "Barron's Springs." By 1886, however, the post office had become "Barren Springs." Southeastern: VA-100 at VA-608

Bethany: Near Austinville, Bethany's name originated in 1846 when Elizabeth P. Chaffin donated land for what became the "old" Methodist church at Bethany. In about 1902-1904, a second church was built on a lot adjoining the original meeting house. The name of the church comes from the Bible—Bethany is a village east of Jerusalem that was frequently visited by Jesus Christ and is closely associated with the final scenes of His life. Southern: VA-69 at VA-608

Blacklick: A post office opened at Blacklick as early as 1873. The name stems from the area's black topsoil and two sulphur springs—a lick for wild animals. Northwestern: VA-625 at VA-680

Boiling Spring: The Boiling Spring community takes its name from a creek's reputation for boiling, or gushing, from the ground. Eastern: VA-619 at VA-629

Clark's Summit: A half mile west of Gunton Park, Clark's Summit (or "Clarkes Summit") was named for a man remembered as Mr. Clark, the owner of a large roadhouse frequented by early travelers, probably prior to the establishment of the railroad in the mid-1800s. Northeastern: westernmost crossroads of VA-610 and VA-613

Crawfish Valley: Crawfish are crustaceans that look like little lobsters. They make homes in mud and beneath rocks in mountain streams like Reed Creek, a New River tributary lying deep in the Jefferson National Forest. One area of Reed Creek between Brushy Mountain and Walker Mountain goes by the name "Crawfish Valley" and is accessed by hiking trails. The "Brushy" name comes from the mountain's thick undergrowth. Northwestern: USFS-727-2, near VA-625

Crockett: In about 1872, James S. "Iron Jim" Crockett requested a railroad depot to be built to ship iron bars. In turn, he gave his name to the Crockett community. Western: VA-625 at VA-690

Crockett's Cove: Not to be confused with the railroad town called Crockett, the Crockett's Cove area was named for John Crockett, a settler in the 1770s. Northeastern: VA-600, near Cove Creek

Favonia: The post office at Favonia originated in 1892, a time when the U.S. Postal Service requested that single words be used for location names. Such a restriction has often left maps with odd names such as this one, likely derived from the word *favonius*, a Latin term meaning "of the west wind." First postmaster Ellen C. Walton wrote the word *favonia* in heavy cursive resembling calligraphy on the community's post office application. Favonia is five miles west of the Wythe County Courthouse. North-central: US-52, near VA-680

Galena: Paying reference to local lead mines, the name "Galena" comes from a common, heavy mineral that is the principal ore of lead. Southeastern: US-52 at VA-619

Grahams Forge: David Graham (1800-1870) purchased iron forges and furnaces in 1826, and the surrounding area became known as "Grahams Forge." Eastern: VA-619 at Reed Creek

Gunton Park: M. B. Gunton directed the local coal-mining operations of the Summit Coal and Iron Co. at Gunton Park in the early 1900s. Northeastern: easternmost crossroads of VA-610 and VA-613, near railroad and Pulaski County

Huddle: Three Huddle brothers were among the settlers of Wythe County in the late 1700s. One brother, Gideon Huddle, and his wife, Elizabeth, purchased land near Cripple Creek in 1795, and their family name is remembered at Huddle. South-central: VA-642 at VA-643

Kent: In the late 1700s, Joseph Kent built a two-story brick house, called "Kenton," at what became the Kent community. Central: north end of VA-704, east of Wytheville

Lone Ash: Once a flag stop on the railroad line that became the New River Trail State Park, Lone Ash was named for a large, lone ash tree standing in the area. Southeastern: VA-622, near New River

Major Grahams: An exotic house built for David Graham in about 1840 was inherited by his son, Maj. David Pierce Graham, a Confederate officer who embellished the structure and inspired the name for the local community. The house is listed on both state and national landmark registers. Southeastern: VA-626 at VA-619, along Cedar Run

Max Meadows: Col. John Buchanan named "Mack's Meadows" for William Mack, a German who settled on Reed Creek, near the Max Meadows area, in about 1745. Just a few years after the community's post office was established, Robert Hanson served a short stint as postmaster, from 1868-1869, and is believed to have changed the place-name's spelling to "Max Meadows." Central: VA-121 at VA-614

Murphyville: South of Rural Retreat's railroad tracks, Murphyville was once primarily a neighborhood of black residents. It takes its name from the family of Wayman Murphy, a former slave. West-central: VA-616 (Murphyville Rd.) at VA-689 (Sage Rd.)

Petunia: The flowery name "Petunia" originated in 1890 when Robert Kyle Shores opened a post office at what became the western edge of Wytheville. But Petunia might have adopted another name—first postmaster Adam H. Shores, Robert's son, wrote "Shoresville" on the community's post office application, though that name was scratched out and "Petunia" was put in its place. Central: VA-656 (Petunia Rd.) at US-11

Pierce's Mill: David Peirce (not Pierce) built a mill on Cripple Creek in the early 1800s. The operation became the center of the Pierce's Mill community. South-central: VA-641, west of VA-94

Poplar Camp: Stories say that Poplar Camp took its name from a local poplar tree. Southern: US-52 at VA-69

Porters Crossroads: This place was named for a lifelong resident, Samuel "Hutch" Porter (1799-1893). South-central: VA-94 at VA-619

Rackettown: Legend says that feuding between bootleggers once inspired locals to call a community "Rackettown," because racket was all they ever heard. Southeastern: VA-607, west of VA-772

Siloam: Sometimes called "Siloam Church," Siloam is a small residential community. The word *siloam* is a Biblical reference meaning "sent." The Gospel of John 9:7-11 tells the story of Jerusalem's Pool of Siloam, where a blind man gained sight after following Jesus Christ's order to wash mud from his face in the pool. Eastern: VA-94 at VA-634

Staley Crossroads: The Staleys were among the early settlers of this area. Martin Staley acquired a license to operate a tavern here in 1773. Western: US-11 at VA-90

Stroupes Store: When Henry C. Stroupe opened a retail business in about 1900, the surrounding area became known as "Stroupes Store." Central: VA-684 at VA-690

Walton Furnace: The name "Walton Furnace" comes from George Walton, a prominent landowner, and an iron furnace that operated in the 1800s. Southern: VA-630 at VA-631

West Piney: An abundance of pine trees inspired this name (sometimes known simply as "Piney"). Central: VA-645 at VA-648

Wyrick Spring: E. R. Wyrick built a fence on some marshy property he acquired in 1876 and accidentally opened up a spring, which he later used in a business partnership to bottle and sell water. In 1911, M. S. Bennett of Abingdon built a 30-room hotel at Wyrick Spring. The hotel remained a popular destination until 1935; it was torn down in 1957. A small brick building labeled "Wyrick Spring" in bold silver letters marks the site of the old resort. Western: VA-625 (Wyrick Spring Rd.), one mile south of the railroad at Crockett

NEW RIVER VALLEY

Ah, the New River. It widens and thins, again and again, on its northward journey from North Carolina to Virginia's Pulaski County, where a dam on the river forms the all-impressive Claytor Lake. Below Claytor Dam, the New River meets the Little River, which drains Floyd County. Then the New flows along the border of Montgomery County and the City of Radford before coursing through a Giles County gorge.

The ancient New River is the unifying theme running through the four counties and one city traditionally defined as Virginia's New River Valley. The river is a retreat, especially, for the valley's college students at Virginia Tech or Radford University. Yet this river's name may be misleading—geologists note the New as one of the oldest rivers in the world.

FLOYD COUNTY

Created in 1831 from part of Montgomery County, with a portion of Franklin County added later, Floyd County was named for John Floyd, Virginia's governor from 1830 to 1834. The county's oasis of tall, wavy grass and rolling hills escaped practically all forms of commercialism in the 20th century, despite its proximity to Roanoke's industrial sprawl on the north and the ever-growing population center of Christiansburg on the west. For about 383 square miles Floyd forms a quaint quilt of farms, fields, and fences.

FLOYD Quiet and unpretentious, Floyd is a favorite off-beat destination for Blue Ridge Parkway travelers looking for a real-life version of the fictional Mayberry, North Carolina. And Floyd comes close. The town's Floyd Barber Shop, for one, is among local landmarks attracting camera-clicking cruisers. But the Mayberry charm also mirrors the sheer size of this town, the namesake county seat, which stretches only about a mile in any of four directions from the main crossroads of US-221 and VA-8. Floyd is home to Floyd County's sole traffic signal and about 400 residents, according to the 2000 census.

What you'll find here is more like Mayberry with a touch of tie-dye—Floyd is flavored by a counterculture of so-called hippies and back-to-the-land people who discovered this place in the 1960s and 1970s. Eventually, many members of this counterculture opened businesses catering to tourists who use Floyd as a pit stop between the Blue Ridge Parkway and I-81 Exit 114. Others established self-supporting farms and raised organic crops. Yet, by the end of the 20th century, many of the counterculture transplants had blended into the community with such transparency, they had become practically indistinguishable from natives whose family roots could be traced to the county's first settlers.

Looking for a life "away from it all" seems to have a long-standing tradition in Floyd. On the town's southern horizon stands a peak known as Stocker's Knob. According to local legend, that knob was settled by a man named Stocker who came here to avoid the Revolutionary War.

Originally called "Jacksonville" in honor of President Andrew Jackson, the town was first incorporated in 1858 and then rechartered in 1892. Jacksonville was renamed "Floyd" in 1896.

Getting here from I-81 Exit 114 takes about a half hour on VA-8. En route, amid endless hills dotted with cattle and Christmas trees,

Floyd suddenly appears like an oasis—a sign of civilization centered by the 1951 Floyd County Courthouse, 100 E. Main St. Near that brick structure, Floyd's downtown sports an old-fashioned hardware store, a country diner, and a mix of shops selling coffee, spices, and vegetarian items. No business—not even Floyd's handful of fast-food outlets—boasts a gaudy sign.

Floyd's art community unites at the Jacksonville Center, a showcase for wildlife paintings and other artwork off VA-8, a half mile southeast of the Floyd stoplight. Aside from keeping the "Jacksonville" name alive, this nonprofit center includes a gallery with an open-air feel in the Old Jacksonville Barn, a former dairy facility.

Going northeast on US-221, away from the stoplight, the village of Floyd disappears into a long line of white ranch fences and farms. Two miles north of the main Floyd crossroads is the Pine Tavern, where scraggly pines front an old-time motor court. Painted white with pine green trim, the Pine Tavern dates to the late 1920s and rents rooms without air-conditioning. A restaurant was added in the 1930s and often features live music.

More music can be found at the heart of town. At the Floyd Country Store, 206 S. Locust St., well-worn double doors lead to a casual theater outlined by folded metal chairs. The atmosphere gets hot when fiddling and flat-footing take center stage during the Friday Nite Jamboree. These music shows originated in 1983 when two of the store's former owners gathered on Fridays to play bluegrass music. Eventually, a regular audience and other musicians joined the fun and gave birth to the Jamboree at this 1913 store building, known for many years as "Cockram's."

What's to See

Rakes Millpond: Thick rhododendron grows along the banks of a pond once used by 19th-century miller Jarman Rakes, who operated

117

Dam at Rakes Millpond, off the Blue Ridge Parkway

a long-gone gristmill about 2.5 miles north of Tuggle Gap. Tradition says that Rakes allowed his customers to fish for brook trout in this pond while they waited for their grist. The mill's foundation and the milldam's man-made waterfall are at the edge of the Blue Ridge Parkway, between mileposts 162 and 163.

Rocky Knob and *Rock Castle Gorge:* Some days, it seems, you can stand on the Floyd-Patrick county line at Rock Castle Gorge and see all the way across eastern Virginia. Surveying beyond the Blue Ridge, Virginia's mountains slowly descend to the flatlands. On mornings when clouds roll in like ocean waves, looking out over the Rock Castle Gorge can be as equally exciting as watching the sunrise on the Atlantic coast.

The Rock Castle Gorge is east of the Blue Ridge Parkway in Patrick County. The parkway runs along its rim as the road teeter-totters on the spine of the Floyd-Patrick county line. The gorge is named for something early settlers found—six-sided quartzite crystals shaped like castle towers. For serious hikers, the 10.8-mile Rock Castle Gorge Trail connects three parkway overlooks and makes a strenuous leap into the canyon.

Near Mile 168, three miles south of the parkway's entrance on VA-8 at Tuggle Gap, Rocky Knob overlooks the gorge and the eastern horizon's sweeping mountains. A half-mile spur trail leads to Rocky Knob's 3,572-foot summit. The trail ends at an old wood-and-rock shelter built by the Civilian Conservation Corps in the 1930s and used back when the Appalachian Trail passed through here. The moderate Rocky Knob trail makes an exhilarating pre-breakfast workout. Try

to see the sunrise from this properly named peak, a place where chunks of rock stand vertically.

At Parkway Mile 167, the National Park Service operates the Rocky Knob Campground, a facility offering about 100 campsites. At Parkway Mile 174, the park service offers Rocky Knob Cabins, open during summer with non-air-conditioned accommodations.

The small Rocky Knob Visitor Center, at Parkway Mile 169, is usually open May to October.

Smart View Recreation Area: The Trail Cabin is a landmark at the Smart View Recreation Area. Perched atop the Blue Ridge, the 1890s structure was named for a local Trail family.

Early settlers used the name "Smart View" because there's a "right smart view" here when looking into Virginia's Franklin County. Such an assessment is especially true from the Trail Cabin's location at the Smart View Recreation Area, operated by the National Park Service. Smart View sits at Blue Ridge Parkway Mile 154.5, or 10.7 miles north of Tuggle Gap's entrance on VA-8. A moderate 2.6-mile trail encircles the area's picnic tables and shade trees.

MEADOWS OF DAN While the post office at Meadows of Dan is in neighboring Patrick County, the area called "Meadows of Dan" blankets much of modern-day Floyd County, especially in the southeastern corner along the Blue Ridge Parkway. Attractions, including the famous Mabry Mill, carry this address. The main crossroads is where VA-614 meets US-58, less than a mile from the Floyd County line, near the Meadows of Dan entrance to the Blue Ridge Parkway.

View from Rocky Knob, off the Blue Ridge Parkway

Trail Cabin at the Smart View Recreation Area, north of Floyd

From the Blue Ridge Parkway's Meadows of Dan entrance at US-58, go north for 3.9 miles. Turn left on VA-799 (Conner Grove Rd.) and go 1.4 miles. Turn left on VA-604 (Halls Store Rd.) and travel another 1.4 miles. Turn left on VA-727 (Moles Rd.) and go about one mile to a low saddle in the ridge, near the eastern slope of the mountain. Look for a sign with END STATE MAINTENANCE on it and turn right on the narrow, single-lane gravel access road. Go about one mile uphill to the parking area. The summit trail begins beyond a pile of small boulders.

Chateau Morrisette and *Villa Appalaccia:* Chateau Morrisette Winery might seem a little doggy; a pup's picture fronts a flag hanging from the huge winery building, and wines go by names like "Black Dog Blanc" and "Our Dog Blue." Yet this canine connection lends a laid-back air to the winery, named for the dog-loving family of William, Nancy, and David Morrisette. The Morrisettes first planted grapes in Floyd County in 1978. Their winery opened in 1983 and produced about 100,000 gallons of wine in 1999.

At Chateau Morrisette's popular, upscale restaurant, reservations are mandatory to ensure seating during the Blue Ridge Parkway's peak tourism seasons. A separate winery building doubles as a hospitality hall for tours and tastings.

In 1989, a nearby vineyard, also off the Blue Ridge Parkway, was established at Villa Appalaccia Winery, a much smaller operation centered by a two-story Italian Tuscan country house, an architectural style that blends beautifully with the greenery of the Blue Ridge.

The area is named for the meadows at the head of the Dan River, a watercourse that, by separate accounts, either remembers a Saura Indian chief called "Danaho" or is a reference to the ancient tribe of the Danites, as told in the Bible's Joshua 19:47.

What's to See

Buffalo Mountain Natural Area Preserve: Buffalo Mountain can be easily seen in most parts of Floyd County and for at least 20 miles along the Blue Ridge Parkway. Abruptly rising from rolling hills, Buffalo Mountain is named for its humpback shape, said to resemble the back of a buffalo. The peak is part of the 1,000-acre Buffalo Mountain Natural Area Preserve, managed by the Virginia Department of Conservation and Recreation. Open to visitors, the preserve includes a summit trail built on an old roadbed. The path is easy to follow but should be given a moderate rating, at least, for its harsh ascent—it gains about 600 feet in elevation in little more than a half mile.

A bench with an information kiosk is about one third of the way to the top, but don't stop there. A true reward—a *Sound of Music*-style vista—awaits the climber. Atop this 3,971-foot peak, you can see much more than simply the green valley of Floyd County. Up here, it seems like you're standing on top of the world. Look for Virginia's highest point, Mount Rogers, on the distant western horizon. Look for the Roanoke Valley to the north and North Carolina to the south. The Blue Ridge is to the east, but so is some brush, slightly blocking the 360-degree view.

The mountain is capped with rocks pocked with small holes, and this almost treeless peak is often subject to subalpine winds and temperatures. The peak's prairie-like glades provide a haven for rare plants and animals.

Atop the hump of Buffalo Mountain in southern Floyd County

Chateau Morrisette Winery

🚗 Chateau Morrisette is 6.2 miles north of the Blue Ridge Parkway's Meadows of Dan entrance on US-58. At Parkway Mile 171.5, turn left on VA-726 (Black Ridge Rd.), then immediately turn left on VA-777 (Winery Rd.). The winery is on the right.

At Parkway Mile 170.3, Villa Appalaccia is 7.4 miles north of the Meadows of Dan entrance, on the right along VA-720, a loop that slides into Patrick County for about one mile.

Mabry Mill: The unforgettable Mabry Mill looks like a postcard that you can walk through. It's no coincidence that the visage of the gorgeous, water-powered mill shows up on countless postcards, plus paintings, brochures, and tourism pamphlets promoting Virginia and the entire Blue Ridge Parkway. National Park Service rangers deem it the most photographed place on the parkway. And, on a typical summer day, you can see evidence of that claim as crowds with cameras scramble across the grassy hillsides. Some people even belly crawl to the bank of the millpond, to find just the right angle.

Others hang out here on Sunday afternoons in the summertime to hear musicians play old-time Appalachian tunes. A short trail leads past farm implements, a blacksmith shop, and a moonshine still. Also on-site is a short-order restaurant, open spring to fall, with a screened-porch dining room shaded by rhododendron.

Water spills down the mill's wooden raceway, providing power to convert corn into meal, just like Edwin B. Mabry began doing in 1910, when he diverted water from a couple of different streams to make his mill's waterwheel turn. Mabry, known commonly as "Uncle Ed," was a miller as well as a chair maker, a farmer, and a blacksmith. Mabry and his wife operated this mill, making grist and sawing wood, until 1935. About a decade later, the park service restored Mabry Mill as a display area. It's at Parkway Mile 176.1, about 1.5 miles north of the Meadows of Dan entrance on US-58.

Slate Mountain Presbyterian Church: The Rev. Bob Childress used native fieldstone to construct Slate Mountain Presbyterian Church, one of six churches he built in or near Floyd County. Childress served as a preacher in this area for 30 years, until his death in 1956, and actively converted mountaineers from their ways of drinking and fighting, as told in Richard C. Davids's book *The Man Who Moved a Mountain.* A map outlining the locations of the "Bob Childress Churches" is available at the Rocky Knob Visitor Center, on the Blue Ridge Parkway at Mile 169.

🚗 Go north on the Blue Ridge Parkway for 6.2 miles from the Meadows of Dan entrance on US-58. At Mile 171.5, turn right on VA-726 (Rock Church Rd.) and follow to the VA-758 (Willis Rd.) crossroads. The church is on the Floyd-Patrick county line.

Mabry Mill on the Blue Ridge Parkway, near Meadows of Dan

Alum Ridge: Alum springwater and the area's alum deposits are the reasons for the name "Alum Ridge." A post office was established here in 1877. Central: VA-740 at VA-750

Camp Creek: The name "Camp Creek" might be a reference to a stopping point, or camp, for early travelers. Central: VA-615 at VA-689

Check: Originally, residents wanted to call the Check community's post office "Checkers," because a local store was a meeting place for residents who loved playing checkers. Postal officials didn't like that name, but they did accept the slightly shorter "Check." Northern: VA-642 at US-221

Conners Grove: Also known as "Conner Hill," this community's name originates from the family of Daniel Conner, who settled in the area circa 1773. Southern: VA-776 at VA-799

Copper Hill: Copper ore gave the name to Copper Hill. In the 1800s, Robert L. Toncray was among the area's early prospectors. Northeastern: VA-796 at US-221

Copper Valley: Like Copper Hill, Copper Valley's name comes from the region's copper-mining industry during the 1800s. Western: VA-740 at VA-787, near Little River

Duncan: Arriving in about 1783, Blanche Duncan was a settler who gave his name to this community along Indian Creek. Western: VA-730 at VA-766

Greasy Creek: A post office existed at Greasy Creek in 1840. Legend says that the area's name comes from hunter James Burk, who killed so many bears along the creek in the mid-1700s that the water became greasy with blood. Southwestern: VA-624 (Shady Grove Rd.), near VA-622 (Indian Valley Rd.)

Haycock: The Haycock community is near a mountain called "The Haycocks," said to resemble the form of three haycocks (conical piles of hay) or hay shocks (thick, bushy masses). About a mile south of Haycock lies Woods Gap, a pass some say is named for Col. Abraham Wood, an explorer who is believed to have crossed the Blue Ridge at this point in about 1654. But the "Wood" name might (or also) refer to the family of Richard Wood (1769-1859), who lived at Woods Gap in the early 1800s. Eastern: VA-615 at VA-635

Hemlock: This community's name probably stems from a local abundance of the evergreen hemlock. Northern: VA-653 at VA-660

Huffville: The name "Huffville" may remember Henry Huff, who came to the Floyd County area from Pittsylvania County, Va., in about 1807. But one account says that the name is owed specifically to Easom Huff, a local schoolteacher in the late 1800s. Northern: VA-610 at VA-672

Indian Valley: Many arrowheads have been found in Indian Valley, which is believed to have once been the summer hunting ground for the Kanawhay (Kanawha) Indians. Western: VA-622 at VA-787

Kings Store: Wallace King (1900-1991) and his family once operated a general store inside a wooden A-frame building, and the nearby crossroads became known as "Kings Store." Northeastern: US-221 at VA-661

Pizarro: A Pizarro post office opened in 1886. The place-name might be a reference to famous Spanish explorer Francisco Pizarro, who conquered Peru in the 16th century. An earlier post office in the vicinity was titled "Turtle Rock." Established in 1871, it's believed to have taken its name from an outcrop shaped like a turtle. A Turtle Rock Church opened in 1882 and remained active until about 1913. Eastern: VA-681 (Franklin Pk.) at VA-679

Poff: Likely, Poff's name is owed to a family of six German brothers named "Poff" (or "Pfaff"), who were among Floyd County's earliest settlers, circa 1805. Central: VA-615 at VA-817, north of Floyd

Shelors Mill: George William Shelor (1860-1922) built a sawmill on Howell Creek and naturally inspired this community's name. The name "Howell Creek" most likely refers to one or various members of the Howell family who owned land in this vicinity in the early 1800s. Central: US-221 (Floyd Hwy.) at VA-726 (Canning Factory Rd.)

Simpsons: Allen Simpson (1757-1820) was a New Jersey native and early settler in Floyd County, giving his family name to the Simpsons community. His son William Simpson once owned nearly all of the land in the Simpsons vicinity. North-central: VA-610 (Daniels Run Rd.) at VA-653 (Shawsville Tnpk.)

Terry's Fork: A Terry's Fork post office was established in 1879. "Terry" was the surname of some early landowners in this agricultural community. Northern: VA-610 at VA-660

Tory Creek: In about 1878, a Tory Creek post office was established in the southernmost corner of Floyd County. The name was derived from an instance when a number of Tories camped here on a creek bank sometime after the Revolutionary War. Southern: US-58 at VA-620 (Tory Creek Rd.)

Tuggle Gap: In the post-Revolutionary War period, a man remembered only as "Reverend Tuggle" built a home at what became "Tuggle Gap." Eastern: VA-8 at Blue Ridge Parkway

Willis: For years, the post office at Willis was called "Hylton," a name honoring early settler Hardon Hylton. The community became "Willis" in 1894, likely for the family of Jonathan Willis, who settled near the present-day Willis community in 1833. Southwestern: VA-799 at US-221

Wills Ridge: According to tradition, Wills Ridge takes its name from a man named "Wills" (or "Will") who came here from neighboring Franklin County, Va., on hunting trips. A "Will's Ridge" post office was established in 1869. Central: VA-692, south of VA-730

GILES COUNTY

It's easy to sum up the treasures of Giles County. Just think of waterfalls, covered bridges, the home of *Dirty Dancing*, and 37 miles of the New River—exactly what the county's welcome signs promise. The Jefferson National Forest flanks the outer edges of the 360-square-mile area. Giles County's largest towns and communities sprawl at the county's heart, along the parallel paths of the New River and US-460.

Formed in 1806 from Montgomery County, Giles County takes it name from William Branch Giles (1762-1830), a U.S. Senator from Virginia at the time of the county's creation.

DISMAL

The Dismal area was named for the dismal look of the rough and wild land in the southwestern corner of Giles County. Dismal's growing season is short and the soil is poor. The Appalachian Trail and USFS-201 pass through this section of the Jefferson National Forest.

What's to See

Dismal Falls: Splitting its path as it curves around a rock wall, Dismal Creek slips down steps of sandstone at a 40-foot width, then rushes in two flumes into a single whirlpool. The creek makes a total drop of about 12 feet at Dismal Falls, in the Jefferson National Forest. The water here is clean, clear, and stocked with trout. Away from the falls, the creek disappears into the forest, later heading to Bland County and eventually draining to Kimberling Creek and the New River. In summer, the pool below the falls is a popular swimming hole.

🚗 From US-460-Business at the Giles County Courthouse in Pearisburg, follow VA-100 south for 10.4 miles to Poplar Hill. Turn right on VA-42 and go 10.2 miles to VA-606. Turn right on VA-606 and go north for 0.9 miles. Turn right on VA-671, which becomes USFS-201 when it turns to gravel, and follow for one mile to the parking area on the right. A trail leads 50 yards to the falls.

Alternate Route: From I-77 Exit 52 at Bland, follow VA-42 east for 13.8 miles. Turn left on VA-606 and go 0.9 miles to a right turn on VA-671, then follow for one mile to the trailhead on the right.

EGGLESTON

In south-central Giles County, large rock cliffs loom above the New River and give Eggleston its most well-known landmarks. VA-730 spans the river here and affords great views, though early morning fog often hovers above the water and clouds the cliffs.

The earliest known settler at Eggleston was Adam Harman (Harmon). He built a cabin overlooking the New River here, sometime between 1745 and 1750. Harman was born Heinrich Adam Hermann in Germany in 1700 and came to Pennsylvania in 1726. The place he settled, at Eggleston, was earliest known as "Gunpowder Springs," reportedly because the area's spring-water tasted, or smelled, like gunpowder.

In the 1830s, the New River cliffs at Eggleston took on such names as "Caesar's Arch" and "Pompey's Pillar" when the Hygeian Springs Resort was established here. In 1853, a man remembered as "Doctor Chapman" built a new hotel and dance pavilion at the resort, by then known as "New River White Sulphur Springs." The resort's name changed again in 1867, and eventually so did the community's, when Capt. William Eggleston built an even larger hotel at "Eggleston Springs."

In the 1880s, railroad construction at Eggleston required drilling tunnels through rock formations. This daunting task caused such a delay that the Eggleston area earned a nickname—"Stay-Tied." A post office called "Stay Tide" operated here in 1883, but by 1886 the name had changed to "Eggleston."

The springwater resort closed in the 1930s, and its buildings have since been torn down.

GLEN LYN

In about 1750, early settler John Toney called the Glen Lyn area "Montreal," a French word meaning "royal mountain." The north-central Giles County town was later known as "Shumates Ferry," for a ferry operated by Parkinson Shumate. The name changed to Glen Lyn in 1883 when a railroad

Dismal Falls, in the Jefferson National Forest

was built through the region, but the area—or part of it—was called "Hell's Gate" by railroad workers. The word *glen* means "valley," and interpretations of "lyn" (or *linn*) include "steep" and "waterfall." By either combination, "Glen Lyn" aptly describes this town's steep-sided valley, lying between rapids on the New River. Located where US-460 crosses the river near Mercer County, West Virginia, Glen Lyn was incorporated in 1926 and was home to about 150 people in 2000.

What's to See

New River Access: A takeout on the New River at Glen Lyn sits five miles from Rich Creek. Fishing here includes smallmouth bass and sunfish. Heading downstream from Glen Lyn, the New River flows through the slow-moving waters of the isolated Bluestone Lake. It's about seven miles, by water, to follow the river from Glen Lyn to the West Virginia state line.

🚗 From the east side of the US-460 river bridge at Glen Lyn, turn south on a one-lane gravel road at the Glen Lyn Town Park and Campground and follow for a half mile to the ramp, on the right.

MOUNTAIN LAKE

Eastern Giles County's fabled Mountain Lake community contains the only natural lake still existing in Virginia's mountains, one of only two natural freshwater lakes in the state. Up to 100 feet deep, the crystal blue pool covers 55 acres at an elevation of 3,875 feet. Mountain Lake formed in about 7,000 B.C. when a rockslide dammed a small stream at one end of a tiny valley.

Southwest Virginia explorer Christopher Gist made the earliest known written reference to Mountain Lake in 1751. Settlers in the early 1800s used the forest-lined lake's springy basin to salt their cattle, and that's how the lake became known as the "Salt Pond," the name still used to identify the mountain the lake is carved into. A possibly conflicting account says that the name "Salt Pond" was invented by an early belief that this was once the location of a salt lick frequented by elk, buffalo, and deer.

The lavish Mountain Lake Resort Hotel borders the lake. Worldwide audiences fell in love with the Mountain Lake Resort after the box office release of 1987's *Dirty Dancing*. The stately hotel was given a prominent role in that film when the crews of Vestron Pictures came to Mountain Lake in 1986 to capture the "dirty dancing" style of actors Patrick Swayze and Jennifer Grey. Years later, the movie's love story continues to lure tourists here so they, too, can look for the time of their lives. The hotel stands at the center of the community, along VA-613. Getting there from four-lane US-460, between Newport and Pembroke, requires following VA-700 north for seven steep and winding miles.

But *Dirty Dancing* is the stuff of recent times. The lake's reputation as a vacation destination dates to at least 1857, a time when a hotel was reported to be standing here atop Salt Pond Mountain. Along the way, the fledgling resort's Salt Pond became the more attractive-sounding "Mountain Lake," and its ownership changed several times. By the 1930s, William Lewis Moody of Galveston, Texas, had acquired the lake, and in 1936 he used native sandstone to construct the hotel that now centers the 2,600-acre resort. An inscription over the hotel lobby fireplace—THE HOUSE OF MOODY—remembers its founder.

Mountain Lake Resort Hotel, in time, grew famous for its first-class pampering and endless amenities. A foundation established by Moody's daughter Mary operates the resort. Beyond the main hotel building, several multicolored cabins rise from a lawn outlined with stone walkways. Various individuals built these summer homes in the early 1900s. The builders were given a 15-year lease; after the lease was up, the cottages became property of the hotel.

Open late spring to late fall, the resort is known for more than its restaurant or its rooms. About two dozen miles of trails cross the property, including a popular path leading to a 4,361-foot lookout called "Bald Knob," the tallest point in Giles County. Resort attractions include archery, a swimming pool, and lawn games. Various types of boating are available, and a sandy swimming beach lines the lakeshore.

In 2000, the spring-fed lake's level was considerably low, reaching neither the hotel's picturesque gazebo nor a lakefront cottage on an opposite shoreline. That summer, the hotel admin-

Mountain Lake Hotel—the setting of the film *Dirty Dancing*—in eastern Giles County

drop on this wild trout stream, water cascades down a 45-foot-high rock stairway. The creek then winds through thick woods for several hundred yards before finding the 18-foot Middle Falls of Mill Creek. Just below, the creek makes two immediate but much smaller drops before plunging a height of 10 feet at its confluence with the tiny Mercy Branch.

The Falls of Mill Creek are on public property and can be reached from the Appalachian Trail, without leaving the national forest, by hiking down Pearis Mountain toward Narrows. Getting to the falls, though, is easier through the Town of Narrows, where a hiking trail begins at the edge of the national forest. But when going through town, it may be a little tricky to avoid what might be considered trespassing. The Town of Narrows promotes the falls on brochures and a Web site, saying they can be accessed through its publicly owned Town Farm Park. Still, officials have been known to post NO TRESPASSING signs at a gated road leading to the park.

Field trips to the falls are sometimes held during the Narrows Fall Festival. Other times, seek permission through the town office, 131 Center St., if the trail is under development. Be prepared for some off-trail exploration to find the falls—spurs may not be easy to locate.

🚗 From US-460, follow VA-61 west to Narrows, crossing the New River. Turn left on VA-100 (Main St.). Follow through the downtown business district and turn right on North View Street, which becomes VA-652, and follow for about one mile to its intersection with VA-710. Mill Creek is visible at this junction; parking is limited. On foot, follow VA-652 (gravel) on the left side of the creek. Pass a gate marking the Town Farm Park, then bear right through a field, following close to the

istration issued a statement in its newsletter, blaming the low level on a drought that "historically happens every 30 or 40 years." A year later, scientists discovered that water periodically drains, and possibly refills, through a hole in the lake's floor.

North of the hotel property, the Mountain Lake Wilderness encompasses a virtually roadless area of 11,113 acres. Mountain Lake Wilderness is part of the Jefferson National Forest. The area extends to Giles County's neighbors—Craig County, Virginia, and Monroe County, West Virginia—and straddles the Eastern Continental Divide, with some streams flowing to the Gulf of Mexico, and others draining to the Atlantic Ocean. The wilderness area includes a mountain bog, virgin spruce and hemlock, and several hiking trails.

NARROWS

The Town of Narrows, in north-central Giles County, has a fitting name. Here, US-460 and the railroad tracks have just enough room to narrowly pass where the New River cuts a gorge between East River and Peters mountains. Wolf Creek meets the river near this cut, historically known as "The Narrows."

Settlers came to Narrows as early as 1778. A post office opened here in 1873, and the Town of Narrows was incorporated in 1904. Narrows lies at the junction of VA-61 and VA-100 and was home to about 2,100 residents in 2000. The Narrows Fall Festival is held here on the first Saturday of each October.

What's to See

Falls of Mill Creek: The picture-perfect Cascades near Pembroke usually receive the biggest attention from waterfall fans visiting Giles County. But nearly as spectacular—and also inside the Jefferson National Forest—is a half-mile-long series of falls on Mill Creek, at the southern edge of Narrows. At the largest

Middle Falls of Mill Creek, in the Jefferson National Forest

Lower Falls of Mill Creek, near Narrows

Settlers received land grants in Newport as early as 1785. But the first post office here did not open until 1842, about the time this area became known as a "new port" of entrance to southeastern Giles County. Newport, known early on as "Crossroads" and also "Chapmans Mills," was an important junction on stagecoach roads.

Incorporated during the 1871-1872 session of the Virginia Legislature, Newport reached a zenith of commercial activity in the late 1800s. Mills and a blacksmith shop provided an industrial core. Newport's town council improved streets with sidewalks and alleys. But a bad omen arrived in 1902—several buildings were left in ruin by a fire at the center of town. According to one account, the town's charter also burned in the fire. Not much later, commerce began drying up as new roads lured people elsewhere.

The town's incorporation is no longer in force. But the heart of the village, east of US-460 at the crossroads of VA-42 and VA-796, is listed as a historic district on both state and national historic registers.

What's to See

Link's Farm Covered Bridge: One of Virginia's few remaining covered bridges is located west of Newport, less than a mile from the well-traveled US-460. Painted red and measuring little more than 12 feet wide, the Link's Farm Covered Bridge, once known as the "Bradley Bridge" for former owner Samuel Bradley, is no longer part of the main road leading to Mountain Lake.

Built over Sinking Creek in 1912, the 54-foot span has been silent to traffic since 1949. Named for owners J. C. and Betsy Link, the privately owned structure is a drive-by attraction.

🚗 From VA-42 at Newport, follow US-460 west for about two miles and turn right on VA-700. Head north toward Mountain Lake for about a quarter mile. The bridge is on the left, just before the VA-604 intersection. Visitors should park at the edge of the road and respect private property.

Sinking Creek Covered Bridge: Dating to 1916, the single-lane Sinking Creek Covered Bridge spans 70 feet. The romantic red vestige of rural America, also known as the "Clover Hollow Covered Bridge" for its proximity to the Clover Hollow community, was left in place when a new, non-covered bridge was constructed on VA-601 in 1963. Owned by the Giles County Board of Supervisors, the covered bridge was restored and repainted by local citizens in 2000. The "Sinking Creek" part of the name appears because the creek flowing below the bridge at one point sinks beneath the earth's surface.

Also off VA-601, between Newport and the covered bridge, a 20-foot-high milldam splashes as spectacularly as a natural waterfall. In the early 1900s, the dam was part of the Givens Mill, named for owner Hugh Peck Givens.

creek, as the trail slips into a forested area just past an old water reservoir. Follow the trail, staying close to the creek, for another 1.5 miles until reaching the lower falls, located off a short spur on the right.

Back on the main trail, cross Mercy Branch and take a spur on the immediate right to the middle falls. Return to the trail and walk about 500 more yards, going continually uphill and briefly away from the creek to find another spur leading to the 45-foot waterfall, also on the right.

New River Access: A New River boat landing is available near the mouth of Wolf Creek. The landing is part of Camp Success, a rustic park named for a nearby Confederate Army encampment commanded by Brig. Gen. Henry Heth, who successfully turned away a Union invasion of Narrows in May 1862. Boaters should beware of the river's dangerous Class III rapids—the Narrows Falls—near this landing.

🚗 From US-460, follow VA-61 west to Narrows, crossing the New River, and turn right on VA-649. Follow VA-649 for a quarter mile to the Camp Success entrance on the right.

🚗 From US-460 at Newport, follow VA-42 (Bluegrass Trail) east for nearly one mile. Turn left on VA-601 (Clover Hollow Rd.). The milldam is on the right after a quarter mile. Continue for another half mile to the covered bridge, also on the right. Visitors should park at the edge of the road and respect private property.

PEARISBURG

At the crossroads of VA-100 and US-460-Business in the center of Giles County, mountains cradle Pearisburg, giving this courthouse town a towering backdrop. Pearisburg's name remembers Capt. George Pearis, a local ferryboat operator who donated 53 acres of land to establish Pearisburg as the seat of Giles County. Pearisburg's first post office, called "Giles Court House," opened in 1811. The post office name changed to "Pearisburgh" in the 1850s, with the final *H* falling off by 1893.

The Giles County Courthouse, 501 Wenonah Ave., stands at the center of Pearisburg's Old Town District, an area listed on both state and national historic registers. The Old Town District contains more than a dozen buildings, including the courthouse, built with bright red bricks and topped with an octagonal cupola. Monuments honoring war veterans surround the courthouse on a neatly trimmed lawn outlined with a wrought-iron fence. The date posted above the two-story courthouse's front columns—1806—reflects the year the county was formed, not the building's 1836 construction.

The brick Andrew Johnston House, 208 N. Main St., is also on historic landmark registers. Constructed in 1829 as the residence of Andrew Johnston (1771-1838), one of Pearisburg's first store owners, this Federal-style structure is owned by the Giles County Historical Society. Behind the house, the society operates a general-history museum, with displays of various memorabilia and historic photos. Also here is the circa-1857 office of Dr. Harvey Green Johnston, one of Andrew's sons.

Sinking Creek Covered Bridge, near Newport

Link's Farm Covered Bridge, en route to Mountain Lake

For a week during the Civil War, Federal troops used Dr. Johnston's tiny office as their headquarters. But on May 10, 1862, Confederate soldiers caught the Federals by surprise during the Battle of Pearisburg. Two men on each side were killed in a small skirmish downtown, and several were left wounded.

Pearisburg was first incorporated as a town in 1835. The 2000 census counted about 2,700 residents here.

What's to See

Angels Rest: To find an aerial view of Giles County, simply climb to the top of Angels Rest, a 3,633-foot summit on Pearis Mountain. Reaching the top requires a 1.5-mile ascent on a moderate-to-strenuous section of the Appalachian Trail inside the Jefferson National Forest. The climb is a little rocky in places, but after walking a mile through steep and shady woods, hikers can see practically all of Pearisburg.

Nobody seems to know for sure how Angels Rest took its name. Among the stories told is that a poetic early settler coined the title, thinking this lofty perch was a fitting place for angels to reside. Another theory says the name is related to local settlers with the surname Angel.

🚗 From the Giles County Courthouse in Pearisburg, go north on VA-100 (N. Main St.) for 0.4 miles. Turn left on Johnston Avenue, then immediately turn right on Morris Avenue and follow for 0.7 miles. Look for a white blaze and a small sign noting an Appalachian Trail crossing. On the left side of the road, follow the trail uphill from here to the top of the mountain. Parking is limited.

Glen Alton Farm Recreation Area: The remote and inviting Glen Alton Farm includes two houses dating to the 1930s, a U-shaped duck pond, an elaborate system of stone-and-log dams, and several outbuildings. The U.S. Forest Service acquired Glen Alton in 1999. It is overseen by the Jefferson National Forest's New River Valley District and was once the personal retreat of Giles County banker Clarence Lucas. The 304-acre

Andrew Johnston House in Pearisburg

farm is on the headwaters of the North Fork of Stony Creek and is open for picnicking, hiking, and bird-watching.

Forest officials interpret the name "Glen Alton" to mean "high mountain valley." The farm's elevation is about 2,600 feet.

🚗 From the Ripplemead/Pearisburg Exit, follow US-460 east for 1.3 miles. Turn left on VA-635 (Big Stony Creek Rd.) and follow north for 13.4 miles. Turn left on VA-722 (Glen Alton Rd.) and go a half mile (bearing right after 0.2 miles) to a parking area at the gated entrance.

White Rocks Recreation Area: Not to be confused with the White Rocks near Cumberland Gap, the White Rocks Recreation Area in Giles County became part of the Jefferson National Forest soon after it was logged in the 1930s. Named for the large white rocks on a nearby slope, the site includes a 49-space campground, native brook trout in the picturesque White Rock Branch of Stony Creek, and the 1.5-mile Virginias Walk, a trail traversing northeastern Giles County and Monroe County, West Virginia, inside the Mountain Lake Wilderness Area. Entry fees are charged through the forest's New River Valley District.

🚗 From the Ripplemead/Pearisburg Exit, follow US-460 east for 1.3 miles. Turn left on VA-635 (Big Stony Creek Rd.) and follow north for 16 miles. Turn right on VA-613, go 0.7 miles, and turn left on the campground's mile-long entrance road.

PEMBROKE Several theories make a guess on how the Pembroke post office took its name in the 1840s. One says it comes from Pem Lybrooks, an early settler. According to some accounts, Lybrooks was a descendant of Phillip Lyebrook (originally "Leibroch"), whose family came from Holland. Another story, possibly a different version of the same tale, concerns John Lyebrook, a descendant of Phillip, who ran across the name "Pembroke"—possibly in reference to the Earl of Pembroke—and later christened the community "Pembroke" by hanging a sign with that name in the post office.

Pembroke was settled in about 1748, though it would be 200 years until the town was incorporated, in 1948. In 2000, Pembroke was home to about 1,100 residents, living near the intersection of US-460 and VA-623 in central Giles County.

What's to See

Cascades Recreation Area: A visit to Giles County cannot be complete without hiking to the Cascades. But be prepared—getting to this 66-foot-high waterfall on Little Stony Creek requires a four-mile round-trip hike from the parking lot of the Cascades Recreation Area. Entry fees are charged through the New River Valley District of the Jefferson National Forest.

Known as "Little Stony Falls" to visitors in the late 1800s, the Cascades look like a painting come to life. The water here makes a long midair drop and then splashes and spreads, fanning into a dazzling display on a sloping rock wall. The ultra-clean air is perfumed by an evergreen forest and dampened by light mist. This landmark could hardly disappoint any waterfall seeker, any hiker, or any photographer, beginner to pro.

Two hiking trails lead the way to the falls. Both originate from the recreation-area parking lot. The high road runs along a ridge overlooking Little Stony Creek and is a wide, easy-to-follow path with a few moderate elevation climbs. But it is not nearly as scenic as another well-developed hiking trail leading upstream and following close to the edge of the creek. In places, this lower trail crosses the creek on footbridges made of hand-hewn logs. The creek-side path also passes countless water ruffles, chutes, and whirlpools on sometimes slippery, moss-covered boulders. Be forewarned—it is easy to burn up a whole roll of film simply taking pictures of the creek, before making it to the star attraction.

The Cascades commonly attracts crowds on weekends. The falls are popular with young lovers, families, and students from local colleges. Beyond the actual Cascades, a trail leads upstream to the nearly unknown Upper Cascades, an 18-foot-high ledge with three separate spills in an idyllic and isolated area.

🚗 From US-460-West near the Pembroke Post Office, turn right on VA-623 (Cascade Dr.) and follow northeast for 3.4 miles to the Cascades parking area. The two trails to the Cascades are well marked; both span about two miles. To reach the Upper Cascades, follow left on the uphill trail behind the Cascades' main viewing platform and go 200 yards to an intersection with the high-road trail. Turn right and go uphill for a half mile to a fork. Twenty yards after passing a road gate, bear right and descend below a canopy of trees on a 100-yard path to find the upper falls.

Cascade Falls in the Jefferson National Forest

Castle Rock and *New River Access:* Castle Rock is one of the most prominent cliffs on Giles County's portion of the New River. The imposing bluff, with a sharp head, rises about 125 feet above the New River. And, true to its name, it resembles some kind of castle. The cliff can be seen on Pembroke's southwestern horizon, or it can be viewed directly across the river from the A. H. Snidow Park, a public river access near the VA-623 bridge.

Castle Rock lends its name to a church, an insurance agency, and the Castle Rock Recreation Area, which features an 18-hole public golf course, a swimming pool, basketball courts, tennis courts, and picnic shelters, on Castle Rock Road in Pembroke.

The A. H. Snidow Park is a great place to launch a canoe trip. Immediately downstream from the boat landing, the river passes beneath the VA-623 bridge; the water then swings below high cliffs and bypasses a few small islands. From Pembroke, a 15-mile float on this particularly scenic stretch of river leads to a ramp at Rich Creek. Beware of rapids, especially near Narrows.

🚗 From US-460 at Pembroke, follow Snidow Street west through town for about a quarter mile. Bear left on VA-623 (River Rd.) and follow for another quarter mile. Cross the railroad tracks and turn left on a gravel lane leading to Snidow Park just before crossing a New River bridge.

128

Wind Rock in the Jefferson National Forest

Castle Rock and the New River near Pembroke

Wind Rock: In the northeastern corner of Giles County, a short hike along the Appalachian Trail leads to the Wind Rock. This windswept cliff in the Jefferson National Forest provides a panoramic vantage at a 4,100-foot elevation. The rock gives a bird's-eye view of Peters Mountain, a summit along the West Virginia state line, named for 18th-century hunter Peter Wright.

🚗 From the Pembroke Post Office, follow US-460 east for 2.2 miles. Turn left on VA-613 (Doe Creek Rd.) and go north to reach the Mountain Lake Hotel in 4.9 miles. Bear left on VA-613 at the VA-700 intersection and continue northwest for 5.4 miles. Look for the Appalachian Trail crossing and a parking area on the left side of the road. The trail to the Wind Rock starts at a kiosk on the road's right side and follows the Appalachian Trail uphill for 0.3 miles. Turn left after reaching an informal spur inside a small grassy meadow and go 10 yards to the Wind Rock.

RICH CREEK

Among the Rich Creek area's natural resources are five large springs at the source of a stream. This springwater, known for its high quality, naturally yielded the name "Rich Creek," a title later adopted when the Town of Rich Creek was incorporated in 1946. Nearly 700 residents called Rich Creek home in 2000. The town lies along US-460, between Narrows and Glen Lyn, in north-central Giles County.

What's to See

New River Access: The stretch of the New River downstream from Rich Creek includes a few islands and is noted for small-mouth bass, catfish, and rock-bass fishing. The takeout at Glen Lyn is about five miles from Rich Creek.

🚗 The ramp is off US-460-East, about one mile east of the Town of Rich Creek.

Bane: In 1796, James Bane owned land between Sugar Run Mountain and the New River, an area that came to be called "Bane." Central: VA-663 at VA-100

Berton: Berton is a common family name in Giles County and inspired the name of this community. South-central: VA-622, near railroad and New River

Bluff City: Bluffs overlook the New River at Bluff City, the site of the first court of Giles County in 1806. Formerly called "Wenonah," Bluff City was also once called "Free State," because black residents lived here just after the Civil War. Central: VA-640 at US-460, north end of Pearisburg

Chapel: Chapel's first post office opened in 1908, likely borrowing its name from one of a couple of churches in the area. Northwestern: VA-61 at VA-724

Clendennin: Capt. George Clendennin, a pioneer settler and noted Indian fighter, is remembered at Clendennin, an area between Pearisburg and Narrows. Central: VA-641 along Clendennin Creek, near the Appalachian Trail

Clover Hollow: The Clover Hollow area was originally called "Clover Bottom," a name derived from the outstanding fertility of bottomland along Sinking Creek. Southeastern: VA-601 at VA-685

Curve: Both the New River and the railroad make a sharp bend at an area called "Curve." Central: VA-634 (Curve Rd.), near New River

Goldbond: Formerly known as "Olean," in 1945 this area was renamed "Goldbond," the trade name of products made here by the National Gypsum Co. North-central: VA-635 near VA-628, between Kimballton and Interior

Goodwins Ferry: J. R. Goodwin and Brothers, a local general merchant and milling operation near the New River in the 1880s, is what likely gave Goodwins Ferry its name. South-central: VA-605 at VA-625

Hoges Chapel: Known in the late 1800s as "Hoges Store," this community was named for local resident J. T. S. Hoge. Central: VA-613 at US-460

Interior: The Jefferson National Forest blankets Giles County's northeastern corner and includes a small picnic area at a place called "Interior." This place-name may originate from the Interior Lumber Co., which owned major logging operations here when Interior was a stop on the Potts Valley Branch Railroad in the 1890s. Northeastern: VA-635, near VA-802 and Appalachian Trail

Kimballton: Norfolk & Western Railway president E. J. Kimballton visited this area in 1881, and the place was named for him. North-central: VA-635 at VA-684

Klotz: C. A. Klotz organized the Virginia Limestone Corp. in 1916 and gave his name to the Klotz community. Central: VA-635, one mile north of VA-626

Lurich: A post office opened at Lurich in 1898 after a railroad worker named the place for Lou (Lu) Richardson, a young girl. North-central: VA-649, near VA-725

Maybrook: The origin of Maybrook's name is unclear. It may owe the "brook" to the Lybrook (Lyebrook) family, which settled in nearby Pembroke, about five miles west of Maybrook, in the mid-1700s. Or, "brook" might be a reference to a nearby brook flowing into Sinking Creek, which dissects the community. A Maybrook post office opened in 1881. South-central: US-460 at VA-783

Minie Ball Hill: In the Jefferson National Forest, Minie Ball Hill is on the old Salt Sulphur Turnpike, a mountain-climbing route used by both Confederate and Union soldiers to transport materials during the Civil War. Minie Ball Hill marks a site where Union Brig. Gen. George Crook dumped a load of lead bullets on May 12, 1864, because his horses could not pull the extra weight over the area's steep, 3,947-foot elevation. The minié balls, found for years on this hill, are named for ammunition developed by French army officer Claude Minié. Northeastern: VA-613, half mile south of Appalachian Trail

Penvir: Pennsylvania's W. E. C. Merriman named Penvir for Pennsylvania ("Pen") and Virginia ("vir") when he built a railroad in the area, near Wolf Creek. The area's first post office opened in 1902. Northwestern: VA-61 at VA-673

Poplar Hill: Early settler Samuel Shelton moved to the Giles County area in 1774 and cut huge poplar trees to build a log house on what he called "Poplar Hill." South-central: VA-42 at VA-100

Ripplemead: Between Pearisburg and Pembroke, Ripplemead is named for the rippling waters of the New River and the meadows along its banks. Central: VA-636, near US-460

Shumate: William P. Shumate settled near Wolf Creek in 1866, and the surrounding community was named for him. Northwestern: VA-61, west of Narrows

Staffordsville: Ireland's Ralph Stafford came to the Staffordsville area in the late 1700s, and the community took his name. South-central: VA-100 at VA-660

Thessalia: A Thessalia post office opened in 1885. The community's name comes from the Bible's book of Thessalonians. West-central: VA-661 at VA-663

Trigg: Once called "Irish Settlement" for its Irish residents, Trigg was named for early settlers Daniel and William Trigg. South-central: VA-730, near VA-622

Wabash: Members of the Rogers family left North Carolina but never made it to their intended final destination of Wabash, Ind. Undaunted, the travelers chose to form a new Wabash by giving that name to this small community, where a post office was established in 1876. South-central: VA-659 (Wabash Rd.) at Wabash Creek, one mile north of Poplar Hill

White Gate: Cow-covered hills compose the landscape at White Gate. First known as "Rye Meadows" for the rye grass growing in creek bottoms, the community became "Banesville" for early settler John Bane. The village found its present name in about 1842, paying reference to something on Bane's property—a gate painted white. Southwestern: VA-42 at VA-670

MONTGOMERY COUNTY

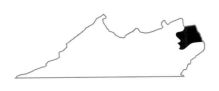

East of US-460, the invisible Eastern Continental Divide runs through Montgomery County and separates the watersheds of the Roanoke River, which flows to the Atlantic Ocean, and the New River, draining west to the Gulf of Mexico. Montgomery County's largest towns, Christiansburg and Blacksburg, are at the apex of the county's 389 square miles. Both towns are in the New River basin, and together they form a mini-metropolitan district along a commercialized strip of US-460.

Formed in 1776 from the now-extinct Fincastle County, Montgomery County was named for Brig. Gen. Richard Montgomery, a hero of the French and Indian War.

ALLEGHANY SPRINGS

Green hills roll to the South Fork of the Roanoke River at Alleghany Springs, a quiet neighborhood near the crossroads of VA-637 and VA-817, in southeastern Montgomery County. The word *alleghany* comes from Native Americans and is commonly interpreted to mean "endless."

In a former life, this area at the edge of Alleghany Mountain was the site of a springwater resort established in 1853. The Alleghany Springs Resort closed in about 1900 after its main hotel burned, but a two-tiered springhouse pavilion, built in about 1890, stands off VA-817 (Gazebo Dr.), about 0.1 miles east of VA-637 (Alleghany Spring Rd.). The springhouse walls are made of entangled rhododendron branches. These untrimmed limbs give a natural look to this odd pavilion listed on both state and national historic registers. The privately owned gazebo, a drive-by curiosity, can be seen from the public roadway.

BLACKSBURG

As the home of Virginia Tech, the state's largest educational institution, Blacksburg is a quintessential college town. The school's 25,000 students give Blacksburg an overwhelming roster of teens and twenty-somethings. Subsequently, college students and the businesses catering to them ignite this mountain village with a youthful zeal that sets it apart from all other places in Southwest Virginia.

Virginia Tech's campus borders downtown Blacksburg's blur of splashy lights—beacons beckoning college students to explore a catchall collection of clothing stores, specialty shops, hair salons, niche restaurants, and pubs along South Main Street. Entertwined with that blend of campus and commerce is a 16-square grid of city blocks listed on both state and national historic registers. The district is outlined by Wharton Street on the east, Draper Road on the west, Clay Street on the south, and Jackson Street on the north. Blacksburg's annual Steppin' Out Festival is held in the downtown area on the first weekend of August, with food, arts, and music.

A longtime landmark on Main Street, the Alexander Black House, was built in 1898 and used for years as a funeral parlor. In 2002, the town acquired the Queen Anne-style home and moved it to a new site, on Draper Road, with plans to showcase the structure as a Blacksburg museum. Nearby, the Price House Nature Center, 107 Wharton St., focuses on flora and fauna as part of the Blacksburg Parks and Recreation Department. The two-story Price House was built from 1840 to 1853 and takes its name from the late Nelson Price, who willed it to the town.

The Blacksburg area was once known as "Draper's Meadows," referring to land owned in the 1740s by settler George Draper. During July 1755, the settlers of Draper's Meadows were all either killed or captured in a raid by Shawnee Indians at what later became the site of the Virginia Tech campus. In 1798, Blacksburg was laid out on land donated by William Black. Officially incorporated in 1871, the town's name was spelled "Blacksburgh" when the first post office opened in 1827; the *H* was dropped by the postal service in 1893.

Blacksburg centers a large valley crossed by two sections of US-460—a bypass and a business route—in north-central Montgomery County. In 2000, about 39,000 residents lived in this Southwest Virginia hallmark.

What's to See

Ellett Valley Recreation Area: Trails loop through a dense,

131

Gazebo at Alleghany Springs

young-growth forest, passing interpretive signs and a rustic amphitheater at the Ellett Valley Recreation Area. Tucked into a residential neighborhood, this 106-acre area is maintained by the Blacksburg Parks and Recreation Department.

On US-460, immediately south of the US-460-Business junction in Blacksburg, turn east on VA-642 (Jennelle Rd.) and follow for 2.1 miles. The entrance is on the right.

Huckleberry Trail: In the early 1900s, the growth of Virginia Tech made a passenger train necessary to serve the Blacksburg campus. By 1904, a spur line leading to Blacksburg was completed and soon became known as the "Huckleberry Railroad."

One account notes that Bill Bland, a local resident who sold fruit to college students, nicknamed this line, saying the train ran so slow, students had time to jump cars and pick huckleberries, then catch the train again en route to campus. But a conflicting story says that the railroad took its name from the wild huckleberries that grew in the Merrimac community, and that when the line was under construction in 1903, locals regularly rode buggies to Merrimac to check on the railroad's progress and pick huckleberries.

The tracks are long gone, but a six-mile rail route remains as the Huckleberry Trail, a flat surface paved with asphalt. Measuring about the width of a car, the public path is ideal for walking dogs, riding bikes, in-line skating, or pushing babies in strollers. The route links downtown Blacksburg to the New River Valley Mall at Christiansburg, passing many neighborhoods, including Merrimac.

Horses and motorized vehicles are not allowed on the trail.

A major entrance to the trail is at a small picnic area near the Blacksburg Area Branch Library, 200 Miller St. Parking is also available at the New River Valley Mall, at the corner of US-460 and VA-114 (Peppers Ferry Rd.).

Pandapas Pond: Pandapas Pond does not have a boat ramp, but canoes can be easily launched at this eight-acre reservoir in the Jefferson National Forest. The pond is named for James J. Pandapas, a Massachusetts native and longtime Blacksburg resident. Pandapas originally developed the land surrounding the pond as a recreational area for employees at one of his Blacksburg businesses. He sold the land to the National Forest Service in 1987.

Fishing here includes bass and bluegill, and the pond is periodically stocked with trout. Walking trails encircle the reeds and trees of the shoreline. Nearby, trails on Poverty Creek welcome bicyclists and horseback riders.

From VA-685 (Prices Fork Rd.), follow US-460-Bypass west for six miles. The entrance is on the left.

Smithfield Plantation: The bright white and immaculate Smithfield Plantation gives a glimpse of Blacksburg's earliest days, when the area stood on the edge of Virginia's westward expansion. The large house was built in the mid-1770s for Col. William Preston (1729-1783), a Revolutionary War officer and member of the House of Burgesses. Covered with wooden shingles and framed by large chimneys, this L-shaped house centers a rolling valley and resembles the Tidewater-style plantation houses seen along the lower James River. The plantation was named for Preston's wife, Susanna Smith Preston. In 1959, a Preston descendant, Janie Preston Lamb, donated the home to the Association for the Preservation of Virginia Antiquities.

Pandapas Pond, an eight-acre reservoir near Blacksburg

Blacksburg's Smithfield Plantation

Furnished with antiques, the Smithfield Plantation is open to visitors, usually from April to December. Costumed interpreters explain the lives of western Virginia's pioneer settlers and showcase locally discovered Native American artifacts. Outside, the home's crisply cut lawn includes an exhibit of three types of wooden fencing—the sharp-edged picket fence, a stockade fence, and the Virginia split rail. Signs also pinpoint outbuildings that are no longer standing, like an office.

🚗 From US-460-Bypass, follow VA-412 (Prices Fork Rd.) east toward downtown Blacksburg for a half mile. Turn right on West Campus Drive and follow for 0.3 miles. Turn right on Duck Pond Drive and go 0.4 miles, then turn right on Smithfield Road and go 0.4 miles.

Virginia Polytechnic Institute and State University: To get a good idea of the massive sprawl of Virginia Tech (as the school is best known) and the majesty of its castle-like buildings, just drive around the oval drill field at the center of the 2,600-acre main campus. The school seems like a small city, with more than 300 buildings and hundreds of research laboratories scattered among 25,000 students and 20 miles of sidewalks. Don't worry if you forget your directions—you can't miss it. Signs all over Blacksburg point to Tech.

Football games starring the Hokies, the home team, are a hot ticket during fall. Games are played at the towering Lane Stadium, a 51,000-seat sports complex opened in 1965 and named for Edward Hudson Lane, a former member of the Virginia Tech Board of Visitors. "Hokie," though, means nothing more than nonsense; an 1896 Tech graduate, O. M. Stull, invented the word as part of a cheer during a spirit contest.

The roots of Virginia Tech can be traced to the Olin and Preston Institute, founded in 1854. This Methodist-affiliated school later reversed its name to "Preston and Olin Institute." Either way, the name honored Col. William Ballard Preston, a local businessman and politician, and Stephen Olin, a Methodist minister. The institute began a new life in 1872 when its facilities were used for the founding of the Virginia Agricultural and Mechanical College, now known officially as the Virginia Polytechnic Institute and State University. The state-supported institution offers more than 70 undergraduate and about 150 graduate programs.

The campus capital is Burruss Hall, a neo-Gothic building full of administration offices. Erected in 1935-1936 with limestone quarried from Montgomery County, the building is named for Dr. Julian Ashby Burruss, university president from 1919 to 1945. Like many other buildings on campus, Burruss Hall was constructed with Hokie Stone, a term referring to several types of limestone commonly found in Southwest Virginia, Tennessee, and Alabama and uniquely used for Tech's building projects.

Tech has operated its own stone quarry since the 1950s. The school also operates many kinds of experimental farms. Agricultural studies, traditionally, comprise a major part of the university's mission. The school, for one, claims fame as the 1925 birthplace of the Future Farmers of Virginia, later used as the model for the Future Farmers of America.

A lifesize Allosaurus skeleton stretching 22 feet greets visitors at Tech's Museum of Geological Sciences, at 2062 Derring Hall, near the corner of West Campus Drive and Perry Street. Other exhibits include gemstones and fossils from across Virginia. The department of art and art history operates the Armory Art Gallery, 201 Draper Rd. Housed in a 1936 brick building, the gallery features rotating exhibits. Also on campus, the Squires Student Center includes the Perspective Art Gallery. The center takes its name from John H. Squires, a member of Tech's class of 1905.

Built in 1937, Virginia Tech's Duck Pond, a popular hangout for students, teachers, and locals, is fed by the waters of Stroubles Creek, a watercourse named for early German immigrant Gaspar Strouble. The pond is outlined with picnic tables, a gazebo, benches, and the draping manes of weeping willows.

Burruss Hall, on the Virginia Tech campus in Blacksburg

CAMBRIA Painted green with red trim, a wooden structure often called the "Cambria Depot" but bearing the name "Christiansburg" stands at 630 Depot St. in Christiansburg. The Italianate-style depot was constructed in 1868 for train passengers. The building is located at the center of Cambria, once an independent, incorporated railroad town with three hotels, two gristmills, a furniture-making business, and a limekiln.

Cambria originated in the mid-1850s as a stop on the Virginia and Tennessee Railroad, and was known earliest as either "North Christiansburg" or "Christiansburg Depot" for its location, just a mile north of the Montgomery County Courthouse in Christiansburg. It's a town that owes its origin to public outcry. That is, several people in this area were opposed to the railroad company's initial plan to lay tracks through the heart of Christiansburg. The complainants said that trains would hurt livestock or children. Rice D. Montague, a landowner, offered the ultimate solution by allowing the railroad a right-of-way across his farm at Cambria. The move provided a railroad bypass for Christiansburg and gave a chance for the new town of Cambria to form.

Situated around Christiansburg's Depot and Cambria streets, the area adopted an odd name, "Bangs," sometime in the 1870s. According to legend, some men departed a train here, then tried to settle a dispute with guns. A bystander reported hearing "bangs," and, later, somebody decided to use that name for a post office. By the 1890s, however, the place was called "Cambria," either to reflect the local mountains' rock formations from the Cambrian geological period, or to remember a city by the same name in Wales. The name "Cambria" refers to Welsh culture or Wales.

Incorporated as Cambria in 1906, the town survived until it was consolidated in 1964 as part of Christiansburg. Local landmarks continue to use "Cambria." As for the depot, it was a freight station through the 1960s. Privately owned, in 1983 the building was saved from razing and then restored and converted into offices. It is listed on state and national historic registers.

CHRISTIANSBURG US-11 runs through Christiansburg's Main Street, a tree-lined thoroughfare closely following the path of the ancient Wilderness Trail. Paying homage to frontier times, Christiansburg remembers its roots on the third Saturday of September with the annual Wilderness Trail Festival.

Still, it's not like Christiansburg is much of a wilderness. Home to about 17,000 people in 2000, the city is a community of suburban and commercial developments stretching from the Blacksburg border on US-460 to the Roanoke River Valley on the east. Christiansburg (or "Christiansburgh" in its earliest days) was founded in 1792 in an area formerly called "Hans Meadows," a name later used to designate a road and housing subdivision. "Hans Meadows" refers to the region's early Germanic migration. Christiansburg's present name honors Col. William Christian (1742-1786), who served in Virginia's General Assembly in 1776.

The Montgomery County Courthouse stands at the center of town, on the corner of US-11 and South Franklin Street. Framed with tan bricks and glass walls, the 1970s-era structure replaced a courthouse torn down in 1979. Across the street sits the 1936 Christiansburg Post Office, one of downtown's registered landmarks. This brick building's lobby features a Works Progress Administration mural, painted in 1938 to depict the early history of the New River Valley, including events of the French and Indian War.

Historic registers also count Christiansburg's South Franklin Street District, a neighborhood centered by a unique brick house called "The Huts." Privately owned, this dwelling with conical roofs originally featured three round rooms, connected with passageways, plus a detached guest hut. Ethel Lawson Rice designed the home in 1919 to look like the native round huts of Africa. To Rice, this house was a constant reminder of the time she and her husband, Will A. Rice, lived in Rhodesia (now Zimbabwe).

Antiques, artifacts, and books explain the history of Christiansburg and Montgomery County at the nonprofit Montgomery Museum & Lewis Miller Regional Art Center, housed in

Christiansburg Depot, in the Cambria section of Christiansburg

a circa-1852 structure originally built as the manse for the Presbyterian Church of Christiansburg. At 300 S. Pepper St., the brick building doubles as the location of a gallery named for Lewis Miller (1796-1882), a folk artist who spent the last 20 years of his life in Christiansburg. Miller's sketches, along with other artists' works, are on display.

Beyond the downtown district along US-460, Christiansburg blends into Blacksburg with hardly a distinction. Near the New River Valley Mall (US-460 at VA-114), several modern restaurants and shopping centers make this a busy place. The Montgomery County Park, a 90-acre site with hiking trails, picnic sites, and a small water park, lies off US-460 at 410 County Rd., between the two towns.

What's to See

Christiansburg Industrial Institute Museum: Celebrated African-American statesman Booker T. Washington (1856-1915) served as education advisor to the Christiansburg Industrial Institute during the last 20 years of his life. Founded in 1866 by Capt. Charles S. Schaeffer and the Friends Freedman's Association of Philadelphia, the institute was the first high school for blacks in Southwest Virginia. Initially a private facility, the school provided instruction ranging from elementary and high school courses to a few with college rank. The Montgomery County School Board operated the institute during its final years; it closed in 1966.

A monument remembering the school's history fronts a small brick museum building that is open by appointment through contacts with the Montgomery County Chamber of Commerce.

🚗 From downtown Christiansburg, follow US-460 (N. Franklin St.) west and look for a historical marker relating to the school's history. Turn left on Scattergood Drive, one block east of Christiansburg High School. The brick museum is on the left at 0.1 miles.

ELLETT

VA-603 meets VA-723 in central Montgomery County, forming Ellett's main crossroads. About a mile north of this residential community, a tiny real estate venture called "New Ellett" developed along the railroad in 1912. The 1906 Virginia Railway Underpass, a one-lane, horseshoe-shaped tunnel spanning 15 feet, links these two Elletts. The tunnel is recognized as a state and national historic landmark for its early demonstration of reinforced concrete on an arched bridge.

"Ellett" comes from Dr. Robert T. Ellett, who took charge of the Civil War hospital at the nearby Montgomery White Sulphur Springs resort in 1863. Ellett and his wife, Sue, had 11 children and lived for many years in Christiansburg.

IRONTO

Despite the fact that its name is on an I-81 exit sign, the actual community of Ironto (pronounced "eye-RON-tow") lies a few miles from the Interstate highway, along VA-647 (Ironto Rd.), between VA-603 (North Fork Rd.) and the railroad in eastern Montgomery County. Ironto was known in the early 1900s as "Burkett," but the railroad flag stop was renamed in 1910-1911. "Ironto" was the name of the adopted daughter of local resident Dabney Burkett.

What's to See

Falls Ridge Preserve: In the deep green Falls Hallow of eastern Montgomery County's backwoods, waters stand almost perfectly still atop a muddy creek bottom. And yet, less than 100 yards below this tranquillity, the creek begins a steady descent, continually sloping for about 80 feet before breaking into two channels and plunging—just a few feet in midair—over a muddy, moss-covered precipice.

These spring-fed, travertine falls, which don't have much water even during a wet spring, are located inside the 655-acre Falls Ridge Preserve, a steep, wooded area donated to the Nature Conservancy by William P. Bradley in 1974. Near the falls lie the ruins of an early industry in the Fagg community—a small lime quarry and kiln that were operated by the late Harry Cleveland Dudley, owner of this property in the early 1900s.

🚗 From I-81 Exit 128 near Ironto, follow VA-603 (North Fork Rd.) west toward Blacksburg for 6.9 miles. Turn left on Falls Ridge Road. Cross a bridge and railroad tracks, then immediately turn left on a rough gravel road, which parallels the tracks and curves to the right. Ford a small stream, then bear left when the road forks. Park on the side of the road near the preserve's entrance sign. Trails start on a road crossing an open, grassy field. Pass into a wooded area at the end of the field, cross a wooden footbridge, and follow a spur trail on the right for about 20 yards to see the falls, or continue straight to the ruins of the lime quarry.

LAFAYETTE

At the confluence of the north and south forks of the Roanoke River, the unincorporated town of Lafayette was originally called "Fayette" when it was laid out in six blocks, circa 1826-1828, along the Alleghany Turnpike. The town was renamed "Lafayette" or "La Fayette" after 1835. Local tradition says that the name honors Gen. Marquis de LaFayette (1757-1834), a French statesman who served in George Washington's army. A common story says LaFayette once spent a night at a home here during the Revolutionary War.

Lafayette prospered through the late 1840s but lost much of its commercial momentum after the Southwest Turnpike bypassed the town. The heart of the village lies along VA-626 and the railroad in east-central Montgomery County.

McCOY

Richard McCoy settled on 400 acres near the New River in about 1782. Within a few years, a community grew near McCoy's home and was named for him and his descendants. McCoy is at northwestern Montgomery County's crossroads of VA-625 and VA-784. In the early 1900s, coal mines operated near here at Brush Mountain.

What's to See

McCoy Falls: Rock islands jut as high as a dozen feet above the New River at the border of Giles, Pulaski, and Montgomery counties. Historically, the Class II-III rapids below these boulders are known as the "Big Falls." To locals, though, this bubbling stretch of whitewater is more commonly called "McCoy Falls" for its proximity to the McCoy community. The New River rolls over these rapids at a quick enough pace to provide a natural flume ride on an inner tube. Still, the water is not so rough that it throws the typical rider into a tizzy.

Bordering the 1,000-foot-wide river, the narrow Big Falls Road gets crowded during warm months, when typical rapid riders include students at nearby Radford University or Virginia Tech.

🚗 From US-460-Bypass in Blacksburg, follow VA-685 (Prices Fork Rd.) west for about three miles. Turn right at Prices Fork on VA-652 (McCoy Rd.) and follow for about seven miles to the railroad tracks crossing the New River at McCoy. Turn right at the stop sign and follow VA-625 (Big Falls Rd.) for about two miles to see McCoy Falls at the center of the river.

MONTGOMERY

The Montgomery community and nearby Den Hill owe their names, in part, to the legendary Montgomery White Sulphur Springs, a resort opened in the late 1840s. Immediately east of Christiansburg near Den Creek, the resort attracted visitors for its springwater, which allegedly produced health benefits. By 1855, the resort's hotel could accommodate several hundred guests.

"Den," by the way, is short for "Devil's Den," a name early settlers called the resort's location, a tiny, narrow valley watered by about 50 springs. When the resort was established, the water here was said to be strange—it steamed and tasted like brimstone and overripe eggs.

The Wilderness Road passed through the Devil's Den just below an odd, craggy cliff that became known as the "Devil's Armchair." On an exposed side of Den Hill, the rocks on the face of the Devil's Armchair are pocked with tiny, eerie-looking crevices. Superstitious locals and resort visitors once believed that the devil sat on this cliff—his "Armchair"—to overlook his "Den."

In 1862, the Civil War interrupted business, and the resort reopened as the Montgomery White Sulphur Springs General Hospital. About 200 soldiers died here during the war and were buried in nearby unmarked graves. The resort opened again after the war, and, by 1874, a Montgomery railroad stop was established near present-day VA-641's railroad crossing. A small train ran from the Montgomery station to the resort. But business slumped during the economic Panic of 1893, and, during that era, a flash flood left buildings soaked and ruined. The resort closed for good in 1904.

A century later, all traces of the resort's buildings were gone at its former site in an east-central Montgomery County valley off VA-641 (Den Hill Rd.), about 1.8 miles northwest of the railroad tracks (or 2.6 miles north of US-11/460). In this vicinity, just below a cut into Den Hill on the right side of VA-641, wooden steps on the west side of the highway lead to a grassy area and a Confederate monument. In 1889, this memorial was erected on the resort grounds to honor the soldiers buried in unmarked graves. The monument was moved in 1949 to its present site, a 20-square-foot plot outlined by a wrought-iron fence and maintained by the Dr. Harvey Black Chapter of the United Daughters of the Confederacy. The monument is atop the Devil's Armchair cliff, which reportedly caved in during the 20th century.

RINER

The intersection of five roads naturally inspired some of the first names for the Riner community, like "Five Points" or "Five Forks." In the 1850s, Riner was renamed "Auburn" and supported a store, a hotel, and a tobacco factory. But the Auburn name was ultimately dropped because another post office with the same name operated elsewhere in Virginia. The community then became "Riner" to honor David Riner, a local farmer who served in the Virginia House of Delegates in the 1880s.

Riner is about four miles south of Christiansburg in southern Montgomery County. It lies at the heart of a wide valley centered by VA-8 (Riner Road). In the 1990s, new housing subdivisions awoke Riner's sleepy status as an agricultural community, though the heart of its old downtown remained largely unchanged from the 1800s. A district listed on both state and national historic registers is located where VA-669 (Union Valley Road) meets VA-671 (Five Points Road)

SHAWSVILLE

Shawsville's name comes from Charles B. Shaw, Virginia's chief engineer when the Southwest Turnpike was built through here in 1847. As a railroad village, however, Shawsville became known as "Alleghany Station," a stopping-off place for travelers who took wagons to nearby mineral-water resorts, including Alleghany Springs, in the late 1800s.

Shawsville is in southeastern Montgomery County where VA-637 joins US-11/460. The unincorporated town grew near the site of Fort Vause, built in about 1754 by Capt. Ephraim Vause (Vaux, Voss, or Vaus). Indians attacked and destroyed Fort Vause in June 1756, taking members of Vause's family prisoner in the process. Capt. Peter Hogg soon rebuilt the fort, and future President George Washington inspected it in October 1756.

What's to See

Camp Alta Mons: The old red cabin known as "Willie Jack's" may not be the most popular site at Camp Alta Mons. But it is practically all that remains of the old Crockett Springs, a resort that once attracted visitors believing its mineral water could produce health benefits. The name "Willie Jack" is from an employee at the Crockett Springs Resort, established south of Shawsville in 1889 and named for the local Crockett family who formerly owned the resort property. One account, in particular, says that 18th-century pioneer Joseph Crockett found this place after retreating from Virginia's Holston Valley, for fear of attacks by Indians.

Crockett Springs closed as a resort in 1939 and has been the location of the 816-acre, Methodist-affiliated Camp Alta Mons since 1957. Alta Mons (the name is Latin for "high mountain") features picnic shelters, a swimming pool, a basketball court, and a campground, plus a pond for fishing and canoeing. The camp is open to the general public but is sometimes closed for church meetings.

The 45-foot-tall Stiles Falls is a beautiful attraction at Alta Mons. This wispy cascade drips over a mossy cliff on the boulder-choked Purgatory Creek. To find it, take a mile-long walk through camp and then hike a half mile on a trail that fords the creek three times. The falls are named for Randolph Stiles, a Civil War veteran who lost his life here while trying to swing across the falls on a vine. Maps of the camp and the trail to Stiles Falls are available at the camp office.

🚗 From I-81 Exit 118-C in Christiansburg, follow US-11/460 northeast for 6.4 miles to Shawsville. Turn right on VA-637 (Alleghany Spring Rd.) and follow south for 5.9 miles. The entrance is on the right, next to the Crockett Springs United Methodist Church, 2842 Crockett Springs Rd.

Bottom Creek Gorge Preserve: Puncheon Run Falls is a braided cataract sliding 200 feet down a crooked canyon wall. It creates a maze through evergreen conifers hugging the side of Bent Mountain, a natural bar-rier between Roanoke and Montgomery counties. Puncheon Run does not form a midair drop—well, not really. This series of chutes looks more like the mountain is crying, with tears parading to the base of the Bottom Creek Gorge.

In 1988, the Nature Conservancy acquired Puncheon Run Falls, alternately called "Bent Mountain Falls," as part of the Bottom Creek Gorge Preserve. A sanctuary for virgin hemlocks and rare fish species, the preserve spans 1,657 acres. About five and a half miles of trails in the preserve are open to the public, but no bikes or pets are allowed. Moderate-to-strenuous hikes lead through a forest and along gorgeous Bottom Creek, a boulder-strewn stream on the headwaters of the South Fork of the Roanoke River in the extreme southeastern corner of Montgomery County. One of the preserve's trails slides past the ruins of an early log home and a pile of stones used for buildings by deserters from the Civil War.

Stiles Falls at Camp Alta Mons

Puncheon Run Falls drops 200 feet at the Bottom Creek Gorge Preserve

In the mid-1800s, Bottom Creek Gorge Preserve was home to a settlement called "Puncheon Camp," which helped inspire the name of the falls. A puncheon is a large barrel.

🚗 From I-81 Exit 118-C in Christiansburg, follow US-11/460 northeast for 6.4 miles to Shawsville. Turn right on VA-637 (Alleghany Spring Rd.) and follow 13.9 miles south to the stop sign at Simpsons in Floyd County. Note: After 7.8 miles, at Piedmont, VA-637 turns to the left, while VA-653 continues straight. Do not turn left on VA-637; stay straight on VA-653.

At the Simpsons stop sign, turn left on VA-610 and go 2.5 miles. At the next stop sign, turn left on US-221 and continue for about seven miles, passing through Copper Hill. Turn left on VA-644 and go 1.1 miles. Bear right on VA-669 and go 2.8 miles. Note: Do not turn on Bottom Creek Rd.

After crossing a small bridge, look for a preserve sign on the left. Drive a short distance on gravel and then park on the shoulder, near a gate. Walk a half mile beyond the gate, uphill, to a kiosk with maps. To reach the waterfall overlook, continue straight for 0.3 miles on the entrance road. Bear left on the Johnston Trail (blazed in red) and go 0.8 miles. At an intersection with the Duval Trail (blazed in blue), bear left and continue for about a quarter mile to the overlook, which is situated about a quarter mile from the actual falls. To get a good view, bring binoculars or a telephoto camera lens.

WHITETHORNE

James Francis Preston built a large brick home fronted by white columns near the New River in 1855. He called the home "Whitethorn." Over time, that name was given to the surrounding area but was spelled "Whitethorne." The community is along VA-623 in the northwestern corner of Montgomery County.

What's to See

New River Access: Just downstream from the mouth of Toms Creek, shade trees hang over the New River's grassy banks near a paved ramp at Whitethorne. Here, the river is flat, wide, and known for smallmouth bass and musky fishing. Going downstream for about seven miles from Whitethorne leads to the Class II-III rapids called the Big Falls of McCoy. A ramp at Pembroke (see the Giles County chapter in the New River Valley section) is about 15.5 miles downriver from Whitethorne.

🚗 From US-460-Bypass in Blacksburg, follow VA-685 (Prices Fork Rd.) west for about three miles. Turn right at Prices Fork on VA-652 (McCoy Rd.) and follow for 3.2 miles. Turn left on VA-623 (Whitethorne Rd.) and follow for one mile to Whitethorne. Continue past an END STATE MAINTENANCE sign, immediately turn left across the railroad tracks, and follow the gravel road for 0.1 miles to the public ramp and fishing area.

YELLOW SULPHUR SPRINGS

Sometime between 1800 and 1810, Charles Taylor constructed log buildings at Taylor's Springs, a small resort serving mountain springwater. The resort was later called "Yellow Springs," deriving its new name from a yellowish-brown sediment perceptible on the bottom of the resort's spring enclosure. In the 1850s, guests arrived by railroad at what by then was known as "Yellow Sulphur Springs."

In 1873, the newly built hotel building at Yellow Sulphur

Old hotel and springhouse at Yellow Sulphur Springs

Springs was destroyed by fire, putting the business into financial hot water. About 50 years later, after a succession of owners, the resort closed its doors, during a time when such spring resorts had lost their popular appeal. In central Montgomery County, the resort property was later used as a shelter for the homeless, as apartments, and as a private residence.

In 2003, a large antebellum hotel building remained standing here. So did a line of cottages, an eight-column gazebo, and a two-lane, open-air wooden bowling alley built circa 1888. The resort site, listed on both state and national historic registers, is considered one of the most intact spring resorts remaining in Virginia. At 3145 Yellow Sulphur Rd., just off VA-643 between Christiansburg and Blacksburg, part of the site operated as an inn again in 2003 but remained under renovation.

Belmont: George Taylor owned land in the Belmont area as early as 1768, but the earliest known reference of the name "Belmont" was not used until 1876; the county school board selected this adaptation of the French *belle monte* (meaning "beautiful mount") when establishing a school here. Central: VA-114 (Peppers Ferry Rd.), two miles west of US-460

Bennetts Mill: M. D. Bennett, the likely source of this community's name, was the postmaster here in the 1880s. The area is where Mill Creek joins the North Fork of the Roanoke River. Incidentally, the Roanoke River is named for an Indian word meaning "shell money." Northeastern: VA-785, near VA-804

Childress: Three brothers—Stephen, William, and Thomas Childress—operated a store here circa 1850. For a while, the local post office was called "Childress Store." Southwestern: VA-600 at VA-693

Elliston: A railroad depot established at Elliston in the mid-1800s was called "Big Springs" or "Big Springs Depot." In about 1880, when this was a proposed steel center on the South Fork of the Roanoke River, the name changed to "Carnegie City," for industrialist Andrew Carnegie. Unfortunately, Carnegie City's manufacturing dreams failed to materialize. And, by the 1890s, the name had changed yet again. The present name refers to Maj. William Mumford Ellis (1846-1921), who married Pearl Tyler (1860-1947), a daughter of President John Tyler. The Ellis family once lived in the Elliston area. Eastern: US-11/460 at VA-631

Fagg: Halfway between Ellett and Ironto, Fagg was established as a railroad stop with a post office as early as 1889. The community name honors George Washington Fagg, the sheriff of Montgomery County in the 1870s and 1880s. Fagg is buried here at the Dudley Family Cemetery. And he is noted as quite a Civil War hero; one account

says, "He captured thirty-four Yankees by himself in Tennessee." Eastern: VA-603 (North Fork Rd.) at Falls Ridge Rd.

Fishers View: The name "Fishers View" refers to an artist named Fisher who studied in Europe and, according to one account, came here in the late 1860s to "make a picture" of Fisher Peak's expansive view. Southern: VA-609 (Fishers View Rd.), near Alleghany Springs

Graysontown: Earlier called "Grayson Mills," Graysontown was named for the family of settler John Grayson. It was established in 1847 with a mill, store, and blacksmith shop along the Little River. Southwestern: VA-613, near Pulaski County

Longshop: The Longshop community, near the New River, was originally called "Long's Shop" for a pair of brothers, Floyd and Joe Long, who operated a local shop here in the late 1800s. Northwestern: VA-652 at VA-655

Lusters Gate: A. W. Luster operated a mill in the 1880s on Indian Run, a tributary of the North Fork of the Roanoke River. But the name "Luster's Gate" refers not to Luster's mill but to a gate blocking a road that led to the mill. Central: VA-785 (Harding Rd.) at VA-723 (Lusters Gate Rd.)

McDonald's Mill: George McDonald's 1850s-era milling operation lent a name to the McDonald's Mill community along the North Fork of the Roanoke River. Northeastern: VA-785 (Catawba Rd.) at VA-630 (Gallon Ridge Rd.)

Merrimac: Legend says that coal from the hand-dug mines at Merrimac fueled the Confederate ironclad ship *Virginia* (aka *Merrimack*) during its 1862 battle with the Union's *Monitor* in the Hampton Roads area of Eastern Virginia. The Merrimac name was later attached to the community. The Merrimac mines had closed by the mid-1930s. Central: VA-657 (Merrimac Rd.), near VA-824

Pepper: Pepper's Ferry once linked Montgomery County to Pulaski County at the site of a modern bridge over the New River. The "Pepper" name, still on maps to designate the river's Montgomery County side, is an honor for Samuel Pepper, who began operating a ferry here in the 1770s. Pepper, incidentally, was a grandfather of Dr. Charles Taylor Pepper (1830-1903), the man for whom the mass-produced soft drink Dr Pepper is named. Western: VA-114 (Peppers Ferry Rd.) at New River

Piedmont: A picturesque dam on Bottom Creek marks the location of Piedmont. The word *piedmont* means "at the foot of the mountain." Southeastern: VA-637 at VA-653

Pilot: In the early 1800s, a community was named "Pilot" for a local merchant, possibly an innkeeper. Later, in the 1880s, Pilot was the site of a short-lived gold rush on nearby Brush Creek. Eastern: VA-612 at VA-615

Prices Fork: Members of the Price ("Priess") family acquired land at Prices Fork as early as the 1740s. Over time, so many Prices owned so much land that a community naturally came to be called "Price's Fork." Central: VA-652 (McCoy Rd.) at VA-685 (Prices Fork Rd.)

Rogers: The Rogers area was likely named for members of a Rogers family buried at the Walters Family Cemetery near the community's main crossroads. South-central: VA-615 (Pilot Rd.) at VA-675 (Elliott Creek Rd.)

Vicker: Known early as "Vicars Switch" and alternately as "Vickers Switch," the Vicker community takes its name from the Vickers (Vicars) family whose patriarch, Elias Vickers, settled on the waters of Crab Creek in 1806. Central: VA-659 at VA-719

PULASKI COUNTY

Pulaski County sits near the middle of Southwest Virginia and, by itself, lends an impression of almost every county in the region. It boasts a heritage of coal mining, railroads, and agriculture, and its landscape is lined with charming small towns, mountain lakes, and scenic views. Spanning about 330 square miles, the county was formed from Montgomery and Wythe counties in 1839. The name comes from Count Casimir Pulaski, who fled the Russian occupation of Poland to serve in the American Army during the Revolutionary War.

ALLISONIA

Named for a local Allison family who were among the area's first settlers, Allisonia lies along the New River and VA-693 in the southwestern corner of Pulaski County. In the early 1900s, the residential community was a center for iron-ore mining operations. The Allisonia Train Depot, built in 1885 and used until about 1952, remains from the town's original heyday. Owners Don and Chipper Holt opened the renovated station as a cozy overnight lodge in 2000, converting the old telegraph office into a kitchen and making a waiting room into a bedroom. The green-and-white depot, near the New River Trail State Park, sits perpendicular to its original site.

What's to See

New River Access: A paved boat ramp leads to the headwaters of Claytor Lake where the New River enters the 21-mile-long reservoir at Allisonia.

🚗 From I-81 Exit 89 near Pulaski, follow VA-100 south for 6.5 miles to Barren Springs. Turn left on VA-608 and follow for 2.5 miles. Bear left at the VA-607 crossroads and follow VA-607 for two miles. Turn left on VA-693 and follow for 1.7 miles to the ramp parking lot on the left.

DUBLIN

About two miles west of Radford, late-18th-century settlers named a place "New Dublin," likely for their homeland of Dublin, Ireland. In the mid-1800s, what became the Town of Dublin was settled in central Pulaski County, just west of New Dublin. In modern times, locals joke that Dublin's name has to do with growth—or how the town keeps "doublin'" every few years. In reality, Dublin's population climbed only about 10 percent from 1990's census count, to nearly 2,300 in 2000.

As one of Pulaski County's major commerce centers, Dublin got its first big boost in the mid-1850s when the Virginia and Tennessee Railroad established a depot here, at the point where the rail line crossed the Giles-Pulaski Turnpike. Incorporated in 1871, Dublin's main crossroads lie where US-11 meets VA-100, near I-81 Exit 98.

What's to See

Claytor Lake State Park: Following a serpentine path for 21 miles, the 4,475-acre Claytor Lake winds through the heart of Pulaski County. Forests and private residences surround the steep banks of this New River reservoir. The lake itself lures fishermen angling for smallmouth bass, spotted bass, and walleye.

Part of the shoreline fronts the 472-acre Claytor Lake State Park. Operated by the state since 1951, this park presents opportunities for hiking, biking, fishing, camping, boating, waterskiing, and picnics. Lifeguards keep vigil on a sandy swimming area bordered by a concrete walk. Nearby, a playground stands in sight of the park's full-service marina. Asphalt roads stream over the hillsides, and pines and dogwoods line much of the park's three miles of lakeshore. White-tailed deer run through the park's oak and hickory forest, and open fields give kids plenty of room to play ball or run with dogs.

Claytor Lake is named for William Graham Claytor (1886-1971), who supervised the $11-million dam's construction in 1939 as vice president of the Appalachian Power Co. The lake's construction meant the end to Pulaski County's oldest settlement, Dunkard Bottom, established in 1744-1745. The site of that village is now underwater, lost between the park and the 130-foot-high Claytor Lake Dam.

Dunkard Bottom was named for three long-bearded mystics

Beach at Claytor Lake State Park, north of Dublin

Chimney of the William Christian home, now a monument at Claytor Lake State Park

called "dunkards." *Dunkard* means either a member of the German Baptist Brethren, a sect of German-American Baptists opposed to military service and taking legal oaths, or it refers to persons who prefer Baptism by immersion, or "dunking." The dunkard trio fled to this area after splitting from a religious sect in Lancaster County, Pennsylvania, and established what may have been the oldest white settlement west of the New River.

Col. William Christian, a noted Indian fighter and brother-in-law of American statesman Patrick Henry, acquired land in the Dunkard Bottom area in 1770 and built a home with five chimneys in 1771-1773. The Christian home stood until 1939, when it was removed as the lake began to fill. Still, one lone chimney, surrounded by lake water, was left standing for 50 years as a tribute to Christian. Appalachian Power officials removed the chimney in 1989, and in 1990 the Pulaski chapter of the New River Historical Society used the stones to reconstruct the chimney as a monument inside the park.

The two-story Haven B. Howe House sits near the chimney monument. Built from brick and native timber in the late 1870s, the home's inviting front porch sports a splendid view of the lake and Claytor Dam. The Howe House is now the park's visitor center. Behind it, look for a gazebo, a popular site for weddings.

The state park offers overnight accommodations, including a dozen lakefront cabins, rustic camping spots, and campsites with full hookups. Annually, the park hosts the Claytor Lake Arts and Crafts Festival during Labor Day weekend. A park entry fee is charged per vehicle at the main gate. A small admission is also charged at the beach, open Memorial Day to Labor Day.

🚗 From I-81 Exit 101, north of Dublin, follow VA-660 southeast for about three miles to the park entrance, 4400 State Park Rd. A boat ramp is off VA-660, just before the park gate.

Randolph Park: Dublin's 90-acre Randolph Park features a water park with slides and a swimming pool. Open since 2001, the county-owned facility also includes large ball fields, tennis courts, a playground, picnic shelters, gazebos, and ponds encircled by 1.5 miles of hiking trails. The park is named for Randolph Alexander, whose daughter, Evelyn, donated land for the site.

🚗 From I-81 Exit 98, follow VA-100 (Cleburne Blvd.) northwest for a quarter mile. Turn left on VA-683 (Alexander Rd.) and go west for a half mile. The park is on the right.

FAIRLAWN Sometimes called "North Radford," Fairlawn is on the northwest side of the New River in eastern Pulaski County, where US-11 meets VA-114. Its restaurants and stores derive much business from the students and faculty of nearby Radford University.

The name "Fairlawn" likely originates from the beauty of the land, or lawn, as it rolls along the river. Fairlawn was the site of a U.S. government-built suburb in the 1940s, when a company called Hercules made ammunition near here during World War II.

What's to See

New River Valley Speedway: NASCAR-sanctioned races are held at the New River Valley Speedway on Saturday nights during spring and summer. Race classes include late-model stock cars, limited sportsman, late-model trucks, pure stocks, and mini stocks. The .416-mile paved oval opened in 1988 at what was once called the "Pulaski County Speedway." The facility seats more than 10,000.

🚗 From Radford, follow US-11 (Lee Hwy.) across the New River through Fairlawn and continue for two more miles southwest of the VA-114 crossroads. The track is on the right, at 6749 Lee Hwy.

NEWBERN

Early Swiss settlers called a place in central Pulaski County "New Bern," spelling the name with two words to signify its newness in relation to the Bern of Switzerland. In 1810, Adam Hance created a town here on his 1,000-acre plantation by marking off 28 lots fronted by the Wilderness Road. By 1839, an assortment of businesses and homes had grown near Hance's home, and the thriving town was designated the seat of the newly formed Pulaski County.

But Newbern would lose its place of prominence. The courthouse burned in 1893, and, by 1895, the county government had been moved to Pulaski. Still, many structures from Newbern's courthouse years remain standing along VA-611 (Wilderness Rd.), in a mile-long linear district listed on both state and national historic registers.

Adam Hance's own house, at the center of Newbern, is now the Wilderness Road Regional Museum, operated by the New River Historical Society. It's a nonprofit showcase of antiques and artifacts.

But the Hance House, actually, is a pair of the town's earliest structures that were joined into a singular, 99-foot-long building in 1851. Fronted by the Wilderness Road, its creaky hardwood floors have served as a post office, a boarding house, a general store, and a private residence. The museum's upstairs office—not regularly open to the public—is one place that even boasts a legend. The office was a gambling room when the Hance House served as a stagecoach tavern. One night, during a card game, a man lost his life here by gunfire. Sometimes, museum officials say, an unexplained "racket" can be heard in this room.

On six sprawling acres, the Hance House lawn contains a collection of outbuildings, including a barn, a buggy shed, a smokehouse, a primitive kitchen, and a slave cabin. Perhaps the most handsome is the Stagecoach Building, also known as the "Granary." The weatherboarding on this circa-1818 structure makes it look modern, though its original doors, roof, floor, and stone foundation remain.

The main museum building faces VA-611 at the town's main crossroads with VA-697, about a half mile northeast of Cleburne Boulevard. Near this intersection is the old county jail, a ghostly structure made of bricks and topped with a gray tin roof. The two-story jailhouse, built circa 1842, was the site of at least two hangings, including one of a man accused of stealing grain from the granary behind the Hance House. The jail stands behind a vacant field that was the site of the burned-down courthouse on Newbern's Courthouse Square.

Also on the town's main street, next to the Newbern Church of God, is the Newbern Reservoir, an odd brick structure resembling a beehive. This water tank, built in 1870, was used when water was pumped through wooden pipes to hydrants along the town's main thoroughfare.

On the second weekend of each October, Newbern celebrates its heritage with the Newbern Fall Festival of Arts and Crafts.

NEW RIVER DEPOT

Gen. Gabriel Wharton owned most of the land in the New River Depot area when the unincorporated town was settled circa 1869 with the opening of a store, a post office, and a hotel along a waterfront business district. New River Depot saw its greatest growth in the 1880s, when it was home to a primarily black population. It's alternately known as simply "New River" and is located along VA-624, near the railroad and the river.

Several stories, incidentally, circulate on how the New River took its name. One version says this became the "New River" in the days of pioneer settlement, a time when the isolated mountains of Southwest Virginia were called "New Virginia."

Old Pulaski County Jail at Newbern

PULASKI Tree-lined streets front Victorian-style mansions in the courthouse town centering Pulaski County. The large homes are evidence of Pulaski's initial prosperity as an industrial center and major rail destination between Bristol and Roanoke.

In the mid-1850s, the railroad arrived at what became known as "Martin's Tank," a place named for Robert Martin, who owned a plantation where a water tank was used to refill locomotives. The name evolved to "Martin's Station" when a post office was established in 1870. In 1884, the area became "Pulaski Station" to match the county name. Incorporated as "Pulaski City" in 1886, the town was known simply as "Pulaski" by the early 1900s.

Pulaski grew along the south side of Peak Creek, a New River tributary slipping through town from the county's western mountains. From 1884 to 1886, the Pulaski Land & Improvement Co. rechanneled Peak Creek and built a stone embankment. That wall helped develop land on the creek's north side, an area originally considered too marshy for much of anything.

Built with gray sandstone culled from Peak Creek, the 1896 Pulaski County Courthouse, 52 W. Main St., is topped with a bell/clock tower and stands as a grand example of Romanesque architecture. A triple archway also made of Peak Creek sandstone marks its entrance; the arches were originally built for the Pulaski County display at the 1607-1907 Jamestown Exposition in Jamestown, Virginia. In 1989, fire gutted the courthouse, but its stone walls survived. The courthouse interior was rebuilt within three years and features a small historical museum showcasing local artifacts. The museum is open during regular business hours of the current courthouse, built in 1958 at 45 Third St. NW.

Besides its place as the seat of the county government since 1895, Pulaski has historically been known as a factory town at the crossroads of US-11 and VA-99. Downtown thoroughfares are straight and flat, giving this place a big-city feel, even though only about 9,500 people lived here in 2000. The town's Main Street boasts a cosmopolitan flair, too, with its thriving mix of gift shops and restaurants. Elevating that ambiance is the Fine Arts Center for the New River Valley, 21 W. Main St., a non-profit gallery of arts and crafts.

Pulaski's own minor-league baseball team plays at Calfee Park, built in 1935 on Fifth Street and named for Ernest W. Calfee, a Pulaski mayor. Another Pulaski mayor, C. V. Jackson, is memorialized in the name of Jackson Park, a small green space with a gazebo, a fountain, and a World War I cannon, at the corner of Washington Avenue and First Street.

Jackson Park overlooks railroad tracks near the Pulaski Railway Station, 20 S. Washington Ave. Built by the Norfolk & Western Railway circa 1887, the antique station is characterized by fanciful detail, including the castle-like appearance of its arched doors. The structure was donated to the town in 1989 and was restored by 1994. The interior houses model railroads, books, and historic photographs at the Raymond F. Ratcliffe Memorial Museum, another place named for a Pulaski mayor. Outside the depot, Dora Highway Park features a railroad caboose, a small playground, a basketball court, and park benches.

Dora Highway leads to Dora Junction, a former railroad stop on the southeastern edge of Pulaski. Dora takes its name from a daughter of a "Mr. Mills," a construction foreman at the Dora Furnace, an operation used by Pulaski's early manufacturing industry. Dora Junction is off VA-99 at Xaloy Way, about two miles north of I-81 Exit 94. The Dora Junction site is the northern terminus of the New River Trail State Park.

What's to See

Draper Mountain Overlook and Wayside: US-11 snakes across 3,332-foot Draper Mountain at the southern edge of Pulaski and passes through a 20-acre public park, the Draper Mountain Overlook and Wayside. Just below the summit, about two miles north of I-81 Exit 89, the overlook's south side gives a sweeping view of Drapers Valley, and the north side faces the Town of Pulaski.

Built in the 1930s by the Works Progress Administration, this wayside remained a popular getaway for its first few decades, attracting both uneasy riders staving off car sickness, and drivers wanting great scenery. But, by the early 1990s, the site's stone walls were crumbling, and the top of Draper Mountain was riddled with so much trash that more beer-can collectors than sightseers seemed to come here. Closed and then cleaned up, the overlook reopened in 1997. The improved site features park benches, short trails, and restrooms.

Pulaski Railway Station, at the center of Pulaski

Gatewood Park and Reservoir: In western Pulaski County, mountains packed with pine trees rise as much as 600 feet above the Gatewood Reservoir. Created in 1960-1961 as a water source for the Town of Pulaski, this pristine lake is the centerpiece of the 740-acre Gatewood Park, an enclave totally surrounded by the seemingly endless evergreens of the Jefferson National Forest. The park was named for Andrew Warwick Gatewood, a local director of public works.

Remote and romantic, Gatewood includes a 42-site campground, hiking trails, a snack bar, picnic sites, a playground, and a gravel ramp for launching small boats. Paddleboats, fishing boats, and canoes can be rented from the first weekend of April to the last weekend of October, the only season the 162-acre lake is open to boating. Bank fishing for largemouth and smallmouth bass, crappie, bluegill, and catfish is allowed year-round, 24 hours a day.

🚗 From I-81 Exit 94, follow VA-99 north for 3.8 miles, bearing right to continue straight on Third Street in downtown Pulaski. Turn left on Randolph Avenue and follow for one block, turn right on Magnox Drive and follow for three blocks, and then turn right on Magazine Street and go one block. Turn left on VA-710 (Mount Olivet Rd.) and go 2.4 miles to a fork in the road. Bear right at the fork and continue 5.2 miles to the park entrance.

Harry DeHaven Park: Built near the apex of a lakeside residential community, the Harry DeHaven Park flanks the banks of Claytor Lake's south side, overlooking some of the widest waters in Southwest Virginia. Anglers know the T-shaped fishing pier here as a place to hook striped bass.

The park's name comes from a longtime employee of the Pulaski County School System. Outlined with a swimming area, plus picnic tables inside a pine forest, this county-owned park sits on a peninsula dubbed "Harry's Point" for former owner Cecil Harry. On site are two fee-free boat ramps with courtesy piers.

🚗 From I-81 Exit 94 at Pulaski, follow VA-99-South for 0.1 miles. Turn left on Rt. F047 (Old Route 100 Rd.) and go 0.4 miles. Turn right on VA-672 (Lowmans Ferry Rd.) and follow for 3.7 miles. Turn left on VA-693 (Lead Mine Rd.) and follow east for 3.1 miles. Turn left on VA-605 (Little River Dam Rd.) and go two miles. Turn left on VA-663 (Owens Rd.) and follow for 3.8 miles. Turn left on VA-757 and go 0.2 miles. Turn left on VA-831 and enter the park.

Alternate Route: From I-81 Exit 105 at Radford, follow VA-232-North for a few yards. Immediately turn left on VA-605 (Little River Dam Rd.) and follow for 6.5 miles. Turn right on VA-663 (Owens Rd.) and go 3.8 miles. Turn left on VA-757 and go for 0.2 miles. Turn left on VA-831 and enter the park.

Alum Springs: In the late 1800s, Alum Springs took its name from a long-gone resort serving alum springwater. Northwestern: VA-643 at VA-601

Belspring: The flow of a large spring inspired the name "Belspring." Local tradition says that a ringing sound, like a bell, made the spring flow, and it became known as "The Bell Spring." Another account says that the actual spring made a ringing noise as it "tinkled" out of the hills on the C. S. Kirkwood farm. In the 1890s, the area was known as "Churchwood" after C. S. Kirkwood donated land for a railroad station. Railroad officials derived this new name from the Scottish word *kirk*, meaning "church." After 1906, the crossroads was called "Belspring." Northeastern: VA-600 at VA-617

Boom Furnace: Located among old iron-ore mines that operated in the 1890s, Boom Furnace (sometimes called "Boone Furnace") is named because a furnace here would make a big boom when started. Southwestern: VA-607 at VA-608

Draper: In 1755, Shawnee Indians captured John Draper's wife at Draper's Meadows, or what is now Blacksburg, in Montgomery County. Draper later found his wife living with the family of an Indian chief. He paid a ransom for her, and in 1765 the couple moved to a log cabin in what became the Draper, or "Drapers Valley," area. Central: VA-651 at VA-658

Dry Branch: A stream called Dry Branch empties into the New River at Dry Branch, an area named because water in the branch doesn't flow much, sometimes even drying up. Northeastern: VA-600, near VA-602

Highland: The name "Highland" likely refers to this scenic community's setting at the highland foothills of Cloyd's Mountain, a peak named for the family of Joseph Cloyd. On May 9, 1864, during the Battle of Cloyd's Mountain, near Highland, Cloyd's two-story home became a Civil War hospital and a headquarters for Union Brig. Gen. George Crook. Confederates under the command of Brig. Gen. Albert G. Jenkins lost a fight with Crook, who successfully severed the railroad at Dublin after Jenkins had lost 538 men. Northeastern: VA-627 (Highland Rd.), about a mile east of VA-100

Hiwassee: The name "Hiwassee" is derived from the Cherokee *ayuwaski*, meaning "savannah" or "meadow." Southwestern: VA-693 at VA-777, near the New River Trail State Park

Mack Creek Village: The Mack Creek community lies at the mouth of Big Mack Creek, near the New River. This place was named for Alexander Mack, an early settler. A peak called Macks Mountain is near the creek's headwaters. Southwestern: VA-655 at VA-693

McAdam: The true derivation of "McAdam" may be lost, but one tale says that railroad workers were at their wits' end when trying to assign names to different stops along the line. And, while here, one man said it didn't "make a damn" (Mc-A-dam) what this one would be called. Central: Rt. F047 (Old Route 100 Rd.), near VA-672

Mountain View: In 1885, Mountain View Methodist Church was established along the old Wilderness Road, between Newbern and the New River. The southern horizon of the church property affords, indeed, a good mountain view. East-central: VA-611, near VA-615

Parrott: John H. Parrott was an owner of a coal mine that opened at Parrott in the late 1800s and closed in 1935. Northeastern: VA-612, near VA-606

Reed Junction: The name "Reed Junction" may pay homage to the reeds growing along Big Reed Island Creek, which enters the New River at Reed Junction. By another account, the creek's name may be owed to early settler James Reed. Southwestern: Mile 13 of the New River Trail State Park, southwest of Allisonia

Snowville: Asiel Snow left Massachusetts and settled near the Little River circa 1830. The area surrounding Snow's home soon became known as "Snowville." By the early 1850s, Snowville flourished as a tiny town, bustling with the production of iron ore, lumber, and wool. But its growth failed to snowball, largely because the railroad bypassed the community in the late 1800s and sent commerce elsewhere. Even so, the original grandeur of the town's heyday remains visible in the architecture of the Snowville Historic District, an area listed on both state and national historic registers. Eastern: VA-693, near Montgomery County

Weldon: "Weldon" is the name of a farm and a home belonging to the family of Dr. Henry Moss Bentley in the late 1800s. Bentley's son, Maj. Williams Weldon Bentley, inherited the property. Northwestern: VA-738, near VA-640

CITY OF RADFORD

Radford is poised with a split personality. The campus of Radford University, outlying apartment houses, and college-related businesses saturate the eastern half of the city, while industries and permanent residents—"townies," as the students say—are at home on Radford's West End. These halves of Radford are joined at the city's main crossroads, where US-11 (East Main Street) meets VA-232 (West Main Street).

Radford's division between east and west seems ideal. But the city unites on the second Saturday of each October, when Radford University and the municipal government sponsor the Radford Highlanders Festival. This event includes Scottish Highland games, children's activities, and music by pipe and drum bands. The festival happens on the university campus near Radford's traditional downtown along Main Street, a sharply dressed district that reflects how this independent city looked not long after its incorporation in 1892.

Early names for Radford included "Lovely Mount," for a local tavern, and "Ingles Ferry," for a New River charter launched by William Ingles in 1762. The railroad reached here in 1854, and the area became known as "Central Depot," because it was equidistant by rail between Lynchburg and Bristol. By 1890, what had been called "Central City" was renamed "Radford," for Dr. John B. Radford, a local physician and civic leader.

Radford's nickname, "The Heart of the New River Valley," is fitting for its location. The city, which was home to about 16,000 people in 2000, is sandwiched between Pulaski County and Montgomery County, with the New River marking its northern and western boundaries.

The river winds around the edge of Bisset Park, a city-owned green space off Berkley Williams Drive, near US-11 (East Main Street). The 58-acre park includes ball fields, picnic shelters, a playground, a swimming pool, a walking trail, and a gazebo. The park's name honors David Bisset, Sr., a longtime director of Radford's parks department.

Near Grove Avenue and Connelly's Run, a rocky New River tributary, the entrance to the 54-acre Wildwood Park sits almost directly opposite Bisset Park, off US-11. In 1930, Alleen Carper, a student at Radford State Teachers College, created the name "Wildwood" for a contest. The city-owned sanctuary includes about two miles of trails. One path traces a grassy field where rabbits run, while another ascends a hill to the gated opening of Adams Cave, a grotto mined for saltpeter during the War of 1812 and used for burials by Native Americans during the Late Woodland Period.

What's to See

Glencoe Museum: Radford's Glencoe Museum is housed in an Italianate-style brick home with a large Victorian parlor. The museum sits high on a hill above the New River and Radford's West End. Gen. Gabriel Colvin Wharton (1824-1906) built the Glencoe home in the 1870s, just across the river from New River Depot, a Pulaski County settlement developed by Wharton during the same era. The name "Glencoe" remembers Glencoe, Scotland, a village that was the ancestral home of Wharton's wife's family; the word comes from the Gaelic *gleann comhann*, meaning "narrow valley."

Operated by the nonprofit Radford Heritage Foundation, the museum includes exhibits of Native American relics, folk art, and historical artifacts of Radford and greater Southwest Virginia.

🚗 From I-81 Exit 105, follow VA-232 (W. Main St.) into Radford for three miles. Turn left on Robertson Street, then turn almost immediately right. The museum is at 600 Unruh Dr.

New River Access: The New River calmly winds its way around Radford, with no major rapids between Claytor Dam and Radford University's Dedmon Center. South of Radford in neighboring Montgomery County, a public river access sits just below Claytor Dam. Two miles downstream is a municipal ramp. An access near the Dedmon Center is about six miles down from Claytor Dam.

🚗 From I-81 Exit 105, immediately turn left off VA-232 onto VA-605 (Little River Dam Rd.) and go south for about a half mile to the upper boat ramp, on the right, just downstream from Claytor Dam. Beware of changing water conditions at the dam.

Glencoe Museum in Radford

To reach the municipal ramp from I-81 Exit 105, follow VA-232 (W. Main St.) into Radford for about 1.5 miles. Turn left on Cowan Street and follow for 0.1 miles. Turn left on River Street and follow for a quarter mile to the ramp.

To reach the ramp near the Dedmon Center from Radford University on US-11 (E. Main St.), follow University Drive north for a quarter mile, crossing the bridge over the railroad tracks. Turn left on Pulaski Street and follow to the street's end at a gravel parking lot.

Outdoor Drama *The Long Way Home:* Shawnee Indians kidnapped Mary Draper Ingles in July 1755 during a bloody attack on Draper's Meadows, a settlement that is now part of the Virginia Tech campus at Blacksburg. Ingles, 23, was taken about 800 miles away from her husband, William. The couple's two young sons were also taken prisoner and soon separated from their mother.

Indians forced the woman to make salt at what is now Big Bone Lick, Kentucky, near present-day Cincinnati, Ohio. But, in getting there, Ingles had watched for landmarks and noticed the Indians' travel patterns along the banks of rivers; such notes proved important.

In October, Ingles and an unidentified old Dutch woman escaped while unguarded. Together, these women foraged for food like roots and berries. Ingles's strength, alone, would prove superhuman. Not only did she lead the pair through wilderness, but, twice, she staved off the old woman's attempts to strangle and cannibalize her. After 43 days, the old woman now fallen behind, Ingles climbed into a Giles County cornfield owned by Eggleston-area settler Adam Harman, a family friend who reunited Ingles with her husband. She lived to age 83.

Centuries later, her story continues to be told. Summertime productions of an outdoor drama remembering Ingles's journey were first staged in 1971 at Radford's Ingles Homestead Amphitheater. The play, titled *The Long Way Home,* is based on an adaptation by Earl Hobson Smith.

For about 30 years, community volunteers staged the play—until a fire consumed the amphitheater. For one summer, the show was relocated to Radford High School but was then put on hiatus. By 2004, new productions were being planned with assistance from the Radford Chamber of Commerce.

Radford University: Brick buildings reflect a Colonial design at pedestrian-friendly Radford University, a state-supported institution with about 9,000 students on its main campus, near the junction of US-11 and VA-177.

The university began life in 1910 as the State Normal and Industrial School for Women. In 1924, it became the Radford State Teachers College. In 1944, the college became a branch of nearby Virginia Tech at Blacksburg. When that union dissolved in 1964, the school became simply Radford College.

By 1979, Radford College had grown into Radford University. The school's academic reputation consistently grew as well, along with the campus itself. New buildings were added and old ones were expanded. By 2003, the campus contained about 35 buildings on its main 76-acre site, and the university offered more than 100 undergraduate and about 45 graduate programs.

Aside from academics, Radford is known for athletics. Radford has no football program, but basketball is a big deal. Radford's team, the Highlanders, plays home games at the university's athletic complex, the Donald N. Dedmon Center, a unique facility opened in 1981 under a fabric roof supported by air. The center seats 5,000 and is named for a longtime university president.

As Radford's president (1972-1994), Donald N. Dedmon relaxed restrictive rules that had grown unpopular with students during the 1960s. In 1972, under Dedmon's tenure, the school turned coeducational. Consequently, Radford's social life awakened, after years of existing as a tightly disciplined women's school under the direction of Charles Knox Martin, Jr., another longtime college president (1952-1972).

The administration building is named for Martin. U.S. presidents are honored in the names of Washington, Jefferson, Madison, and Tyler halls. Local pioneers are remembered in the names of Ingles and Draper halls. Radford's tallest building and the university's most recognizable landmark is the 13-story brick dormitory, Muse Hall, built in 1969-1970 and named for Leonard G. Muse, rector of the college's board of visitors during the 1960s.

Art exhibits can be found at several galleries, on or off campus, including the Bondurant Center for the Arts, 1129 E. Main St., a facility donated to the Radford University Foundation in 1997 by the Ken Bondurant family.

Muse Hall, the tallest dormitory at Radford University

APPENDIX A: FESTIVALS IN SOUTHWEST VIRGINIA

Festivals and celebrations are held in communities all over Southwest Virginia. Usually, a local chamber of commerce is the best contact for festival information.

March:
Maple Festival/ Whitetop/ Grayson/ Last weekend

April:
Redbud Festival/ Honaker/ Russell/ Date varies

May:
Trail Days/ Damascus/ Washington/ Weekend after Mother's Day
Ramp Festival/ Whitetop/ Grayson/ Third Sunday
Homecoming Celebration Day/ Cripple Creek/ Wythe/ Fourth Saturday
Plumb Alley Day/ Abingdon/ Washington/ Saturday before Memorial Day
Pound Heritage Days/ Pound/ Wise/ Memorial Day weekend
Raid at Martin's Station/ Elydale/ Lee/ Second weekend

June:
Clinch River Days/ St. Paul/ Wise/ First weekend
Best Friend Festival/ City of Norton/ Second week
Chautauqua Festival/ Wytheville/ Wythe/ Third Saturday
Nickelsville Days/ Nickelsville/ Scott/ Last weekend
Grayson County Fiddlers Convention/ Elk Creek/ Grayson/ Last weekend

July:
Jubilee Festival/ Ivanhoe/ Wythe/ First weekend
Fourth of July Parade/ Taylors Valley/ Washington/ Date varies
Independence Day Celebration/ Independence/ Grayson/ July 4
Hungry Mother Arts and Crafts Festival/ Marion/ Smyth/ Third weekend

August:
Rich Valley Fair and Horse Show/ Rich Valley/ Smyth/ Date varies
Carter Family Memorial Festival/ Maces Spring/ Scott/ First Saturday
Coal/Railroad Days/ Appalachia/ Wise/ First weekend
Steppin' Out Festival/ Blacksburg/ Montgomery/ First weekend
Virginia Highlands Festival/ Abingdon/ Washington/ First two weeks
Old Fiddlers Convention/ City of Galax/ Second week
Virginia-Kentucky District Fair/ Wise/ Wise/ Date varies
Fries Fiddlers Convention/ Fries /Grayson/ Third weekend

September:
Tri-State Gospel Singing/ Breaks/ Dickenson/ Labor Day weekend
Coal Miners Reunion/ Pocahontas/ Tazewell/ Labor Day weekend
Claytor Lake Arts and Crafts Festival/ Dublin/ Pulaski/ Labor Day weekend
Duffield Daze/ Duffield/ Scott/ Labor Day weekend
Guest River Rally/ Coeburn/ Wise/ Labor Day weekend
Labor Day Celebration/ Saltville/ Smyth/ Labor Day weekend
Labor Day Gun Show and Flea Market/ Hillsville/ Carroll/ Labor Day weekend
Chilhowie Community Apple Festival/ Chilhowie/ Smyth/ Date varies
Old Fashion Day/ Dryden/ Lee/ Second Saturday
Cedar Bluff Heritage Festival/ Cedar Bluff/ Tazewell/ Third Saturday
New River Festival/ Fries/ Grayson/ Third Saturday
Wilderness Trail Festival/ Christiansburg/ Montgomery/ Third Saturday
Rhythm and Roots Reunion/ City of Bristol/ Third weekend
Burke's Garden Fall Festival/ Burke's Garden/ Tazewell/ Last Saturday
Grayson Highlands Fall Festival/ Rugby/ Grayson/ Last weekend

October:
Fall Festival/ Baywood/ Grayson/ First Saturday
Fall Festival at Bush Mill/ Nickelsville/ Scott/ First Saturday
Narrows Fall Festival/ Narrows/ Giles/ First Saturday
Russell Fork Autumn Fest/ Haysi/ Dickenson/ First weekend
Mountain Foliage Festival/ Independence/ Grayson/ Second Saturday
Radford Highlanders Festival/ City of Radford/ Second Saturday
Wilderness Road Festival/ Elydale/ Lee/ Second Saturday
Molasses Festival/ Whitetop/ Grayson/ Second Sunday
Newbern Fall Festival of Arts and Crafts/ Newbern/ Pulaski/ Second weekend
Mountain Dew Days/ Marion/ Smyth/ Date varies
Wise County Famous Fall Fling/ Wise/ Wise/ Date varies
Bridle Creek Fall Festival/ Bridle Creek/ Grayson/ Third Saturday
Home Crafts Days/ Big Stone Gap/ Wise/ Third weekend

APPENDIX B: LAKES IN SOUTHWEST VIRGINIA

(Lake/ Location/ County/ Size [in acres])

Bark Camp Lake/ Dungannon/ Scott/ 48
Bear Creek Reservoir/ Wise/ Wise/ 38
Beartree Lake/ Damascus/ Washington/ 11
Big Cherry Reservoir/ Big Stone Gap/ Wise/ 250
Byllesby Reservoir/ Hillsville/ Carroll/ 335
Claytor Lake/ Dublin/ Pulaski/ 4,475
Clear Creek Lake/ City of Bristol/ 46
Flannagan Reservoir/ Haysi/ Dickenson/ 1,145
Gatewood Reservoir/ Pulaski/ Pulaski/ 162
Hale Lake/ Comers Rock/ Grayson/ 5
Hidden Valley Lake/ Hidden Valley/ Washington/ 61
High Knob Lake/ High Knob/ Wise/ 5
Hungry Mother Lake/ Marion/ Smyth/ 108
Lake Jack Witten/ Tazewell/ Tazewell/ 52
Lake Keokee/ Keokee/ Lee/ 92
Laurel Bed Lake/ Saltville/ Smyth/ 300
Laurel Lake/ Breaks/ Dickenson/ 12
Lincolnshire Lake/ Tazewell/ Tazewell/ 25
Lovill's Creek Lake/ Cana/ Carroll/ 55
Mountain Lake*/ Mountain Lake/ Giles/ 55
Norton Reservoir/ City of Norton/ 10
Oxbow Lake/ St. Paul/ Wise/ 10
Pandapas Pond/ Blacksburg/ Montgomery/ 8
Pound Reservoir/ Pound/ Wise/ 154
Rural Retreat Lake/ Rural Retreat/ Wythe/ 90
South Holston Lake/ Abingdon/ Washington/ 1,600 (in Va.)

Note: Locations listed indicate nearest town or community. Some sizes are approximate.

*All lakes are located in public-access areas except Mountain Lake, which is privately owned but can be accessed through a resort open to the public and can also be seen from a public roadway.

APPENDIX C: WATERFALLS IN SOUTHWEST VIRGINIA

(Falls/ Location/ County/ Height [in feet])

Bickley Falls*/ Castlewood/ Russell/ 40
Big Falls/ Lebanon/ Russell/ 15
Big Tumbling Creek/ Saltville/ Smyth/ 15
Cabin Creek*/ Greendale/ Washington/ 35
Cabin Creek/ Rugby/ Grayson/ 25, 50
Cascades/ Pembroke/ Giles/ 66, 18
Chestnut Creek Falls/ Hillsville/ Carroll/ 10
Chestnut Mountain/ Damascus/ Washington/ 20
Comers Creek Falls/ Sugar Grove/ Smyth/ 15
Crab Orchard Branch*/ Coeburn/ Wise/ 22
Devils Fork Falls/ Fort Blackmore/ Scott/ 25
Dismal Falls/ Dismal/ Giles/ 12
Fall Creek*/ Dungannon/ Scott/ 35
Falls Hill*/ Greendale/ Washington/ 35
Falls Mills Falls*/ Falls Mills/ Tazewell/ 15
Falls of Alavardo Road*/ Damascus/ Washington/ 15
Falls of Chestnut Ridge*/ Meadowview/ Washington/ 25
Falls of Little Stony/ Dungannon/ Scott/ 24, 12, 30
Falls at Swede Tunnel/ Coeburn/ Wise/ 15
Falls Ridge*/ Ironto/ Montgomery/ 80
Fox Creek Falls/ Troutdale/ Grayson/ 10, 15
Gap Creek Falls/ Cumberland Gap/ Lee/ 100
Garrett Creek Cascades*/ Greendale/ Washington/ 25
Laurel Branch Cascades/ Dungannon/ Scott/ 18
Lick Log Branch/ Coeburn/ Wise/ 40
Logan Creek*/ Meadowview/ Washington/ 35
Mill Creek/ Narrows/ Giles/ 45, 18, 10
Peach Bottom Falls*/ Independence/ Grayson/ 100
Phillips Creek/ Pound/ Wise/ 15
Puncheon Run Falls*/ Shawsville/ Montgomery/ 200
Ramey Falls/ Clintwood/ Dickenson/ 18, 25
Rowland Creek Falls/ Sugar Grove/ Smyth/ 150
Russell Creek Falls*/ St. Paul/ Wise/ 50
Stiles Falls*/ Shawsville/ Montgomery/ 45
Straight Branch/ Damascus/ Washington/ 14
Tank Hollow Falls/ Cleveland/ Russell/ 30
Toole Creek*/ White's Mill/ Washington/ 30, 45
Twin Hollows Falls/ Saltville/ Smyth/ 35
Whitetop Laurel/ Damascus/ Washington/ 10
Wilson Creek/ Rugby/ Grayson/ 25, 30

Ramey Falls near Clintwood

Note: Locations listed indicate nearest town or community. Most heights listed are approximate.

*These falls are, or may be, located on private property but can be seen from a publicly accessible roadway, trail, or streambed. Some falls may not be visible at all times of the year, due to foliage. Accessing these noted falls beyond a publicly owned or publicly accessible roadway, trail, or streambed may be trespassing.

APPENDIX D: SOUTHWEST VIRGINIA TOURISM RESOURCES

Abingdon Convention & Visitors Bureau
335 Cummings St.
Abingdon, VA 24210
800-435-3440 / 276-676-2282
www.abingdon.com/tourism

Abingdon Vineyard and Winery
20530 Alvarado Rd.
Abingdon, VA 24211
276-623-1255
www.abingdonwinery.com

Appalachian Trail Conference
P.O. Box 807
Harpers Ferry, WV 25425-0807
304-535-6331
www.appalachiantrail.org

Arts Depot
314 Depot Sq.
P.O. Box 2513
Abingdon, VA 24212-2513
276-628-9091
www.abingdonartsdepot.org

Barter Theatre
133 W. Main St.
Abingdon, VA 24210
276-628-3991
www.bartertheatre.com

Bear Creek Reservoir
Wise, Va.
276-328-6353

Beartree Recreation Area
3714 Hwy. 16
Marion, VA 24354
276-388-3642

Town of Big Stone Gap
505 E. Fifth St. South
Big Stone Gap, VA 24219
276-523-0115
www.bigstonegap.org

Big Walker Lookout
8711 Stony Fork Rd.
Wytheville, VA 24382
276-228-4401
www.scenicbeauty-va.com

Birthplace of Country Music Alliance Museum
Bristol Mall
500 Gate City Hwy., Suite 140
Bristol, VA 24201
276-645-0035
www.birthplaceofcountrymusic.org

Blacksburg Parks and Recreation
615 Patrick Henry Dr.
Blacksburg, VA 24060
540-961-1135
www.blacksburg.gov/recreation

Bland County Administration
P.O. Box 510
Bland, VA 24315
276-688-4622 / 800-519-3468
www.bland.org

Bluefield College
3000 College Dr.
Bluefield, VA 24605
800-872-0175 / 276-326-4212
www.bluefield.edu

Town of Bluefield
P.O. Box 1026
Bluefield, VA 24605
276-322-4626

Blue Ridge Parkway
199 Hemphill Knob Rd.
Asheville, NC 28803
828-298-0398
www.nps.gov/blri

Blue Ridge Travel Association of Virginia
468 E. Main St., Suite 300-A
P.O. Box 2589
Abingdon, VA 24212
276-619-5003 / 800-446-9670
www.virginiablueridge.org

Breaks Interstate Park
P.O. Box 100
Breaks, VA 24607
800-982-5122 / 276-865-4413
www.breakspark.com

Bristol Convention and Visitors Bureau
20 Volunteer Pkwy.
Bristol, TN 37620
423-989-4850 / 888-989-4850
www.bristolchamber.org

Bristol Virginia Parks and Recreation
1501 Euclid Ave.
Bristol, VA 24201
276-645-7275
www.bristolva.org

Buchanan County Chamber of Commerce
P.O. Box 2818
Grundy, VA 24614
276-935-4147

Camp Alta Mons
2842 Crockett Springs Rd.
Shawsville, VA 24162
540-268-2409
www.altamons.com

Carroll County Chamber of Commerce
P.O. Box 1184
Hillsville, VA 24343
276-728-5397 / 888-728-7260
www.thecarrollchamber.com

Carroll County Historical Society & Museum
P.O. Box 937
Hillsville, VA 24343
276-728-4113

Carter Fold
P.O. Box 111
Hiltons, VA 24258
276-386-6054
www.carterfamilyfold.org

Cave House Craft Shop
279 E. Main St.
Abingdon, VA 24210
276-628-7721
www.cavehousecrafts.com

Town of Cedar Bluff
P.O. Box 807
Cedar Bluff, VA 24609
276-964-4889
www.cedarbluffva.org

Chateau Morrisette Winery
P.O. Box 766
Meadows of Dan, VA 24120
540-593-2865
www.chateaumorrisette.com

Town of Christiansburg
100 E. Main St.
Christiansburg, VA 24073-3029
540-382-6128
www.christiansburg.org

Claytor Lake State Park
4400 State Park Rd.
Dublin, VA 24084
540-643-2500
www.dcr.state.va.us/parks/claytor.htm

Clinch Mountain Wildlife Management Area
Saltville, Va.
276-944-3434

Country Cabin
P.O. Box 67
Wise, VA 24293
276-679-3541

Crooked Creek Wildlife Management Area
Woodlawn, Va.
276-236-6391

Cumberland Gap National Historical Park
P.O. Box 1848
Middlesboro, KY 40965-1848
606-248-2817
www.nps.gov/cuga

Town of Damascus
P.O. Box 576
Damascus, VA 24236
276-475-3831
www.damascus.org

Dickenson County Chamber of Commerce
P.O. Box 1989
Clintwood, VA 24228
276-926-6074 / 800-665-1260

Dye's Vineyards
Rt. 2, Box 357
Honaker, VA 24260
276-873-4659
www.dyesvineyards.com

Emory & Henry College
P.O. Box 947
Emory, VA 24327-0947
276-944-4121
www.ehc.edu

Fields-Penn 1860 House Museum
208 W. Main St.
Abingdon, VA 24210
276-676-0216

Fine Arts Center for the New River Valley
P.O. Box 309
Pulaski, VA 24301
540-980-7363

Floyd Country Store
206 S. Locust St.
Floyd, VA 24091
540-745-4563
www.floydcountrystore.com

Floyd County Chamber of Commerce
P.O. Box 510
Floyd, VA 24091
540-745-4407
www.visitfloyd.org

Galax-Carroll-Grayson Chamber of Commerce
608 W. Stuart Dr.
Galax, VA 24333
276-236-2184
www.gcgchamber.com

Galax Tourism
111 E. Grayson St.
Galax, VA 24333
276-238-8130
www.ingalax.net

Gatewood Park and Reservoir
Pulaski, Va.
540-980-2561

Giles County Chamber of Commerce
101 S. Main St.
Pearisburg, VA 24134
540-921-5000

Giles County Historical Society & Museum
208 N. Main St.
Pearisburg, VA 24134
540-921-1050

Glencoe Museum
600 Unruh Dr.
P.O. Box 1412
Radford, VA 24143
540-731-5031

Grayson County Tourism & 1908 Courthouse
107 E. Main St.
Independence, VA 24348
276-773-3711
www.graysoncountyva.com

Grayson Highlands State Park
829 Grayson Highland Lane
Mouth of Wilson, VA 24363
276-579-7092
www.dcr.state.va.us/parks/graysonh.htm

Greater Bluefield Chamber of Commerce
P.O. Box 4098
Bluefield, WV 24701
304-327-7184
www.bluefieldchamber.com

Harmon Museum
P.O. Box 113
Woodlawn, VA 24381
276-236-4884

Harry W. Meador Jr., Coal Museum
E. Third St. & Shawnee Ave
Big Stone Gap, VA 24219
276-523-9209

Heart of Appalachia Tourism Authority
112 Shawnee Ave.
P.O. Box 207
Big Stone Gap, VA 24219
276-523-2005 / 888-798-2386
www.heartofappalachia.com

Higginbotham House Museum
P.O. Box 175
Tazewell, VA 24651
276-988-3800
www.legacyadvocacy.org

Historic Crab Orchard Museum & Pioneer Park
Rt. 1, Box 194
Tazewell, VA 24651
276-988-6755
www.craborchardmuseum.com

Historic Grist Mill and Restaurant
P.O. Box 1610
Cedar Bluff, VA 24609
276-964-9691
www.historicmill.com

Historical Society of Washington County Library
306 Depot Sq.
P.O. Box 484
Abingdon, VA 24212-0484
276-623-8337

Hungry Mother State Park
2854 Park Blvd.
Marion, VA 24354
276-781-7400
www.dcr.state.va.us/parks/hungrymo.htm

Interstate Railroad Private Car No. 101 &
   Lonesome Pine Tourist Information Center
619 Gilley Ave.
P.O. Box 236
Big Stone Gap, VA 24219
276-523-2060 / 800-867-1355

The Jacksonville Center
P.O. Box 932
Floyd, VA 24091
540-745-2784

Jefferson National Forest:
Headquarters
5162 Valleypointe Pkwy.
Roanoke, VA 24019
540-265-5100
Clinch Ranger District
9416 Darden Dr.
Wise, VA 24293
276-328-2931
New River Valley Ranger District
110 Southpark Dr.
Blacksburg, VA 24060
540-552-4641
Wythe Ranger Station
155 Sherwood Forest Rd.
Wytheville, VA 24382
276-228-5551

Jeff Matthews Memorial Museum
606 W. Stuart Dr.
Galax, VA 24333
276-236-7874

John W. Flannagan Dam and Reservoir
Rt. 1, Box 268
Haysi, VA 24256-9739
276-835-9544

John Fox, Jr. Museum
117 Shawnee Ave. East
Big Stone Gap, VA 24219
276-523-2747

Lee County Chamber of Commerce
P.O. Box 417
Pennington Gap, VA 24277
276-546-2233
www.leecountyvachamber.org

Log House 1776 Restaurant
520 E. Main St.
Wytheville, VA 24382
276-228-4139

Lonesome Pine International Raceway
10800 Norton-Coeburn Rd.
Coeburn, VA 24230
276-395-5001
www.lpraceway.com

Mabry Mill
266 Mabry Mill Rd. Southeast
Meadows of Dan, VA 24120
276-952-2947

Town of Marion
P.O. Box 1005
Marion, VA 24354
276-783-4113
www.marionva.org

Martha Washington Inn
150 W. Main St.
Abingdon, VA 24210
276-628-3161
www.marthawashingtoninn.com

Montgomery County Chamber of Commerce
New River Valley Mall
612 New River Rd.
Christiansburg, VA 24073
540-382-4010
www.montgomerycc.org

Montgomery Museum &
 Lewis Miller Regional Art Center
300 S. Pepper St.
Christiansburg, VA 24073
540-382-5644

Morgan-McClure Motorsports Museum
26502 Newbanks Rd.
Abingdon, VA 24210
276-628-3683
www.morgan-mcclure.com

Mountain Lake Resort Hotel
115 Hotel Circle
Pembroke, VA 24136
800-346-3334 / 540-626-7121
www.mountainlakehotel.com

Mount Rogers National Recreation Area:
Damascus Caboose
276-475-3233
Green Cove Depot
276-388-3386
Jennings Visitor Center
3714 Hwy. 16
Marion, VA 24354
800-628-7202 / 276-783-5196
www.southernregion.fs.fed.us/gwj/mr/index.htm
Whitetop Station
276-388-2919

Museum of the Middle Appalachians
123 Palmer Ave.
P.O. Box 910
Saltville, VA 24370
276-496-3633
www.museum-mid-app.org

Town of Narrows
P.O. Box 440
Narrows, VA 24124
540-726-3020
www.townofnarrows.org

Natural Tunnel State Park
Rt. 3 Box 250
Duffield, VA 24244-9361
276-940-2674
www.dcr.state.va.us/parks/naturalt.htm

Nature Conservancy of Virginia
490 Westfield Rd.
Charlottesville, VA 22901
434-295-6106
www.nature.org

New River Trail State Park
176 Orphanage Dr.
Foster Falls, VA 24360
276-699-6778 / 276-236-8889
www.dcr.state.va.us/parks/newriver.htm

New River Valley Speedway
6749 Lee Hwy.
Radford, VA 24141
540-639-1700
www.nrvspeedway.com

City of Norton
P.O. Box 618
Norton, VA 24273-0618
276-679-1160
www.nortonva.org

Town of Pearisburg
112 Tazewell St.
Pearisburg, VA 24134
540-921-0340
www.pearisburg.org

Pocahontas Exhibition Mine and Museum
P.O. Box 128
Pocahontas, VA 24635
276-945-2134

Pulaski County Chamber of Commerce
4440 Cleburne Blvd.
Dublin, VA 24084
540-674-1991

Town of Pulaski
P.O. Box 660
Pulaski, VA 24301
540-994-8600
www.pulaskitown.org

Purely Appalachia Crafts Center
409 Front St. East
Coeburn, VA 24230
276-395-5160

Radford Chamber of Commerce
27 W. Main St.
Radford, VA 24141
540-639-2202
www.radfordchamber.com

City of Radford
619 Second St.
Radford, VA 24141
540-731-3603
www.radford.va.us

Radford University
P.O. Box 6916
Radford, VA 24142
540-831-5324
www.radford.edu

Raymond F. Ratcliffe Memorial Museum
20 S. Washington Ave.
Pulaski, VA 24301
540-980-2055

Rex Theatre
113 Grayson St.
P.O. Box 544
Galax, VA 24333
276-236-0668
www.rextheatergalax.org

Richlands Area Chamber of Commerce
1413 Front St.
Richlands, VA 24641
276-963-3385

Rooftop of Virginia Craft Shop
206 N. Main St.
Galax, VA 24333
276-236-7131

Town of Rural Retreat
P.O. Box 130
Rural Retreat, VA 24368
276-686-4221
www.townofruralretreat.com

Rural Retreat Lake Park
Rural Retreat, Va.
276-686-4331

Russell County Chamber of Commerce
P.O. Box 926
Lebanon, VA 24266
276-889-8041
www.russellcountyva.org

Town of St. Paul
P.O. Box 66
St. Paul, VA 24283
276-762-5297

Saltville Tourism
P.O. Box 730
Saltville, VA 24370
276-496-5342
www.saltvilleva.com

Scott County Chamber of Commerce
P.O. Box 609
Gate City, VA 24251
276-386-6665
www.scottcountyva.org

Settlers Museum of Southwest Virginia
Atkins, Va.
276-686-4401

Shot Tower Historical State Park
176 Orphanage Dr.
Foster Falls, VA 24360
276-699-6778
www.dcr.state.va.us/parks/shottowr.htm

Smithfield Plantation
1000 Smithfield Plantation Rd.
Blacksburg, VA 24060
540-231-3947

Smyth County Chamber of Commerce
124 W. Main St.
P.O. Box 924
Marion, VA 24354
276-783-3161
www.smythchamber.org

Smyth County Museum
P.O. Box 710
Marion, VA 24354-0710
276-783-7286

Southwest Virginia Museum Historical State Park
P.O. Box 742
Big Stone Gap, VA 24219-0742
276-523-1322
www.dcr.state.va.us/parks/swvamus.htm

The Tavern
222 E. Main St.
Abingdon, VA 24210
276-628-1118
www.abingdontavern.com

Town of Tazewell
P.O. Box 608
Tazewell, VA 24651
276-988-2501
www.townoftazewell.org

Tazewell Area Chamber of Commerce
Tazewell Mall Box 6
Tazewell, VA 24651
276-988-5091

Thomas J. Boyd Museum
295 Tazewell St.
Wytheville, VA 24382
276-223-3331

The Trail of the Lonesome Pine Outdoor Drama &
    June Tolliver House
P.O. Box 1976
Big Stone Gap, VA 24219
800-362-0149 / 276-523-1235

University of Virginia's College at Wise
1 College Ave.
Wise, VA 24293
276-328-0100 / 888-282-9324
www.uvawise.edu

Villa Appalaccia Winery
752 Rock Castle Gorge
Floyd, VA 24091
540-593-3100
www.villaappalaccia.com

Virginia City Pioneer Town & Gem Mine
P.O. Box 542
Wytheville, VA 24382
276-223-1873
www.vacity.com

Virginia Department of Conservation
    and Recreation
203 Governor St. Suite 213
Richmond, VA 23219-2094
800-933-7275 / 276-676-5673
www.dcr.state.va.us/parks

Virginia Department of Game and Inland Fisheries:
Blacksburg
Draper Aden Building
2206 S. Main St. Suite C
Blacksburg, VA 24060
540-951-7923
Marion
1796 Hwy. 16
Marion, VA 24354
276-783-4860
Richmond
4010 W. Broad St.
Richmond, VA 23230
804-367-1000
www.dgif.state.va.us

Virginia Intermont College
1013 Moore St.
Bristol, VA 24201
276-669-6101 / 800-451-1842
www.vic.edu

Virginia-Kentucky Opry
724 Park Ave. Northwest
Norton, VA 24273
276-679-1901

Virginia Tech
Blacksburg, VA 24061
540-231-6000 / 540-231-3200
www.vt.edu

Virginia Tourism Corporation
901 E. Byrd St.
Richmond, VA 24219
800-847-4882
www.virginia.org

Washington County Chamber of Commerce
179 E. Main St.
Abingdon, VA 24210
276-628-8141
www.washingtonvachamber.org

Wilderness Road Regional Museum &
    New River Historical Society
5240 Wilderness Rd.
P.O. Box 373
Newbern, VA 24126-0373
540-674-4835

Wilderness Road State Park
Rt. 2, Box 115
Ewing, VA 24248
276-445-3065
www.dcr.state.va.us/parks/wildroad.htm

William King Regional Arts Center
415 Academy Drive
P.O. Box 2256
Abingdon, VA 24212-2256
276-628-5005
www.wkrac.org

Wise County Chamber of Commerce
765 Park Ave.
P.O. Box 226
Norton, VA 24273
276-679-0961
www.wisecountychamber.org

Wohlfahrt Haus Dinner Theatre
170 Malin Dr.
Wytheville, VA 24382
276-223-0891 / 888-950-3382
www.wohlfahrthaus.com

Wolf Creek Indian Village and Museum
Rt. 1 Box 1530
Bastian, VA 24314
276-688-3438
www.indianvillage.org

Wythe Raceway
164 Racetrack Rd.
Rural Retreat, VA 24368
276-686-4261
www.wytheraceway.com

Wytheville Convention & Visitors Bureau
P.O. Box 533
Wytheville, VA 24382
276-223-3355 / 877-347-8307
http://visit.wytheville.com

Yellow Sulphur Springs
P.O. Box 151
Blacksburg, VA 24063
540-953-2977
www.yellowsulphursprings.com

SELECT BIBLIOGRAPHY

Books

Addington, Luther F. *The Story of Wise County, Virginia.* Johnson City, Tenn.: The Overmountain Press, 1988.

Addington, Robert. *History of Scott County, Virginia.* Kingsport, Tenn.: Kingsport Press, 1932.

Albert, Henry E. *Log Cabin Heritage.* Pulaski, Va.: B.D. Smith & Bros. Printers, Inc., 1976.

Alderman, John Perry. *Carroll 1765-1815: The Settlements.* Hillsville, Va.: Alderman Books, 1985.

Armstrong, Joan L., and Mack H. Sturgill. *Smyth County Tours.* Marion, Va.: by the authors, 1982.

Axelson, Edith F. *Virginia Postmasters and Post Offices, 1789-1832.* Athens, Ga.: Iberian Publishers, 1991.

Bales, Hattie Byrd Muncy. *Early Settlers of Lee County, Virginia and Adjacent Counties,* vol. II. Greensboro, N.C.: Media Inc., Printers and Publishers, 1977.

Ball, Bonnie. *Stickleyville Its Early History People, and Schools.* Aransas Pass, Tex.: Biography Press, n.d.

Barrett, Theodosia Wells. *Pioneers on the Western Waters.* Bristol, Tenn.: Service Printing Co., 1978.

Benner, Bob, and David Benner. *A Canoeing & Kayaking Guide to the Carolinas,* 8th ed. Birmingham, Ala.: Menasha Ridge Press, 2002.

Bland County Centennial Corporation. *History of Bland County.* Radford, Va.: Commonwealth Press, 1961.

Bond, Avery, and Martha Nichols. *Town of Fries.* Collinsville, Va.: Collinsville Printing Co., n.d.

Bowman, Owen. *Carroll County, Virginia: The Early Days to 1920.* Virginia Beach, Va.: The Donning Co. Publishers, 1993.

Brown, Nancy Clark, and Rhonda Robertson. *History of the Pound.* Pound, Va.: Historical Society of the Pound, 1993.

Bucklen, Mary Kegley, and Larrie L. Bucklen. *County Courthouses of Virginia: Old and New.* Charleston, W.Va.: Pictorial Histories Publishing Co., 1988.

Burke's Garden Homemaker's Club. *Seasonings of Time.* Burke's Garden, Va.: Burke's Garden Homemaker's Club, 2001.

Carroll County Genealogy Club. *Carroll County Heritage, Volume One: 1842-1994.* Hillsville, Va.: Carroll County Genealogy Club, 1994.

Carroll County Genealogy Club. *Carroll County Heritage, Volume Two: 1842-1997.* Hillsville, Va.: Carroll County Genealogy Club, 1997.

Cohen, Stan. *Historic Springs of the Virginias: A Pictorial History.* Charleston, W.Va.: Pictorial Histories Publishing Co., 1981.

Cox, Clara B., ed. *A Special Place for 200 Years.* Blacksburg, Va.: Blacksburg Town Council, 1998.

Crush, Charles W. *The Montgomery County Story.* n.p.: by the author, 1957.

Davis, Edward H., and Edward B. Morgan. *The Virginia Creeper Trail Companion: Nature and History along Southwest Virginia's National Recreation Trail.* Johnson City, Tenn.: The Overmountain Press, 1997.

Dickenson County Heritage Book Committee. *The Heritage of Dickenson County, Virginia 1880-1993,* vol. I. Waynesville, N.C.: Don Mills, Inc., 1994.

Farrar, Emmie Ferguson, and Emilee Hines. *Old Virginia Houses: The Mountain Empire.* Charlotte, N.C.: Delmar Publishing, 1978.

Fields, Bettye-Lou, ed. *Grayson County: A History in Words and Pictures.* Independence, Va.: Grayson County Historical Society, 1976.

Fleenor, Lawrence J. *The Bear Grass.* Big Stone Gap, Va.: by the author, 1991.

Fleenor, Lawrence J. *Driving the Wilderness Trail.* Gate City, Va.: Daniel Boone Wilderness Trail Association, Inc., 2000.

Floyd County Heritage Committee. *Floyd County, Virginia Heritage.* Summersville, W.Va.: S.E. Grose & Assoc., 2001.

Friend, Robert C. *Giles County: A Brief History.* Pearisburg, Va.: Giles County Chamber of Commerce, 1956.

Giles Research Group. *Giles County, Va., History-Families,* vol. II. Marceline, Mo.: Walsworth Publishing, 1994.

Givens, Lula Porterfield. *Highlights in the Early History of Montgomery County, Virginia.* Pulaski, Va.: B.D. Smith and Bros. Printers, Inc., 1975.

Givens, Lula Porterfield. *Christiansburg-Montgomery County, Virginia: In the Heart of the Alleghanies.* Pulaski, Va.: Edmonds Printing, Inc., 1981.

Greater Newport Rural Historic District Committee. *Tall Tales and Short History of Newport, Virginia.* Newport, Va.: Greater Newport Rural Historic District Committee, 1996.

Greever, Ida R. *Sketches of Early Burke's Garden*. Radford, Va.: Commonwealth Press, 1974.

Hagemann, James A. *The Heritage of Virginia: The Story of Place Names in the Old Dominion*. Norfolk, Va.: The Donning Company/Publishers, 1986.

Hall, Louise Fortune. *A History of Damascus, Virginia 1793-1950*. Abingdon, Va.: The John Anderson Press, 1950.

Hamilton, Emory L. *Old Mills of Far Southwest Virginia*. Coeburn, Va.: Virginia Printing Co., 1973.

Hanson, Raus McDill. *Virginia Place Names*. Verona, Va.: McClure Press, 1969.

Harrington, Susan J. *Virginia Highlands*. Dover, N.H.: Arcadia Publishing, 1997.

Holston Territory Genealogical Society. *Families of Washington County and Bristol, Virginia 1776-1996*. Waynesville, N.C.: Don Mills, Inc., 1996.

James, Emma Jane Wright. *Glimpses of Appalachia's Past*. Appalachia, Va.: by the author, 1988.

Johnson, Charles A. *Wise County Virginia*. Norton, Va.: Norton Press, 1938.

Johnson, Clint. *Touring Virginia's and West Virginia's Civil War Sites*. Winston-Salem, N.C.: John F. Blair, Publisher, 1999.

Johnston, David E. *A History of Middle New River Settlements and Contiguous Territory*. Huntington, W.Va: Standard Ptg. and Pub. Co., 1906.

Kearfott, Clarence Baker. *Highland Mills*. New York: Vantage Press, Inc., 1970.

Kegley, F. B., and Mary B. Kegley. *Early Adventures on the Western Waters: The New River of Virginia in Pioneer Days 1745-1800*, vol. I. Orange, Va.: Green Publishers, Inc., 1980.

Kegley, Mary B. *Glimpses of Wythe County, Va*. Wytheville, Va.: Kegley Books, 1986.

Kegley, Mary B. *Wythe County, Virginia: A Bicentennial History*. Marceline, Mo.: Walsworth Publishing, 1989.

Kent, William B. *A History of Saltville*. Saltville, Va.: by the author, 1955.

Keokee Extension Homemakers. *The Village of Keokee*. Keokee, Va.: Keokee Extension Homemakers, 1975.

Killen, Linda. *The Whartons' Town: New River Depot, 1870-1940*. Radford, Va.: Radford University/College of Arts and Sciences, 1993.

King, Nanci C. *Places in Time Volume II: Abingdon, Meadowview & Glade Spring, Virginia*. Marion, Va.: Tucker Printing, Inc., 1994.

King, Nanci C. *Places in Time Volume III: South from Abingdon to the Holston*. Marion, Va.: Tucker Printing, Inc., 1997.

Kiwanis Club of Coeburn. *Coeburn Area History*. Coeburn, Va.: Kiwanis Club of Coeburn, 1994.

Laningham, Anne Wynn. *Early Settlers of Lee County, Virginia and Adjacent Counties*, vol. I. Greensboro, N.C.: Media Inc., Printers and Publishers, 1977.

Lawson, D. Geraldine. *Rough Side of the Mountain*. Huntington, W.Va.: University Editions, Inc., 1996.

Lee County Historical and Genealogical Society, Inc. *Bicentennial History of Lee County Virginia 1792-1992*. Waynesville, N.C.: Don Mills, Inc., 1992.

Leslie, Louise. *Tazewell County*. Johnson City, Tenn.: The Overmountain Press, 1995.

Linkous, Clovis. *Twelve Stones for Belmont*. Fort Wayne, Ind.: by the author, 1976.

Lord, William G. *Blue Ridge Parkway Guide: Rockfish Gap to Grandfather Mountain*. Birmingham, Ala.: Menasha Ridge Press, 1998.

Loth, Calder, ed. *The Virginia Landmarks Register*, 4th ed. Charlottesville, Va.: University Press of Virginia, 1999.

Lucas, Roderick Lewis. *A Valley and Its People in Montgomery County, Virginia*. Blacksburg, Va.: Southern Printing Co., 1975.

Miller, Hattie. *A Story of Newport and Its People*. Blacksburg, Va.: by the author, 1978.

Neal, J. Allen. *Bicentennial History of Washington County, Virginia 1776-1976*. Dallas: Taylor Publishing Co., 1977.

1908 Courthouse Foundation. *Bicentennial Heritage Grayson County, Virginia, 1793*. Independence, Va.: 1908 Courthouse Foundation, 1995.

Nunley, J. Shannon. *Clinch Mountain Memories*. Mendota, Va.: by the author, 1991.

Oermann, Robert K. *A Century of Country*. New York: TV Books, 1999.

Owens, Pauline. *Buchanan County History: A Past to Remember, A Future to Mold*. Marceline, Mo.: Walsworth Publishing, 1983.

Pendleton, Lee. *Indian Massacres in Montgomery County 1755-1756*. n.p.: by the author, 1968.

Pendleton, William C. *History of Tazewell County and Southwest Virginia 1748-1920*. Richmond, Va.: W.C. Hill Printing Co., 1920.

Phillips, V. N. *Bristol Tennessee/Virginia: A History—1852-1900*. Johnson City, Tenn.: The Overmountain Press, 1992.

Pollard, Edward Alfred. *The Virginia Tourist*. Philadelphia, Pa.: J.P. Lippincott & Co., 1870.

Pratt, D. C. *Russell County, Virginia's Bluegrass Empire*. Bristol, Tenn.: King Printing Co., 1968.

Prescott, E. J. *The Virginia Coal and Iron Company*. Big Stone Gap, Va.: by the author, 1945.

Presgraves, James S., ed. *Wythe County Chapters*. Pulaski, Va.: B. D. Smith and Bros. Printers, Inc., 1972.

Reedy, Dennis, and Diana Reedy. *Haysi, Virginia: Community and Family History*. Haysi, Va: by the authors, 1998.

Reedy, Dennis, ed. *Mountain People and Places: Dickenson County, Virginia*. Clinchco, Va.: Mountain People and Places, 1994.

Reedy, Dennis, ed. *School and Community History of Dickenson County, Virginia*. Johnson City, Tenn.: The Overmountain Press, 1994.

Research Committee, Giles County Historical Society. *Giles County Virginia: History and Families*. Marceline, Mo.: Walsworth Publishing, 1982.

Roberts, Virginia Finnegan. *Mountain Lake Remembered*. Austin, Tex.: Nortex Press, 1994.

Roberts, W. Keith, et al. *The House by the Wilderness Road*. Dublin, Va.: Pulaski Printing Co., 1998.

Russell County Heritage Book Committee, Inc. *The Heritage of Russell County, Virginia 1786-1986*, vol. I. Marceline, Mo.: Walsworth Publishing, 1985.

Russell County Heritage Book Committee, Inc. *The Heritage of Russell County, Virginia 1786-1988*, vol. II. Marceline, Mo.: Walsworth Publishing, 1989.

Salmon, Emily J., and Edward D. C. Campbell, Jr., eds. *The Hornbook of Virginia History: A Ready-Reference Guide to the Old Dominion's People, Places, and Past*, 4th ed. Richmond, Va.: The Library of Virginia, 1994.

Salmon, John S. *A Guidebook to Virginia's Historical Markers*. Charlottesville, Va.: University Press of Virginia, 1994.

Scott County History Book Committee. *Scott County Virginia and Its People, 1814-1991*, vol. I. Waynesville, N.C.: Don Mills, Inc., 1991.

Scott County History Book Committee. *Scott County Virginia and Its People, 1814-1998*, vol. II. Gate City, Va.: Scott County History Book Committee, 1998.

Shearer, Katharine C., ed. *Memories From Dante: The Life of a Coal Town*. Abingdon, Va.: People Incorporated of Southwest Virginia, 2001.

Shifflett, Crandall A. *Coal Towns*. Knoxville, Tenn.: University of Tennessee Press, 1991.

Smyth County Heritage Book Committee. *Heritage of Smyth County Virginia 1832-1997*. Waynesville, N.C.: Don Mills, Inc., 1997.

Spiker, Linda McHone. *Max Meadows, Virginia: Destined for Glory*. Pulaski, Va.: Edmonds Printing, Inc., 1990.

Summers, Lewis Preston. *History of Southwest Virginia 1746-1786, Washington County 1777-1870*. Johnson City, Tenn.: The Overmountain Press, 1989.

Sturgill, Mack H. *Hungry Mother: History and Legends*. Marion, Va.: Tucker Printing, 1986.

Sutherland, Elihu Jasper. *Meet Virginia's Baby: A Pictorial History of Dickenson County, Virginia*. Clintwood, Va.: by the author, 1955.

Tate, Leland B. *The Virginia Guide*. Lebanon, Va.: by the author, 1929.

Taylor, Kathleen Robinson. *They Say . . .* North Tazewell, Va.: Clinch Valley Printing Co., Inc., 1999.

Tazewell County Historical Society. *Tazewell County Heritage Vol. 1, Tazewell County, Virginia 1799-1995*. Summersville, N.C.: Shirley Johnson-Grose/Walsworth Publishing, 1995.

Varhola, Michael J. *Everyday Life During the Civil War*. Cincinnatti, Ohio: Writers Digest Books, 1999.

Virginia Atlas and Gazetteer. Yarmouth, Maine: DeLorme, 2000.

Virginia Center for Coal & Energy Research. *Virginia Coal: An Abridged History*. Blacksburg, Va.: Virginia Tech, 1990.

Washington County Historical Society. *From Indian Villages to Electronic Villages: Washington County . . . from A to Z*. Abingdon, Va.: Washington County Historical Society, 1998.

Wax, Don. *Welcome to John Fox, Jr.'s Lonesome Pine Country, Third Printing (Revised)*. n.p.: by the author, 1996.

Webb, Munsey W. *Norfolk and Western Railway Company North Carolina Branch*. Pulaski, Va.: Edmonds Printing, Inc., 1995.

Weeks, Ross, Jr. *Virginia's Tazewell County: A Last Great Place*. North Tazewell, Va.: Clinch Valley Printing Co., 2000.

Wells, Dianne. *Roadside History: A Guide to Kentucky Highway Markers*. Frankfort, Ky.: The Kentucky Historical Society, 2002.

Willis, Ninevah J. *Carroll County Schools*. Hillsville, Va.: Carroll County Historical Society, 1992.

Wilson, Goodridge. *Smyth County History and Traditions*. Kingsport, Tenn.: Kingsport Press, 1932.

Wise County Historical Society. *The Heritage of Wise County and the City of Norton 1856-1993*, vol. I. Waynesville, N.C.: Don Mills, Inc./Walsworth Publishing, 1993.

Wise County Historical Society. *The Heritage of Wise County and the City of Norton 1856-2001*, vol. II. Wise, Va.: Wise County Historical Society, 2001.

Wood, Dr. Amos D. *Floyd County: A History of Its People and Places*. Blacksburg, Va.: Southern Printing Co., Inc., 1981.

Worsham, Gibson. *Montgomery County: Historic Sites Survey, Vol. I and II.* July 1986. File at Virginia Tech Library, Blacksburg, Va.

WPA Virginia Writers' Program. *Virginia: A Guide to the Old Dominion.* Richmond: Virginia State Library and Archives, 1992.

Writers Program of the Works Progress Administration. *Historical Inventory, Floyd County, 1937-38.* n.d. File at Floyd County Public Library, Floyd, Va.

Writers Program of the Works Progress Administration. *Historical Inventory, Russell County.* File at Russell County Public Library, Lebanon, Va., n.d.

Zwonitzer, Mark and Charles Hirshberg. *Will You Miss Me When I'm Gone?* New York: Simon & Schuster, 2002.

Articles & Research Papers

Addington, Luther F. "Chief Benge's Last Raid." *Historical Sketches of Southwest Virginia, Publication 2.* Wise, Va.: Historical Society of Southwest Virginia, 1966.

Brown, Douglas Summers. "The Legendary Hermit-Hunter of Whitetop Mountain." *Virginia Cavalcade.* Summer 1977.

Cary, Leona H. "Derivation of Place Names in Giles County." File at Giles County Historical Society archives, Pearisburg, Va., 4 November 1975

Hamilton, Emory L. "Frontier Forts." *Historical Sketches of Southwest Virginia, Publication 4.* Wise, Va.: Historical Society of Southwest Virginia, 1968.

Herman, Bernard L. "Washington County Grist Mills." *The Historical Society of Washington County, Va. Publication Series II, No. 12, 1974-75.* Abingdon, Va.: Historical Society of Washington County, Virginia, Inc., 1975.

Hillenbrand, Ann. "The Bondurant Center for the Arts: Dedication to Community Art Education." *Expressions.* Christiansburg, Va.: New River Arts Council, January-March, 2000.

Hoback, Michael R. "Blackwell Chapel: A Mountain Community." File at Historical Society of Washington County archives, Abingdon, Va., 3 November 1980.

Hunter, Elizabeth. "Saving the Courthouse." *Blue Ridge Country.* Roanoke, Va.: Leisure Publishing Co., May 2000.

Keister, Susie Reed. "A History of Newport, Virginia." File at Giles County Historical Society archives, Pearisburg, Va., n.d.

Lutts, Ralph H. "The Changing World of Saltville." *Virginia Explorer.* Spring-Summer 1992.

Maggio, Carina. "History of Hamilton." Mendota, Va., n.d.

"Names Along the Line." *Norfolk and Western Magazine.* December 1948.

Price, Charles Edwin. "Death in the Afternoon." *Blue Ridge Country.* Roanoke, Va.: Leisure Publishing Co., May 1998.

Reedy, Dennis. "How Places in Dickenson County Got Their Name." Haysi, Va., n.d.

Sarvis, Will. "Green Cove Station: An Appalachian Train Depot and Its Community." *Virginia Cavalcade.* Autumn 1992.

Schroeder, Joan Vannorsdall. "An Extraordinary Woman, and Equal to Any Emergency: Mary Draper Ingles' Return to Virginia's New River Valley." *Blue Ridge Country.* Roanoke, Va.: Leisure Publishing Co., March 1998.

"Southwest Virginia: A Mountain Treasure." Special edition. *Virginia Wildlife.* February 1996.

Tennis, Joe. "Sweet Virginia Breezes." *Blue Ridge Country.* Roanoke, Va.: Leisure Publishing Co., May 1997.

Worsham, John Gibson, Jr. "A Place So Lofty and Secluded." *Virginia Cavalcade.* Summer 1977.

Newspapers

Associated Press. "'Quiet and Peaceful' Development Bypasses Former Montgomery County Coal Mining Community." *Bristol Herald Courier.* Bristol, Va., 5 April 2000.

Berrier, Ralph, Jr., and Mark Morrison. "The Woodstock of Bluegrass." *The Roanoke Times.* Roanoke, Va., 14 August 1994.

"Bicentennial." Special edition. *Clinch Valley News.* Tazewell, Va., 5 July 2000.

"Bicentennial Edition." Special edition. *Montgomery County News Messenger.* Christiansburg, Va., 1 July 1976.

"A Blue Ridge Mountain Labor Day" Special edition. *Carroll County News.* Hillsville, Va., 30 August 2000.

Bowman, Rex/Media General News Service. "Coal Memories." *Bristol Herald Courier.* Bristol, Va., 26 September 1999.

Bowman, Rex/Media General News Service. "Hikers Welcomed to Wythe Mountains." *Bristol Herald Courier*. Bristol, Va., 23 October 2001.

Bryant, Laura. "Byways Tour: Western Grayson County." *Galax Gazette*. Galax, Va., 6-8 November 1992.

Cox, Jim. "Old Schoolhouse Begins New Chapter." *Bristol Herald Courier*. Bristol, Va., 4 September 1994.

Dellinger, Paul. "Boat Ramp, Fishing Dock Dedicated at Park on Claytor Lake." *The Roanoke Times*. Roanoke Va., 13 May 1999.

Elledge, Glenna. "They're Working This Way." *Smyth County News*. Marion, Va., 26 February 1994.

Evans, Stephen B. "Southwest Virginia Hamlet Faces Question: To Be or Not to Be?" *Bristol Herald Courier*. Bristol, Va., 27 October 1997.

Evans, Stephen B. "Town Residents Added a Page to Virginia History." *Bristol Herald Courier*. Bristol, Va., 5 November 1997.

Hall, Susan Harris. "Branch of Lee Family Was Once Established in Floyd on Honor Grant to Light Horse Larry." *The Floyd Press*. Floyd, Va., 8 April 1937.

"How Stiles Falls Got Its Name." *Montgomery County News Messenger*. Christiansburg, Va., 19 December 1968.

Miller, Kevin. "Who'll Stop the Drain?" *The Roanoke Times*. Roanoke, Va., 2 June 2002.

"Mountain Empire Crossroads." Special edition. *Bristol Herald Courier*. Bristol, Va., 27 February 1994.

Padgett, Owen. "Black, Gaping Hole in Fancy Gap Mt. Isn't the Attraction it Used to Be." *Galax Gazette*. Galax, Va., 23 April 1968.

"Progress '99." Special edition. *Scott County Virginia Star*. Gate City, Va., 31 March 1999.

"Pulaski County Centennial Edition." Special edition. *Southwest Times*. Pulaski, Va., 13 August 1939.

Reeves, Jason. "It's Just Bloomed." *Bristol Herald Courier*. Bristol, Va., 2 April 2001.

Sanders, Frank. "History of Saltville." *Saltville Progress*. Saltville, Va., 29 October 1970.

Sanders, Frank. "History of Saltville." *Saltville Progress*. Saltville, Va., 7 January 1971.

Sanders, Frank. "History of Saltville: What's In a Name?" *Saltville Progress*. Saltville, Va., 24 November 1966.

Sanders, Frank. "History of Saltville: What's In a Name—Part II." *Saltville Progress*. Saltville, Va., 1 December 1966.

Sanders, Frank. "History of Saltville: What's In a Name—Part III." *Saltville Progress*. Saltville, Va., 8 December 1966.

Sanders, Frank. "History of Saltville: What's In a Name—Part VI." *Saltville Progress*. Saltville, Va., 29 December 1966.

Still, Kathy. "One Town's Rebirth." *Bristol Herald Courier*. Bristol, Va., 13 June 1999.

Tennis, Joe. "Along the Banks of the Beaver." *Bristol Herald Courier*. Bristol, Va., 30 August 1998.

Tennis, Joe. "Barn Dance." *Bristol Herald Courier*. Bristol, Va., 16 November 1997.

Tennis, Joe. "Clinchport: Rampaging River Once Submerged Virginia Town." *Kingsport Times-News*. Kingsport, Tenn., 17 October 1993.

Tennis, Joe. "The Hills of Home." Special edition. *Bristol Herald Courier*. Bristol, Va., 23 February 1997.

Tennis, Joe. "In the Middle of Everywhere . . . Mendota." *Bristol Herald Courier*. Bristol, Va., 12 July 1998.

Tennis, Joe. "Irises Call it Home." *The Roanoke Times*. Roanoke, Va., 18 May 1991.

Tennis, Joe. "Lost Colleges of Southwest Virginia." *Bristol Herald Courier*. Bristol, Va., 14 July 1996.

Tennis, Joe. "Oil! Lee County Still Pumping Highest Volume in Old Dominion." *Bristol Herald Courier*. Bristol, Va., 3 July 1994.

Tennis, Joe. "Singer's Visit Rekindles Movie Memories." *Bristol Herald Courier*. Bristol, Va., 24 April 1997.

"Town of Saltville 1896-1996." Special edition. *Saltville Progress*. 22 February 1996.

Wilson, Goodridge. "The Southwest Corner." *The Roanoke Times*. Roanoke, Va., 15 June 1941.

Wilson, Goodridge. "The Southwest Corner." *The Roanoke Times*. Roanoke, Va., 25 August 1958.

"Wyndale Began as Prestons." *Washington County News*. Abingdon, Va., 4 March 1971.

Web Sites

Angleberger, Tom. "Parrott." *New River Valley Current/The Roanoke Times*. 2000. http://www.newrivervalley.com/profiles/par.html (24 December 2003)

Cagle, Sarah. "Pilot." *New River Valley Current/The Roanoke Times*. 2000. http://www.newrivervalley.com/profiles/pil.html (24 December 2003)

Chataigne's Virginia Gazetteer and Classified Business Directory 1888-89. http://www.ls.net/~newriver/va/cvb1888.htm (24 December 2003)

Hamilton, Emory L. "The Slaying of John Douglas at Little Moccasin Gap." http://www.rootsweb.com/~varussel/indian/15.html (24 December 2003)

Henson, E. L. "A Brief History of Wise, Virginia." *The Official Web Site for Wise County Government.* 2003. http://www. wise county.org/wise_history.htm (24 December 2003)

Howell, Isak. "Preserving a Feeling of Remoteness." *The Roanoke Times.* 2000. http://www.newrivervalley.com/newriver/nrpre.html (24 December 2003)

James-Henderson, Yvonne. "VA Cities, Counties and Towns." 1997. http://www.rootsweb.com/~varockbr/vatown.htm (24 December 2003)

Johnson, Jill. "Lafayette." *New River Valley Current/The Roanoke Times.* 2000. http://www.newrivervalley.com/profiles/laf.html (24 December 2003)

Matusevich, Melissa. "Auburn Middle and High School." *Montgomery County Public Schools.* http://pixel.cs.vt.edu/melissa/ amhs.html (24 December 2003)

Miller, Jeff. "Origins of West Virginia Place Names." *History of West Virginia.* 12 October 2003. http://members.aol.com/jeff560/places.html (24 December 2003)

"Notes on the History of the Town of Dublin." *Town of Dublin, Virginia, U.S.A.* http://www.rootsweb.com/~vapcgc/doc/Dublin.html (24 December 2003)

Pathways for Radford. "Yesterday." *Welcome to Wildwood Park!* 27 June 2002. http://civic.bev.net/pathways/wildwood/yesterday (24 December 2003)

Patterson, Kathy Largen, and Charles E. Patterson. "Guide to the New River Trail by Kathy And Charles." *Cherry Creek Cyclery & More.* 3 July 2001. http://www.cccyclery.com/geninbg.htm (24 December 2003)

Rocky Gap High School. The Bland County History Archives. 2000. http://www.bland.k12.va.us/bland/rocky/gap.html (24 December 2003)

Special Collections Department, University Libraries. "Manuscript Resources for Montgomery County, Virginia, History at the Special Collections Department of the University Libraries at Virginia Tech." 10 July 2002. http://spec.lib.vt.edu/specgen/mcguide.htm (24 December 2003)

Weaver, Jeffrey C. "Grayson County Postmasters." April 1998. http://www.ls.net/~newriver/va/graypo.htm (24 December 2003)

Weebers, Hans A. M. "William Mumford Ellis." 14 October 1999. http://users.legacyfamilytree.com/USPresidents/6692.htm (24 December 2003)

Miscellaneous

"A People, a Path, a Gateway. Tour Guide." Brochure. Chilhowie, Va.: Town of Chilhowie, Va., September 2002.

"Civic Monument and Sports Hall of Fame: Wall of Honor." Booklet. Wytheville, Va.: Withers Park, 17 December 1993.

Correspondence by Melody Savage, Research Assistant, Postal History, Corporate Information Services, United States Postal Service, Washington, D.C., to Robert C. Wininger, Gate City, Va., 24 January 1998.

"Historical Map of Montgomery County, Va." Roanoke, Va.: Roanoke Historical Society, 1970.

"Historic Tazewell, Virginia: A Walking Tour." Brochure. Tazewell, Va.: Tazewell County Historical Society, n.d.

Lawson, Pat. "Historical Map of Floyd County, Va." Roanoke, Va., 1992.

"Olde Towne Pearisburg Established 1808." Brochure. Pearisburg, Va.: Olde Towne Pearisburg Association, January 1995.

"Our Home, Sweet Home in the Mountains." Brochure. Troutdale, Va.: n.d.

"Pine Mountain Trail Guide, Birch Knob Section, First Edition." Booklet. Whitesburg, Ky.: Pine Mountain Trail Conference, Inc., n.d.

"A Tourist's Guide to Historic Appalachia, Virginia." Brochure. Appalachia, Va.: n.d.

"Unlock the Door to the Hidden Heart of Appalachia! Lee County, Virginia." Brochure. Pennington Gap, Va.: Silent E Design, n.d.

Williams, Daisy N. "Self-Tour Map of Historic Newbern." Brochure. Newbern, Va.: Newbern Promotional Bureau, 1994.

INDEX

162

OTHER BOOKS OF INTEREST

VIRGINIA HISTORY

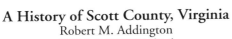

A History of Scott County, Virginia
Robert M. Addington
ISBN: 0-932807-67-4
$24.95 / Hardcover

History of Southwest Virginia 1746-1786 Washington County 1777-1870
Lewis Preston Summers
ISBN: 0-932807-43-7
$42.50 / Hardcover

History of Tazewell County and Southwest Virginia 1748-1920
William C. Pendleton
ISBN: 0-932807-39-9
$32.50 / Hardcover

Annals of Southwest Virginia 1769-1800
Lewis Preston Summers
ISBN: 0-932807-80-1
$74.95 / Hardcover
Two Volumes

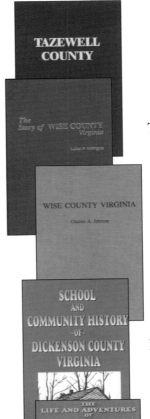

Tazewell County
Louise Leslie
ISBN: 1-57072-031-2
$34.95 / Hardcover

The Story of Wise County, Virginia
Luther F. Addington
ISBN: 0-932807-30-5
$24.95 / Hardcover

Wise County, Virginia
Luther F. Addington
ISBN: 0-932807-29-1
$27.95 / Hardcover

School and Community History of Dickenson County, Virginia
Edited by Dennis Reedy
ISBN: 1-57072-010-X
$21.95 / Hardcover

The Life and Adventures of Wilburn Waters
Charles B. Coale
ISBN: 1-57072-003-7
$5.95 / Trade Paper

Appalachian Genesis
The Clinch River Valley from Prehistoric Times to the End of the Frontier Era
Richard Lee Fulgham

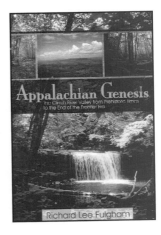

Appalachian Genesis: The Clinch River Valley from Prehistoric Times to the End of the Frontier Era is a documentary of a unique place and time in early American history. It is also a book as exciting and fun to read as an adventure novel. Fulgham's story is of epic proportions, spanning not centuries but millennia and even epochs, as the river valley is first shaped by nature into a paradise for all living things—then shaped by humans into a war zone where Native American, British, French, Colonial, Tory, and Patriot forces regularly collided in bloody conflicts. Americans can read *Appalachian Genesis* and understand what happens in the country today by studying what happened in one of its river valleys yesterday.

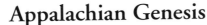

ISBN: 1-57072-088-6 / $24.95 / 6 x 9 Hardcover / 166 pages

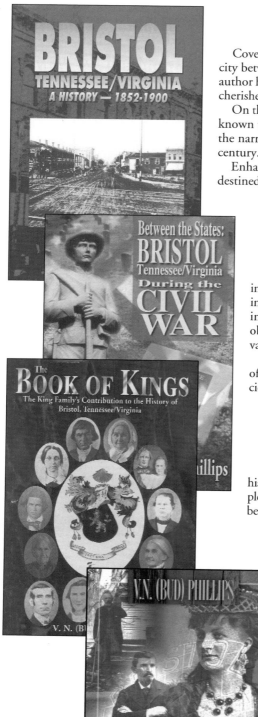

Bristol Tennessee / Virginia
A History 1852-1900

Covering Bristol's formative years, this is the story of people and events surrounding the rise of this city between two states—the town Joseph R. Anderson, its founder, wanted to call "Paradise." The author has endeavored to "tell it like it was" without fear or favor, showing no undue regard for long-cherished but undocumented historical traditions that have grown up over the years.

On these pages you will meet a cross section of Bristol's ancestry, ranging from the noble and well-known to the humble and obscure. Containing a myriad of facts that will be of wide local interest, the narrative offers more than a little insight into the human condition as it existed during the last century.

Enhanced with numerous old photographs, this carefully researched and well-written volume is destined to be the standard reference on Bristol for years to come.

ISBN: 0-932807-63-1 / $27.95 / 6 x 9 Hardcover

Between the States: Bristol Tennessee / Virginia During the Civil War

This second in a series of books on Bristol's history gives a vivid account of her most trying years—the Civil War period. It begins with a look at slavery as it existed in the new town in those years just prior to the beginning of the war. For a town its size, Bristol had a surprising number of slaves. Information given in the opening section of the book was largely obtained from the writings of two persons who lived in the new town at that time. Thus a valuable insight into slave life is given by those who saw it firsthand.

The author has endeavored to show how this great civil conflict affected the everyday lives of local citizens. An effort is made here to show that Bristolians suffered more from the atrocious acts of roving bands of bushwhackers than by the invasion of conquering Yankees.

ISBN: 1-57072-068-1 / $24.95 / 6 x 9 Hardcover

The Book of Kings

The Book of Kings is much more than a portrait of a pioneer family; it is actually another history of Bristol viewed from a different angle. It would be virtually impossible to write a complete history of this city without including a record of the pioneer King family. Likewise, it would be very difficult to write of this family and not become involved in general Bristol history.

ISBN: 1-57072-083-5 / $29.95 / 6 x 9 Hardcover

Pioneers in Paradise
Legends and Stories from Bristol Tennessee/Virginia

The fourth installment in the history of Bristol, Tennessee/Virginia, *Pioneers in Paradise* is a compilation of tales centered around the people who lived, worked, and died in the young town on the border.

This collection includes historical references to the days of the stagecoach, tales of prostitution—one of the vices common at the time—evidence of Bristol ghosts, and narratives about the people who lived in the Town of Bristol in its beginning days. Some of the stories come straight from interviews with the early citizens, while others include documentation from actual court cases or personal diaries. Each narrative provides a small glimpse into the day-to-day life in a town almost named "Paradise."

This unique portrayal of the people and their ways is truly the best of the Bud Phillips historical books of Bristol, because it lets the reader experience life as it was when the town was known as "hell on the border."

ISBN: 1-57072-234-X / $29.95 / 6 x 9 Hardcover